MW00779151

The Non-Existent Manuscript

Studies in Antisemitism

The Non-Existent Manuscript:
A Study of the *Protocols of the Sages of Zion*

Cesare G. De Michelis

Translated by Richard Newhouse

Published by The University of Nebraska Press, Lincoln and London
for The Vidal Sassoon International Center for the Study of Antisemitism (SICSA),
The Hebrew University of Jerusalem

© 2004 by The Vidal Sassoon International Center for the Study of Antisemitism,
The Hebrew University of Jerusalem

Originally published as *Il manoscritto inesistente: I "Protocolli dei savi di Sion":
un apocrifo del XX secolo* © 1998 by Marsilio Editory, S.P.A. in Venizia.
This English edition is revised and expanded.

Library of Congress Control Number: 2003111392
ISBN: 0-8032-1727-7 (cloth)

Manufactured and distributed by The University of Nebraska Press for
The Vidal Sassoon International Center for the Study of Antisemitism (SICSA)
The Hebrew University of Jerusalem
Mount Scopus
91905 Jerusalem
Israel

Editing and typesetting: Alifa Saadya

Table of Contents

Introduction to the English Edition

This work is *not* concerned with the formation of the myth of the "Jewish Plot" nor even with the story of the myth's incredible success through the wide circulation of the *Protokoly sionskix mudrecov* (PSM, Protocols of the Sages of Zion). Both these aspects have already been the subject of many publications, of which the benchmark remains *L'Apocalypse de notre temps* (1939) by H. Rollin, scholar and officer in the French secret services. Over recent years there has been a growing number of contributions on the subject, among which there are disquieting new symptoms of a renewed exhumation of PSM, such as *Tajnye sily v istorii Rossii* (St. Petersburg 1996) by the noted scholar of ancient Russian culture, Ju. Begunov.

Naturally the texts from between the two world wars that investigated the problem of the PSM[1] constitute the basis for using the term "historic" for the present research. Furthermore a renewed visitation to the materials of the "Bern Trial," which has revealed some surprises, has proven fruitful. What immediately springs to mind among the more recent publications is first of all S. Dudakov's able and erudite *Istorija odnogo mifa* (Moscow 1993), which follows the development of the idea of the "Jewish Plot" in 19th-century Russian literature. As regards the history of the PSM and its diffusion, it is necessary to cite at least the chapters on the PSM in *Russia and Germany, Hitler's Mentors* (New Brunswick, N.J. 1965) by W. Laqueur of the Center for Strategic and International Studies in Washington; N. Cohn's *Warrant for Genocide* (London 1967); the deft booklet of Ja. Tazbir, that illustrious Polish historian of the Reformation, *Protokoły mędrców Syjonu. Autentik czy falsyfikat?* (Warsaw 1992); and that impressive work of documentary history by P. A. Taguieff, *Les Protocoles des sages de Sion. Faux et usages d'un faux* (Paris 1992).

Effectively from the point of view of the origins of the fake, its date and attribution, matters have remained more or less fixed where they were left sixty or so years ago by Rollin (who in turn was returning to the speculations of A. du Chayla of 1921), that is, the hypothesis—in itself plausible but never proven[2]—of the compilation of the work in Paris, about 1887, under the aegis of P. I. Račkovskij along with the foreign section of Oxrana.[3]

The question of the origin of the PSM cannot be studied separately from the definition of the text and a proper interpretation. Otherwise, as has happened, faced with the impossibility of proceeding further into the insoluble problems, the idea imposes itself that, everything considered, the history of the use of the text is more important than the text itself, and has thus ended up with the passive acceptance, at least in part, of the trap of mystification. It is this which has driven me to undertake the research that I now place before the attention, and naturally the judgment, of the reader.

After twenty-odd editions had appeared in Russia between 1903 and 1912, the PSM ventured out into the world at large in 1919 with the German, Swedish, Polish, English, Hungarian, and French editions. The first Italian edition appeared in February 1921. Among the later editions which appeared in many languages there was even one in Yiddish, which has offered the opportunity for not disinterested inferences.[4]

However, the origins of the PSM have remained enveloped in mystery; the only thing that appears certain is that it derives from a French manuscript, purloined and copied in a conspiracy, or else compiled by the Russian Secret Service, which does not make the mystery any more accessible. Might it have itself been part of its own mystification?

Consequently I have intended to shed light on the even more obscure aspects of the PSM, moving not indeed—as has been fruitlessly attempted many times—among the many contradictory sources (secret archives, renegade Jews, spies, mystic writers, femme fatales, ink-stained manuscripts, anonymous translators, etc.) that have accompanied this phantasm. These are all things that I prefer to see as the "literary frame" around the insertion of an invented text into the grand romance of history. Rather, I wish to consider the sole element that cannot lie: the text itself, its linguistic nature, its construction and the modalities of its tradition. The parent work has therefore had as its point of departure the restitution of the text of PSM following current ecdotic principles, which is an operation as obvious and banal as it has been systematically overlooked. The text that appears in the appendix is so reconstructed and is notably different from that previously in circulation, especially from the Nilus edition.

Only after facing that problem does it appear possible to attempt a new reading of the text, reinserting into it the linguistic coordinates and the surrounding culture of which it is a product. It will then also be possible to make a contribution concerning the question of its diffusion in Italy, given that the author is Italian.

In doing this it has not been my intention to flee from the inherent drama of the story so as to retire to the ascetic halls of philology. Rather it has been the link between the academic and civil obligations that has proved to be the essential stimulus for this research.

What stimulated this work was my reading Ja. Tazbir's volume in 1993 along with some not very convincing aspects of N. Cohn's essay and some "literary" suggestions raised by reading Umberto Eco's *Foucault's Pendulum.* Reading S. Dudakov's book in 1994 led me to expand into a wider project what had originally been intended to be a limited incursion into the textual history of the PSM. Other than consulting Italian libraries and archives I have undertaken research in Moscow, Paris, Jerusalem, and Tel Aviv.

Between 1994 and 1997 I presented various stages in the progress of this study before audiences in various places, and have found the support of audiences and readers an encouragement to proceed along my chosen path.

I am grateful to the Vidal Sassoon International Center for the Study of Antisemitism of the Hebrew University of Jerusalem who have undertaken the publication of the work in Israel and are responsible for this English edition. I am also grateful to Roberta De Giorgi.

This book is dedicated to the memory of my father, Eurialo, and to Pastor Tullio Vinay.

Cesare G. De Michelis
Rome, February 2000

NOTES

1. L. Wolf, *The Jewish Bogey and the Forged Protocols of the Learned Elders of Zion* (London 1920); Ju. Delevskij, *Protokoly Sionskix mudrecov. Istorija odnogo podloga* (Berlin 1923), B. Segel, *Die Protokolle der Weisen von Zion kritisch beleuchtet* (Berlin 1924); S. Livingston, *Protocols of the Wise Men of Zion* (London 1934); H. Bernstein, *The Truth about "The Protocols of Zion"* (New York 1935); V. Burcev, *"Protokoly sionskix mudrecov," dokazannyij podlog* (Paris 1938); J. S. Curtiss, *An Appraisal of the Protocols of Zion* (New York 1942).

2. H. Bint attributes the compilation to M. Golovinskij, according to the testimony recently discovered by M. Lepexin. Lepexin's discovery, however, does not add anything to what was known since 1934; cf. C. G. De Michelis, "Una storia che si ripete," *La Repubblica,* 21 November 1999.

3. The popular term for the Tsarist Secret Police: *Oxrannoe otdelenie,* or *Oxranka.*

4. *Di "Protokoln" fun Zikney Tsion: Di greste provokatsye in der yidisher geshichte* (Warsaw 1934). A. Ivanov slyly asks himself: "To whom and in what way could the dissemination of 'an antisemitic forgery' be of service especially among the

Jews?," "Na vsjakix mudrecov dovol'no protokolov," *Russkij vestnik* 15 (1991). It is enough, however, to read the title in its entirety to understand that it was a form of "innoculation" (or perhaps only editorial opportunism), at the time of the Bern Trial.

CHAPTER 1

The First Editors

In his monograph on the PSM, N. Cohn concludes his examination of its origins thus:

> Often, in searching to clear up the initial history of the *Protocols* one encounters ambiguities, uncertainties and enigmas. There is no call to be overly worried, [because] the true importance lies in the great influence it has exercised on the history of the 20th Century (1969, 77).

This is a point of view that is now generally accepted. P. A. Taguieff writes in a similar vein (1992, 1:8):

> If today we must renew our studies of the *Protocols* it is less to resolve certain problems that remain to be resolved regarding their origin…than to enquire into the imperviousness of this mythical construct to rational criticism.

Notwithstanding the ambiguities and uncertainties, the two scholars are convinced, along with the previous writings on the subject (Rollin [1939], 1991, Laqueur [1965] 1991), and along with contemporary and later writings (Tazbir 1992, Eco 1994), that

> it is practically certain that the *Protocols* were forged between 1894 and 1899, and most probably in 1897 or 1898. This was certainly in France (Cohn 1969, 73).

or in other words

> In Paris in 1897–1898…by the Tsar's Secret Police, the *Oxrana,* run in France by Petr Ivanovič Račkovskij (Taguieff 1992, 1:17).

In attempting to resolve the "enigmas" about the origins of the PSM, nothing must be taken for granted. Therefore, neither the compilation in Paris around 1897 by Račkovskij and his agents, nor even less the existence at some imprecise date of a mysterious Jewish headquarters must be taken on trust, but one must turn one's attention to the text and its transmission. Jouin (1922) has given a collation, albeit brief, of two differing editions (N and B), while the more serious contribution of I. Čerikover has remained unpublished.[1] The PSM is a text which is subdivided into a number of paragraphs[2] which vary according to the editions between 22 and 27, with various comments of the "translator" attached, plus two notes on the text and a gloss.[3] In fact, according to current opinion, the PSM is the Russian translation of a text that was originally written in French, handed down on one side in the "complete" and "corrected" editions published in 1905 by S. Nilus, and on the other in that abbreviated or "corrupted" version published first by P. Kruševan in 1903, then anonymously in 1905, and subsequently by G. Butmi in 1905–1906. The Russian translation dates back to 1901, and thus the tradition of the text may be portrayed as follows[4]:

French archetype
1897 (?)

Russian translation
1901 (?)

Kruševan edition
1903

Nilus edition
1905

Anonymous edition
1905

Butmi edition
1905–1906

The opinions of "zealots" and "critics" diverge on the history of the text prior to the archetype. While for some it would appear that the manuscript has been extracted by chance from the documents of a mysterious Jewish and/or Masonic organization, for others it is none other than the hoax contrived by Račkovskij. In synthesis, this is the outline of the presumed origins of the most celebrated apocrypha of the twentieth century, which must now undergo textual verification.

***

How many "editions" of the PSM exist and how do they differ? I have traced five between 1903 and 1906, to which should be added two "shortened versions": one, published several times in 1905 and 1906, while the other appeared as a monograph in 1917.

The critical literature on the PSM, however, mentions others which I have not managed to see. Therefore, it is difficult to say if we are dealing with different editions, the reprinting of the aforementioned texts, or mere "bibliographical ghosts." The first, *Rol' evreev i evrejstvujuščix v russkoj revoljucii,* is supposed to have appeared in the newspaper *Kazanskij Telegraf,* but there is no sign of it in the relevant editions.[5] Another edition may have appeared in Moscow in 1905 with the title *Drevnie i novye protokoly sobranij Sionskix mudrecov,* if indeed we are not dealing with a corrupt version of the title of A2. However it has proved untraceable.[6] A third edition, which appeared in Kazan (*Vyderžki iz drevnix i sovremennyx protokolov Sionskix mudrecov Vsemirnogo obščestva Fran-Massonov*), is attributed by some to Butmi, and would appear to be a reprint of A1.[7]

It only remains to examine the five noted sources and the two "shortened editions." It will be possible to establish the relationships between them (and consequently to advance concrete hypotheses concerning both the date and the provenance of the text) only after having studied them in detail, and in particular after ascertaining if the variants should be considered more or less "insignificant" as Dudakov (1993, 261) would like to have it.

The PSM appeared for the first time in September 1903 in nine installments in the extreme right-wing St. Petersburg daily, *Znamja,* founded in February by Pavolakij (Pavel) Aleksandrovič Kruševan (1860–1909),[8] who was an antisemitic journalist of Moldavian origin. He was also the publisher of *Bessarabec,* and in 1903 had instigated the pogrom of Kišinëv.[9] Already a member of *Russkoe sobranie,*[10] he was president of the *Sojuz russkogo naroda* of Bessarabia,[11] and, finally, a member of the Second Duma. This edition, even though anonymous, will be cited with his initial (K).

The newspaper headline was *The Jewish Programme for the Conquest of the World,*[12] but the title of the document (attributed to the "translator") of *Protokoly zasedanij "vsemirnogo sojuza franmasonov i sionskix mudrecov"* (The protocols of the sessions of the "World Alliance of Freemasons and of the Sages of Zion") comes from the introduction and the final note.[13]

The internal segmentation is more articulated in the nine installments of the newspaper, but it is not expressly indicated. Between the caesurae separating one installment from another and the more or less marked spaces within each installment (three asterisks, a line, a simple white space), one can count in fact twenty paragraphs. In two cases, however, the indentation marked as the beginning of a new paragraph is unequivocally such (8: "today we shall begin with the repetition…", and 22nd: "I shall pass today to the means of reinforcing..."),[14] so that the segmentation of this edition, which coincides only in part with succeeding ones, results in 22 chapters (as in the Apocalypse).[15]

The concluding note of the publisher (not that "of the translator," which forms part of the PSM) affirms that the "Second Part" was published with cuts. From this comes the assertion that we are dealing with a "shortened version" compared with the "complete text" which, according to the "Vulgate", would be taken from the other editions. This partly reflects a more complex textual situation. "Cuts" are found also elsewhere, both with respect to the original text and to the same K. Here one asks how had it proved possible to reconstruct it. If one takes the expression "Second Part" literally ("Protocols" 12th–22nd), one notes in K the absence of a large number of passages found elsewhere (in particular in the "Protocols" 16, 18, 19, and 22). We have no assurances, however, that we are dealing always with "cuts." In line with this principle one must retain as omissions in K (compared with the archetype) only the missing parts that contain calques in Joly's text, or instead refer back to his copy.[17] In total, these are around 8%, with an effective prevalence of the second part (12–22: 12%) over the first part (1–11: 4%).

To sum up, K certainly shows some "cuts," but not in any different way from those of the other editions (even if they are more consistent) and above all they are not limited to the "Second Part." Thus it appears more congruous to read the forward, which shows some intervention, as a preventive measure for a later retouching of the text which would appear to a future reader not as an "addition" but, precisely, as a "restoration." This implies that, for some reason, the publication of K had been rushed, and done from a text that was still not considered definitive, which is confirmed by certain textual peculiarities.

For example, one comes across a certain degree of frequency in the repetitions or duplications, which are then later emended or reduced to a stylistic device. This brings to mind a phase of elaboration in which the compiler had not yet decided which of the two variants to employ. The semantic nature of the variants excludes any possibility that one is dealing with any uncertainties entertained by the supposed translator. However, the most relevant idiosyncrasy of K, which too supports the above hypothesis, is its abnormal linguistic nature, later by stages normalized, and in particular:

the lexical, morphological and/or syntactical anomalies; and

the presence of Ukrainianisms such as the preposition "v" transformed into "u" in the pre-consonantal position[18] and the lack of the letter doubling in the borrowings. Furthermore, the recurrent "*goevskij*" (for "*gojskij*") is more Ukrainian than Russian.[19]

Because it is to be excluded that similar anomalies should be all imputed to the original, or that a text written in correct Russian might have been systematically corrupted by the publisher, it must be that K reflects the primitive version and therefore the closest to the protograph or original. Therefore, it is the closest to, but not "the" protograph, as the omitted passages demonstrate.

Immediately afterwards, in 1904 (censorship pass: 3 November 1903), K's first protocol was republished in the second volume of I. Lutostański's (Ljutostanskij: 1835–1912) *Talmud i evrei* (3rd ed.), where it was presented as an extract of the Masonic-Zionist protocols *Iudejskie tajny* "translated from the French" (L). The text is identical, with the correction of the errors more marked and the correct use of double letters, but also with some brief omissions and the odd corruption.[20] While this proves useless from an ecdotic point of view, it does present some interest from the point of view of the historical reconstruction of the text.

K makes a lengthy disappearance from the scene, and its existence was only "rediscovered" at the time of the Bern Trial (1934).

The second edition of the PSM, which we shall call A1, appeared anonymously in the pamphlet *Koren' našix bedstvij*[21] under the title of *Vyderžki iz drevnix i sovremmennyx protokolov Sionskix medrecov Vsemirnogo obščestva Fran-Masonov* (Excerpts[22] from the ancient and modern Protocols of the Sages of Zion of the World Society of Freemasons). This was published by the printers of the Headquarters of the Guards and of the Military district of St. Petersburg,[23] and presented to the censors already in printed form. It received its "no objection" on 9 December 1905,[24] and preceded, even if by very little, the publication of N.

It is the fullest text of the PSM that has appeared. The *Translator's Gloss* (here without title) is very similar to K, but with the addition of a note that has given rise to many inferences: "translated from the French, 9 December 1901." A1 is overall fairly close to K, but the textual material is subdivided into 27 "chapters" (like Leviticus), rather than into 22. One's attention is drawn to various redundancies, more relevant in the recorded "protocols" (16, 18, 19 and 22), and in the parts in common the dictation is substantially followed, with the correction of the most notable errors,[25] the correct use of double letters, but also with the intrusion of misunderstandings.[26] One further notices elsewhere modifications (still limited) in the tenses of the verbs, which, in a piece of discourse that is largely schematic, introduce not insignificant variations in meaning.

The edition is pretty incorrect, with printing errors and brief gaps caused by omoteleutus rather than intentional cuts; the first line of page 71 is actually printed at the bottom of the page. The text is presented without so much as a line of introduction or comment, which renders it impossible to advance any possible hypothesis concerning the identity of the publisher. Judging from the hyper-correctness, it is possible only to infer that the publisher may have worked on a text similar to K (or to its copy) and that he himself may have been uncertain as to the use of double lettering through Ukrainian interference.

Silence has also reigned a long time over A1. After a brief mention in *Luč sveta* (1920: 103), studies of the PSM have exhumed it at the time of the Bern Trial (cf. Rollin 1991, 35).

Another anonymous edition, which is therefore designated A2, appeared in Moscow in 1905[27] from the lithographic presses of I. I. Paškov, and bearing the title *Drevnie i sovremmennye Protokoly sobranij Sionskix Mudrecov* (The ancient and modern Protocols of the Meetings of the Sages of Zion). If it is not possible to give a precise date for the booklet, it is instead possible to fix the publication as being not before October, through a phrase found in the Introduction which says that, while in Russia one goes with joy to death "for the fatherland and the Tsar,"

> this October, in a France now governed by the anarchy of the capital of Zion, entire regiments have refused to go to on active service (p. 9).[28]

The PSM are presented by an unknown editor who, as K had already done, warns the reader of the incorrect linguistic nature of the dictated text.[29] He attaches an untitled introduction, which repeats in some insertions information and remarks from the *Translator's Note,* where for the first time the design of the "symbolic serpent" appears, with the motto in Russian (p. 11).[30]

One can note certain inconsistencies; e.g., in the context of a speech in which the Jews are always referred to in the third person. In a passage (p. 5) one reads: "but *we,* Jews"; neither is it clear to what the note "St Petersburg, 4 November. Translation by Semenov" refers, at the end of a text in which it says: "with *us* in Russia" (p. 9).[31] There follows a *Covering Letter,* a mere variant (repetitive) of the *Translator's Note.*

If K was subdivided into 22 chapters and A1 into 27, this edition arranges the text into 24.[32] Compared with A1, there are more textual additions than in

K (some of which are unknown in the rest of the tradition[33]). Some of these prove to be omissions with respect to both of the others, and some of them filter out rude and unfortunate expressions.[34] In one of these (between the 2nd and the 3rd "Protocols"), together with a quotation from Nehemiah, the first "Translator's Note" disappears, and the second (on Marxism, Darwinism, and Nietzscheism) is shortened.

Noticeable among the most important modifications is the removal of the only *internal* indication of the fact that the writing of the PSM does not date back to the last years of the 19th century, but rather to the beginning of the 20th century.[35] Moreover, the passages that refer to the origins of the plans for the Temple of Solomon are left out.[36] Significant also are the finishing touches of "Frenchness" and later temporal transpositions.

A2 therefore derives from a text parallel to K and A1, but contains considerable interventions, which cannot but prove that K and A1 cannot have their provenance from A2 or its copy. The proof of this is the many textual details from the cases of *lectio facilior* (cf. *Note on the Edition*). One also therefore comes across interpretations that follow more closely the text of Joly. Here there are corresponding passages not found in K and A1 as well as phrases containing expressions from Joly, which are absent in the preceding editions.

The first sentence of the *Note,* here taken out of context and which, as has been said, has been transposed to the beginning as a *Letter,* is collocated at the end of the PSM and modified to identify the mysterious "sages" in the upper orders of Freemasonry. In any case, as Rollin (1991, 35[37]) has already revealed, such modifications are not "insignificant," but are surprising "for a text on which such importance has been conferred."

This edition has passed unobserved until recent years.

The fourth edition of the PSM, to be named N, was edited by Sergej Aleksandrovič Nilus (1862–1929), the descendant of a family of Swedish origin and already well-known as the publisher of the *Conversation with Motovilov* by Serafim of Sarov. N is the version that then served from 1918 onwards for the diffusion of the text worldwide. It appeared with the title *Protokoly sobranij*[38] *sionskix mudrecov* (The protocols of the meetings of the sages of Zion) in the 12th chapter (*Antixrist, kak blizkaja političeskaja vozmožnost'*) of the second edition[39] of the book which had made him famous as a mystical writer and zealous convert: *Velikoe v malom* (Carskoe Selo, 1905[40]). It was then reprinted various times. [41] After the Revolution, the 1911 reprint was taken by a German Russian émigré magazine, *Luč sveta* (1920), then it came out in Berlin in 1922, in Paris in 1927, and from there it was reintroduced into post-Soviet Russia.

The name of Nilus has remained so linked to the PSM that he has even been taken as being the author. (This thesis, already widely held in contemporary Russian journalistic circles,[42] was taken up in the West by S. Reinach,[43] then maintained on stylistic grounds by the writer A. Kuprin.[44]) Once the attribution to "the forger Nilus" fell through, he was then cited as the "editor" of the PSM (by General P. Krasnov; cf. Cohn, 169, 179), or the "discoverer" and real interpreter. In any case, he was considered to be the most authoritative publisher (cf. again Romano 1992, 148, Vol'skij 1993, 43 and Begunov 1996, 73).

In reality, N is only a variant of A2, in which the division is into 24 chapters. The *Translator's Note*[45] appears, reworked but recollocated in its place, as a note to his name ("All this has been obtained from *my* correspondent...."). The first phrase uses a form which is closer to A1 than to A2[46] to attribute the text to the mysterious "representatives of Zion of the 33rd degree." As in A2, N omits the long passage of the 2nd Protocol which contains the quotation from Nehemiah and the first "translator's note." It inserts, however, the second, with some modifications, *into* the text. In the 4th Protocol (7th of A1, 6th of A2, and N), a phrase from Joly was badly translated into Russian. A2 seeks to correct this by producing almost a nonsense, and N recognizes the mistake, but not being able to restore it, omits the anomalous term, reducing the list of nouns to a couple.[47] One comes across a similar case in the 10th Protocol.[48]

As far as the other modifications go, some are relatively marginal. For example, where K, A1, and A2 indicate with initials the supposed interlocutors of the mysterious reporter, N uses the impersonal form. Others concur both lexically and morphologically in a later cleanup of the text. Furthermore, even N has "solitary"[49] additions present.

N is distinguished in a marked way from K and A1,[50] but in part also from A2, essentially by the following characteristics:

the Old Testament references are eliminated and details relevant to the pre-Christian era which go back to the "Solomonic" origins of the PSM[51];

the French (and "Francophone") characteristics are accentuated in the text[52]; and

later movements in time take place in the sequencing of the plan, introducing a notable change in the sense of the text.

Čerikover's indications were taken up again by Rollin (1991, 35) according to whom N (but also in part A2) were "more European than Russian, while the editions of *Znamja* and of Butmi [identified by him with A1: C.D.M.] were rather more adapted to fit the Russian internal politics of that time." They appear, therefore, to be substantially correct, once agreed that we are not dealing with the second deriving from the first. However, they are extremely partial and insufficient to fully validate the textual operation begun by A2 and completed by N.

In perfecting the "linguistic cleansing," accentuating the "French" traits of the Jewish project for world domination, shifting attention onto the *mudrecy,* who are no longer those of the Solomon's Temple but rather of the *Alliance Israélite Universelle* or of the Zionist movement, N had all the requirements for supplanting the preceding editions and acquiring the role of the privileged source of the PSM. The story of its success, beginning from just after the First World War, coincides almost completely with that of the PSM.

The fifth edition of the PSM was by Georgij Vasil'evič Butmi de Kacman[53] (1856–1918?), landowner, retired officer, and friend of Kruševan with whom he was among the founders of the "Alliance of the Russian People," and later held to be "a very well-known writer, very patriotic, incapable of knowingly entering on a intrigue based on suspect material" (*Protocols* 1934, 11).[54] The fifth edition will be called B.

It appeared at the end of 1905 (the *Preface* is dated 5 December) or the beginning of 1906[55] in the pamphlet *Obličitel'nye reči. Vragi roda čelovečeskogo* published by the "Alliance of the Russian People," with the title *Protokoly izvlečennye iz tajnyx xranilišč Sionskoj Glavnoj Kanceljarii* (Protocols dealing with the secret deposits of the Central Chancellery of Zion). It then had other editions.[56] From the third (*obrabotannoe,* not simply *ispravlennoe*), which we shall call B3, a different sequence of the Protocols is introduced, evidently to offer the readers the text as it might have appeared in the "original."[57] This is a reworking of the text which makes one suppose that Butmi had a greater familiarity with the text than the other publishers, but that has no relevance to our purposes, since the "natural" sequence (1st, 2nd, 3rd, etc.) not only is common to K, A1, A2, N, and B (first two editions). It also follows the order of the passages copied from Joly, (of which obviously there is no mention), which show the original order.

B has close parallels with A1,[58] beginning with the subdivision into 27 Protocols (and not 22 or 24), in such a way as to lend support to the idea that Butmi might be the publisher also of A1.[59] However, there is no lack of differences consisting of omissions and differing interpretations and also of micro-variants which connect B to A2 and N. Moreover, B also contains isolated additions,[60] and it does not seem likely that the same publisher would have published the same text at so short a distance of time in two editions, which while they are similar, are so contrasting.

A partial reprint of B3 is included in the fifth chapter (*Izloženie evrejskoj politiki noveješčego vremeni*) of Demčenko, 1906,[61] of which the preface is dated 30 September. This will be designated as D. The variants are insignificant, and such as to convince one that one is dealing with a *descripta,* interesting only from a historical-cultural point of view, but irrelevant from an ecdotic one.

B has maintained a fair presence in the history of the PSM. In Russia it fulfilled one of its functions at the time of its appearance,[62] but it had some success also in the West, in Germany,[63] and in France, where Butmi had contacts before the war.[64] Jouin's version (1922) was reprinted several times,[65] and has given rise to some discussion on the relationship between B and N.[66]

Xar'kov's review, *Mirnyj trud,* published in No. 8 of 1905 (censor's visa: 28 September 1905) a "shortened edition" of the PSM presented by N. Mordvinov at St. Petersburg in a meeting of the *Russkoe sobranie* as the "speech of one of the leaders or administrators of the Jewish people, read in the meetings of the heads of Zionism": *Tajny politiki, sposoby ee dejstvij i rezul'taty, dostignutye eju pri pomošči nauki i lželiberalizma* (Translation from the French, 1902).[67] This we shall call R2.

The typed copy kept in the library of A. Striževᴠ (published by Begunov 1996, 102–114; R1) was probably earlier and came from Warsaw and bears the signature of General G. Skalon, Governor of the Kingdom of Poland between 1905 and 1914. This is not so much because the Warsaw copy is "more correct and complete than that of St. Petersburg" (Begunov 1996, 99),[68] but for the fact that interpretations in it are found to be closer to K.[69] Begunov, convinced that the PSM hark back to the 1880s, claims that one is dealing with a genuine document, dependent certainly on the PSM, but developed autonomously in French by a mysterious economist who was a Jew and a Mason,[70] even if the "Russian" traits are even more marked than K, A1, and B. The Warsaw version and that of St. Petersburg are two different Russian translations.[71]

R is an abridgement of the PSM, as the same Begunov shows in comparing some passages of R1 and of N. However, it does not derive from N, but rather from K or better, from its copy. In fact, there where it indicates the elimination of restless politicians under the directives of Israel, besides the addition of "Count Murav'ev,"[72] one notes the listing of Carnot, *Gambetta,* Faure, and McKinley. In the corresponding passage (the first "Translator's Note," omitted from A2 and N) the name of Gambetta appears only in K and A1, but A1 was presented to the censor in St. Petersburg more than two months after the publication of R2. R also keeps two passages which hark back to the protograph or original, which K omits (cf. *Note on the Edition*).

The text was probably drafted by a person who spoke Russian with Ukrainian interference as the creator of K did. One sees, for example, the strange use of the word *oslušnik,* in the phrase: "if among them there is a spy[73] or a traitor." This "concise edition" of the PSM reappeared in serial form in the course of 1906 in a magazine and in a booklet (R3 and R4),[74] and attests to an even more confused state of the "story" of the PSM, both for the extreme freedom in the reworking of the text and for the dating of the presumed "translation" (1902) which should no longer take into account the indication of A1 and B (9 December 1901). However it is important also because of the extracts, or the interpretations, absent in K, which find comparisons in the other editions, and which assure us of their closeness to the primitive level of the PSM.

Finally Begunov (1996, 66–71) reports another "concise edition" of the PSM,[75] which appeared (together with an anti-Russian Masonic document believed to have been written in the United States in 1871[76]) in a brochure (pp. 1–7) published in Moscow in 1917: *Izvlečenie iz protokolov 1-go Sionistskogo kongressa, byvšego v Bazele v avguste 1897 g., doložennyx Sovetu starejšin "Knjazem izgnanija" Teodorom Gerclem* (Extract from the Protocols of the First Zionist Congress, held at Basle in August 1897, shown to the Council of the Elders of the "Prince of Exile," Theodor Herzl). This will be designated I.

One is dealing here with an anthology of extracts from certain "Protocols."[77] Begunov (1996, 423) is convinced that he has in his hands a genuine document, come across casually in Russia at the time of Herzl's trip (1903); that is to say, another translation. However, one only needs to read the first sentence to understand that one is dealing with an extract from N.[78] One is led to the same conclusion by the nature of a biblical quotation in Latin (Proverbs 8.15: *"Per me reges regnant"*; 4th) which I, like N, corrupts into *"regnat."*

If I is dependent on N, not only is it not a translation, but it is a forgery compiled after December 1905. Its appearance in 1917 offers however an interesting date. It was that year that Nilus "discovered" that the PSM had been edited by Herzl. Therefore either I is the source of the "discovery" or it is a new hoax created to render the discovery plausible.

NOTES

1. *Les Protocoles, leur origine et leur diffusion* (1934). The only copy that has been traced (WL, London) has now disappeared. I shall, however, make references to the quotations in Rollin 1991 and Cohn 1969; the conclusion we draw is that only three sources had been taken into account (K, N, and B).

2. The paragraphs are not marked by K; A2 uses progressive Roman numerals; and A1, N, and B mark them *protokoly.*

3. Their presence in all the editions but above all, the absence of a "translator" (cf. Chap. 2) proves it belongs to a primitive "convoy."

4. Bugunov (1996, 423), who has taken into account all the data immersed in the preceding "apparitions" of the PSM, proposes a more complex diagram, in which the "line" of Nilus indicates the best text: in it, however, the greater part of the evidence is given as "missing" or "lost."

5. Demčenko (1906, 34) indicated in numbers 3895–3898 and 3902, from 26–29 January and 1 February 1906 (the numbers cited correspond to 22–26 and 29 January 1906, where the PSM does not appear). Demčenko claims that the text should be "absolutely identical" to that of Butmi, and therefore of no interest in our researches.

6. The information is baldly stated in Nilus (1995, 2:471), while Begunov (1996, 73) specifies that the shelfmark of the RNB was <34.50.4.1004>, adding, however, that since 1970 the book has been missing, therefore its "compositions and sources are unknown."

7. Thus Begunov (1996, 73; he dates it 1907), who also attributes A1 to Butmi. In *Literatura o evrejax* (1995), 307 the edition refers to 1906 and is explicitly indicated as a reprint of A1.

8. Cf. A. Čancev, *Kruševan P. A.,* in RP, Vol. 3 (1995), 172–73: the author of short stories and novels, he wrote also under a pseudonym (cf. Masanov Vol. 4 (1960), 256).

9. As a result of which in July he was the target of an assassination attempt by Pinxus Daševskij.

10. Cf. Raskin, *Nacional'naja pravaja* 1992, 8. The *Russkoe sobranie,* founded on 26 January 1901, was the first of the so-called "Black Hundred" political groups, to which many right-wing writers and journalist belonged (cf. Stepanov 1992, 32–33).

11. Stepanov 1992, 98.

12. Which takes its title from the 2nd Russian edition (1880) of Osman Bey's 1873a edition.

13. On the basis of an unsubstantiated gloss by Dudakov, the editors of Nilus 1995 (2:473–77) attribute it to the selfsame Nilus.

14. As thus they are maintained, except with a different numeration, in the other editions.

15. I shall refer to this from now on. Cf. the *Note on the Edition.*

16. "We are printing the second part of these protocols in a notably reduced form."

17. Cf. the *Note on the Edition*.

18. E.g., 5, 17: «порядок у них» (A2, N omit; B: «в», 61: «агенствами, у которых централизуются» (A1, A2, N, B: «в»).

19. I thank W. Moskovich for suggesting this.

20. E.g., «права» per «плана».

21. Cf. 1 Tim. 6.10, «корень всех зол» (cf. Nilus 1899).

22. As M. Men'šikov (cf. Chap. 2) presents the document as being offered to him by a mysterious and "refined" lady.

23. Without drawing hasty conclusions, it must be remembered that the brother of the presumed "first publisher" of the PSM, M. P. Stepanov, was a General of the Guards.

24. Nilus 1995, 2:472

25. Not all, however: cf. (3rd) the persistence of «борятся» for «борются».

26. The Jewish management of politics (1st) «имеет право заменить ужасы войны менее заметными *кознями*, которыми мы поддерживаем террор» which becomes in A1 and remains in N and B) «...*казнями*». The term *terror* has an exclusively political force, and not as it is sustained with the "executions" (*kazni*), but rather with the "conspiracies" *(kozni)* of a "strategy of terror."

27. Its "precedence" with respect to A1 is more heraldic rather than necessarily chronological.

28. Cf. the polemic which had exploited in France with the news that "committees of Hervéian propaganda [from the French Parliamentary Deputy G. Hervé] are designing posters to send to conscripts to persuade them not to fulfill their military service" ("Contre la patrie," *Le Temps,* 8 October 1905).

29. "We are printing all of this manuscript without modifications or corrections of any sort, given that it is not possible to say that the translation of the language in which the original was written was not very good: there are incomprehensible and illiterate passages; but we have preferred to leave the manuscript intact, since its entire style with all its imperfections, almost reinforces the credibility of its authenticity" (p. 1).

30. According to G. Bostunič (1928), the first "plan" (up to "Petersburg") may have appeared in Ljutostankij 1902–1905, but (at least in the example I have consulted) there is no trace of it.

31. Masanov 1958, 3:105, reports three "Semenov," but this could obviously mean another. Perhaps the indication referred to the *Covering Letter,* or to the text itself, or it chanced to appear by error at the end of the Introduction.

32. In the Bible, there are three books of 24 chapters each: Joshua, II Samuel, and the gospel of Luke. If there is a "biblical" intention, it certainly concerned the book of Joshua.

33. For example: (1): "how are the laws of the Creator, since Nature is only a synonym for God."

34. For example (17) a clumsy phrase on the Christian religion is omitted ("our most dangerous adversary in the doctrines on the spiritual world and on the life to come").

35. K, A1 «что может быть не скоро, может быть **к концу века** и далее» / A2: «*что будет через не мало времени, а может быть до того времени пройдет* **целый век**» (to say "towards the end of the century" obviously means to write at the beginning of the 20th century). The phrase comes from Joly ("*Dans combien de temps s'accomplira-t-elle?—"Avant un siècle*"), but here we are dealing with a recurrent *topos* in conspiracy literature.

36. For example, (13) omits: "at the time in which our sages constructed the program of their actions for tens of centuries."

37. Speaking of N, very similar to A2 (which he does not know).

38. In the title: *zasedanij* (as in K: "Sessions").

39. According to some (Cohn, Taguieff, Tazbir) the first edition of Nilus's book harks back to 1901, with that of 1905 being the third and not the second edition. The information comes from Fry 1931, 93 and is without foundation.

40. The *nulla osta* of the censor is "28 September 1905, but the *Postface* is dated "Optina Pustyn', 24–25 October 1905." The book came out at the end of December.

41. *Bliz grjaduščij Antixrist,* Sergeiev Posad 1911 (2 printings) and 1912 (2 printings), *Bliz est' pri dverex,* Sergiev Posad 1917.

42. Referring to the years 1905–1910, I. Kolyško wrote to Vl. Burcev on 7 September 1934: "When…this author's name [Nilus] was mentioned all over," in *Nikolaevsky mss.,* 14, 9–6. I thank S. Garzonio for having procured for me this material from that archive.

43. In an article in *Opinion,* 26 June 1920.

44. "The Jews or the Judaised Russians obtained from Mr. Kuprin…an article included in the "La cause commune" ["Obščee delo"] to demonstrate that the style of the PSM was in no way different from the other writings of Nilus, which would then prove that he was the sole author of the PSM" (Jouin 1922, 136).

45. Without title in N: in Nilus 1911 as *Neobxodimye raz"jasnenija* (Necessary explanations).

46.   K, A1 «протоколы написаны» A1: «подписаны...Сионскими представителями»

      A2: «подписали Сионские представители 33»

      N: «*Подписано Сионскими представителями 33 степени*».

47.   Joly: "protecteur, **promoteur** et rémunerateur"

      K, A1: «покровителем, **проводителем** и вознаградителем».

      A2: «покровителем, **праводателем** и вознаградителем».

N: «*покровителем и вознаградителем*».

The verb *provodit'* means "to lead," and something of the sort "guide" should mean the non-existent *provoditel'* (R1 keeps the term seeking to make it plausible: «**проводителя** на посты»), not indeed "promoter", which would be *načinatel'* (Makarov 1887 offered *popečitel'* or *staratel'*). Whoever used Joly's text evidently not only had poor French, but also little Russian. *Pravodatel'* from A2 (not joined; in any case *zakonodatel'*) means something like "legislator."

48. The expression "***entreprise de publicité***" has been translated (K, A1, and A2) by "*predmet*" ("object," instead of *predprijatie*, "business"), which obviously does not make sense, and N corrects with a more plausible but equally arbitrary "*produkt*" ("product," "fruit").

49. E.g., (10th): "If at present we have known how to control the minds of the *gojim* societies to the point where all see world events through the colored lenses of the glasses we have put over their eyes, if now there do not exist for us in any state locks which might impede our access to the so-called (by the stupidity of the *gojim*) state secrets, what will happen when we shall be the recognized owners of the world in the person of our universal king? Let us return to the press."

50. All agree on the divergence between K and N, except Dudakov (1993, 265) who identifies N with K: "the Nilus version with its preface was published for the first time in the St. Petersburg newspaper *Znamja* (1903)." Following such indications, the editors of Nilus 1995 (2:471) asserted that "however, the publication in *Znamja* may be taken as the first of those edited by Sergej Aleksandrovič."

51. E.g., (1st): K, A1, A2 «Во времена величия Греции» / N: «***Еще в древние времена***».

52. E.g., (19th) K, A1, A2: «будет заведывать [A2 add.: каждый департамент,] каждый округ» / N: «*будет заведывать каждый департамент (**французское административное деление**)*». But N (3rd) introduces a reference to the French Revolution absent in K, A1, and A2: «Вспомните французскую революцию, которой мы дали имя "великой"»; now the usage of calling it "Great" (*Velikaja francuzskaja revoljucija*) is exclusively Russian and in not found in French.

53. From the old family of Boutmy, who came from Gand, and were descended from Étienne-Philippe-Joseph (born 1753) who in 1772 in Russia, where he was Lt. Major in the Army and a Knight of St. Vladimir, added to his surname that of his mother assuming the title, Baron de Katzmann: cf. S. Clercx, "Les Boutmy, une dynastie de musiciens belges au XVIII siècles," *Revue belge d'archéologie et d'histoire de l'art* 13 (1943). In the German translation of a monograph he was said to be a native of Jampol im Podolien.

54. The argument recurs, not only for Butmi but also for Nilus; its weakness is already indicated by Benigni (1921): "The authenticity of the document is based on

the good faith of the Russian publisher Nilus and his companion C. [*sic*] Butmi. It is too little.... There remains the internal criticism of the document itself."

55. *Literatura o evrejax* (1995, 289) indicates 1905, while Taguieff (1992, 1:366) January 1906. The two things need not be in opposition, especially since 31 December 1905 in the old calendar corresponds to 13 January 1906 in the new.

56. *Vragi roda čelovečeskogo,* 2nd ed., St. Petersburg 1906; 3rd, St. Petersburg 1906; 4th, St. Petersburg 1906; 5th, St. Petersburg 1907.

57. The order is: 1, 11, 10, 8, 2, 5, 21, 18, 3, 6, 12, 13, 14, 9, 17, 19, 16, 15, 20, 22, 25, 26, 27, 23, 24, 7, 4; Butmi does not even explain why his edition is in 27 "protocols," while that of Nilus (which even cites: *"The Magnificent among the Dregs and the Anti-Christ as an Imminent Political Possibility. Note by an Orthodox,* Carskoe Selo 1905," 87, note) is in 24.

58. Identical apart from the titles (in A1 proper title, and in B subtitle): "Where the root of contemporary disorder lies in the social ordering of Europe in general and Russia in particular," absent in K, A2, and N.

59. Extremely similar to K ("Butmi's version is almost exactly the reproduction of that of *Znamja*"). B is still more similar to A1, and "Čerikover...holds that it is the first edition of the version given by Butmi" (Rollin 1991, 35).

60. E.g., (2nd): "At present not a single Ministry can hold on to power if we do not support them with a recommendation behind them, or of the people."

61. Ethnographer and geographer (1842–1912; cf. his *O navodnenii Aralo-kaspijskogo nizmennosti* [Kiev, 1900]); he also studied the Ukrainian Question (*Pravda ob ukrainofil'stve* [Kušnerev 1905]) and was occupied in politics, from a position close to *Sojuz Russkogo naroda* (see also *Po povodu našej smuty* [Kiev 1905]).

62. Apart from its use in D, Cf. Ja. B[*ulan*]ov, "Vinovniki revoljucii," *Moskovskie vedomosti,* 21 March 1906: "For all those that have had the possibility to read the splendid book of Mr G. Butmi, *Vragi čelovečstva";* cf. also V. Protopopov, *V poiskax zemli obetovannoj,* Spb. 1908, "in the analysis of the Zionist movement and of its future author uses very fully G. Butmi's book" (Dudakov 1993, 170).

63. Cf. *Luč sveta* (1920): 103.

64. Jouin IV, 1922, 136. "It was in 1912 that he consigned, in Paris, the Russian Edition of his *Protocols* to M. *** who had kindly passed them on.... From then on Mr G. Butmi did not return to Paris, but his son Étienne was here two years ago." The story of the PSM is enriched in this way by another mysterious personality, this M. ***, of whom—to my knowledge—no one has ever bothered to establish the identity. Perhaps we are dealing with A. Chabry, with whom Butmi was in correspondence. (cf. Butmi 1898, 14–15).

65. Cf. Taguieff 1992, 1:370–72: RISS Paris 1934, 2 *Action Fatima-La Salette* (Seignosse 1965. Published privately, France 1970s) *Revision,* No. 3–7 (1989).

66. The hypothesis of Msgr. Jouin is the most recurrent: "the two translators had in their hands, in 1901, the incomplete pages of the French manuscript and trusted in the same sources" (1922, 136).

67. A reactionary and antisemitic review. In 1907, the volume *Evrei v istorii* by A. Šmakov, and the same *Tajny politiki* were republished in a monograph.

68. In reality, in each of the two, one notes passages missing from the other, and those present only in R1 effectively prevail, and R2 attests interpretations closer to the archetype.

69. E.g., (repeatedly): "*antisemizm*" for "*antisemitizm*."

70. Not so the editors of Nilus 1995 (2:472).

71. The nature of the variants excludes it. As regards the thesis that in R one is dealing (in French) with the French "original" of the PSM, it clashes with the fact that *in the text,* the first "Translator's Note" appears to have been reworked.

72. And, in R1, of a mysterious "B"; Mixail Nikolaevič Murav'ev (1845–1900), a Russian Foreign Minister who died suddenly on January 10 after drinking a coffee.

73. *Oslušnik* in Russian means "disobedient"; in Ukrainian *osluxatisja,* "listen to, eavesdrop," explains the improper use of the Russian lemma on the part of a Ukrainian speaker in the sense of "one who eavesdrops," a "spy."

74. Respectively, "Reč'odnogo iz rukovoditelej...." (trans. from the French, 1902), in *Samoderžavie* (Kiev) 1–5 (1906) and *Evrejskaja politika i ee rezul'taty* (Kremenčug, printed by A. Dikovskij, 1906). All three editions, therefore, appeared in Ukraine (Xar'kov, Kiev, and Kremenčug), which, given the presence of Ukrainian-isms in the higher levels of the text (K) and those found in R, leads one to think of an origin in the circles in which the protograph had been produced. R2 shows variations closer to Joly than R1, which seem to come from the "third" production (A2, N, and R2) «люди всех *мнений, всех [R2: направлений и] доктрин», rather than K, A1, B, and R1: «люди всех доктрин»; cf. Joly: "*hommes de toute opinion et de toute doctrine*") but which come from the protograph.

75. *Literatura o evrejax* (1995, 166) registers it in the section dedicated to the First Zionist Congress, therefore concerning the (supposed) intervention of Herzl.

76. A. Pike, *Izlečenie iz Opredelenija "Svjatejščego Velikogo Sobranija Zaslužennyx Masonov", sostojavščegosja v 1871 godu v g. Čarl'stoune, SŠA,* which came from *Morals and Dogma of the Ancient and Accepted Scottish Rite of Free-Masonry* (Charleston, S.C., USA, 1871). Albert Pike (1809–1891), Grand Master of the Supreme Council of the USA, Southern Jurisdiction, gives an anthology on the Masonic system, but the text published in Russian in 1917 (reprinted by Begunov 1996, 50–52) does not figure. The image "Luciferine" used by Pike comes from L. Taxil, *Le diable au XIX siècle* (1892–1895). Msgr. L. Meurin, an admirer of Taxil and author of *La Franc-Maçonnerie, synagogue de Satan* (1893), uses as the key to his accusations the name and the apocryphal writings of Pike, and the same road was

followed by D. Margiotta, *Le Palladisme, culte de Satan Lucifer* (Grenoble, 1895), known to the Russian "Black One Hundred"; cf. Stepanov 1992, 30. E. Šabel'skaja used this tradition in his novel *Satanisty XX veka* (1912). Moreover, B3 records Pike as the occupant of the "Holiest throne of the Supreme Patriarch of Universal Masonry." Nilus 1911 (cf. *Luč sveta* (1920): 318) also follows the theme when he cites the "Black Pope,"... "a certain Jew, A. Pike," who had established the cult of Bafomet and of the Anti-Christ at Charlestown.

77. According to N: 1, 3, 4, 5, 7, 8, 9, 10, 11, 12, 14, 15, 17, and 23.

78. 1, 201–204: K, A1, B: 1, 201–204: K, A1, B: «Во времена величия Греции мы впервые крикнули слово "свобода"»

A2: «Во времена величия Греции мы *среди народа* впервые крикнули слов*а*: "свобода, *равенство и братсьво*"».

N, I: «*Еще в древние* времена мы *среди народа* впервые крикнули слова "свобода, *равенство, братство*"».

CHAPTER 2

The "Unknown Witnesses"

There are various sources of "evidence" according to which the editions of the PSM mentioned up to now should in some way depend on preceding witnesses, and which among other things would prove the existence of a text prior to 1903. However, no such witnesses have come to light, and they will thus be indicated as "unknown witnesses."

The first "unknown source" (*Drevnie i sovremennye protokoly sobranij*[1] *Sioniskix mudrecov* [The ancient and modern protocols of the meetings of the sages of Zion]) harks back to the years 1895–1897, and is designated S after its publisher Stepanov.

The *kamerger* Filipp Petrovič Stepanov (1857–1932), Executive Councillor of State, was Procurator of the Muscovite Section of the Holy Synod and member of Sojuz Russkogo naroda. His brother, General Mixail Petrovič (1853–1917),[2] was attaché to Elizaveta Fedorovna, the sister of the Empress and wife of the Tsar's uncle, the Grand Duke Sergej Aleksandrovič.

In a sworn statement made in Yugoslavia on April 17, 1927, Stepanov declared that:

> In 1895, the retired major Aleksej Nikolaevič Suxotin [1848–1903], who had the neighboring estate to mine in the Tula Province, sent me a manuscript copy of the PSM. He told me that a lady friend of his (whose name he did not divulge), and who had lived in Paris, had found it there at a friend's (I imagine, a Jew) and before leaving Paris had secretly made a translation, a single copy of which she then brought with her to Russia, and had given to him, Suxotin. First he ran off 100 copies on a duplicator, but this edition proved hard to read, and he therefore decided to produce it at a printer's but without indicating the date, the location, or the printer. I was helped to do this by Arkadij Ippolitovič Kelepovskij, who at that time carried out special duties for the Grand Duke Sergej Aleksandrovič. He gave it in 1897 to be printed by the Provincial Governor's printers.[3] S. A. Nilus reprinted these protocols in his book with a suitable comment (cited in Begunov 1996, 77).

The anonymous lady has since been identified as Justina Glinka (1844–1918), a diplomat's daughter, once a contributor to *Oxrana* through the offices of General Orževskij[4] and a follower of the theosophist Blavatskaja. Stepanov would thus have been only the final link in the chain, after the Jew, the lady, and the retired major Suxotin. Naturally, the edition would have been free from the usual editorial information.[5]

Stepanov's story is highly suspect. However, it has been believed because it finds confirmation in a note in Nilus, who had been introduced at Court through Stepanov's brother, Mixail, who introduced him to his future wife, a distant relative of his. This is found in the 1917 edition (*"He is near, he is at the door"*) which indicates Suxotin as the "source":

> In 1901, I had the occasion to gain access to a manuscript entitled...The Protocols of the Meetings of the Sages of Zion, and it was brought to me by Aleksej Nikolaevič Suxotin now deceased (remember in your prayers, O God-fearing reader, the soul's repose of boljarin Aleksij[6]), already Marshal of the Nobility for the District of Čern', and later governor of Stavropol'.... Incidentally, Suxotin informed me that he had also received a copy of the manuscript from a lady who lived permanently abroad, and that this lady was a landowner of Čern (I remember that he told me also the name, but I have forgotten) and that she had obtained it by very mysterious means (perhaps in fact by theft).

It is Chayla's opinion that *this* mysterious lady was not Glinka, but rather the cousin and sometime lover of Nilus, N. A. Volodimerova née Matveeva (1843–1932); in his memoir: *Mme. K*[omarovskaja].[7] Rollin (1991, 33) gives a clear bill of health for the Stepanov Edition (and thus the role of Suxotin), except for entertaining doubts about the date:

> A note attached to the apparatus used for this print run [*scil.*: the duplicator], which was found in the library of V. V. Pašukanis [1879–1919],[8] indicates that it was printed prior to the first edition.

Rollin identifies it as that in *Znamja* (1903), but it is much more probable that the note (if it does in fact refer to the Stepanov edition) refers to a 1905 edition (A1, A2, or N). The same note "indicates that this print run was made with the participation of Račkovskij" (ibid., 483), which poses other problems.[9] For his part, Cohn (1969, 70) records that

> a copy of the duplicated text still existed at the time of the Bern Process in 1934. It is found in the Pašukanis Collection of the Lenin Library in Moscow, and the Soviet authorities sent a four page photostatted copy[10] to the tribunal.... Boris Nikolaevskij is sure that

we are really dealing with a duplicated copy of Stepanov.... Unfortunately it can no longer be examined.... However the Wiener Library possesses a German translation of the extract sent to Bern.[11] This shows that text must have been practically identical to that prepared later by Nilus.

Even if the duplicated print run has disappeared and the printed edition is untraceable, S might be identical to N for still another reason. On November 23, 1919, a "White" newspaper, *V Moskvu!,* printed at Rostov-na-Donu published an article that revealed a so-called secret dispatch on the Jewish financing of the Bolshevik Revolution[12] sent in December 1918 from French counterespionage in the United States to the French Government (cf. Begunov 1996, 194–97): two passages of the *Sekretnye Sionskie protokoly, izd. 1897*[13] are quoted. Although brief, they are sufficient to identify where they come from. This is particularly so of the second (from the 7th Protocol),[14] which coincides point by point,[15] and only with N, with variants and additions not only with respect to the original text, but also of the nearest witness (A2). All this shows definitively the hoaxed character of the document, but here there is interest for another side of the question.

Stepanov's story diverges from the preceding versions of the origin of the PSM.[16] If it had arrived in Russia, already translated, in 1895, it would not have been possible to collocate it with the First Zionist Congress (1897). It is not possible to understand why A1 and B refer the translation to 1901, nor why Nilus claims to have received the manuscript from Suxotin only in that year. Above all, Men'šikov's 1902 article would not make sense when it talks of a completely unknown document, while at that time the PSM would already have passed through four or five people's hands, over and above the journalists mentioned by Men'šikov and it would already have been published twice.

Instead of progressing further into the quicksands of the various stories about the origins of the PSM, we shall remain fixed on two aspects of the text. First, if the text (at least the duplicated one sent to Bern) was "practically identical" to N, as everything leads us to suppose, it must have been a successor to K (1903), and probably not published before 1905. Secondly, the title of S ("The Ancient and Modern Protocols of the Meetings of the Sages of Zion") is identical to that of A2 (1905),[17] and together with it takes the road from "true forgery" to "forged truth" (cf. *infra*).

Brazol' and Nožkin write of an 1897 edition because in 1917, Nilus had "revealed" that in that year the PSM had been read at Basle by Theodore Herzl.[18] It is this, therefore, which suggested to Stepanov to give the publication date of his presumed edition as 1897, and not the reverse with the "document" quoting Stepanov's edition, as Begunov (1996, 423) has it.

S (in its duplicated form) could have some grounds for his theory, but in terms rather different from those considered up to now. The data referred to by L. Wolf,[19] which is neither proved nor should be ignored, and which sustains that, immediately prior to N (December 1905), "The Protocols first appeared in the shape of small pamphlets or broadsheets," and therefore the copy sent by the Soviet authorities to Bern in 1935 might be one of those booklets. In which case even the involvement of Račkovskij could be well-founded (as Vitte narrates). However, it does not refer to the time of his Parisian activities, but rather to that of his rehabilitation. In July 1905, he was nominated Director of the Police Department, with special responsibilities for political affairs.[20]

Until a copy of one of those leaflets is found, all must remain vague. As far as the testimony of Stepanov goes, it would appear that this close acquaintance and almost relative of Nilus, had most probably tried at the distance of more than 20 years to enhance that version with a false declaration.

A second "unknown witness" is the French manuscript that Nilus would have shown in 1909 to Armand Alexandre de Blanquet du Chayla (in Russia Aleksandr Maksimovič: 1885–1945)[21] during his stay at Optina Pustyn', claiming it to be the "original" of the PSM. This will be designated F. If the mysterious lady had carried into Russia the *translation* of the PSM, which then came into Nilus' hands via Suxotin, how could Nilus also have had the *original*?[22] Cohn, despite believing Chayla's testimony, affirms that "there is no proof that [the French edition] had ever left France" (1969, 72). Moreover, many still think (Romano 1992, 148; Vol'skij 1993, 39; and Begunov 1996, 423) that this may be the "original," as Chayla claims that Nilus asserts. Nevertheless it has disappeared, and only uncheckable notes affirm that it may have been conserved in the archive either of Florenskij[23] or Koncevič.[24]

This "unknown witness" poses serious doubts as to the trustworthiness of Chayla and indeed of the very existence of a "French original."

On May 12–13, 1921, Chayla published in *Poslednie novosti* (The latest news), his Russian newspaper in Paris, the article "S. A. Nilus i 'Sionskie Protokoly,'" republished in French on May 14 in *La Tribune Juive* (the paper of the Jews in Russia) as "Serge Alexandrovitch Nilus et les "Protocols des Sages de Sion." Among the many inaccuracies, two are particularly noteworthy: the surname of the ex-lover of Nilus (Komarovskaja rather than Volodimerova[25]), and the date of the first edition of the PSM edited by Nilus (1902 rather than 1905).

As regards the former, the coincidence of the erroneous indication of the surname of an acquaintance, the Countess Komarovskaja with whom the Niluses had stayed at Černigov from April 1926 till May 1928 is striking.[26] Chayla's information seems to have been garnered from a second hand note, which had confused *Natalija* Volodimerova with Ol'ga *Komarovskaja*.

As regards the latter error, it cannot be considered a "lapse of memory" because the same information recurs in the preface of the German edition of Nilus's book (1919) and independently from any possible derivation from Chayla or from his source, the aforesaid Preface. However, both are explicable in relation to Men'šikov's article (1902; cf. *infra*).

Certainly independent from it, however, is Chayla's (exact) information that *The Magnificent among the Dregs* appeared in the Red Cross Press of Carskoe Selo. However, to say such, one only needs to have had a copy of the book in one's hands, while *Luč sveta* claims it was printed by the press of the Laura of Saint Serge. Finally, as Hagemeister (1995, 157) explains, the false note by which Nilus (1991, 60) would have gone to Germany in the winter of 1918–1919 and settled in Berlin, manifestly refers to Sergej Sergeevič [1883–1941], who was Nilus's son.

Therefore, Chayla says that he had known Nilus, who showed him F, in February 1909 (when they both lived at Optina Pustyn'.[27]).

> On the first page one noted a large very lilac bluish stain. One had the impression that at some time an inkwell had been overturned on it.... The paper was thick and yellowish, the text was written in French by many hands and, it appeared to me, with different inks.... Reading the text I was struck by some special particulars in the text. There were spelling errors and, above all, some of the grammatical construction was not French. Too much time has now passed to be able to say whether the text contained any Russianisms. One thing is beyond doubt, the manuscript had been edited by a foreigner.[28]

Chayla says that he did not believe for an instant that that crude hoax could be "The Charter of Anti-Christ" as he said Nilus claimed, and he considered it with the utmost annoyance to be a fake. Whether it had been edited in Paris by Račkovskij, whom Nilus had nominated as the person who had confided the manuscript to Mme. K[omarovskaja], or whether it was a translation carried out in Russia, it was undoubtedly a fake. A fact to which he was only too happy to attest once the "PSM case" exploded.

However, before Count Chayla, there was also Princess Katarzyna Radziwiłłowa (1858-1941; pseudonyms: Count Paul Vassili[29] and Hildegarde Ebenthal) who said she had seen F. She was an adventuress who had been condemned in 1900 for fraudulent cheques and the swindling of *"wyrachowana kokietka."*[30] She gave an interview on February 25, 1921 to the *American Hebrew,*[31] claiming to have personally seen F in Paris in 1904 or 1905, through the offices of Matvej Golovinskij,[32] who would have been the compiler of it with Ivan Manasevič-Manuilov,[33] on behalf of Račkovskij.[34] According to her, these (who meanwhile had both died) had done nothing more than rework a prior forgery produced in 1884 by General P. V. Orževskij in the ambit of the "secret services." Princess Radziwiłłowa described it thus:

> The manuscript was in French, handwritten but by differing hands, on yellow colored paper. I remember perfectly that, on the first page, there was an enormous blue ink mark.[35]

The declaration of the Polish princess was subsequently confirmed by an interview (*American Hebrew,* 4 March 1921[36]) with an American woman who at that time was with her in Paris, one Henrietta Hurlbut, who declared herself to be an "anti-Semite" and therefore not suspicious. However, the testimony of the two ladies was immediately challenged by Vl. Burcev,[37] because at the time neither Golovinskij nor Račkovskij were in Paris: the former had remained there only until 1900 while the latter until October 1902. As regards Manuilov (the only one at that time in Paris), he was one of Pleve's men and "a mortal enemy of Račkovskij and his protector Vitte," and thus it must be excluded that "he could have dedicated himself to such work in behalf of Račkovskij" (Rollin 1991, 453). This is without taking into account the additional fact that the PSM had appeared in print in *Znamja* in 1903 and that Men'šikov had already spoken of it in *Novoe vremja* in 1902.[38]

What is striking is the "singular coincidence" between the testimonies of Chayla and that of Radziwiłłowa (yellowish paper, different handwritings, large ink mark). General Aleksandr Nečvolodov (1864-1938[39]), who supported the authenticity of the PSM with alacrity, had no doubts: "Mr. du Chayla lies, similarly Princess Radziwill and Mrs Hurblut [*sic*]" (1924, 299). He cites as evidence an article, "The Homecoming of the Cossacks," which appeared a year later in another emigrants' paper (*Slovo,* 18 September 1922) in which it is stated that Chayla had been an agent of the Bolsheviks in the (White) Cossack Army on the Don, that in 1920 he had been tried, condemned, and pardoned by General Vrangel'[40] and that "at present" he was employed in the repatriation of Cossacks who had emigrated "under the orders of Čičerin."

According to N. Markov, following the sentence of April 1920, Chayla had been expelled from the Crimea (and not shot) because he was a French citizen. He then moved to Bulgaria and made contact with the Soviet Agent "Karlikoff," and during the Bern Trial *L'Action nationale* (29 December

1934) published a report that Chayla had then returned to the already Soviet Russia in 1922–1923 in the company of the journalist Joël de Montclair and Professor Erwin Grimm. All this contradicts Chayla's story, who in turn denied these accounts. However the charges in the Crimea actually existed and according to a note of V. X. Dvatc (in Nilus 1995, 2:269–70), the go-between between Čičerin and "the Russian Bolshevik of French nationality Chayla" was the President of the Bulgarian Council, Stamboljski. A suspect source therefore (first "agent provocateur," then Čičerin's agent)[41] like Radziwiłłowa. Nečvolodov (a rabid judeophibe, but not a fool) adds:

> Mr. du Chayla says he arrived in Lyon from the Crimea[42] by way of Constantinople in early April [1921]; now, even without wishing it, one is struck by the fantastic speed of his movements.

He arrived in time to have had the opportunity, in little more than a month, 1) to see "by chance" Msgr. Jouin's edition (the second French edition of the PSM) in the window of a bookshop in Lyon; 2) to buy and read it; 3) to study the then-current polemic; 4) to write a long record (seven newspaper pages, 18 book pages); 5) to make contact with two separate newspapers; and 6) to write, correct, and publish the articles.

From this breadth of information on this Russified French nobleman who was converted to the Orthodox Church and fought for the Whites, but worked for Čičerin, there arises the suspicion that Chayla may have intervened in the matter piloted by the Soviet "Secret Services." This was with the purpose of confirming from an unexpected quarter the substance of Radziwiłłowa's declaration, of which he repeats word for word the characteristics of the mysterious manuscript (F), even though her interviews appeared prior to his arrival in Europe, and along with her and him knowing nothing of K (1903), nor of Joly's method of compilation, which would be revealed only three months later on August 18, 1921.

At the time, Nilus was in the Ukraine at Vl. Ževaxov's (Polovinkin 1995, 264) and was not in a position to read the French emigrant press.[43] However, had he been able to, he would probably have substantially endorsed Chayla's story because, opportunely adapted, it did no more than confirm what he had always sustained in his writings from 1905 onwards.[44]

In reality, Chayla's memorandum offers no new information on the origins of the PSM and on Nilus's edition. The allusion to Pope Pius X's encyclical among the material on Antichrist was easily exhumed from Nilus 1905, 308 or 1911.[45] The collection of esoteric symbols (the "Musée de l'Antéchriste")[46] does no more than back date to 1909 that which anyone could extract from Nilus 1911, as in fact Chayla himself says.[47] As regards the Tarot cards (mystery VII, "the Cart")[48] given as an icon for the antichrist,[49] Nilus had taken it from the book of "a cabalistic Masonic Jew, written in French" which appeared in 1856; in other words Éliphas Lévi.[50]

The suspicion arises, therefore, that in 1909, at Optina Pustyn', Chayla had not yet seen anything at all, which does not exclude, obviously, that he knew Nilus. Rather some additions to the book *Na beregu Božej reki. Zapiski pravoslavnogo* (Sergiev Posad 1916)[51] tell of his conversations on the "mystery of iniquity" with a Frenchman already converted to Orthodoxy a year before who had resided at Optina "already for eight months" (Nilus 1995, 1:259), evidently Chayla. The conversation is dated September 4 and another October 30 (ibid., 268), but there are no records of earlier conversations, while Chayla declares that he met Nilus immediately after his arrival in January. According to Nilus's account, the conversation had touched on the imminent coming of the Antichrist, but not the PSM (even less F). Learning this on February 27, 1938, Chayla wrote to V. Burcev denying that he was "the Frenchman" in question.

> 5) the information in the book *Na beregu svjatoj* [*sic*] *reki* does not apply to me. It deals with the French Abbot Morel, whom I believe visited Optina a year before me[52] (Nilus 1995, 2:265).

If, despite this, one takes Chayla's testimony on F in good faith, in 1909 he did not see the "French original" of the PSM, but rather a version from the Russian carried out to enhance the authenticity of the text. If, however, we are to believe Nilus, then the Franco-Russian Count's intervention is merely a move to deny the authenticity of the PSM; in other words a "false testimony."

Does this perhaps mean a reopening of the whole question of the authenticity of the PSM, as Nečvolodov (and behind him the anti-Jewish press) wanted? Absolutely not; it rather means that there had never ever existed a "French original."

Indeed, why should it ever have existed? Why should the Russians, even if they were spies and living in Paris, have wanted to use French for a forgery destined to circulate in Russia? An "unearthed manuscript" which can be circulated only in translation is the most obvious means for passing off an apocrypha as genuine. The thesis that the PSM had originally been written in French served only to assert its authenticity. It became superfluous once it was known to be a fake.

The story of the "French original" accompanied the PSM from its conception. Men'šikov wrote in 1902:

> A French journalist happened on them, and from him, in some way, they arrived in the hands of my refined hostess. According to her, she translated fragments of the precious documents into Russian.

With some variations, this is supported by Kruševan (1903):

> A manuscript was sent which turned out to be the translation of the protocols.... We do not know how, when, or in what way the minutes of this sitting could have been transcribed in French, and precisely who transcribed them.

Together with the warning that one had to do with "a not entirely happy translation with obscure passages," with "a bad translation," probably to justify the halting Russian. Therefore, from Anonymous from St. Petersburg and from Butmi ("translation from the French"), moreover, from the Muscovite Anonymous (1905, 1) who underlines the defects of the "translation"; and also from Nilus (1905, 394):

> All that had been obtained...from the secret deposits of the Central Chancellery of Sion, which one at present finds on French soil.

Curiously, the critics of the PSM, who should have been led to restrain all those fakers or emissaries of fakers, and, why not, declare F (of which Chayla speaks) a "forgery of a forgery," have passively accepted the idea that the PSM had been published in French. However, the examination of the Russian text poses difficulties difficult to overcome.

Moreover, the title itself, *Protokoly sionskix mudrecov,* already evident in Men'šikov 1902 (and repeated from L, 1904) begs the question as to why *protokoly* — that is, it is necessary to explain why we are not dealing here with proper "minutes"[53]:

> The title of the manuscript does not fully tally with its contents. They are not minutes [*protokoly*] of a meeting, but the lecture, subdivided in sections, of someone holding power (Nilus 1905, 322),

and not *otčety* (reports),[54] *zapiski* (notes, statements), or similar?

Evidently the alloglottic character of the term should suggest from the title onwards that one is dealing with something translated. However, the Russian *Protokol* does not derive from the French *protocole* (which at the turn of the century did not then mean "minutes"[55]) but rather from the German *Protokoll.*[56] Probably according to the original idea of dating the PSM back to the distant past, the expression had been dug up by the compiler for a paronomistic calque on the current title of an antique Russian text published by I. Franko in 1899, *Proročestva ellinskix mudrecov* ("Prophesies" of the pagan philosophers [the Greeks] regarding Christ).[57]

In the second place, the extracts dealt with from Joly's pamphlet show various misunderstandings which consequently produce nonsense (cf. chapter 3), and if all the PSM were to have had a translation from the French, there should have been many more of them, which is not the case. Moreover, nor this would not be incongruous with the idea of the work of an educated Russian in possession of an authentic Hebrew document, and even less that of an operation conducted by the "secret services."

While the "Russifications" introduced in the rendering of some of Joly's passages can be easily explained:

II *"de la tyrannie"* / «самодержавие»;

III *"le prince souverain"* / «царствующие»;

   "règne"/ «царство» (and derivations);

IV *"de son haut"*/ «помазание Божим избранием»

it is easier to imagine the supposed French forms (and their own requirements) of perfectly Russian expressions that recur elsewhere[58]:

1st «владыка»

3rd «кулачество» [59]

9th «комитет министров» [60]

19th «герои и **богатыри**»,[61] etc.

Even the metaphor of "gold" ("riches," "money," but based on the *Gold Standard System* adopted in Russia in 1897) is suspicious: in the face of one isolated case of correspondence Joly/PSM,

4th *"...autre culte que l'or"* / «культ золота»,

l'argent in French (which should be *den'gi*) does not become either *den'gi* nor *serebro* (silver), but rather *zoloto* (gold):

21st "la plus grande puissance des temps modernes, l'argent"

   «величайшая современная сила — золото»,

with the purpose of immediately rendering the reference to the golden monometalism introduced from Vitte (*Leitmotiv* of the economic ideas of the PSM) in an already stated compositional (and linguistic) context.

Furthermore, whether in the passages dealt with by Joly, or in those outside them, and certainly in K, A1, A2, and B, Frenchifications abound. However N manages to inset others, both "political"[62] and "cultural"[63] with the intention of reinforcing the impression of "a text translated from the French."

There are, then, particular forms of late 19th-century Russian lexis, side by side with typically Russian expressions like *vladyka* or *bogatyr'*, which it would be difficult to imagine coming from a French version (*klassicizm*, for "classics," *vino* for "vodka," *stački* for "trusts," *anarxija mysli* for the expression "anarchists of the idea").

However, more than all this, two general considerations bring us to exclude it. First, the presence of duplications in the higher stratum of the text among which the compiler had still not made his choice. These are often at such a distance from each other as to exclude the idea that one is dealing with two different renderings of the same term. Second, the subsequent freedom of re-elaboration (with additions, modifications, cuts, and adjustments), already pointed out in A1 and B, but particularly marked in A2 and N.

The story of the "translation from the French," functioning as the accreditation of a forgery,[64] was probably suggested by the fact that the PSM had in reality been largely plagiarized from a French text: Joly's *Dialogue*. The "unknown witness" of which Chayla speaks becomes a strong argument against the French origins of the PSM. Had he really seen F, it would have been a Russian version; had he not seen it, then we are dealing with a lie invented about another lie to invalidate it.

The third "unknown witness" is that of which Mixail Osipovič Men'šikov (1859–1918) speaks in *Novoe vremja* (7 [20] April 1902): "Zagovory protiv čelovečestva," one of his first "Pis'ma k bližnim"—the column he wrote from December 9[20], 1901,[65] and which we shall denominate M. It is the first definitely datable information we have concerning the PSM.

Men'šikov had a certain reputation as a publicist. A Tolstoyan when young,[66] on friendly terms with Semën Nadson, Anton Čexov, and other writers of the time, he was editor of *Nedelja,* which, if it no longer followed a radical democratic line, was still populist-liberal. He collaborated on *Rus* and then on *Novoe vremja,* the reactionary daily published by A. Suvorin. In his *Diaries* (7 April 1918; cf. 1993, 91), he establishes a parallel between himself, whom he felt to be underestimated by public opinion, and V. Rozanov, noted for his anti-Jewish opinions,[67] and who was, despite this, considered a "great writer." In the 1890s, he underwent a complete political change of heart (similar to Kruševan and Nilus, and the same Račkovskij, who, when young, had embraced the "Left"), to the extent of joining the extreme Right. Between 1901 and 1903, he joined the *Religiozno-filosofskie sobranja,* which was already close to *Russkoe sobranie,* and was one of the founders of the *Vserossijskij nacional'nyj sojuz* (from 1911 the "Russian Nationalists' Party"), an assortment of relatively "moderate" monarchists who, however, held "equal rights for Jews inadmissible" (*Programmy* 1995, 368). The *Sojuz Russkogo naroda* published one of his "Letters to a Neighbour" *(Drevnie dokumenety po evrejskomu voprosu),* extensively based on Chamberlain [1899] 1913). Among all those who had anything to do with the PSM, he alone paid a price: he was shot as a *pogromščik* at Valdaj near Novgorod on September 7[20], 1918.[68]

The 1902 article has a curious "twist." Before coming to the PSM, it speaks of a mysterious pilgrim[69] who announced the imminent Parousia. However, what is most singular is the article's incipit, a phase in inverted commas *("Nel'zja ob"jat' neob"jatnogo"),* which is an almost literal quotation from Koz'ma Prutkov, the celebrated author, and fruit of a literary hoax: "*Nikto neob"jatnogo obnjat' ne možet.*"[70]

In the second part, Men'šikov tells of being in contact with a mysterious lady who had shown him M, which she had obtained as a result of a burglary in Nice.[71] He had translated it into Russian, and then succinctly revealed its contents:

> Ever since 929 BC, a secret plot against the entire human race has been organized in Jerusalem by King Solomon and the Jewish Sages. The Protocols of this plot and the commentary on them were conserved in the greatest secrecy, passing down from one generation to the next.... The conclusion was that under King Solomon the leaders of the Jewish people had decided to force the rest of humanity to submit to their power and to establish the permanent rule of King David over them. A secret alliance was formed to dominate, above all, the business and industry of the peoples of the world. Dispersed throughout the world, the Jews set themselves the task of concentrating the capital of all the countries of the world into their hands with the purpose of using it to squeeze, as with tentacles, the masses to serve them. With a truly diabolic astuteness, which outmatched that of the Jesuits, the Jews worked to undermine the foundations of order and of Christianity with the propaganda of liberalism, cosmopolitanism, and anarchy, and then, when they had finally achieved power, would have forced all humanity to submit to the most cruel despotism that the world had ever seen. It had taken a millennium and a half[72] to destroy the ancient pagan kingdoms; now the end of Christianity is also nigh.

Commenting on the horrendous plan, the lady had also exposed to him the theory of the "symbolic serpent" with words similar to those that we come across in the *Translator's note*:

> According to the lady's assertion, Judaism is really the serpent predicted in the Apocalypse [12.9] and this serpent slithers from one country to another. France, Germany, and England are already in its suffocating coils. Now the head of the serpent can be found in St. Petersburg itself.

However Men'šikov concludes his writings denouncing the apocryphal character of the document:

> The authenticity of the *Protocols* is denied by the style. I have been dealing with manuscripts[73] for many years and can through their style fairly rapidly divine the nature of the author. In this case, it only

requires a glance at the "Protocols of the Sages of Zion" to divine that it came from a place and time far from that of King Solomon....

and informs us finally not to be the only person in on the secret:

> Since, according to the lady, revealing such a tremendous secret would put my life in immediate danger, I must warn my assassins that an exact copy of these same protocols is in the possession of a journalist in St. Petersburg, and perhaps not one only.

Men'šikov is hardly mentioned[74] in the vast literature surrounding the PSM, and when he is, he appears only as an early "unmasker" of the PSM:

> Even the leaders of the "black one hundred" like...M. Men'šikov, whom Ju. Glinka tried to convince in 1902 that the PSM was really stolen from her in Nice, "the Jewish capital," rejected the clumsy fake (Dudakov 1993, 266).[75]

That article (perhaps only "noted" but not read) probably suggested to Chayla, or someone for him, to date the first Nilus edition as 1902. The antisemitic literature was then used to validate the far-off appearance of the PSM, which would then be backed up by S and M:

> For now it seems that only the fact of the printing of the *Protocols* for the first time has been sufficiently proved...to be in 1897, and that from the appearance in the press of comments about it by the famous publicist M. Men'šikov in his "Letters to a neighbour," published in the newspaper *Novoe Vremja* in 1901–1902 (Ževaxov 1939, 45).

However, it is clearly evident that the sense of that article is different and much more relevant. Above all, it testifies that at the beginning of April 1902 the PSM were not yet published and that up to that point neither Račkovskij, nor Suxotin or Stepanov, nor Nilus, or even the "journalists" to whom they refer, and whom it would be legitimate to identify as Kruševan and Butmi, had anything to do with it. The essential date is therefore the declaration of forgery concerning the PSM *as he would have known it*: and Men'šikov, thanks to the mysterious lady, would have known the text of a plot ordered by Solomon and his "Sages" in 929 BC.

Why therefore 929 BC, the date taken from the *Translator's Note,* and why therefore is it in all the editions of the PSM? The only grand assembly of King Solomon with the headss of Israel recorded in the Bible (I Kings 8.1–2) refers to the consecration of the Temple, in the twelfth year of his forty-year reign. However, this has never been placed so late as 940–901 BC by either Byzantine,[76] Romano-Germanic,[77] nor modern Biblical criticism.[78] There is, however, a basic text in the Slav-Orthodox culture, and the Russian one in particular, which may have produced such anomalous dating. It is Chapter

XIII of the *Vita Constantini* which contains the story of "Solomon's Chalice" (placed in the Temple on the same occasion: cf. I Kings 7.48–50), and on which the prophecy of the advent of Christ 909 years later[79] had supposedly been engraved. Either due to misreading or a printing error (consequently "929" for "909"[80]), in all probability the compiler took the date from there; from a source that, though hardly "scientific," was most authoritative for the Russians.

And why "Sages"? The passage speaks of "the elders…and the heads" of Israel.[81] In the Old Testament, the "sages" (wisemen, *mudrecy*) are mostly those of the neighboring peoples (Egyptians, Babylonians[82]), and in Old Russian (away from the Biblical text) *mudrec* means, if anything, "philosopher," with the term *filosof* reserved for the designation of doctors of the church (Constantine/Cyrill is a *filosof*, while the Greeks are *mudrecy*). Here is confirmation, therefore, of the model of the *ellinskie mudrecy*, and the exact translation of the PSM should be "The Minutes of the Philosophers of Zion." To avoid the incongruity that one therefore registers (if they are ancient they are not Jews, and if they are modern they are not philosophers), the English translation and then the Italian and Spanish ones have added the words "Elders" ("Learned Elders,"[83] "Savi Anziani,"[84] and "Sabios Ancianos,"[85] respectively), which do not appear in the Russian[86] and have then been shortened to "elders," with the omission of the original term.[87] Such a substitution is not without its heuristic aspects. On it one bases, among other things, Cohn's (1969, x) psychoanalytic interpretation which attributes to the PSM the identification of "Jew" with "*wicked* father."[88]

But in M, the *mudrecy* have to be those of Solomon's Temple, and only later (modifying the plan of the text) did they become "the unknown superiors" to whom are accredited the highest Masonic grade in the Scottish Rite "ancient and accepted" ("…from the 33rd grade").

In conclusion, the text of the PSM that Men'šikov asserted that he had come to know from the mysterious lady is not that which we know. Only in this way can we explain his accusation of "forgery," as being not a text going back to the time of Solomon but rather one passed off as being such (by modern Jews, who would not have been the true authors). This, moreover, is the reason for the diction of A1 and A2: *[Extracted from] Protocols ancient and modern…*, which depend on M's assertion that Men'šikov knew and used it. That is to say, it would be ancient because it harks back to Solomon's times, as well as modern because it had been elaborated up to the present by the leaders of the plot. Furthermore, it also arose from the haste of Nilus to erase any signs remaining of such an original formulation. This, emphasizing the reference to the epoch of the Old Testament, followed the line of Chamberlain ([1899] 193, 449), which Men'šikov knew of and used.[89]

All this means that in April 1903, the PSM were still in the process of elaboration, and they were in the form of a "true forgery" (a *forgery,* attributed to Solomon and "his *sages,*" which would have in reality been compiled by mysterious Jews. While subsequently—perhaps only for the difficulty of maintaining some slight plausibility, already called in question by that "929 BC"—there was created a "forged truth"; that is to say a *fake* document to be attributed to the same Jews, as a *true* guide to their collective activity.

From this also arise the slips in the temporal co-ordinates. The "true forgery" harking back to the tenth century BC would have been much more credible had it contained traces of elaboration down to the date of the "theft" (the "American, Japanese, and Chinese canons" [5th], the "case" of President Loubet [9th], the reversal of the Dreyfus trial's verdict on appeal [15th], etc.).[90] However, to verify the "forged truth," one would need to fix the drafting in recent times and in a precise place, where it would be no longer open to modification. Moreover, by casting aside the veil (in particular, as regards the edition of 1905, which cast a shadow over those of 1903), one adds to the concern to backdate to the last possible moment to show the "prophetic" character of the PSM in relation to the revolution taking place.

In the end it was, as a last resort, the France of the Dreyfus Affair, at the time of the First Zionist Congress (1897), which was chosen.

NOTES

1. In Nilus 1995, 2:471 and in Begunov 1996, 77: *Drevnie i sovremennye protokoly vstreč sionskix mudrecov* ("reunions," or rather "meetings"), for the re-trans. by Nikolaevskij cited in Cohn [1967] 1969, trans. into Russian in 1990.

2. Author of *Selo Il'inskoe,* M. 1900, and of *Xram-usypal'nica velikogo knjazja Sergeja Aleksandroviča,* M. 1909.

3. It is unclear whether it was at Tula or Moscow. The alleged intervention of the Grand Duke's assistant had induced some (Nilus 1995, 2:471) to suppose that the missing edition may have been produced at Moscow, while others (Begunov 1996) retain that it must be Tula.

4. Rollin 1991, 371. Orževskij was the Secretary of the Minister of the Interior, General Čerevin, and his contacts with Glinka went back to 1884.

5. A duplicated printing could pass unnoticed, but a printed work would have had to have been sent to the Central Libraries of St. Petersburg and Moscow.

6. In the 1905 edition, Suxotin does not appear; in the 1911 edition, there is a note on "*boljarin* Aleksij," from which we come to know the name but not the surname. Dudakov (1993, 265) asserts, without any evidence, however, that Butmi would have received a copy of the PSM from Suxotin.

7. In Taguieff 1992, 1:59: "For personal reasons Suxotin became the weathervane that indicated for the reader the mysterious lady, Mrs. K."

8. Secretary of the "Musaget" series, and from 1916 owner of a Muscovite publishing house associated like the former with symbolism.

9. According to Vitte (vol. 2 [1923]: 73), Račkovskij was involved in the forgery at the Ministry of the Interior "of provocative proclamations of all types, in particular with a content calculated to incite *pogroms* against the Jews," but that was from October 1905. Are the fly sheets of which we are speaking part of these provocations?

10. Cf. the letter of A. S. Tager (3 January 1935, *Berner Prozess,* 13:21): "The photocopies of a duplicated manuscript, conserved in the Lenin Library, with the title: *Alte und moderne Protokolle der Versammlungen der Weisen von Zion.*"

11. The Head Librarian of the WL in London informs me that at the moment this is also missing, and while there is one at the WL in Tel Aviv; all researches have proven fruitless.

12. V. Nožkin, *Kto tvorec prokljatoj "russkoj" revoljucii;* the "document" was then inserted by F. Vinberg in the book *Krestnyj put'. I. Korni zla,* 2nd ed. (Munich 1922, 30–35); Cohn (1969, 93) has already shown that one is dealing with another mystification.

13. On November 30, 1918, B. Brazol' compiled a report for the American secret service called *Bolshevism and Judaism* which cited a *Secret Zionist Protocol* of 1897 (cf. Taguieff 1992, 1:81; the title came from the edition of A. Rodinov, *Sionskie protokoly (*Novočerkassk 1918); cf. Taguieff, ibid, 366), where "Zionist" is rendered *sionskij* and the singular is merely an error. Whence, in this case, the indications of Nožkin.

14. *Incipit:* «К действиям в пользу широко задуманного нами плана...», *explicit:*   «...мы ответим американскими или китайскими или японскими пушками» (ibid., 197).

15. With one minimal variant: "*tajno*" for "*v tajne*".

16. Cf. Dudakov 1993, 153.

17. This gives rise to the suspicion that S and A2 are the same. That is to say that Stepanov may be the anonymous editor of the third edition of the PSM printed in 1905 in Moscow, the city in which he was living.

18. The *Extract* attributed to Herzl (1) contained the last sentence of the extract cited above ("In other words, to recap": cf. Begunov 1996, 69).

19. "The Jewish Peril," *The Spectator,* 19 June 1920, 788.

20. Ganelin, in *Nacional'naja pravaja (*1992), 76.

21. According to *Poslednie novosti* (12 May 1921) he will be the author of "some researches in French on Russian culture on religious and Slavonic problems"; the only printed works by him that I know of are *Un conflit d'opinion en Suède* (St. Petersburg 1912) and the French translation of: S. Em. Mgr. Antoine [Xrapovickij], Archevêque de Volhynie et de Jitomir, *L'idée morale des dogmes de la T. S. Trinité* (...) (Paris 1910).

22. It is commonly known that the PSM published in Russia were "extracts" from the "original" *Protocols*. If Nilus had the "original," however, this in turn should have been an "extract," which would be compatible with the story of the clandestine version copied in haste, but not with the one of the burglary.

23. Hagemeister 1996, 6. Florenskij's archive in effect has Nilus's papers, which include a note taken from a conversation between Serafim of Sarov with Motovilov (*Antixrist i Rossija*) published in *Moskovskij literator,* 21 November 1990 (rpt. in Nilus 1995, 2:429): the rumor might have started from here.

24. Begunov (25 April 1997) wrote to me: "His [*Nilus's*] manuscript of the translation and the original of the text [F]...have been found in the USA. It is going to be sensational: Nilus's archive rescued by Koncevič!" Ivan Koncevič (1893–1965) married a niece of Nilus's wife, E. Karcova, in 1935; he taught at the Orthodox Seminary in Jordanville, New York (USA) and is the author of *Optina Pustyn' i ee vremja* in which he published unpublished notes by Nilus from the materials sent in 1925 to Germany (cf. Nilus 1995, 1:213). The fact that part of Nilus's archive is in the United States does not imply that the "original" of the PSM is kept there: while one hopes that this material will be published as soon as possible (which will allow us to examine textually the nature of F), one can obviously wonder why this has not happened yet.

25. In the article he designated her 'Madame K" and only later the initial was resolved in the full surname (cf. Taguieff 1992, 1:50): her name had never been so, since she was born Matveeva; first name and patronymic (Natal'ja Afanas'evna), though, were correct. In her deposition (29 October 1934, *Berner Prozess,* 1:38) she is mentioned as *Frau Ladimirowna Komarowski* with a patronymic very similar to her real surname instead of "Afanas'evna"; I cannot find a reason for this.

26. Cf. Hagemeister 1995, 150 and Polovinkin 1995, 232. At the beginning of 1938, Nilus's widow, Elena Aleksandrovna, moved to Kola in order to follow Komarovskaja and died there a few months later (cf. N. Karcova, *S. A. Nilus. Kratkoe žizneopisanie* [1969] in Nilus 1995, 1:46).

27. The Niluses stopped at Optina Pustyn' from September 1, 1907 to May 14, 1912 (Polovinkin 1995, 263). As far as Chayla is concerned, a note of *Letopis' skita* of June 2, 1909 certifies that it had arrived "last winter" (Chayla says "end [Hagemeister 1995, 155 rectifies: beginning] of January"), and another one that he went back to St. Petersburg on October 19, 1909 (ibid. 278; in a note of October 30,

1909, Nilus [1995, 1:269] says that he left "the next evening" but this actually happened on November 2 [ibid. 2:271]).

28. Begunov (1996, 76) arbitrarily deduces "but not a Russian," exactly what Chayla implied.

29. This pseudonym concerns three other people involved in the PSM affair who knew each other: Il'ja Cion (who, in the 1895 answer to Vitte, however, described as slanderous the idea that he was the author of *La Société de Saint Pétersbourg* which had appeared in 1886 and was signed by "Comte Wasili"), Ju. Glinka, and J. Adam; the Russian secret police pointed out as co-author (along with Radziłłowa) of *La Société de Saint Pétersbourg,* Glinka (therefore called back to Russia), but maybe it was Adam (using documents provided by Princess [Elena Petrovna Trubeckaja] Demidova di San Donato; cf. Begunov 1996, 91). On this subject, cf. Świerczyńska, "Hrabia Paul Vasili i księżna Katarzyna Radziwiłłowa," *Teksty,* 5 (53) (1980).

30. PSB, vol. 30 (1987).

31. Reported on April 1, by *La Tribune juive*; it reaffirmed the revelations of March 15 with an article about *Les Protocoles des Sages de Sion* in *La revue Mondiale.*

32. Contributor to *Le Figaro* in Paris (1865–1920) and agent of the Russian Secret Service.

33. Journalist and playwright of Jewish origin (1869–1918; he used various pseudonyms, among them "Maska"); an *Oxrana* agent, he reached the grade of College counselor and was intimate with G. Rasputin; executed by the Bolsheviks.

34. He is quoted here for the second time (after the article of the *Varšavskoe slovo* of 17 July 1920; cf. chap. 7) in relation to the PSM: Chayla's witness refers to 1909, but was publicized only in May 1921 and S. Svatikov's and Vl. Burcev's (cf. Cohn 1969, 52–53; they might, however, relate to "The secret of Judaism") concerning conversations held in 1917, but were submitted during the Bern Trial.

35. I quote (from Nečvolodov 1924) the text of *La tribune juive*; in *La revue mondiale* (6, 1921) it tells again that it was "a notebook with yellowish paper and a large stain of blue ink on the front page."

36. Later *La Tribune juive,* 1 April 1921.

37. *La Tribune juive,* 29 April 1921.

38. Instead of backdating the episode using the "jokes of memory," we had better ask ourselves why Radziwiłłova produced this date: it is very likely that she wanted to pretend that she had seen the PSM *before* they had been printed and she obviously only knew of the 1905 edition (A1, A2, N).

39. Author of various books; cf. Bibliography in this volume.

40. The accusation was of instigating the Cossacks' hostility against the non-Cossack military units of Southern Russia in the General Staff's paper, *Donskoj vestnik* (cf. Nilus 1995, 2:244).

41. On the obscure figure of Chayla, cf. Hagemeister 1996, 133–36. Given that his testimony is useful also to the "zealots," Nilus (1995, 2:244) dedicates a chapter to him with the telling title: *Lžeč, vozveščajuščij pravdu* (The liar who proclaims the truth).

42. Vrangel's army was defeated on November 17, 1920 and detachments fled from Crimea immediately afterwards. As has been said, such an account is at least suspicious.

43. Nilus kept up correspondence, via a third person, with friends abroad until the mid-1920s, even if "he wrote rarely" because "one must be extremely prudent" (Ževaxov 1939, 33). The sole contact *from* the West was a parcel in the post which he received from H. Ford, the American industrialist who had remained "hypnotized" by the PSM (cf. Hagemeister 1991 and Polovinkin 1995, 204), and whose articles in the *Dearborn Independent* (really written by August Müller, cf. Rollin 1991, 611) appeared between May and October 1920 and were collected in volume form *(The International Jew)* in November of that year. The package is likely to be in the same period, and therefore before the interventions of Chayla. According to Ževaxov 1939, 38, "Nilus died...without knowing that his *Protocols* were already spread all over the world and that they had made him world famous" (an opinion refuted by Hagemeister cit.: "Nilus knew that his edition of the *Protocols* was translated and diffused in the West").

44. At the time of the Bern Trial, Nilus's son treated Chayla as a "perfidious liar" and a "calumniator" (cf. *Introduction to Les Protocols des Sages de Sion*, 1943, in Taguieff 1992, 2:658). However that is essentially in relation to his mother, Mme K. (that is, N. A. Volodimerova), who denied any contact whatsoever with Račkovskij.

45. In one of the encyclicals published immediately after accession to the papal throne by Pius X, the prophesy of the fatal epilogue of the world in the person of the Antichrist who, according to the Roman Pontiff, has already been born: "A close observer" etc. Cf. *Luč sveta* 1920, 179). The text of the Encyclical (4 October 1903) goes: *"Haec profecto qui reputet, is plane metuat necesse est, ne maiorum quae supremo tempore sunt expectanda, sit perversitas haec animorum libamentum quoddam veluti exordium; neve filius perditionis, de quo Apostolus loquitur (II Thess. II, 3), iam in hisce terris versetur. Tanta scilicet audacia, eo furore religionis pietas ubique impetitur.... "*

46. "From materials prepared for the edition" (from 1911, obviously, given that in the 1905 edition, nothing of the sort is found; cf. Taguieff, 1:1992, 55).

47. "Almost all these observations were included in his 1911 edition of the *Protocols*" (Taguieff 1992, 1:5).

48. And not *"la carte du Roi"* (Chayla, ibid., 57).

49. "The sacred number seven; victory, rule, holiness. World Sovereign of the present century," in *Velikoe v malom* (rpt. by Nilus 1911, Novosibirsk 1994, 525–26).

50. "The most important figure in the history of the occult in modern times" was in fact not Jewish, rather he had studied to be a priest and was called Alphonse-Louis Constant (1810–1875), and "Jewish-ized" his name around 1852. The work in question is *La Rituel de la haute magie* (1856).

51. A copy, with the added autograph of Nilus, was sent into Germany in 1925. The notes, used for the Bern Trial, were published in Nilus 1995, 1:213f.

52. Chayla should have realized that the unexpected note by Nilus put his testimony on shaky ground, but Gustav Morel could not have visited Optina "a year before" Chayla, that is in 1908, because he died in Smolonsk in August 1905 (cf. A. Tamborra, *Chiesa cattolica e Ortodossia russa* [Alba 1992], 384).

53. Men'šikov 1902 uses the lemma ("the *Protocols* of these conspiracy") not in the sense of "minutes," but rather (according to the second meaning given in SSRLJA, 11:1475) of "documents attesting to some fact, a happening"; the same applies in the *Note*: "This design and the *Protocols* have been obtained...."

54. In the note in the calce to the text of A2 (one is dealing with the *Note*) instead of *"protokoly"* one reads *"otčety"*; and are indicated as such in the Russian translation of L. Müller's "Introduction," *Luč sveta* (1920): 100–65.

55. The first French editions adopted the form *protocol,* without the *e,* which is a mere borrowing: *"Protocols," Procès verbaux...* (Gohier 1920); *Les "Protocols" des Sages* (Jouin, 1920); and *"Protocols"*...(Lambelin, 1921). The (French) difficulty in understanding the term is confirmed by Confino (1938, 16) who underlines: *"the word* Protocole *means procès-verbaux in German and in Russian."*

56. Vasmer, *Russkij etimologičeskij slovar'* (St. Petersburg. 1996), 3:383 considers both derivations plausible, in their turn obviously coming from the Greek. He gives more credence to the second for the semantic reasons given above.

57. I. Franko, *Apokrifi i legendi z ukraïn'skix rukopisiv,* vol. 2 (L'viv 1899); cf. N. Kazakova, *"Proročestva ellinskix mudrecov" ix izobraženija v russkoj živopisi XVI–XVII vv.* in TODRL (Moscow and Leningrad) 18 (1961).

58. I am referring to the restored text, but this occurs also in the additions: for example (21st) in A1, A2, N, and B there is a heading (absent in K and not derived from Joly) which ends with a Russian proverbial usage: «не встретилось [должно лежать] *ни сучка, ни задоринки*», that is, "there are no hindrances," but literally "there should be *neither branches nor obstacles."* If the French translation had been similar to that used by Lambelin (1921): "le moindre obstacle"*),* it would have obviously been translated «...не встретилось *препятствия*», without returning to the proverbial form.

59. In Makarov 1884, the lemma «кулачестьво» is absent, while «кулак» is rendered with *"accaparreur";* but Makarov in 1887 translates *"accaparreur"* not with «кулак» but with «скупщик».

60. Until 1905 in Russia there was a "Committee", and not the "Council" (*sovet*) of Ministers.

61. The French translation of Lamberlin, *"les héros mêmes,"* becomes, according to Makarov 1887, *"Samye geroi."*

62. «округ» / «департамент [французское административное деление]»; «в журналистике» / «в формах хотя бы французкой журналистики».

63. «партизаны» / «Тартарены». Even the first term ("one of the first supporters of some movement or direction", cf. SSRLJA, 9:225) is a Frenchification, but in use from 1762; the second comes from the name of the character in the novels of A. Daudet (*Tartarin de Tarascon*) which in Russian, but not in French, is synonymous with "chatterboxes, self-important politicians" (cf. KLE, 2, col 729).

64. Ford 1939, 64 in fact wrote: "the proof that the *Protocols* are Russian in origin has no other purpose than to render them likely."

65. An anthology of the "Letters to a neighbour" was republished in Moscow in 1991; cf. the review of S. Šumixin, *Professionaly i "kul'turtregery," Novoe literaturnoe obozrenie,* 12 (1995): 347–50).

66. Cf. M. Gor'kij: "Men'šikov filled his book *O ljubvi* with Tolstoj's ideas" ("O S. A. Tolstoj," *Russkij sovemennik,* 4 [1924]: 169); cf. also his essay on Tolstoy in Men'šikov 1899 and the article "Lev Tolstoj kak žurnalist," in *Novoe vremja,* 13 July 1908. For his later attitude to Tolstoj see in his *Diary* (10/23 March 1918): "God sent Lev Tolstoj to Russia, but he was an arch-aristocrat and he revealed himself to be a bad savior" (Men'šikov 1993, 53).

67. At the time of the Bejlis Affair (1913) because of his articles he was expelled from the Philosophical-religious Society.

68. Cf. Men'šikov 1993, 6.

69. "A mysterious old man, of whom I know neither the name, nor the patronym, nor the surname": Dudakov (1992, 407) identifies him with Nilus, even though he was younger than Men'šikov, who it would have been difficult in 1902 to have called *"starik"* (Nilus was 40!). This vice of "ageing" Nilus returns in the *Preface* to the German edition (*Luč sveta* 1920, 102) who mentions him as "an old man [*starik*] in his seventies." In reality, he was not even 60 at that time.

70. The titles of Chapter 17 of *Vyderžki iz zapisok moego deda* (1859), in *Sočinenija Kozmy Prutkova,* (Moscow, 1955), 169. This idiomatic expression means "you can't know everything."

71. "Recently they were kept hidden in Nice...but...they were stolen and fell into the hands of a French journalist and from him, in some way, to my refined hostess." The story of the theft was then repeated, but always making reference to Paris.

72. The calculation divides the history of humanity into two cycles of fifteen centuries each: from Solomon to the fall of the Roman Empire (10th century BC to

5th century AD), and from the fall of the Roman Empire up to the present day (5th century AD to the 20th century AD).

73. Men'šikov had attended the Naval Technical Institute at Kronštadt leaving it as a Naval Lieutenant. He retired in 1892, and in 1898 he was still publishing books such as *Havens of the Cliffs of Abos and of the Eastern Part of Aland* (Men'šikov 1993, 5). Neither these, nor the role of journalist undertaken later, would have given him much practical experience with manuscripts.

74. His name does not even appear once in the seminal work of H. Rollin, and is equally absent in Taguieff.

75. Following certain baseless rumours, one arrives at the picture offered by Putilov (1994, 167): "According to the claim of a contributor to "Novoe vremja" [*Men'šikov*], Ju. Dm. Glinka already had the PSM in her hands in 1881" (?).

76. Cf. Capaldo 1990a, 955, n. 31: "the twelfth year of Solomon should fall between 1041 and 1019 BC."

77. D. Petavius (*Rationarium temporum*, vol. 2 [Venetiis 1749], 360) compresses the reign of Solomon between 1014 and 974 BC: the twelfth year would therefore occur in 1003 BC.

78. The most accepted dates, even taking into account that "the number [*of the forty-year reign*] was probably rounded up," are 965–926 BC. Solomon "died during the year between the autumn of 926 and the autumn of 925 BC," and this is important because "in the history of Israel his death is the first event of which we are able to establish the date" (M. Noth, *Storia d'Israele,* It. trans. [Brescia, 1975], 277–78). Therefore, the twelfth year would have fallen in 954 BC. The late 19th-century biblical scholar, F. Schaff (*Dizionario biblico,* It. trans. [Florence 1891], 456) showed the dates of Solomon to be 1017–977 BC, and Bostunič (1928, 251) placed them 1015–975 BC. Therefore, the twelfth year would fall between 1006–1003 BC.

79. For the explanation of this anomalous "909 BC" (cf. again Capaldo 1990a, 956f.) who convincingly refers to a "process of degradation of the numeric part" of the inscription, hypothesizing that the original reading was "1019."

80. At the time several manuscripts were passing through the printers, and this makes the confusion between a "0" and a "2" plausible. For the same reason, in the path of the "symbolic serpent," the August date of birth varies from "63" to "69" BC (cf. Chap. 6). The error could also depend on one of the popular publications which appeared in 1885, marking the millennium of the death of Metodius.

81. In the Massoretic, respectively, *zeqēnim* and *sárîm;* in the Septuaginta, «τους πρεσβυτερους ... χαι ...τους αρχηγους», which give «старейшины и начальники» both in the Sl.–eccl. of the Ostrožskaja which is in the Russian of the Synod. ("sages" in Hebrew is *hakāmīm).*

82. Cf. Genesis 41.8, Daniel 2.12.

83. The translation which appeared in the United States is not so: *Men of Wisdom* and *Wise Men* (1920). The use of *Elders* for *starejšiny* also introduces a disturbing interference with the wholly different concept of *starcy* (authoritative monks).

84. Not, however, the Milan editions of 1938 and 1944 and those of Rome, Brescia, and Lucera 1972, and of Padua 1976.

85. In this way the 1938 edition, printed in Rome and derived from the Italian one of Preziosi. Otherwise (from 1927) only *Sabios*.

86. Nor, obviously, in the translations into other Slav languages: cf. Polish *mędrcy,* Czech *mudrci,*and Croat *mudraci.*

87. Laqueur's 1965 Russian edition (1991, 130) leads to the final Aporia: "... *rukoj starejšin (mudrecov) Siona,"* that is, the mysterious personages come to be called "Elders," carrying in parenthesis the denomination "Sages" as an incongruous definition of the original. Butmi (in Butmi N. 1914, 13) seeks to make it all add up by explaining that the *"mudrecy iudejskie"* are the "Scribes and Pharisees."

88. "Why is the propaganda…concentrated to such an extent on the fable of a body of pitiless "elders"...?"

89. "Never has a people given of its personality such a perfect and sincere images as that which the Jews have left in the Bible. Men'šikov (1908, 8) paraphrases this as: "The Holy Scripture of the Jews…is a complete charge sheet against their race."

90. Men'šikov, moreover, cites the Boxer Rebellion in China (1900), and the "translator" the killing of McKinley (1901), which R still manages without problems to include in the text.

CHAPTER 3

Text and Subtext

On June 8, 1920, the London *Times* launched the PSM with a review by Wickham Steed[1] ("A Disturbing Pamphlet: a Call for Enquiry") in the English edition, which substantially validated its authenticity. Again in the *Times,* Philip Graves's articles from Constantinople ("The End of the Protocols," 16–18 August 1921) revealed that they were dealing with a forgery. He had been informed by a "Mr X" (Mixail Raslovlev, 1893–1987)[2] that the text had been extensively plagiarized from a French pamphlet attacking Napoleon III, the *Dialogue aux enfers entre Machiavel et Montesquieu* by Maurice Joly (Bruxelles 1864).[3]

Since then, many texts have been indicated as material on which the PSM were based. Rollin (1991, 28): from the *Monita privata Societatis Iesu* by Hieronim Zahorowski[4] to *The Testament of Peter the Great* (1812)[5]; Cohn (1969, 37) has indicated as a "trailblazer" a series that runs from Barruel and the "Letter of Simonini"[6] through Herman Goedsche *(The Rabbi's Speech),* the Frenchmen Gougenot des Mousseaux, the abbé[7] Chabauty, Drumont,[8] Msgr. Meurin,[9] the renegade Russian Jew Brafman (1869), the uprooted[10] Englishman Osman Bey (1873), and including the Russified Pole Lutostański[11]; to all these should be added Benjamin Disraeli, Earl of Beaconsfield.[12]

U. Eco (1994, 172) has traced an ingenious scheme of borrowings and influences among whom, together with a good number of those already mentioned, are also A. Dumas and E. Sue. In this line of inquiry, the most pertinent reconstruction has been made by S. Dudakov (1993), which has followed the formation and the diffusion of the myth of the Jewish conspiracy in Russian 19th-century literature, with findings that arrive very close to the ambience and epoch of the PSM. This is a good indication of the "frame of reference" which is, moreover, offered by the texts cited by the first publishers and from contemporary Russian anti-Jewish media circles.

However, speaking of the "subtext," one must distinguish between the different levels on which one must collocate the texts that furnished the PSM with its overall design and the concrete material for the forgery. Those that suggested the general idea and its form, should be referred to as the first level. On the second level should be considered those that effectively have been used, even if not indicated by footnotes, in the organization of the contents. On the third level should be considered those which can be precisely matched with the text.

The level that presents the greatest investigative difficulty is the second when one considers the difficulty in distinguishing the specific source of an idea or a concept from the simple echoing of widely diffused ideas and concepts. The question of the "French original" then assumes a particular relevance. If "the creator of the PSM wrote in French and lived in France," he would certainly have "got[ten] much from the tradition of French political anti-Semitism" (Cohn 1969, 28). However, if the premise is invalidated, even if one assumes that a Russian, in Russia, had been able to take advantage of the same tradition, it loses its central role.

***

The great "historic forgeries" are certainly among the texts that have furnished the framework of reference of the PSM. Alongside the *Secret Warning* or the *Testament of Peter the Great,* there is also, going back in time, the *Constitutum Constantini* or the *Decretales pseudo-Isidorianae,*[13] while, coming to the 20th century, the Russian success of the *History of Jacobinism* by Abbé Barruel[14] should not be forgotten, or the forged commentary by Napoleon on Machiavelli's *The Prince,*[15] or indeed the *Pol'skij katexizis.*[16]

However, alongside these "forgeries," a work which is certainly not a forgery must be considered: *Der Judenstaat* (1896) by Theodor Herzl.[17] The name of Herzl is obviously linked to the question of the nexus between the PSM and Zionism, and in particular the First Zionist Congress (Basle 1897. Some translations are entitled *The Zionist Protocols*[18]). This is (apparently) challenged by a phrase that one reads at the beginning of the *Translator's Note* (omitted in A2 and N): "Not to be confused with the representatives of the Zionist Movement."[19] However, that phrase was not intended to contradict the idea of the mysterious "unknown superiors" of the supposed Jewish plot with that of the delegates of the Zionist Congress, and as such to distinguish the "Sages of Zion" of the time of Solomon from the protagonists of the Jewish National Movement at the end of the 19th century.

It is therefore completely coherent to suppose that the PSM were constructed to give life to the myth of the Jewish plot by "parodying" the fundamental text of the real Jewish program to found a state to gather together the Jewish Diaspora,[20] even if at first the scenario denied that the "Sages" were exponents of the Zionist movement.

In the Preface to the fourth edition of his pamphlet, Butmi said the same thing, but from a different point of view, and as a check to guarantee the authenticity of the PSM:

> This idea ["to obtain benefit for Israel at the expense of the other peoples" — author's note] is identical to that which flows from every line of the noted work *The Jewish State* by Dr. Herzl, the founder of modern Zionism.[21]

Many internal elements validate this interpretation. There is Herzl's (1992, 26) citing of Darwin; the formulation of a targeted pedagogical policy ("Right from the beginning we shall educate the children as we would wish them to be" [ibid., 53]); the detailed discussion of economic policy with thoughts on progressive taxation (ibid., 36); the denunciation of the "Members of Parliament as chatterboxes" (ibid., 93); and finally, the essentially monarchical conception of a future Jewish State ("I am a firm supporter of monarchical institutions"). In 1896, Herzl wrote that "politics should always be conducted from above" [ibid., 93][22]). However, above all, there is the idea of a "project to which everything must make reference" (ibid., 38), similar to the plan of which the PSM speaks (or rather the Program, as it is presented in *Znamja*), accompanied by a paradoxical and above all unequivocal "eulogy to antisemitism."

> Only repression reawakens in us the sense of belonging to our lineage (ibid., 38), the antisemites also work for us. They only have to continue along their path, and the desire of the Jews to emigrate will awaken where it is yet to be, and will be reinforced where it is already present (ibid., 77).

This finds confirmation in the 7th Protocol ("antisemitism is necessary to guide our younger brothers") and in the *Note* ("The administration of Zion has made a felicitous use of the antisemitic movement"). To draw the right conclusions from this passage (which has the most delicate implications, one of which is the same accusatory use made of it by the PSM), one must take into account the fact that those pages were written by Herzl under the influence of events such as the Russian persecutions of the 1880s and the Dreyfus trial.[23] It is true that these were dramatic, but without doubt they were less devastating than the śo'ah (Shoah), and also the terrible *pogromy* which were unleashed on Russia from 1903 onwards and in particular during the civil war of 1919-1920.[24]

The structure of the "forgery" therefore rests on the intentional distortion of Herzl's project. By the declaration of the desire to set up a State, the forger implies that the Jews had, in reality, the intention of dominating the States ("Next year in Jerusalem[25]" = the closing of the cycle of the "symbolic serpent"). In fact, as the antisemitic Frenchman R. Lambelin, editor of the PSM, wrote:

> "next year in Jerusalem!" was a sort of pious invocation…. It awaited…Theodor Herzl to give to this formula a concrete meaning, substituting real possibilities for vague hopes.[26]

Such is the meaning of the quotation of Nehemia (9.22–25) in the 2nd Protocol (according to K, A1, and B: "You have given them kingdoms and peoples…": not in Canaan alone, but in the whole world!), which takes on the function of the "thematic key" in the ancient Russian texts.[27]

Taguieff (1992, I, 172) comes to an analogous conclusion:

> Behind the appearance of a national liberation movement aimed at resolving the "Jewish Question" by the creation of a Jewish State, the conspiracy theorists postulate the existence of a secret project for world domination. It is for this reason that the presentation of the *Protocols* as the minutes of a secret sitting of…the Zionist Congress… or as the exposition of the real Zionist program, intended for internal circulation, is most in agreement with the axioms of the conspirators.

The compilation of the PSM, as we are seeking to show, is in reality connected with the Zionist movement and with its Congress, but not, however, with the First Congress (1897) but rather with the Fifth (1901), which, establishing the basis for the acquisition of land in Palestine, passed from the "theoretical" to the "executive" phase of the plan.

On the other hand, while the first publication (from 28 August [9 September] 1903) is concomitant with the pogrom of Gomel',[28] it also happens shortly after the Sixth Zionist Congress (Basle, 9 [22]-15 [28] August) and, a few weeks later, Herzl's trip to the Russian Empire,[29] during which he obtained Vitte's[30] authorization for the creation of an office in Russia for the Jewish Colonial Trust (28 July [9 August]), which was followed by his enthusiastic welcome in Vinjus (3 [16] August).

Passing to the "second level," one notes that the most repeated assertion— that the strategic purpose of the plot would be "the conquest of the world in a pacific way[31] [by the Jews]"—gives rise to a calque on the central thesis of Osman Bey's book, *The Conquest of the World by the Jews* (1873).

Another text which acts as background for the PSM is the novel *Biarritz* (1868–76) by H. Goedsche (1815–1878), part of which was immediately translated into Russian.[32] From this was extrapolated the scene in the Jewish cemetery in Prague[33] which, reworked, was presented as a "document" with the title *The Rabbi's Speech* and published in the appendix to B (*Reč ravvina k evrejskomu narodu*).[34] The publication of the *Rabbi's Speech* in the appendix of PSM by one of the possible authors to "demonstrate" their authenticity excludes, in my opinion, that it had had been used in their compilation in the sense of the "third level." It appears more convincing to refer to it as being of the "first level," and thus to see it "as the framework which the author of the PSM had used in adapting M. Joly's Dialogue" (Rollin 1991, 558).

Even comparing the PSM with Barruel can offer some contrasts. One sees, for example, the phrase that concludes N ("Our Sovereign must be an exemplar of irreproachability") which Jouin (1922, 4:177) had already compared to Barruel's *Instructions for the Grade of Regent* ("Un Régent Illuminé sera l'un des hommes les plus parfaits. Il sera prudent, prévoyant, rusé, irréprochable"). Precisely however, for at least in this case we are dealing with a supplement to A1 (we do not come across the phrase in either K or B), which is then modified in A2 and N.[35] This alerts us to the fact that not all the corresponding passages necessarily go back to the original text of the PSM. One comes across a similar case in the 16th Protocol, where one alludes to the "law of the example," which Rollin rightly (1901, 338) refers to the debate that arose over *Les lois de l'imitation* (1890) by G. Tarde (1843–1904). The passage does not appear in either K or R and, not containing calques from Joly, should be considered a supplement to the common original of A1, A2, N, and B.

The texts which narrate the discovery of the "secret of the Jews" need to be related to the original idea of the "framework," namely, the incredible means employed to be able to come into possession of such a top secret document as the PSM. They are re-elaborated in various forms which M. Baxtin defines as coming from "spy and eavesdrop" literature, and which imply a "third person" (other than the author and the protagonist) who was responsible for "discovering the hidden mechanism,...discovering the most intimate secrets," and who could be the rogue, the adventurer, the servant, the prostitute, the courtesan, or the parvenu.[36] One may be dealing with hidden witnesses of the meeting at the Jewish cemetery at Prague (as in Goedsche), or with the thief of the top-secret material from the premises of the Alliance Israélite Universelle in Paris (as in Osman Bey 1883). Among these variants, and very similar to that which was then effectively diffused in the original of the PSM, is the interweaving of the short story of S. Efron-Litvin, *Sredi evreev* (1896), concerning the false Jew of Curland who, introduced as governess into the house of a rich Jew, discovers in the old man's forbidden room the archive of the Jewish plot. Dudakov noticed this (1993, 136), but in such a form that it appears completely upside down:

> As becomes clear 10 years later [that is to say in 1906–1907], at the bottom of the interweaving of the story [of Efron-Litvin] one finds the literary version of the theft of the PSM.

It is as if the story of the governess were a reflection of the stories of the mysterious ladies (Glinka, "Komarovskaja") entering into possession of the PSM. To tell the truth, little else (Dudakov 1993, 139) seems to change the view:

> The interweaving of the story of Litvin, which came to the attention of the Russian public in 1897–8, *anticipated* in a surprising way the version of the theft of the PSM, which appeared in the early 1900s, and the tactic and strategy of "world *qahal*"—confirmed at the "documentary" level of the "letters" addressed (*to the old man*)—the texts of the *Protocols* themselves.

If one continues to believe that the PSM were forged in 1897, one can hypothesize (even with some contradictions, and a little forcing of the date) that the "framework" of the PSM was of fundamental use in the interweaving of Efron-Litvin.[37] However, if one holds that the PSM were composed (and not only published) in 1902–1903, the relationship is reversed with the story of Litvin furnishing the material for that of Men'šikov and then Nilus.

The influence of the novels of F. Bulgarin cannot then be excluded; not so much the *Ivan Vyžigin* (1829) as the *Mazepa* (1833–1834) with its theme of the "Jewish-Jesuitical-Gynecratic" plot of which the protagonist would be the instrument, expressed in tones which (apart from the role of the Jesuits; cf. Chap. 8 onwards) one finds in the PSM:

> The world is not governed by force, as those that have been initiated into the secrets of politics think, but by the cunning that has force at its disposal. Catholic Europe is governed by the Jews, the clergy, and women, that is to say, coin, prejudice and passion. These springs are invisibly connected between themselves in a marvelous machine that moves the world.[38]

With the repeated mention of "depraved women" in the service of Zion (1st and *Note*), Bulgarin's idea has suggested later variants in which one finds the erotic imaginings of the belle époque, which is one of the rare passages that raise a smile in the dark universe of the "sages." The original phrase in the *Note* ("with the help of dissolute Jews, Spanish women") had been earlier extended (X): "of Jewesses who passed themselves off as

French, Italian, Spanish") then completed in (Y): "who are the best transmitters of the dissolution of manners. Presently among the best female agents [agentši] of Zion are [the beautiful] Otero, Sakharette [?], Sarah Bernhardt, and others." (N omits the example following the conditions not to reveal real names, thus one finds the complete phrase only in A2[39]).

No less relevant to a correct exegesis of the text are the micro-notes. From Tolstoj comes the "pedagogic policy"; from Dostoevskij[40] (in particular *The Legend of the Great Inquisitor*) the voluntary renunciation of liberty by the masses; from John Stuart Mill "the despotism of the majority"; from N. Vagner "the aristocracy of science and wealth"[41]; and from S. Šarapov[42] and I. Cion[43] the financial policy.

Cross-checking with the texts of A. Chabry (1896–1897) and Chamberlain ([1899] 1913) can serve not only for a more perspicacious reading of certain passages, but also as evidence in the attribution of the forgery. In particular, Chabry's expression:

The feudal lords of international finance protect this monopoly [of loans] *as a sword of Damocles suspended over the peoples,*[44]

appears as in the original in a passage in the 19th Protocol:

the loans hang like a sword of Damocles over the heads of the governed.

Beside the image of the serpent to indicate the Jewish plot, taken from *L'Usure suprême* (1896), there is the observation on the indifference as to the material of the circulating money.[45] Then there is the thesis that poverty forces the people to submit more or less to slavery or serfdom[46] and the "sword of Damocles." All this should persuade us to transfer the calques in Chabry from the second to the "third level," thus giving greater weight to the participation of Butmi in the creation of the PSM.

Moreover, by way of Joly, the PSM present us with calques on extracts from Machiavelli and Montesquieu (essentially from *The Prince* and *L'Esprit des lois*) which then form exchanges between the two protagonists in the *Dialogues*.

As regards Joly's *Dialogue,* the importance of his use in the PSM largely passes over the fact that it proves the plagiarism, and that one is dealing with a forgery.

In fact, one is not dealing with a practically unknown work, which arrives in Russia (however without the *Épilogue en sept Dialogues* [1870])[47] "nobody knows how," that is to say, via the "secret services."[48] It had been reprinted several times in French,[49] had been immediately translated into German[50] and several years later into Spanish.[51] It was itself the subject of a fair amount of writing.[52] As regards A, it had acquired a certain amount of fame through being cited in the supplement of *La France maçonnique de 1889* by L. Taxil.[53] The "actors" of this belated "dialogue of the dead" (in their turn following a firm tradition[54]) were well-known in Russia, also as characters in that literary genre, while Machiavelli's reputation underwent a sudden flowering in Russia in the second half of the 19th century.

In conclusion, while the discovery, in 1921, that Joly's pamphlet lay hidden beneath the PSM was apparently casual,[55] it was in fact the case that any text of this genre, however it fell into their hands, would have attracted the attention of the Russians at the turn of the century. Rollin (1991, 335) writes:

> If one places the PSM alongside the measures taken from Count Vitte and the criticism to which they were subjected, one becomes aware that among all the economic, financial, and social considerations associated with Maurice Joly's *Dialogue,* the author of the PSM has kept only those that could be adapted to Russia, and the additions made to the *Dialogue* only concern the Russia of the years 1892–1902.

The discussion regarding the "rarity" of Joly's text proves vain, and above all serves only the interests of zealots ("Joly's book passed completely into oblivion," Creutz 1934, 6),[56] or those same people who circulated the myth that Joly, too, was Jewish (Maurice Joly was circumcised with the name Moses Joël," ibid., 7).[57]

The methodical use of Joly's text in the compilation of the PSM (one French academic even denies that one can speak of a simple plagiarism, but rather a forgery following the procedure "that the French situationists later called a "maspérisation"[58]) can be delineated progressively from the beginning:

1. D. "Laissons…les mots…pour nous en tenir aux idées"

1 Pr. «Отбросив лишние фразы будем говорить толко о значении каждой мысли»

until at the end:

24 D. "[le prince] personnifie…la Providence dont les voies sont inconnues"

22 Pr. «в лице царствующего…как бы судьбу с ее неведомыми путями»

As Cohn has noted (1969, 49–50):

with fewer than a dozen exceptions, the order of the copied passages remains the same as that of Joly's book as if the forger had functioned by commencing at the beginning of the *Dialogue* and had gone on mechanically transcribing one page after the other in his "protocols, according to this plan[59]:

1.	Protocol 1-ɪ	Dialogue 1–3	pp. 8–28
2.	Protocol 2–3, ɪɪ	Dialogue 3	pp. 28–33
3.	Protocol 4, ɪɪɪ	Dialogue 4	pp. 38–45
4.	Protocol 5–7, ɪv–vɪ	Dialogue 4–7	pp. 45–76
5.	Protocol 8-vɪɪ	Dialogue 7	pp. 76–78
6.	Protocol 9-vɪɪɪ	Dialogue 7	pp. 78–79
7.	Protocol 10-ɪx	Dialogue 7–8	pp. 80–88
8.	Protocol 11–12, x	Dialogue 8–9	pp. 92–103
9.	Protocol 12–13, x–xɪ	Dialogue 9–10	pp. 104–124
10.	Protocol 14, xɪɪ	Dialogue 11–12	pp. 125–149
11.	Protocol 15, xɪɪɪ–xɪv	Dialogue 12	pp. 149–153
12.	Protocol 16–17, xɪv–xv	Dialogue 12–13	pp. 153–161
13.	Protocol 17, xv	Dialogue 13	p. 164
14.	Protocol 18, xv	Dialogue 13	p. 165
15.	Protocol 19, xv	Dialogue 13	pp. 166–169
16.	Protocol 20, xvɪ	Dialogue 16	pp. 195–197
17.	Protocol 21, xvɪɪ	Dialogue 16–17	pp. 198–207
18.	Protocol 22, xvɪɪɪ–xɪx	Dialogue 17	pp. 211–213
19.	Protocol 23, xx	Dialogue 18–20	pp. 219–253
20.	Protocol 24, xxɪ	Dialogue 21	pp. 262–269
21.	Protocol 25–26, xxɪɪ–xxɪɪɪ	Dialogue 22	pp. 271–277
22.	Protocol 27, xxɪv	Dialogue 22–24	pp. 280–298

The other side of this regularity is, however, the extreme inconstancy in their use. If some protocols are almost entirely copied from Joly's text, in others the quotations are sporadic and in one (14th) almost absent. The French text[60] is adapted in the PSM with recurring alterations, which at times appear to be really and truly errors in translation[61]:

ɪ	"vie libre"	— «собственная [rectius: *свободная*] жизнь»
ɪv	"phraséologie"	— «физиономия [rectius: *фразео-логия*]»
	"promoteur"	— «проводителем [rectius: *начи-*

		нателем]»
VII	"dérangera le mécanisme"	— «избрали [rectius: *извратили*] концы...механизма»
IX	"droit d'amendement"	— «право допроса [rectius: *поправки*]»
X	"entreprises de publicité"	— «предмет [rectius: *предприятие*] гласности»
	"libraire"	— «библиотекарем [rectius: *книгопродавцем*]»
	"journeaux"	— «журналы [rectius: *газеты*]»
	"trois cents pages"	«300 листов [rectius: *страниц*]»
	"annexes[62] du journalisme"	— «пристежки [rectius: *приложения*] к журналам»
XII	"ceux qui sont...connus"	— «тех которые...знают [rectius: *известны*]»
XV	"l'organization judiciaire"	— «законодательства [rectius: *судебная система*]»
	"paternel"	— «отеческой [rectius: *патерналистской*]»
XVII	"l'apologue du dieu Wishnou"	— «апология [rectius: *аполог*] божка Вишну

The way Joly's text has been used, (at times followed pedestrianly, at others, with considerable jumps), puts one in mind of an indirect use, using some form of resume compiled earlier and by others. This would explain the lack of homogeneity in the comparisons. At any rate, in order to proceed with a minute collocation to a reconstruction of the text, it is essential to identify all the passages of the PSM traced to Joly's text. From this point of view, the exemplification offered by Cohn is fairly limited,[63] while an almost complete review (of N however) was carried out in 1933 by the Legal Section of the Swiss Jewish League.[64]

The attempts to identify the copy that was used for the forgery have proved fruitless — whether one wants it to be the same copy which was in the hands of Raslovlev at Constantinople (as the initials "A. S." on the binding would indicate,[65] or the fact that the plagiarism begins at page 8 of Joly's text[66]), or whether one wishes it to be the copy in the BNF,[67] with markings which in part indicated passages then reprised in the PSM.[68] One is dealing in this instance with a copy on which I have worked in microfilm, and the markings in the margin (rare, and little concerned with the passages effectively taken from the PSM) have evidently been made by a casual reader, or one wishing to understand the nature of the plagiarism, if not in fact only wishing to leave his mark on the "Parisian" original of the text.

NOTES

1. Cf. Taguieff 1992, 1:39: not by Robert Wilton, as Laqueur 1990, indicates, 1990, 397.

2. Cf. J. F. Moisan in Taguieff 1992, 2:196; Fry believed he had identified him as a Mr. "Korost."

3. The articles were collected in a booklet, *The Truth about "The Protocols"* (London 1921) also translated into Russian, *Pravda o "Sionskix protokolax"* (Paris 1922).

4. The work of a Polish Jesuit expelled from the order, published first (Crakow 1614) as a translation from the Spanish.

5. It appeared in L*** [Lesur], *Des progrès de la puissance russe* (Paris 1812) (and reproposed by É. Drumont, *La Libre parole,* 4 September 1896), and perhaps of Polish origin: cf. *Les auteurs du testament de Pierre le Grand* (Paris 1872) and B. Mouravieff, *Le Testament du Pierre le Grand* (Neuchâtel 1948).

6. The 1806 apocrypha which informs Barruel of the Jewish nature of the plot he is describing; cf. Miccoli 1997, 1391–94.

7. *Judaïsme et la Judaïsation des peuples chrétiens* (Paris 1869).

8. *Les Juifs, nos maîtres* (Paris 1880).

9. *La France juive* (Paris 1886).

10. *La Franc-Maçonnerie, Synagogue de Satan* (Paris 1893).

11. *Vopros ob upotreblenii evrajami-sektatorami xristianskoj krovi dlja religioznyx celej,* (Moscow 1876); *Talmud i evrei (*Moscow 1879); *Sovremennyj vzgljad na evrejskij vopros* (Moscow 1882). On Lutostański, see F. Borisov, *Ippolit Ljutostanskij. Ego žizn' i dejatel'nost'* (Kiev 1912).

12. In his novels, he "exposes the plan for a Jewish empire in which the Jews would have assumed the position of the dominant caste" (Arendt 1996, 105) and was thus a darling of antisemitic writing. His "racial opinions...were...the fruit of the specific secularisation of assimilated Jews" (ibid., 103). Šmakov 1897 dedicates an entire chapter to him *(Veniamin d'Izraeli. Etjud po teorii i praktike Talmuda).*

13. At the end of the 19th century, there was great polemic interest in the suspect "sources" of the Roman Papacy (cf. e.g., M. Orlov, *Liber Pontifacalis kak istočnik dlja istorii rimskogo papstva* [St. Petersburg 1889]). The false *Decretales* came into play over "Pope Joan."

14. *Volterjancy; ili Istorija o jakobincax,* 12 vols., transl. by P. Domogatskij, (Moscow 1905–1809); and *Zapiski o jacobincax* (Moscow 1806–1808).

15. "Knjaz' ili vladelec, sočinenie Maxiavelja s zamečanijami Napoleona Bonaparta," in *Russkij vestnik,* 1–6 (1817).

16. Probably compiled in circles close to M. Murav'ev Vilenskij (called the "hangman") who repressed the Polish Revolt in 1863.

17. Russian trans. 1896. His other works appeared in Russian before the compilation of the PSM (1902–1903), until in 1905 in Belostock, there appeared a *Polnoe sobranie rečej i statej o sionizme.*

18. Ljutostanskij places it in the section of his work (1904) dedicated to Zionism. The *Preface* to the German edition puts the PSM "in direct relations with the Zionist movement." S. Poliakoff entitled an article "Le 'Times' et les procès-verbaux sionistes," *La tribune juive,* 21 March 1920. In the United States they were first noted as *Zionist Protocol* and the second German edition (edited by T. Fritsch [Leipzig 1924]) was entitled *Die zionistischen Protokolle.* However, one must remember the confusion between *sionistskij (*Zionist) and *sionskij* (of Zion); cf. Chap. 11, n. 17.

19. The same Butmi (1906a, 87) denied the denial: "In vain the translator asks...not to confound the sages of Zion with the representatives of the Zionist Movement.... The Zionism of Herzl is associated with the Masonry of 1900, which was diffused in Russia and had become the principal arm of the propagation of internal submission...following the plan of the sages of Zion."

20. P. Nora (*Le thème du complot* [1981], in Taguieff 1992, 2:459–71) compares the two texts but, convinced that the PSM hark back to 1897–1898, finds only a typological parallel ("*The Jewish State* shows in positive the plate that the PSM shows in negative").

21. Cited in Jouin 1922, 4:5.

22. Only later, with the Utopian novel *Altneuland* (1902) does Herzl embrace a democratic future for his concept of the State of Israel.

23. On the question of the "use" of antisemitism by Judaism, cf. the observations of H. Arendt (1996, 10f.).

24. Cf. B. Lecache, *Quand Israël meurt...* (Paris 1927).

25. Cf. Herzl 1992, 28: "This is our ancient motto. Now it is necessary to show that from the dream an idea may arise as bright as day." Jouin (1922, 199) makes it explicit thus: "Jerusalem should not be the capital of a Judea restored to the Jews, but the capital of a world super-government."

26. R. Lambelin, *Les victoires d'Israel* (Paris 1928), 104.

27. Cf. R. Picchio, "The Function of Biblical Thematic Clues in the Literary Code of 'Slavia Orthodoxa,'" in *Slavia Hierolymitana,* 1 (1977).

28. It broke out on August 29 [Septembre 10], the day on which the second instalment of the PSM appeared in *Znamja* in St. Petersburg.

29. Where he arrived on July 27 [August 8]; cf. Herzl 1990, 334f.

30. Who on that occasion declared himself to be a "friend of the Jews."

31. For "in a pacific way" read "in a financial way."

32. "Do Sedana," in *Novosti. Gazeta dlja vsex* (1871), dir. N. S. L'vov.

33. *Evrejskoe kladbišče v Prage* (St. Petersburg 1872): "The content of the legend — says the editor — is not an invention of Radcliffe [*Goedsche*]," which would have only reworked the real fact in an artistic form. The following year it was reprinted by *Kievljanin,* 17–24 April 1873. (cf. Klier 1995, 440), and there were then other reprints in 1876 and 1880 (Cohn 1969, 16).

34. Butmi (1906a, 84) relates that the *Discourse* (published in *Le Contemporain,* July 1881, was sent to *Novorossijskij Telegraf,* but in Russia it had already been in circulation for ten years, that is "the Russian anti-Semites were the first to have the idea to pass off the story for a authentic copy" Cohn 1969, 16). Dudakov (1993, 142, 169–70) records that they were submerged among the others: Osman Bey 1873, Wolski 1887, Demčenko 1906, A. Kalužskij (*Družeskij sovet evrejam* [St. Petersburg 1906]), S. Rossov (*Evrejskij vopros* [St. Petersburg 1906], V. Protopopov, *V poiskax zemli obetovannoj* [Kazan' 1908]).

35. In A1, it was the King (*car'*) who had to renounce everything to be *bezuprečnym.* In A2, "exemplarily reprehensible [*bezuprečna*]" must be the *opora čelovečestva* (the firm base of humanity, p. 86). N substitutes it with the *Vladyka naš,* which should be *primerno bezuprečen.*

36. M. Baxtin, *Formy vremeni i chronotopa v romanse* (1937–1938), Italian trans. in *Estetica e romanzo* (Turin 1979), 272. Among the forms of the romance there is also that of "publishing a manuscript written by no one knows who...and found nobody knows where and by whom" (ibid., 308).

37. Cited by A2 (p. 7) for the theatrical script *Syny Izrailja* (1900, written together with V. Krylov), which gave rise to a scandal (cf. Dudakov 1993, 139).

38. Bulgarin 1990, 516–17.

39. Svatikov, giving his opinion on the censor (*Berner Prozess* 1, 453, 30 October 1934), confirmed that they were also present in N *"Tänzerin Oterof,... Sachardm und...Sarah Bernhardt."*

40. Whose anti-Jewish positions evidently attracted Judaeo-phobes: Ljutostanskij (1904, 326) cites, for example, the phrase from a letter to N. Griščenko of 28 February 1878 (in PSS 1988,30:1) "Also, the Jew and his *qahal* are really like a plot against the Russians!" As also does the commentator regarding another passage in which Dostoevskij cites the *qahal* (PSS 1983, 25:389), he bases himself on Brafman 1869, who possessed them in his library.

41. Dudakov 1993, 254.

42. Ibid., 182.

43. *S. Ju. Vitte i ego proekty zlostnogo bankrotstva pred Gosudarstvennym Sovetom* (Paris 1896) and *Kuda vremenščik Vitte vedet Rossiju* (Paris 1896, French trans., *Où la dictature de M. Witte conduit la Russie* [Paris 1897]).

44. A. Chabry, *L'accaparement monétaire et l'indépendance économique* (Paris 1897), 20.

45. A. Chabry, *Avant-propos* of the tradition of A. Del Mar, *Les systèmes monétaires* (Paris 1899), 1: "monnaies...de matières si dissemblables: or, argent, cuive, étain, porcelaine, cuir, carton, etc."; cf. PSM (19th) «мы введем...валюту, будь она деревянная или бумажная, это безразлично».

46 A. Chabry, *L'accaparement...* cit., 31: "*Le premier outil pour assurer la domination de l'homme sur l'homme a été la chaîne, et l'on eut l'esclavage. La securité des sociétés permit à quelques-uns de remplacer la chaîne de fer par celle de la loi qui attachait au sol, à la glèbe, et l'on eut le servage. Le développement de la société et des bésoins...firent de ces bésoins une chaîne suffisamment solide pour permettre la moderne liberté.... Enfin le dernier système...c'est la dette!, qui fait que le débiteur ne travaille plus que pour son créancier*"; The corresponding text of the PSM (3rd: «Народы прикованы к тяжелому трудубедностью сильнее, чем их приковывало крепостное право и рабство: от последних они освободились, от нужды и горя они не оторвутся» derives from Joly (*"Il y a des populations...rivées au travail par la pauvreté, comme elles l'étaient autrefois par l'esclavage."*) One is dealing however with a crossed quotation, which "serfdom" *(krepostnoe pravo)* and the pursuit of liberty *(osvobodilis')* show like a watermark the presence of Chabry beside that of Joly.

47. *Le Gaulois,* 30 April 1870 and *La Cloche,* 2–10 May 1870: cf. Rollin 1991, 286–89.

48 Taguieff 1992, 2:693f. published in facsimile the essay of R. Lambelin, *Maurice Joly et les "Protocoles"* (1921), with annotations from the pen of M. Raslovlev: the passage that says: "*il* [*scil.* Raslovlev] *avait acheté ce livre* [of Joly, author's note] *à un ancien officier de l'"'Okhrana" refugié en Turquie et celui ci le tenait d'un policier corse mis autrefois par la France au service de la Russie"* is underlined, commented on in the margin with two question and exclamation marks and initialled ["?! ?! R."]. The anonymous *Avant-propos de l'éditeur* (in Rollin 1991, vii) affirms that "without doubt, when *(in 1864)* the *pamphlet* of Joly appeared, the correspondents abroad of the *Oxrana* made it come to St. Petersburg," but that does not mean that *therefore* the forger, in 1902–1903), was an agent (the GRB possess a copy of the reprint of 1868, with the code «И н 58-20/66»).

49. There were immediately three other editions (1865 and 1868). It was reprinted in 1948, 1968, 1987, and 1992.

50. Leipzig 1865.

51. Buenos Aires 1898.

52. J. Rentsch speaks favorably about it in *Totengespräch in der Literatur* (in *Lukian-Studien,* 1895).

53. But Joly had been dead for 11 years; cf. Rollin 1991, 277.

54. The placing together of the two names begins with Voltaire: cf. Gentile 1972. The work of J. Venedey (1805–1871), *Macchiavel, Montesquieu und Rousseau* (1850) is a ponderous treatise in two volumes, not a "dialogue," as W. Creutz has it (1934, 8) following prompting from Fry 1931, 123.

55. One of the "artificial explanations" of the plagiarism, already put forward by Nečvolodov 1924 (then by Bostunič 1928, 113), consisted of hypothesizing that the author of the PSM (Gincberg) would have knowingly used Joly's text, in such a way that when the other ways of making the PSM apocryphal had failed, they would have commissioned someone in Constantinople to "discover" the plagiarism.

56. The reason indicated by Raslovlev was different according to Ph. Graves: "Mr. X maintained that it must be rare, because if it had not been, anyone who might have read the original would immediately have understood that the *Protocols* were a plagiarism" (cf. Cohn 1969, 47). However, another reason is the "rarity" of a French text from 1864 in Russia in 1902 (and what is more, in Constantinople in 1921), while another is its extreme bibliographic rarity. If you like, it is merely another clue to the fact that the PSM were compiled in Russia and not in France.

57. The thesis put forward by A. Douglas (*Plain English*, 27 August 1921), even though denied at the time, is again today repeated in Russia (Nilus 1995, 3:480: "French journalist of Jewish origin"). From here comes another "artificial explanation": the *Dialogue* and the PSM are "similar to one another" because they both depend on a remote tradition of *Jewish* thought; or the "discovery" of E. Evseev ("Čto skryto za "Bibliej sionizma," *Sovetskaja kul'tura,* 25 September 1979) that even Herzl would have used the *pamphlet* of Joly cryptically in *Judenstaat* (cf. Nilus, 1995, 2:479).

58. M. Bounan, *L'État retors,* in M. Joly, *Dialogue...* (Paris 1992).

59. The first numeration is referred to K, the second and the third respectively to A1/B and A2/N; the pages of Joly are indicated according to the *first edition* of 1864.

60. The modalities of use could give rise to the doubt that the forger had not used the French text, but rather a translation, for example the German one (1865), but a few checks make one abandon it:

Fr. *"Qui contient entre eux ces animaux dévorants qu'on appelle les hommes?"*
Ger. *"Wer vermag die Menschen zu zügeln?"*
Rus. «Что сдерживало и руководило этими хищными животными, которых зовут людьми?»

61. Also from the Latin: Proverbs 8.15: *"per me reges regnant"* trans.: «через меня [rather than *мною*] царствуют цари».

62. The PSM interpret in the sense of "supplements to newspapers and reviews" (пристежка is an obsolete term and means "attached" rather than "something added") but elsewhere, Joly uses the word *annexes* (e.g., *"annexes de la police"*) in the sense of "complement" and not "supplement," and the sense should be that the *brochures*

undertake the same role as newspapers and reviews, and not that they are "free inserts." The Russian translation should therefore be «пополнения к журналистике».

63. N. Cohn's book effectively leaves itself open to some reservations, which, however, have been put forward by the antisemitic journalist with the aim not of a scientific criticism of his work, but rather to confer renewed credibility on the PSM: cf. J.L.M. [Jean-Louis Martin?], "Nouvelle controverse autour des Protocoles," *Lectures Françaises,* (1967), 124–25, cit. in Taguieff 1993, 2:781f.

64. *Confrontation der "Geheimnisse der Weisen von Zion" ("Die Zionistischen Protokolle") mit ihrer Quelle "Dialogue aux Enfers entre Machiavel et Montesquieu"* (Basle 1933).

65. The *Times* supposed that "it was the precisely the copy belonging to Suxotin [which Nilus had indicated at the beginning of the copy of the PSM in his possession; author's note] which had served for the plagiarism," hypothesizing that "Račkovskij *had* transmitted it to Suxotin together with the manuscript of the forged PSM" (cf. Nečvolodov 1924, 310).

66. "We know that the first pages are missing from the copy of the *Dialogues*, found at Constantinople in 1921. Now the *Protocols* begin *ex abrupto* from page 8 of the *Dialogues* of Joly" (Charles 1939, 19). In reality, only the title page was missing, and the *Simple avertissement* (Genève, 15 October 1864) being present there should also have been pages 1–7.

67. Signed "8° Lb 56. 1469" and not "L. 566, 1469", as indicated in Tazbir 1992, 51. The other two copies of the BNF are: "Rés. Lb 56. 1469 [1865]" and "8° Lb 56 1469A."

68. Cf. Cohn 1969, 74; cf. the reply from the "plotters" side of J.L.M., *Nouvelle controverse*, cit. p. 785, substantially acceptable on this point: "how many researchers have pored over this book?... The signs of which Cohn speaks could have been made by anyone.... He who wishes to prove too much...."

CHAPTER 4

Localization of the Text

The circumstances of the forgery and the first distribution of the PSM, consisting of the secret compilation, the launch in *Novoe vremja* in 1902, the different political contexts in the 1903 edition and of the reworkings of 1905–1906 all imply an interweaving between the manuscripts, the various editions, and the eventual publications in fly-sheets, which seem to carry us back to the dawn of civilization in the world of books and publishing.

One is dealing with an "open tradition" consisting of five redactions (three "complete" and two "shortened"). Nevertheless, it is possible to return fairly closely to the archetype, restoring it on the basis of common material reduced to the best interpretation and integrated with extracts from the passages of Joly's pamphlet (however conserved), as well as on the basis of those which, finding comparisons in the first "short redaction," are related to the higher level of the compilation.[1]

With the primitive draft of the PSM, one can concentrate one's attention on its origins, seeking above all to define its spatial-temporal location.

Therefore, the current opinion is that

the Protocols were forged in Paris in 1897 or at the beginning of 1898" (Rollin 1991, 356),

even if the same Rollin does not exclude outright that they could have had their origin in St. Petersburg (ibid., 227), while elsewhere (ibid., 334) he seems to indicate 1901 as the possible date of the compilation.[2]

This dating (1897) and that location (Paris) support, in turn, the attribution of the forgery to Račkovskij who, as Radziwiłłowa indicates, would have taken advantage of the collaboration of Golovinskij and Mansevič-Manuilov. Račkovskij would then have used Nilus's ex-lover (as Chayla refers to her), or, in other words, Ju. Glinka (as one says in emigrant circles[3]) to enable it to reach Russia.

This scenario is contradicted by the following facts:

In the 12th Protocol, it is said that the final triumph of the plot will take place "probably not soon, perhaps towards the end of the century [*k koncu veka*]." Saying "towards the end of the [*present*] century" means that the writer is working at the beginning of the 20th century and not at the end of the 19th century.

A passage from the 5th protocol ("to one of them [*European states*] we have shown our capacity for attacks") most probably alludes to the regicide of King Humbert I of Italy (July 29, 1900). Moreover, in a "translator's note" to the 2nd protocol, the assassination attempt on the American President McKinley is mentioned (September 14, 1901). However, if the PSM is not a translation, there is no translator and the note should be attributed to the compiler and therefore the PSM are after that date.

All five "complete" editions speak of a President of the Republic to be elected who, to be better controlled, should have in his past "something of Panama." Charles (1939, 28) has revealed that the allusion must refer to Émile Loubet,

> elected on February 18, 1899,… whom the people of Paris, on his return from Versailles, greeted with shouts of "Panama, Panama."

To make this fit with the hypothetical date of 1897–1898, Rollin puts forward that all this

> could have been inspired by his election as the President of the Senate in March 1896, which made him a candidate for the Presidency of the Republic (1991, 356).

However, the PSM speak of a *President of the Republic,* and the scandal of Panama in 1892 was worldwide news with the election of Loubet. The PSM, therefore, are later than that date. If one then takes into consideration the fact that Loubet was on a state visit to St. Petersburg in May 1890 and if, as we believe, the PSM were compiled in Russia, the subject of "Panama" was repeated for the occasion by the Russian press[4] and was probably created then. The PSM, therefore, are not before that date.

From the oral testimony of "the mysterious lady" Men'šikov in 1902 affirms that

> all the happenings of the last years…*the Chinese Rebellion,* all that has occurred…has been the work of the forces of this tremendous being, of the forces of Judaism which slither snakelike throughout the world.

The allusion to the "Boxer Rebellion" (1900–1901) is not found in the PSM.[5] Here it is inserted as a comment on the "true forgery" (a forgery which has been passed off as genuine), but with the "true forgery or original forgery" being before the "forged truth," the drafting should not be prior to that year. In any case, the article of Men'šikov (7 [20] April 1902) proves that at that date the PSM, as we know them, had still not yet been "forged."

The year 1901 is a watershed in the history of the Jewish Movement,[6] and "the events at the end of 1901, and in particular from 1902–1903, are closely connected with the increase in Jewish land possession and the growth of Zionism" (Briman 1998). Now in the first news items in the PSM, subsequently found in all the editions, a whole series of elements relative to the end of 1901 recur. Men'šikov mentioned the contacts with the mysterious lady in the winter of 1901–1902. K, A1, B, and R cite (the first three in the notes, the fourth in the text) facts which happened up to September 1901. A variant of the *Translator's Note* of A2 and N, concerning the imposition on Turkey of improved conditions for all Christians except Catholics, is based on a captious reading of the Franco-Turkish Accord of October 1901.[7] Nilus repeatedly claimed to have had the text since 1901.[8] Lastly A1 and B end the *Translator's Note* with "translated from the French 9th [22] December 1901." If the text is not a translation, what does that precise date mean?

The Fifth Zionist Congress took place in Basle on December 13–17 [26–30] 1901.[9] This was of considerable importance because it was then that the *Qeren Qayemet le-Yisra'el* was founded for the purchase of land in Palestine, which was the first concrete step towards the creation of a Jewish State. The Judeo-phobic world was deeply shocked by this; Men'šikov wrote in *Novoe vremja* (20 December 1901 [2 January 1902]):

> The Jews have been historically defunct for a long period, and the last two millennia of their existence ruled by the Talmud and the Qahal have been so desolate and gray that there is in them no living seed that could "be reborn." For the rest, those who live will see.

A few months later a certain "Infolio" harped on the same theme (*Mysli vslux. Evrejskoe vozroždenie,* ibid., 12 [25] April 1902); in a very similar way to a passage in the *Translator's Note.*[10]

At the beginning of April, Men'šikov published an article on the PSM which opened with quotation from Koz'ma Prutkov. This was almost as if saying in code to the "adepts" that "it is only a humorous invention." If, as we believe, it was the *ballon d'essai* for the "launch" of the forgery, and if, as we have tried to show, the PSM were a parody of Herzl's *Judenstaat* then carried out on the thematic framework of *The Rabbi's Speech* and in the textual style of Joly's *Dialogue,* everything then leads us to hold that they were originally conceived as a (presumed) document destined for that Fifth Congress. It was thus the response of an alarmed awareness that Zionism was becoming something serious.

One should add the fact that N. Mordvinov, in introducing the "short edition" of the PSM (R2, September 1905), presented it as a "translation from the French, 1902." Even if one does not, with Begunov, credit its authenticity, one must conclude that at the time, when A1 and B, which had the "translation" of the PSM as December 1901, had still not yet appeared, nothing in fact opposed a reference to the appearance of the text in 1902.

There is another reason which induces us to conclude that the PSM were not prior to 1902. That year I. Ljutostanskij published the first volume of his book *Talmud i evrei,* in which the chapter dedicated to the plot ("Ob evrejskom masonstve") gathered together all the available writings up to that moment. However there is no trace of the PSM, even if this would have been the "ideal reader," also because he was a member of the "Imperial Orthodox Society for Palestine" around which gathered many of the future zealots of the PSM, including the brother of that Stepanov who would have been its publisher in 1897. Furthermore, when the second volume (1904) included the PSM (1st Protocol) in the section dedicated to "Zionism," it used the text of K.

The conclusion appears to be as simple as it is obligatory. The PSM was compiled between April 1902 and August 1903. Indeed, at the second date they had not yet been "finished." Kruševan used them as concomitant to the August pogrom, and not the April one.

All this finds confirmation in a detail from the first edition of N to which insufficient attention has been paid. The half title of the chapter that contains the PSM goes:

12.

АНТИХРИСТЪ,

какъ близкая политическая возможность

(ПРОТОКОЛЫ ЗАСѢДАНІЙ СІОНСКИХЪ МУДРЕЦОВЪ).
1902-1903 гг.

Such strange dating[11] is confirmed in the acts of the Bern Trial, in which it is reported (evidence of Svatikov) that the text presented to the censors had had as its title *"Die Sitzugen der Weisen von Zion vom Jahre 1902 bis zum Jahre 1904"* (that is to say, 1902–1903).[12] This among other things explains the wording *"zasedanija"* (sessions) in place of *"sobranija"* (meetings). This has been ignored because everybody (Svatikov included) was involved in discussing the hypothesis of Račkovskij. However, in light of what has been shown so far, that is to say, that the Nilus manuscript *still* bore the real date of the *composition* of the PSM, then passed off as that of the presumed "conferences" (being a residue of the "true forgery"), without canceling it when it went to the printers, even though he had written contextually (ibid., pp. 322 and 405) that he had had the text from 1901 onwards.

***

Collocating the dating of the PSM not to 1897–1898 but to 1902–1903 invalidates the sophisticated but arbitrary reconstruction put forward by Chayla (1921),[13] then elaborated by Rollin ([1939] 1991, 356) and taken up by Cohn ([1967] 1969, 75–77) concerning the intrigue against Mr. Philippe. It is also the link with the story of Račkovskij's intrigues against Il'ja Cion.

Following such a version,[14] at the beginning there would have been his pamphlet against Vitte, this too forged from Joly's "Dialogue of the Dead." Il'ja Cion would have entered into the affair because in 1897 the agents of Račkovskij (protected by Vitte) had burgled his villa in Switzerland, Mont-Riant (Territet, Vaud), carting away many papers, and that

> would have been well able to furnish the occasion to attribute the editing of the PSM to Vitte's personal and implacable adversary making believe that that "document" had been found among those stolen (Rollin 1991, 428).[15]

In 1895 the implacable polemic against Vitte[16] had cost Cion his Russian citizenship. Nor can it be excluded that one or more of his books may have entered into the dossier which the creator of the PSM made use of. However, advancing this hypothesis turns the link upside down. Račkovskij had compiled the PSM by reworking a pamphlet by Cion, then transmitted it to Nilus (that is to say, via the "lady" and why not Suxotin) thus giving him a means to combat Mr. Philippe,[17] who had acquired too much influence over the Tsar and his consort, as a result of their eagerness for the "miracle" of a male heir. Following this reconstruction, Nilus would have been introduced at Court "at the end of 1901 or at the beginning of 1902."[18]

However the *žizneopisanie* of Nilus[19] registers his arrival at court not in 1901–1902, but rather in June 1905, when Mr. Philippe was not only no longer in Russia,[20] but was close to death (July 20 [August 2], 1905[21]), and for two years his influence had been supplanted by that of S. Serafim of Sarov, who was canonized on June 18, 1903. Finally, in 1904, the long awaited heir, Aleksej, had been born.

To tell the truth, the first formulation of the hypothesis connected to the intrigue against Mr. Philippe[22] did not entail chronological difficulties, but did not consider the role of Nilus and foresaw as the author of the PSM not Račkovskij (who had only transported it to Russia), but rather the "magician" Papus, and as Rollin (1991, 453) has shown, that is unbelievable for completely different reasons.

The PSM came to the notice of Nicolas II in 1906,[23] when he expressed his first reactions of enthusiastic approval:

> What profound thought! What foresight! What a precise realization of the program! Our 1905 is truly under the direction of the Sages. There can be no doubt of their authenticity. Everywhere is seen the directing and destroying hand of Judaism.[24]

Then, when he knew of the hoax, he, in vexation, condemned it:

> Sequestrate the *Protocols.* One cannot carry forward such a pure cause (*scil.:* the struggle against the Jews) with dirty tricks.[25]

Even independently of the date on which Nilus effectively had the PSM in his hands and contrary to what he himself claimed, I believe that to be in 1905.[26] If indeed the text was composed between 1902 and 1903, the whole edifice constructed by Chayla, Rollin, and Cohn collapses.

Assuming this dating further means excluding that the PSM might be ascribed to Račkovskij, who was recalled to St Petersburg in October 1902, and in the course of that year had drawn up the appeal of the so-called *Ligue pour le salut de la Patrie Russe.* His son, Andrej Petrovič, denied unheard that his father had anything to do with the PSM,[27] while the disappearance of his name in the *affaire* is linked to the rather suspect testimony of Radziwiłłowa and Chayla (1921).

On the other hand, the document entitled *Tajna evrejstva* (dated February 10, 1895[28]) can be laid at Račkovskij's door. This was produced by Russian agents in contact with French esoteric circles at the end of the century[29] and arrived in Russia, into the hands of General Petr Čerevin (1837–1896) by the same means (Ju. Glinka[30]) later followed by the PSM. However, it may be supposed that the other testimonies on the role of Račkovskij in the origins of the PSM (by H. Bint, by Lopuxin or A. Harting[31]) in reality concern this second text. *The Secret of Judaism* is not a "forgery" but a secret report connecting the origins of the "Judao-Masonic Plot" (in whose existence it firmly believes) with the Sect of the Essenians, describing its organizational structure with able "technical" expertise, but above all paying attention to suggesting measures against the Russian revolutionary movement, which was sponsored in its opinion by Freemasonry, which in turn was directed by the mysterious Jewish "secret society." This report seems to have circulated somewhat outside official Russian government circles.[32]

No investigation, either before[33] or after the 1917 Revolution,[34] has ever ascertained the involvement of the *Oxrana* in the drafting of the PSM[35] (as the "zealots"[36] are determined to record). This would, however, be in singular contrast with the difficulties encountered by Nilus in obtaining the Censor's placket (Rollin 1991, 34). Furthermore, it would have been strange that the "secret services" would have had to have recourse to Kruševan's "rag" of a paper to disseminate it.[37]

Cohn, picking up on a note in Rollin (1991, 442), puts forward another consideration to validate that Račkovskij had a part in the invention of the PSM, or at least "some contact with Nilus or with a copy of the manuscript of the *Protocols* in [*his*] possession." The point in question is this: in Nilus's text presented to the Censor, there is the phrase

> Naturally, the Head the Russian Agency [*in Paris*], the Jew Efron, and his agents, also Jews, have not referred this matter to the Russian Government.[38]

The commission authorized the publication of N on condition that all the proper names were removed, in that way not even Efron's[39] name appeared. Now, Cohn argues, Efron's name is not found in the other editions,[40] therefore

> the reference to Efron was introduced on purpose in Nilus's manuscript, and this can only have been done or inspired by some personal enemy of Efron.

And since Efron can be identified with the "blackmailer" "whose cheek still bears the signs of slaps received in 1889" (as is said in the appeal of the "League for the salvation of the Russian Fatherland"), there appears to be no doubt that "the mention of Efron in Nilus's manuscript is to make one think of some link" between Račkovskij and Nilus.

The fact is that if such a link were to have been established in 1905 (when Račkoskij returned to favor, and *perhaps* took part in the dissemination of the PSM), it would not imply his participation in the drafting of the text. It remains to be seen if the mention of Efron should necessarily lead us to accept the existence of contact between Račkovskij and Nilus.

Akim Efron [Effront] (1859–1909) was an informer for Vitte in Paris, and as we see from A2 (p. 13) the "missing information" effectively refers to a passage in the *Note* in which it is said that, despite knowing of the existence of the Central Chancellery of Zion "on French territory,"

> naturally the head of the Russian Foreign Secret Service, the Jew Efron, and his agents, also Jewish, have still not referred this to our ministry.[41]

Even Rollin, who does not know A2, is given pause by the "coincidence" of which Cohn (1991, 442) speaks, but without in fact making much of it (something which, of itself, need not say much). The violently hostile line adopted to Vitte's politics throughout the PSM, and the presence of Efron's name in A2, however, permit us to see the malevolent mention as another element against Vitte (a friend "of the Jews,"[42] and against whom, in August 1905, the Russian Right was launching new barbs for having negotiated the peace with Russia on terms judged by them to be unacceptable). This does not, however, imply an intervention by Račkovskij, and therefore any direct contacts between him and Nilus.

Račkovskij, therefore, has nothing to do with the matter. The PSM were compiled between 1902 and 1903, certainly in Russia and in all probability in St. Petersburg. There can be no doubt that they are a forgery, but wide-ranging investigation also shows that there is no evidence that they emanated from the *Oxrana*. So, from whom and why?

NOTES

1. Cf. the *Note on the Edition.*

2. Commenting on the passage which deals with the "world economic crisis," he cites an interview given by Vitte to the newspaper *Le Gaulois* (18 May 1901) which said: "Such was the crisis that, it would appear, inspired the author of the PSM."

3. Cf. Cohn 1969, 71, which sends one back to L. Fry (Eng. ed., 1931), 87–89.

4. F. Bulganov, "Emil' Lube," *Novoe vremja,* 2 [15] May 1902.

5. It occurs, however, in the novel *Petersburg* by A. Belyj (1913); the wording "American, Chinese, and Japanese" at the end of the 5th Protocol (destined for not short-lived success as a result of the Russian-Japanese War of 1904–1905) instead referred to the protests of Japan, England, and the United States in the autumn of 1902 against the Russian pretensions on Manchuria.

6. "Nacionalističeskij 'uklon' Bunda," in *Soblazn socializma,* [ed. by A. Serebrennikov] (Paris and Moscow 1995), 274.

7. Cf. "Le conflit franco-turc. Le conflit en voie d'arrangement," *Le Temps,* 3 September [27 October] 1901.

8. Probably because he wanted to show that he too had come into early possession of the PSM. The first English translation dated the PSM to 1901.

9. Cf. *Predvaritel'noe izvestie o 5 kongresse,* (Xar'kov 1901), M. Šapošnikov, *Vsemirno-evrejskij kongress sionistov v Bazele,* (Xar'kov [n.d., but 1902]), I. Sapir, *V kongress sionistskogo Obščestva,* (Odessa, n.d.); cf. *Literatura o evrejax* (1995), 168–69.

10. "which gave the possibility of creating a world alliance of Zionists which *now* [my italics, C.D.M.] has thrown away the mask."

11. "Nilus…had categorically affirmed that the lectures had been held not in 1897 but in 1902-3" (Cohn 1969, 45); "Nilus gives as the dates the years 1902-3" (Hagemeister 1985b, 155) contrary to all the information from himself and others referring to the origins of the PSM.

12. *Berner Prozess* 1:453 (30 October 1934).

13. In Taguieff 1992, 1:59–60.

14. Judged "very unlikely" even by Ganelin, in *Nacional'naja pravaja* 1992, 108.

15. Cohn (1969, 76) modified the inference, saying that "it is certainly possible that they have found [among Cion's papers] an adaptation of Joly's book."

16. *M. Vitte et les finances russes* (Paris 1895). His other interventions are: *La France et la Russie* (Paris 1891); *La Russie contemporaine* (Paris 1891); *Nichilisme et anarchie* (Paris 1892); *Itogi finansovogo upravlenija I. A. Vyšnegradskogo* (Lausanne 1892); *Histoire de l'entente franco-russe* (Paris 1895); *Kuda vremenščik Vitte vedet Rossiju* (Paris 1896 [French trans. 1897]); *S. Ju. Vitte I ego proekty zlostnogo bankrotstva pred Gosudarstvennym Sovetom* (Paris 1896 [French trans. 1896]); *Les finances russes et l'èpargne français. Réponse à M. Vitte* (Paris 1896). None of these has anything to do with Joly's pamphlet.

17. Who was presented to the Tsar at Compiègne in September 1901. What would have then happened to Račkovskij, if we make him the compiler of the PSM in 1897?

18. Chayla 1921, in Taguieff 1992, 1:60; and Cohn 1969, 59.

19. Polovinkin 1995, 261.

20. Cf. L. Tixomirov (*Diary*, 16 November 1902): "The Filippeide is over. Philippe is no more, not only at Livadija, but in Russia itself. Thanks be to God. However, how was he able to understand this story?" (Nilus 1995, 2:495).

21. Amal'rik 1984, 65.

22. "Axeron" 1920.

23. Cf. Nilus 1995, 2:318.

24. Words in the margin of his copy of the PSM.

25. When he found himself isolated with his family, and Z. Menšted gave the ex-Tsarina a copy of *Velikoe v malom,* the ex-Tsar made a note (27 March 1918): "Yesterday I read aloud the book by Nilus on the Anti-Christ, to which are joined the Protocols of the Jews and the masons, — a fairly up-to-date read" ("Tsar Nicolas II reads S. A. Nilus," in Nilus 1995, 2:320).

26. Ževaxov (1939, 76) says that Nilus presented the PSM to Grand Duke Sergej Aleksandrovič in January 1905, which would indicate the time at which he acquired it; Hagemeister (1991, 55) maintains that a phrase from a letter of Nilus in April 1905 ("I not only declare that the disaster will arrive, but I know it, I know where and from whom it will come and what awaits us in the near future") refers to the PSM, which

therefore would have already been in his possession. Moreover, some of the modifications to the text common to the "second" and the "third" editions ("the government of the parishes," the "fluctuation of the rouble") relate to the evolution of the political situation in Russia, which moves the re-exhumation of the PSM (even by Nilus) to the summer of that year. The dependence of L on K, and of R on its antigraph, confirm that until halfway through 1905 it had still not yet been "re-exhumed."

27. In a letter to Burcev (from 28 December 1937, in Nilus 1995, 2:264) Chayla affirms that "the son of Račkovskij denies Natalja Afanas'evna had anything to do with any occult circles in Paris, an acquaintance who was supposed to act as a cover for the sending of the work of the gentlemen collaborators of Račkovskij." According to Helebrandt (1991, 6) "the claim of the son of Račkovskij that his father has nothing to do with the PSM, it is irrelevant."

28. Published by G. Sliozberg (who had it in his hands in 1922) in Delevskij 1923, 138–58.

29. The whole of the first part derives from the hypothesis of Fabre d'Olivet (1767–1824), taken up by Saint-Yves d'Alveydre (1842–1919), the "master" of Papus; cf. Webb 1976, 236) and from E. Schuré, *Les grands Initiés* (1887).

30. Cf. Confino 1938, 17; Cohn 1969, 75; and Webb 1976, 222.

31. Cf. Rollin 1991, 482.

32. On the mss. was Stolypin's annotation: "I do not judge it useful to communicate this document to the Emperor. Proceeding with the struggle inadmissible" (Confino 1938, 17).

33. The "Lopuxin Report" on Zionism (1903) makes no allusion to the existence of the PSM, "nor does one find any trace in the archives of the Police Department" (cf. Rollin 1991, 220). When Stolypin ordered an inquiry into the origins of the PSM (1906), it "certified its being a forgery" (Ganelin, in *Nacional'naja pravaja* 1992, 99), but no involvement of the "Secret Services."

34. The most intensive were conducted at the time of the Bern Trial.

35. "The archives of the *Ochrana* in the Hoover Institute at Stanford University reveal nothing, and the same holds true for the private archives of Račkovskij in Paris (now lost) examined by B. Nikolaevskij between 1930 and 1940" (Cohn 1969, 77).

36. Cf. *Les Protocols des Sages de Sion,* "Introduction" (1943; in Taguieff 1992, 1:658): "all attempts made to accuse Račkovskij, or in general the Russian Police, have failed miserably."

37. Barrucand 1992 expresses himself contrary to the hypothesis of a police origin for the PSM, for the same reasons. In the story by Reznik (1988, 102; cf. chap. 5) it is rather Kruševan who offers them to Pleve ("little more the twelve months") before his death, therefore in June–July 1903).

38. Cf. Cohn 1969, 60–61.

39. In the Acts of the Bern Trial (1:452; deposition of Svatikov, 30 October 1934) the name is corrupted into *"ein Herr* Jeffrow." Cohn (1969, 61) rightly identifies the place where the phrase was inserted into the *Translator's Note.*

40. Cohn, however, does not know A2.

41. The "Jew Efron," ex-attaché of the Empress Aleksandra Fedorovna (cf. "France & Russie," *Le Gaulois,* 18 May 1901), was the Director of the Russian Police Agency (different from the Foreign Section of the Oxrana). Her work is probably referred to in a passage from the PSM (17th): "the Police Officer, who at present, in the system which we have worked out, impedes the government from knowing the truth."

42. Cf. Šmakov 1912 (*Evrei i S. Ju. Vitte*), 562.

CHAPTER 5

The Origins of the *Protocols*

Now that the "material evidence" (the text) and "the time and place of the crime" (the dating and localization) have been ascertained, it only remains to confront the principal question of "who did it and why?"

Above all, one must clear up the role of Nilus, who appears in all discussions on the PSM in which he features, if not as author, as the "best publisher." In post-Soviet Russia, his "figure, strong and luminous" as a "writer and Orthodox ascetic"[1] commands renewed credit,[2] which excludes "any possibility of hoaxing on his part,"[3] and this gives a hypothesis of trustworthiness, if not to his editing of the PSM, at least to the text itself.

Hagemeister (1991, 49–50) justly laments that

> the biographical information, in particular on the origins of Nilus and the last years of his life, are scarce, untrustworthy and often contradictory.

Our problem—which cannot be faced without an adequate documentary base, but today is notably improved thanks also to the work of the same Hagemeister—is not so much in reconstructing Nilus's biography, but in being accurate as to his role in the whole business of the PSM.

Two images have been presented. There is, on one side, the hagiography of the "eminent religious writer" (Nilus 1995, 1:3), and on the other side, criticism of the religious maniac on the verge of paranoia. The origins of the first lies in the interwar writings of the fascist-supporting émigrés (Ževaxov 1936), and this has been taken up by followers of the present day Russian Right (Vol'skij 1993, Strižěv 1993, Begunov 1996). The origins of the second is, on the other hand, the lacerating portrait by Chayla, which speaks of his "hallucinations," (in Taguieff 1992, 1:55), then to be confirmed by Cohn (1969, 63) with his formula of "the religious eccentric," and so on to in Tazbir (1992b, 73: "a maniacal mystic") and in Dudakov (1993, 144: "a religious fundamentalist"). Whether he was a saint or a dangerous fanatic, both of these hypotheses shed light on his good faith in standing as guarantor for the PSM.[4] Instead it is this that rightly needs to be examined. Nilus (1905, 405) claims to have had the PSM from 1901 and to have waited four years before publishing it.[5] However the PSM are from 1902–1903, and his is a variation of the third edition, and makes no allusion to the first of 1903.

Nilus has given at least four versions of the origins of the PSM and how it came to him.[6] It is sufficient to stop at the first two, the other two being manifestly "secondary." An addition to the *Translator's Note* (by himself, dating it 1902) indicates as the source his presumed "correspondent" (p. 394), who can be seen as coinciding with the "dear person, already dead" (*Vmesto predislovija,* 1905; p. 321), later mentioned in Suxotin,[7] or on the other hand as not. Being contextual, in the first case the two versions jointly negate each other. In the second case, the first version (the "correspondent" is obviously false, but implicitly so is the second (the "dear person"[8]), nor is it possible to make them agree because in that case the "correspondent" would be the mysterious lady who had given the PSM to the "dear person"; that is to say, no longer a correspondent of Nilus. Therefore, neither of the two correspondents is true, and the later confirmations (in the first place by Stepanov, 1927[9]) prove to be none other than later "inventions" to validate the authenticity and the late appearance of the PSM.

Nilus has notably revised the PSM, with omissions and additions, inserting in the text a note "by the translator," attributing it the *Note.* These are all things on which he had to keep quiet if he wanted to maintain that his edition was the "original." Among the additions, moreover, the "francophone" ones give the lie to the knowledge that we are dealing with a *Russian* text that was being passed off as a *French* one.

Nilus had headed his edition with a comment that proposed the reading of the PSM against the background of Vl. Solov'ev's *Antichrist,* which is to be regarded (as we shall see) as manifestly incongruous.

Finally, Nilus lived in Soviet Russia for twelve years and his fame as the publisher of the PSM was widespread. He was arrested several times,[10] but was always released. We know nothing of his interrogations, nor what he might have said to get off ("up to now the papers have not been traced," Polovinkin 1995, 5). All this casts over him a shadow of doubt.[11] He died in his own bed at Krutec (Polovinkin 1995, 265–66), a village near Aleksandrov, remaining unharmed by the threats that would have hung over anyone who had only had the PSM in his hands.

Nilus therefore is not only not the "best publisher" of the PSM, but has all the appearance "lying knowing to be lying." His role in the origins of the PSM is nil, even if the role played by the diffusion of his edition proved to be decisive.

Now we are able to return to the text.

In the West, the myth of the "Jewish Plot" coincided from 1919 with the PSM. However Dudakov has shown with due evidence that, from 1902, such a myth was already formed and indeed "established" in Russia.[12] The purpose of the PSM was therefore to convalidate it definitively in the eyes of its readers with a "document,"[13] in a variant which also involves Vitte and his politics. To manage this, the exponents of the Russian radical Right had at their disposal everything they needed at St. Petersburg, without having to have recourse to the services of the *Oxrana,* and even less so any abroad.

In the early years of the century, a series of events occurred that tied in significantly with the framework offered by the PSM. In January 1901, the Minister of the Interior, Pleve, ratified the Statute of *Russkoe sobranie,* the aristocratic organization, "the forerunner of all the agrarian monarchist parties" (*Programmy* 1995, 419), which in its Statute (drawn up—incidentally—in 1905) echoed the fundamental motif of the PSM: the "Jewish Question" would have to be resolved separately from that of other nations,

> given the long-lasting natural hostility between Judaism and Christianity and the non-Jewish nations, and *the Jewish aspiration for world domination* (ibid., 422; my italics, C.D.M).

In February 1902, the student movements renewed their activities in various cities and held their first Pan-Russian Congress with openly subversive intentions, raising fears of a new wave of terrorism.[14] On April 2, Sipjagin, the Minster of the Interior, was assassinated. On March 10, the conservatives succeeded in invalidating the election of Gor'kij as a member of the Academy of Sciences, and there was the outburst over the bitter "case" of the banning of *Meščane,* which had opened in February, in the provinces. On December 18, there was the first night of *Na dne* and the right-wing press pointed out in Gor'kij those traits of "degenerate literature" of which the PSM speaks.[15]

In May, the President of the French Republic, Loubet, paid a state visit to Russia which was to guarantee the "balance of power not only in Europe <u>but also in the Far East</u>."[16] (But wait a moment, the Right asked itself: Are we to be protected from the "Chinese and Japanese cannons" thanks to a Masonic and in practice Judaized France?) In addition, in July, the King of Italy, Victor Emanuel III, undertook a state visit to Russia, and that called to mind the assassination of his father.

On September 29, 1902, Zola died and the press comment turned to the "Dreyfus Affair." Two months later, Butmi published another essay on the Gold Standard.[17] Ioann of Kronštadt[18] published a violent attack on Tolstoj who had been excommunicated by the Orthodox Church[19] the year before, and in 1901 Tolstoj had written the "pedagogic" letter in which, among other things, he judged "impious" historic sciences, concluding that "they should be excluded from the curriculum."

In September 1902, the "Pan-Russian Zionist Congress"[20] was held at Minsk. The November issue of the émigré review *Osvoboždenie* contained an essay by "the Professor" (P. Miljukov) comparing Russia with France on the eve of the Revolution.[21] On January 31, 1903, on the occasion of the bicentenary of the Russian press, the Government rejected an appeal for the abolition of censorship, which underlined the importance of the Russian press. On February 26, the Government *Manifesto* was published granting toleration to non-Orthodox confessions, which was felt by some to be a recognition of freedom of conscience and as such was fiercely opposed by the Right. Over Easter, April 19 and 20, the pogrom of Kišinëv broke out. This is the context in which the PSM was produced, and of which it bears fatal traces.

Vl. Burcev, in a letter addressed to A. Amfiteatrov, who had emigrated to Italy,[22] at the time of the Bern Trial summed up his idea of the origins of the PSM thus:

> In the nineties, Russian anti-Semites had contacted Račkovskij about the Jewish problem. Together, they composed something on the Jewish problem, and among other things also composed the PSM. Their means was the writer Matvej Golovinskij. I imagine Manuilov would have helped while Račkovskij directed the matter. In 1900–1902 this manuscript arrived in Russia. Nilus, a fanatical anti-Semite who then lived in Optima Pustyn', authenticated it. Nilus had contacts, if not actually with the Court and the Tsar, with people close to the Tsar, among them Meščerskij.

Even though this has been worked out by "one in the business," this scenario depends uncritically on more-than-suspect sources, in particular K. Radziwiłłowa. For his part, I. Kolyško (right-wing journalist, in his time "closer in *his* sympathies to those favorable to anti-Semitism than to those opposed to it")[23] had, a few days before, summed up to Burcev the opinion he had formed of the PSM as a result of personal recollections of the journalistic scene between 1905 and 1910 as follows:

> The *Protocols* are a hybrid apocrypha from a group of people at the center of which was a certain Nilus, I was told with consternation in the editorial offices of *Novoe Vremja, Peterburgskie Vedomosti* and *Graždanin,* with joy in the editorial office of *Birževye vedomosti,* and with composure in the editorial offices of *Russkoe slovo.*[24]

An analogous version was inserted by A. Belyj in the novel *Peterburg* (1913).

A voice halted him at the threshold:

— Have you understood therefore, madam, the links between the Japanese War, the Jews, and the Mongolian invasion? The insolence of the Russian Jews and the entering on the field of the Boxers are closely connected....

Meanwhile one heard:

— So you have understood, madam, the Jewish-Masonic activities?

The Professor[25] did not hesitate: turning to the mistress of the house, he observed:

— Permit me, madam, to interpose a modest word of science: similar information has a clear source: it comes from the supporters of the pogrom.

The Russian cultural world therefore appeared to have no doubts: the PSM were attributed not to the *Oxrana* but to *pogromščiki* circles.

Everything induces us to hold in its entirety the framework given by Kolyško with the proviso only that in place of Nilus (who, as has been said, was merely the "secondary" publisher of the text), one needs to substitute one or more persons who have been shown to be involved in the PSM affair from the beginning. Furthermore, only two or three names were implicated in the very first phase of their circulation.[26] Those were Men'šikov and the "journalists" who at the same time (1902) were involved with the mysterious document, one of whom is almost certainly Kruševan (who however published the PSM for the first time the following year) and the other, in all probability, is Butmi.

All three belonged to the extreme Jew-phobic Right of the *Russkoe sobranie* which two years later (November 1905) would father the *Sojuz Russkogo* in which Kruševan[27] and Butmi were active, and whose Xar'kov section published an antisemitic booklet by Men'šikov (1908). *Sojuz,* too, said that the "Jewish Question" must be faced separately from that of other nationalities,

given the longstanding natural hostility of Judaism not only for Christianity but also for the non-Jewish nations, and given *the Jewish aspirations for world domination* (*Programmy* 1995, 444; my italics, C.D.M.).

Let us concentrate our attention, however, on M. Men'šikov, who in 1918 was shot for his Jewish-phobic past. In the years of Stolypin (1908–1909), he had been the theorist of Russian nationalism who had inspired the constitution of *Nacional'nyj klub*.[28] He had had some disagreements with his one-time friends who, from the extreme nationalist positions of *Sojuz russkogo naroda,* in 1905 had remained against any form of constitution, to which, however, the "nationalists" were not totally opposed because it would guarantee the predominance of Russians (and Orthodox) over other nationalities (and the other confessions). However, it is difficult that any proof would have remained of his later involvement with the PSM. From the prison of Valdaj he wrote to his wife (1 [14] September 1918; Men'šikov 1993, 227) telling her to "burn from his diaries and letters all that the children should not know." I do not suppose he was referring to love affairs.

Men'šikov knew very well what he was accused of ("articles inciting *pogromy* against the Jews," 5 April; ibid., 229). The next day he wrote:

> The members and the President of the Extraordinary Commission of Inquiry are Jews[29] and do not conceal that my arrest and trial are a vendetta against my old articles denouncing the Jews (ibid., 230).

In a situation of this type, the last thing to do would have been to admit to having taken part *even* in the drafting of the PSM. Learning of his sentence, he wrote that same day:

> Remember—I die a victim of Jewish vengeance, not for some crime, but only for the accusation of the Jewish people, a thing for which they have exterminated even their prophets (ibid., 232).[30]

The letters of those condemned to death are often moving and those of Men'šikov are no exception. He emerges from them as a dignified figure, which obviously does not erase the odious part he had played at the beginning of the century in the "Jewish Question." Here it is interesting to reveal that, even in a period of widespread violence like 1918, the "Men'šikov Affair" follows a precise logic, in singular contrast to the effective impunity reserved for Nilus, both then and later, by the Soviet authorities.

Does this mean that the ČeKa of Valdaj knew of Men'šikov's special role in the antisemitic campaigns of 1902–1903 and that, in particular, they had "secret" information on his involvement in the drafting of the PSM? If this were to have been the case, would there not have remained traces of it? The tragic epilogue of Valdaj, together with the strange article of 1902, however, lead one to hold that it was from *Russkoe sobranie* circles (of which he was a member and in which the first "shortened edition" (R) appeared,) that the PSM really sprung.

This conclusion leads to other considerations.

Men'šikov wrote an article on the PSM (April 1902) *before* Loubet's visit to St. Petersburg (in May 1902), of which the PSM bear traces which, beside the denunciation of the "forged truth" (prior to the "true forgery"), means that he spoke of it before it was published, at least as far as we know. This is, obviously, something he could do only if he were involved in its compilation. Moreover, the "veterotestimentary" line adopted in the first conception of the text is found also in the pages of Chamberlain that Men'šikov knew and made use of.[31] Certainly we do not know if he had already read it in 1902, but some details of the PSM seem to come from there (cf. Chap. 6).

The figure of Butmi appears of no lesser significance. He was reputed by Bostunič to be one of the three "founders" of Russian antisemitism.[32] In the preceding decade, he had been one of the prime exponents of the agricultural world against the Gold Standard System[33] and its Russian advocate, Vitte.[34] In this way he became involved with Šarapov whose ideas[35] "rest at the basis of the economic theory of the PSM" (Dudakov 1993, 182). He had written the preface to a booklet by Butmi (1898b) and had relations also with Men'šikov.[36]

Butmi complained that his writings were more appreciated in the West than in Russia, and it is true that two of his works had appeared in German[37] and one in English.[38] He also had to do with A. Chabry,[39] "noted expert in monetary questions" (Butmi 1904, 231) who, despite obvious differences of context, expressed the same economic-political positions as Butmi.

In *Capital and Debt* there is an image taken from Chabry that (without belittling the "literary" suggestions which will be discussed further below) seems constituted from the image of the "symbolic serpent" In the PSM. Butmi writes:

"In this way the *boa constrictor* swallows an ox, bigger than himself, after having first reduced him with his coils [*kol'ca*] to the dimensions of his jaws. I take this metaphor from A. Chabry *(L'Usure Suprême)*.[40] Speaking of the disasters produced by the Gold Standard, he compared the latter to an enormous boa of gold, whose maw one finds in London *while waiting for its transfer to Palestine* (my italics, C.D.M.). And whose coils encircled the whole world squeezing into gold coins all the contributors and all the debtors" (Butmi 1898b, 14).

The serpent of the Gold Standard which devours agricultural property with its interest on loans is therefore already in Chabry an allegory for the Judaism against which Butmi had inveighed since 1899[41]:

On the pile of those bloody victims of famine is erected the golden citadel of the shameful Jewish dominion. In this way, then, a miserable race which has never given even an idea of genius to humanity, nor a scientific discovery...has in this way this miserable race has become master of the world?

Alongside these passages from Chabry's writings one finds comparisons with the PSM (cf. Chap. 3), which reinforce the idea that Butmi had a hand in their compilation.

As regards Kruševan, who knew Men'šikov from the days of *Nedelja,* he is the "prime suspect," not only because he was the first publisher of the PSM, but above all because in the anti-Jewish campaign of 1903 he had been utterly ruthless.[42] Apart from the brief note of *Znamja,* Kruševan never gave his version of the discovery of the PSM, to which he never returned in the six years that he had still to live, not even to comment on the editions which appeared in 1905. His involvement in the affair has appeared to some more than a mere hypothesis. An interesting "historical novel" based on the figure of Kruševan without any pretence of documentary reconstruction (Reznik 1988),[43] offered a picture very similar to that which has been outlined here. According to Reznik, Kruševan had brought the manuscript of the PSM[44] to Men'šikov to be published in *Novoe vremja,* but he had turned it down, among other reasons because the PSM would have appeared under "work commissioned by us." To this, Kruševan's disdainful reply ("Do you want perhaps to say that it was not I who composed these Protocols?" p. 27), in the narrative context, sounds like an implicit confirmation. The "mysterious lady" of Men'sikov 1902 (but the interweaving into the story of Reznik is placed in 1903!) would have been therefore the "mask" of Kruševan, who (according to the story), after obtaining a notable sum of money from *Novoe vremja,* attempted to implicate Pleve who would, however have given the "via libera" or permission for the publication of the PSM in his not very authoritative paper.

This last part of the narrative reconstruction finds unexpected confirmation in the letter which Aleksandr Tager (1888–1939)[45] enclosed when he sent the material collected in the Soviet Archives to the court expert, C. A. Loosli, for the Bern Trial.[46] The Russian Archives hold originals of the letters Kruševan sent to Pleve, the Minister of the Interior, which

> even though he knew very well that no "protocols" existed, fostered his strong antisemitism and the consequent policy of the pogroms through publishing material of this type in the right-wing press and especially in Kruševan's daily *Znamja.*

Nobody, however, grasped the importance of this. The nexus between Kruševan and the Police Department was also recalled by Briman (1998) who added a very interesting element, which was that Russian Zionism's "post office" was kept by Ja. Bernštejn-Kogan at Kišinëv, and one can well imagine Kruševan's irritation when he came to know (from the Police, who financed his paper) that a sort of Jewish "Secret Service" had set itself up in his own city:

> In [*his*] enflamed imagination, the correspondence, the instructions, the documents, and the circulars of Dr. Bernštejn-Kogan's "Post Office" could be transformed into protocols and directives of the "World-wide Jewish Center," proof of the existence of a "Zionist Plot" against Russia and humanity.

The intervention of the Russian Government would therefore have consisted in contacts with those around Kruševan maintained by Pleve, which makes the involvement of Račkovskij (Vitte's man) even less plausible. As regards the PSM, they would have been compiled on Kruševan's initiative with the complicity and perhaps the help of other representatives of the antisemitic Right. Tazbir also (1992, 51) proposes without relevant objections the attribution of the PSM to Kruševan and/or Butmi. One is always dealing with an hypothesis in an "investigative trial," but one which corresponds much more with the available information than the thesis of a forgery made by *Oxrana* in Paris.

There is a latent contradiction between the conceptual and "literary" plan of the PSM (which shows a certain degree of culture and a not indifferent sense of organization) and their realization, which is tatty, and even linguistically incorrect. However, more than the incorrect Russian, one's attention is drawn to the presence of Ukrainianisms.

Kruševan was originally from Bessarabia (where one in essence speaks Moldavian and Ukrainian, or Russian with strong Ukrainian inflection[47]) and Butmi was born in Jampol (in Podolia) on the borders with Bessarabia, where he had his estates. Both Kruševan and Butmi made use of the services of collaborators and could have trusted one of these[48] with the drafting of a project born perhaps as an (ignoble) "party game" in cahoots with Men'šikov, the most cultivated of the three. Both he and Butmi had good French connections, and both could have suggested the use of Joly's pamphlet. A shortened edition (D) and the first short edition (R) appeared in the same area, Ukraine, as Men'šikov 1908. Furthermore, if the PSM had their source in Kruševan and Butmi's circles, from Men'šikov and Šarapov, it would also explain why they were never caught. When the PSM "affair" burst upon the world after 1919 both had disappeared,[49] while Nilus, admitting that he was not aware of it, had no interest in divulging the true origins of the PSM, which however would have re-dimensioned the whole affair.

Seen in relation to the 1901 Zionist Congress, the events of 1903 (the *pogromy*, the visit of Herzl to Russia, the Sixth Zionist Congress) would have driven Kruševan, with the support of Pleve, to use the PSM in a still rough and ready state.

Then we come to the crucial year 1905, when the text could turn out to be useful in other directions, and someone (Butmi? and whoever are the true publishers of A1 and A2?) "refined" the draft of the PSM to make use of it in relation to current events in Russia.

At this point Nilus became involved (perhaps in reality to distract attention). He was a person of note who was already moving in the right circles with the publication of his *Conversation with Motovilov*[50] (and more generally because of the part he had played in the beatification of St. Serafim of Sarov in 1903). Meanwhile, after the loss of ownership of Zolotarevo, he arrived in St. Petersburg where he succeeded in getting himself introduced at Court. Thus he assumed the role of privileged publisher of the PSM putting it at the disposal of highly placed people in the clerical-political Establishment[51] with the intention of providing a "documentary" basis for those especially evil explosions of antisemitism that broke out in the wake of the "October 17 Manifesto."[52] He thus acquired a certain fame, (questionable if you like, but still fame) which redeemed his gray existence as a bankrupt landowner and failed priest.[53] We know how it all ended.

NOTES

1. Bugunov 1996, 72. However, Bostunič 1928, one of the most implacable Russian antisemites (he became an adviser to Himmler), distanced himself from Nilus, considering him too "philo-Catholic."

2. A full bibliography of the recent reprints of his works and writings on him is in the principal of these which is Nilus 1995, 2:550f.

3. Vol'skij 1993, 29.

4. In the "critical" published material Nilus is mostly considered "a mythomaniac, but not a deliberate forger" (see above, S. Rochcau, *Saint-Sérafim* [Belle Fontaine, 1987], 47).

5. Without, however, saying that the first edition of his book had appeared in 1903, without the PSM.

6. Not taking into account that attributed by him to Chayla (1921), denied by the son: 1. from his correspondent, who had it in France from the deposits of the Central Chancellery of Zion (Nilus 1905, 394); 2. from a deceased acquaintance (Suxotin) who had it in turn from a lady who had stolen it from one of the "most initiated" Masons in France (ibid., 321–22); 3. from an old lady whose deceased son had a

relationship in Paris with a baptized Jewess who had purloined the manuscript from her father, one of the "sages of Zion" (M. Orlova Smirnova, "Poslednie dni Nilusa," *Domostroj,* 45 [1991], then in Polovinkin 1995, 88). 4. through a news leak, at Basle, during the First Zionist Congress of 1897, where Th. Herzl had presented it (Nilus 1917, 88). Even Begunov (1996, 78–80) speaks of "four versions," but counting that referred to by Chayla and omitting that "of Herzl."

7. According to Begunov (1996, 80), in 1905, Nilus had kept quiet about the name of Suxotin for fear of exposing him, given that he "occupied an important post at Stavropol," but a little later (ibid., 91) reported that he had died in 1903.

8. Dated 1905, it would effectively deny the former, which is implausible if that really goes back to 1902, while it is also that of 1905.

9. Whose declaration was confirmed by the daughter, Princess V. F. Golicyna (N. Ževaxov 1936, 23), from the son of N. F. Stepanov (evidence at the Bern Trial, 14 January 1935) and "from a cousin of A. Suxotin *who* says that around 1895…she saw the ms. which a sister of Suxotin was copying" (declaration of 13 December 1936, in Cohn 1969, 72): too many confirmations of a date (1895) which is certainly wrong.

10. At Kiev in 1923, at Pirjatin in 1924–1925, again at Kiev in 1925–1926 (when he was transferred to the Lubjanka of Moscow), then again in Kiev in 1927.

11. The question was raised by S. Žarikov ("Kogda padajut zvezdy," *K toporu,* 5 [1993]) from an extreme Right standpoint as trying to pass Nilus off as a Jew. The editors of Nilus 1995 (2:480) defined this as "at the limits of provocation."

12. Cf. Šmakov 1897 (there is already all of the PSM, except the text of the PSM; completed from an ample *Bibliografija evrejskogo voprosa*) or Ljutostanskij vol. 1, 1902 (in particular the chapter "Ob evrejskom masonstve").

13. I. Kolyško attributes these words to Russian right-wing circles of the time (letter to Vl. Burcev of 7 September 1934, in *Nikolaevsky mss.* 14:9–6): "And it was not the artistic invention of some Wells (*The Martians*) or Jules Verne (*Forty* [*sic*] *Thousand Leagues under the Sea*), but the conspiracy of a whole race, on whose success depended the destiny of Western culture and the destiny of Christianity itself."

14. A. Suvorin wrote in his *Diary* (6 November 1902) "many arrests; in Moscow one awaits the *revolution.*"

15. N. Engel'gardt, "Maksim Go'rkij kak xudožnik," *Russkij vestnik,* 6 (1902); Seren'kij [I. Kolsyško], "Dux vremeni" *Graždanin,* 2 June 1902; a bitter critic of the first Gor'kij was also Men'šikov (1993, 268). Paradoxically, the effective proscription of "degenerate art" by the Nazis in the 1930s (but also undertaken in the USSR, even if under a different name) finished by considering not the "realistic" tendencies of which Gor'kij had been the interpreter, but those "modernist" ones overthrown by him.

16. Letter from R. Morra, Italian Ambassador at St. Petersburg, 23 April 1902 in AS MAE AP (Russia 1899–1905), 343.

17. *Sposoby rasprostranenija zolotoj valjuty* (15 November 1902) in Butmi 1904a.

18. Ioann Il'ič Sergiev (1829–1902), "one of the most intransigent antisemites among the ecclesiastics"; cf. H. D. Löwe, *Antisemitismus und raktionäre Utopie* (Hamburg 1978, 63, cited by Hagemeister 1991, 53) was canonized by the Russian Orthodox Church Abroad [ROCA] in 1964.

19. *Protiv grafa L'va Tolstogo* (St. Petersburg 1902); on the question, see G. Petrov, *Otlučenie L'va Tolstogo ot cerkvi* (Moscow 1978).

20. El'jaševič, in *Nacional'naja pravaja* 1992, 62; see Herzl 1990, 333.

21. *Sovremennoe položenie Rossii i vidy na buduščee,* cited in B. Itenberg, *Rossija i Velikaja francuzskaja revoljucija* (Moscow 1988), 221.

22. In *Amfiteatrov* mss. (14 September 1934).

23. Even if later he changed his opinion; cf. his *Evrei o sebe* (Berlin 1923).

24. I. Kolyško (Bajan) to V. Burcev (7 September 1934), in *Nikolaevsky* mss. Šmakov includes the first three newspapers and the last among the "non-Jewish" press (that is, with antisemitic tendencies, more or less marked), while the *Birževye vedomosti* gloried in the fame of being philosemitic.

25. In which Belyj "impersonated" P. B. Struve; cf. L. Dolgopolov, *Kommentarii to A. Belyj, Peterburg* (Moscow 1878), 373.

26. For reasons already mentioned, these will not include characters such as Ju. Glinka, A. Suxotin, N. Stepanov, nor P. Račkovskij and his agents.

27. Cf. Stepanov 1992, 98: to one F. Volovej, who opposed him for the Presidency of Kišinëv's section, are sent two armed figures, ready to fire in case of a refusal to hand over the passage.

28. Avrex 1991, 133.

29. Their surnames were: Jacobson, Davidson, Gil'font, and Guba (ibid., 250).

30. In the *Izvestija Vserossijskogo CIK,* 22 September 1918, there appeared the following despatch of the ROSTA: "The shooting of Men'šikov" (Novgorod, 21 September): "The extraordinary field directive has shot at Valdaj the noted Black Hundred journalist Men'šikov. A letter for Prince L'vov [perhaps the last Procurator of the Holy Synod; author's note] was found on him. A monarchist plot has been uncovered with Men'šikov at its head. He was publishing a clandestine Black Hundred newspaper which incited the overthrow of Soviet power."

31. Cf. Chamberlain, *The Jews* ([1899] 1913) with reference to the chapter "The Entrance of the Jews into Western History." In 1907, a 4th ed. of the Russian translation was published in St. Petersburg *(Evrei, ix proisxoždenie i pričiny ix vlijanija v Evrope).* I have not been able to establish when the first edition came out, but naturally Men'šikov would have known it from the original.

32. The others would have been I. Ljutostanskij and A. Šmakov (Bostunič 1928, 72).

33. Cf. Butmi 1896 and 1897b.

34. Cf. Butmi 1906b.

35. In booklets like: *Sredi xozjaev* (St. Petersburg 1896); *Vopros o valjute* (St. Petersburg 1899); *Vopl' golodajuščego intelligenta* (Moscow 1902); *Socializm, kak religija nenavisti* (Moscow 1907). He also published a "Utopian" novel which was proposed as a compendium of slavophile ideals: *Čerez polveka* (Moscow 1901).

36. A. Šarapov, *S Angeliej ili s Germaniej? Obmen mysljami s M. O. Men'šikovym* (Moscow 1908).

37. Butmi 1897 and 1899 (cf. G. Butmi 1904a, v.).

38. Butmi 1898a.

39. Journalist, member of the Society of French Agriculturists, secretary of the French League for Bi-metalism, reactionary Catholic, and Judeo-phobe. He wrote in *La Croix,* among other things, "L'accaparement monétaire," cited in *La monnaie et les "capitalistes chrétiens"* (Paris 1897), *Les rapines monétaires* (Paris 1897), and translated texts against mono-metalism by W. J. Walsh (1894) and by A. Del Mar (1899).

40. *L'Usure suprême, ou les Dangers du crédit à l'heure actuelle* (Paris n.d. [but: 1896]), 12; the title recalls those of the Catholic decadentism of J. Péladan (*La Vice suprême* [1884]).

41. "Umirajuščij Bogatyr'" (10 April 1899), in Butmi 1904a, 222.

42. Cf. Cohn 1969, 78–79; *Znamja* also republished "The Rabbi's Speech" (22. I. 1904).

43. Because, says A, of the attention reserved for Kruševen by "Pamjat'." He wrote in the early 1880s, and was only able to publish it at the end of the decade, once he had emigrated to the United States.

44. A always cites the PSM according to the *Znamja* edition, and not the more widely available Nilus edition.

45. Jurist, formally a collaborator of A. Blok in the commission of enquiry on Tsarist power (cf. SS 1963, 7:285) wrote a volume on *Carskaja Rossija i delo Bejlisa* (Moscow 1933).

46. From 3 January 1935, in *Berner Prozess,* 13:21–26; Tager sent a copy of the memorandum-Lopuxin (*Sionizm* 1903) and the photographs of the cyclostiled run of the PSM which we have cited as S.

47. According to the statistics of 1897, the population of Bessarabia was composed as follows: Moldavians 47.6%, Ukrainians 19.6%, Jews 11.8%, Belrussians 8.1%, Bulgars 5.2%, and Germans 3.1% [others 4.6%]; cf. Ch. Rakowsky, *Il problema della Bessarabia* (Rome n.d. [but: 1927]), 19.

48. For example, N. Zozulin, one of the "two or three most intimate members of the editorial board of *Bessarabec,* which had helped Kruševan in the compilation of his volume *Bessarabija* (Moscow 1903), or "N. L." (N. Abarinov), together with whom Butmi compiled two *Obličitel'nye reči* (Butmi 1906c and Butmi 1906e).

49. I have no definite information on what happened to Butmi, of whom traces are lost with the involvement of his relative in two booklets (N. A. Butmi) of 1914. When his son turned up in Paris in 1920, Msgr. Jouin claimed he was still alive, but, according to a oral communication of S. Dudakov, he had died (also shot?) in 1918.

50. M. Hagemeister, "Il problema della genesi del 'Colloquio con Motovilov' (The problem of the origins of the 'colloquy with Motovilov')" in AA.VV. *San Serafim da Sarov a Diveevo* (Bose 1998) has shown all the dubious circumstances of the Nilus edition, putting forward the suspicion of a forgery stimulated by "the machine of beatification" of which Amal'rik 1984, 65 speaks.

51. The Metropolitan of Moscow had published in the right-wing newspaper *Moskovskie vedomosti* (16 October 1905) an article/homily of proud aversion to the *Manifesto* which would be published the following day, in which the PSM were referred to, in particular with the quotation of the *Translator's Note* according to the A2 and N versions.

52. Cf. D. Klier and Sh. Lambroza, eds., *Pogroms: Anti-Jewish Violence in Modern Russian History* (Cambridge 1992).

53. Nilus was about to be ordained a priest (February 1906) when *Novoe vremja* published an article denouncing his past disorderly life, and the Archbishop Antonij refused him ordination (cf. Hagemeister 1991, 56 and Koncevič [1969], in Nilus 1995, 1:10–11).

CHAPTER 6

An Introduction to the Text

Taguieff proposes that the PSM should be studied from four points of view:

1. Within the framework of a history, typology and psycho-sociology of the theories of the plot, connected with the phenomenon of modern secret societies (late 18th to 19th century) both as fact and myth.

2. Within the framework of the history of antisemitism, and more precisely...of a story of the development of anti-Jewish ideologies in the modern and contemporary age....

3. Within the framework of the history of forgery...linked to police falsifications...or again within the framework of a history of textual impostors and literary hoaxes....

4. Within the framework of a history of the anthropology of devil worship, representations of the devil and of Satanism....

Taguieff indicates, on the contrary, some other essential difficulties of the PSM (conspiracy, antisemitism, forgery, anti-theology) but, shifting from a viewpoint which is more ideological than philological, he offers, in my opinion, an inadequate framework for their exegesis. However, his is an advance on Cohn's "interpretative model" (1969, x and 201f.), which, taking as its basis the category of "collective psychopathology," ends by transferring an intricate textual criticism and cultural historical question into a psycho-analytical one.

The "questions" should be reformulated in such a way as to place the text at the center of attention rather than the ideologemes and the "literary" peculiarities rather than the psychology either of the individual (the sender) or the group (the recipient). Moreover, this is in relation to the reconstructed text, leaving apart the story of the establishment of the myth and that of the succeeding re-elaboration of the text.

Let us first examine some passages that restoration allows us to read in a more correct way than was possible with the vulgate.

1. The Modern Doctrines

The intellectuals [the "gojim"] *are proud of* [their] *knowledge without logical verification, and put into practice all the notions dealing with science, written by our agents with the intention of forming the minds in ways that will prove useful (the translator remembers the successes of Darwinism, of Marxism, of Nietzscheism and the other unproven doctrines).* (11)

N grounds the *Translator's Note* in the text, reworking it thus:

Do not think that our claims are unfounded. Look at the success we had with our construction of Darwinism, Marxism, Nietzscheism. At least for us the mind-building function for the *gojim* of these science studies should be evident.

Darwin, Marx, and Nietzsche are therefore presented by the PSM as "agents of Judaism," though the logic of this is not imediately apparent. The only person possessing the necessary qualities for the role assigned to him is obviously Marx, while Darwin and, above all, Nietzsche do not seem at first sight to fit particularly well with the Jewish plan to dominate the world.

To understand these assertions, one needs to place them in the context of the Russian culture of the time. Darwin, who had been published in Russia since the 1860s, was very popular at "a cultural level typical of Elementary School teachers"[1] and had a major impact on culture from the 1870s.[2] Darwinism's fame for being "progressive" is not, however, sufficient to explain the role reserved for it in the PSM, especially since the doctrine of natural selection possessed characteristics (reducible to "the predominance of the strong over the weak") which would appeal to the "culture of the Right."

In 1882, Nikolaj Vagner (illustrious zoologist, but also author of fables, not to mention an antisemitic novel) published in *Novoe vremja* an obituary of Darwin in which, assuming that history demonstrates the correctness of Darwinian doctrine of the survival of the fittest, he wrote that

victory will come to that wandering, nomad, homeless nation whose tenacious and pliable vitality has been wrought by oppression and hundred of years of persecution.... For some time, [the Jews] have understood that strength lies not in altruism, but in economic principle.... For some time they have sensed that money is the only force that can dominate the world, and they now already possess half the world if not more. Here are the strugglers who provide a shining confirmation of Darwin's principle.

A journalist from a democratic background, Nikolaj Šelgunov, noted ironically that "the man of science" had honored in his own way the memory of the great Darwin, by twisting the theory of evolution into the persecution of the Jews.[3]

It was therefore a double-edged sword, and as such was used by the author of the PSM. Darwinism is a "doctrine at the service of the Jews" not only because it contained the most crude materialism, but above all because it would guarantee them world domination.

As regards Nietzsche, the theoretician of an "anti-Christian antisemitism" (with the idea of a slaves' morality, from within the Judeo-Christian tradition, as opposed to a masters' morality"[4]), seems to lend itself even less to the role reserved for it in the PSM.[5] However, among the perceptions of Nietzsche in Russia, there was also a "Zionist" one, expressed by Mixa Berdičevskij (1865-1921)[6] and also Ašer Gincberg. The nature of this was a sort of identification of the People of Israel within a "collective Superman." The "Zionist Nietzscheism" is at the origin of the idea (attributed to the "translator," but obviously written by the forger himself) according to which the doctrines of Nietzsche had been secretly promoted by the "Jewish Center"; an idea that could only be conceived of in Russia and have a meaning easily accessible to the reader.

Placed alongside the Jew Marx (theoretician of the hegemonic role of the proletariat, that is of mass democracy), Darwin (the natural selection that would guarantee the "primacy" of the Jews) and Nietzsche (the collective superman identified as Israel), are all employed as eponymous heroes of a "philosophy of history" that condemns Christianity with no possibility of appeal, and in particular, Russian autocracy. The idea appealed so much to Nilus that he removed it from the presumed "translator" so as to attribute it directly to the "Sages of Zion."

2. STRIKES AND "CARTELS"

The guarantee of a secure and regular salary, which depends on the bosses and their partners' trusts, have been promoted by us when necessary to distract minds from current affairs and carry on undisturbed that which benefits us. (3rd)

I dwell upon this passage, which is not, however, of crucial importance, because it shows how the text written before the Revolution has been fatally misunderstood in later writing about it. To understand the misunderstanding into which almost all the interpreters have fallen, one needs to say above all that in A2 and N the passage is modified and abbreviated, encouraging the ambiguity:

the guarantee of a secure and regular salary, which depends (N: *placing them in dependency*) on the agreements of the bosses and [*their*] partners.

The key term in this passage (*stačka*) has lost the primary meaning that it still had at the beginning of the century ("[secret] agreement," "cartel"[7]), keeping only its secondary meaning of "strike" which became preeminent and almost exclusive in the post-1917 language of politics. As regards *tovarišč* (which, however, meant "partner" or "assistant," more than "comrade" in the political or trade union sense), it can effectively give rise to some doubts because it is not clear if it refers to the "bosses" or the "workers." This is different from R, which paraphrases the passage following the second meaning. I maintain that the first meaning is more coherent because of the meaning of *stačka* (trust) which in R (especially R2) would give rise to sheer nonsense. Almost all the translations fall into this trap. The Czech one at least shows the nonsense[8] of making the bosses "strike":

na výlukach a stávkách organizovaných podnikateli neb jejich dělnickými soudruhy[9];

but not so the French one:

des grèves des patrons ou des camarades,[10]

and the Italian one,

degli scioperi, di chi gli dà lavoro e dei suoi compagni,[11]

which instead shows us nothing; and for good measure also the Polish one:

od porozumienia między pracobiorcami lub towarzyszami pracy,[12]

which embraces the meaning of *stačka* (*porozumienie*), but not that of *tovarišč*, that renders it as R does (*towarzysz pracy*).

The original sense (underlined by the specification that the "cartel agreements," which were very much in the news at the beginning of the century in Russia,[13] were promoted by the Jews) is that the opiate of "republican rights" would take from the workers that economic peace of mind guaranteed by a social peace secretly organised by the Jewish "shadow government" with the entrepreneurs and their (the entrepreneur's) partners.

3. The Reign of Terror

Our dominion, proceeding by way of a peaceful conquest, has the right to substitute for the horrors of war intrigue, which is less noticeable but more appropriate, and with which we sustain the terrorism which submits the "gojim" to a blind obedience. (1st)

To sum up in a word our system for keeping the governments of the
"gojim" in Europe under control, to one of them we have shown our
force in outrages — in terrorism. ...(5th)

The second assertion is understood to refer to Russia and perceived as
"prophetic," given that the edition of the PSM with the widest circulation (N;
here the same as A2) changes the verb from past to future ("we shall
show...in outrages — in terrorism...."). It is from this that there is the
following note in the English edition: "Note the present state of affairs [1920]
in Russia."[14]

In the reworking of Y (1905), the editor refers to the events of that year,
and has resolved one of the many repetitions ("in outrages — in terrorism")
in an explanatory form ("with outrages, that is to say terrorism"), assigning
the responsibility for the violence of the time to subversive motives alone.
However, if the text runs with the meaning we have restored to it (on the
basis, moreover, of the of the agreed reading of K, A1, and B), what are the
PSM alluding to here?

The hypotheses could be two: firstly, yet another Russian reference (the
attempted assassination of Alexander II on March 1, 1881); secondly, it could
relate to the killings (of Carnot, Gambetta, Faure, and McKinley) recorded in
the first *Translator's Note* to the 2nd Protocol.

The second hypothesis is impracticable because it concerns "exemplary
punishments" of the "servants of the Jews," who are rebels against the
"orders" they had received, and because among them is numbered that of the
American President McKinley, while here it is explicit that European
governments[15] are being spoken of. As regards the first, it appears highly
unlikely, both because of distance in time (some twenty years: too many for a
warning whose efficacy is to bear some relation to its actuality), and because
it is difficult to imagine that the PSM would have treated Russia (the
principle obstacle to the "sages' plan") as one of the European governments.
It is not for nothing that A2 and N, to allow for a "Russian" reading of the
passage, transfer the action into the future, transforming it into a dark
indeterminate threat. The PSM reserved a much more emphatic and decisive
role for the 1881 assassination attempt: it is the first "Russian coil" in the
cycle of the "symbolic serpent."

The passage concerns in all probability the regicide at Monza of King
Humbert I of Italy on July 29, 1900, which made a great impression in
Russia, in particular on right-wing and clerical circles who were united in
their execration of Gaetano Bresci (an anarchist, and therefore a
Freemason[16]) and the enemies of Russian autocracy. The Roman clerical
weekly *La voce della verita* (The voice of truth)[17] had already attributed the

regicide to "Jewish anti-clericalism." In Russia, the attack had profound
reverberations (renewed again two years later, when King Victor Emanuel III
was on a visit to St Petersburg) because Lev Tolstoj had written a powerful
article, "Do not kill him,"[18] that was republished by papers all over the world
and very much so also in Russia, even though it was banned. Tolstoj
maintained that

> it was not necessary to kill the Alexanders, the Carnots, the Humberts
> and others, but one must explain that they themselves are assassins
> and above all one must stop them from killing.

The nexus with the PSM really lies in the list of crowned heads (or
governing heads) which Tolstoj points out as true assassins, among whom
Humbert I is only the most recent example: "Carnot, Faure, McKinley," that
is to say, those in the note to the 2nd Protocol. After he had recorded them
thus, the forger returned to the "last of the list," Humbert I, so as to give rise
to the idea that the conspiracy had all the countries of Europe (and especially
Italy) under control by means of terrorist attacks.

In the light of this "strategy of terror," it is easier to understand the
sentence in the 1st protocol, in which a simple alternative *a/o* (*kazni* for
kozni) is introduced into the common copy of A1, N, and B,[19] and has
reached the public in an almost nonsensical form: "with the executions with
which we support [*podderživaem*] terrorism.[20]

The phrase amplifies a passage from Joly, and is based on the common
passage introduced by Osman Bey according to which the terrorist
movements (nihilists, anarchists) would have been secretly run by the Jews.

4. THE METROPOLITANS

*You say that, if they understand before the time that we are dealing
with, they will take up arms against us; but for this we have in reserve
such a terrifying manoeuvre that (even) the most intrepid souls would
tremble; nothing will remain of the metropolises, we shall blow them
up with all the organisations and the documents of the countries. (7th)*

The conclusion of the 7th Protocol, copied in Joly,[21] has always attracted
commentators who have dedicated to it a not inconsiderable number of
observations, also as evidence for the dating of the text.

The meaning of the verb *frapper* has been rendered *vzorvat'*; *la cité* has
been translated *stolicy*,[22] and if "nothing of it remained," it must mean "they
will blow up together with the documents." It was the editor of the third
edition, not the compiler of the PSM, who associated the idea of "blowing
up" the city to that of an underground mine, giving it the motive of a

"modern devilry" like the subway.[23] However, the original sense was different. It was of a terrorist movement activated by secret powers to crush preventive countermeasures against the planned coup d'état.[24]

Now it is true, on the other hand, that the text later diffused world-wide is N, but the PSM should be read above all in their original form, or only after one has seen how they have been modified in other editions.

5. THE "MYSTERIOUS INTERLOCUTORS"

D. Ž. says that the despotism of which I speak does not accord with modern progress. (4th) To D. A.'s observations that giving pensions to elderly workers will cost the state dear.... (15th)

In both cases, N substitutes the initials with the impersonal form ("They tell us that the despotism...", "To the possible observation that...") and since the PSM were in great part diffused via N, it has never been questioned whether they were generic terms for "N. N." or whether they alluded to actual persons.

In favor of the first hypothesis is the fact that anonymity is the norm in apocrypha, and the initial pretexts for the real names can be only a touch of authenticity conferred at the meetings of which the PSM represent the minutes. However, in favor of the second, there is the fact that only N abolishes them (A2 still keeps them[25]), and only N has the censor's plaquet on condition that the proper names were omitted.

The possibility exists that for the intention of the compiler "D. Ž" and "D. A." were no more than mere variants of "N. N." This is reinforced by the consideration that the reader of the PSM, even though unsophisticated, would have been able to become involved in the game of identification, and every game of this type must presume a solution; so much more so when, in the passages from Joly, the interlocutor is a real person (in the first case explicitly, and in the second implicitly, Montesquieu).

Theoretically, considering the phonetic equivalence ("Ж [Ž]=J French), that "D. Ž." could be a comment on a passage from Barruel's book, which in the *Notes concerning some articles contained in the first two volumes*[26] speaks of the

> letter sent to the Editors of the *British Critic*, by an author who dares not reveal himself except by the initials D. J.

However, apart from the doubts already raised concerning the involvement of Barruel in the PSM, the thing seems denied by the "D. A." which follows, and of which no reference is found in Barruel.

If the initials were inserted to allude to a real person, they must be Russian (otherwise the game would have been in vain), obviously of Jewish origin, and of names and surnames (not then names and patronymics, considering the difficulty in Russian in having names — and therefore patronymics which begin with Ž). Ju. Begunov believed that he could decipher the names of two Frenchmen, assuming the text to be of French origin and taking advantage of the convention (more that of a simple conscript soldier than that of a high-ranking exponent of Judeo-Masonry) of placing the surname before the name. For him, therefore, "D. Ž." indicates Jules Doinel, "friend and collaborator of Papus and Péladan and founder of the Gnostic neo-Cathar Lodge or "Church" in Paris and at Carcassonne" (Begunov 1996, 87),[27] while "**D. A.**" is that **A**ndré **D**upin, Junior (ibid).

The initials must however allude to more of less notable Jewish figures, such as one **D**aniil **Ž**itlovskij (or **Ž**abotinskij),[28] or **D**avid **A**jzman.[29]

6. THE PEDAGOGIC PROGRAM

"Their youth is stupefied through classical education and early deprivation. (1st)

We propose to put in the first place elementary education,[30] the most important of all sciences — the science of the organization of human nature, of social life, which requires the divisions of the workforce." (3rd)

We have touched on...education and training, as the cornerstone of social life. We have rendered through education the "gojim" children stupid, drugged and corrupt. (7th)

We shall render innocuous the first stage of collectivism[31] — the university.... We shall exclude from the teaching program civil law and anything tainted with political problems.... We shall substitute a study of the present and the future for the teaching of the Classics as well as any other study of Ancient History in which there are more bad examples than good.

We shall destroy any freedom for teachers to teach what they like.

The demonstrative teaching system must transform the "gojim" into unthinking, obedient animals incapable of understanding anything "without demonstration." Bourgeois,[32] one of our best agents, has already proclaimed in France the new curriculum of demonstrative education. (16th)

The polemic over "demonstrative education" thus concludes a discussion that involved the entire scholastic system from primary school to university. The other themes faced up to by the "Sages" are: the principles of a social education concerning the divisions of the workforce into classes; the aversion for the teaching of classical culture and ancient history; the removal of "political science" from debate in lecture halls; the hostility to the freedom of teachers to teach what they like and to the autonomy of universities.

Taken together, these proposals present a certain ambiguity, resulting essentially from the fact that it is not clear to what extent one is dealing with a denunciation of intentions attributed to their "Jewish" opponents, and to what extent they instead mirror the "values" of the Russian radical Right. Though not excluding a priori a certain dose of incongruity, due as it may be both to the Joly's underlying text and to the loose control of the system itself, it therefore seems legitimate to see in general lines a fairly coherent design, which can be summarized in the form of "the struggle of the two Tolstojs" (Dimtrij Andreevič and Lev Nikolaevič).

On the one hand, all the points put forward by the "Sages" sound like a latter-day attack on the reforms introduced by Alexander II's Minister of Education, Count Dmitrij Tolstoj (previously Procurator of the Holy Synod, and later President of the Academy of Sciences; 1823–1889). On the other hand, the "Sages" assume that some of the pedagogic choices of the writer, Count Lev Tolstoj (1828–1910) are in harmony with the plans of world Jewry.[33]

Dm. Tostoj was the Minister who reformed — in the reactionary — sense, the entire Russian scholastic system in 1871.[34] He set up the grammar or high schools (which his successor, Deljanov, held to be "dangerous for the lower classes"), in which 41% of teaching time was reserved for the teaching of the ancient languages (the *klassicizm* of which the PSM speaks). This was held to set education as completely free as possible from the complexities of everyday life.[35] In 1880, he worked out a reform of the universities (adopted by his successor under Alexander III) intended to limit academic freedom and the formation of student organizations. In 1878, he subjected the primary school system to rigid police control carried out by inspectors who were vigilant against "tendencies towards criminal political and moral propaganda."[36]

At the end of the century, the entire scholastic framework conceived in the "years of reaction" was giving way. 1901 and 1902 "saw the end of Count Tolstoj's classical lyceum" (Miljukov cit., 836). The university reform never really took off, and in 1900 the new Minister, Bogolepov, admitted the need for "a radical revision of the...academic system" (Miljukov cit., 812). The "most relevant changes" occurred in the primary schools, in which "one was largely conscious of the pressure of new tendencies, before which the old power proved impotent" (Miljukov cit., 837).

These "new tendencies" were those of "demonstrative" education, and, more generally, the pedagogic ideas supported by I. Paul'son's magazine *Učitel'* (1861–1870), and here one comes up against another, more famous Tolstoj.

According to Rollin (1991, 339), the final passage of this Protocol

> is none other than a hurried and incomplete summary of the pages that L. Bourgeois consecrated to the sensory-imaginative educational method of Froebel.[37]

The Russian terms used in the PSM for *visuel (nagljadnoe)* derive from the pedagogic ideas of Rousseau and Pestalozzi (the highest authorities for *Učitel'*) which arrived in Russia with K. Ušinskij. L. Tolstoj had dedicated to *nagljadnoe obučenie (Aschauungsunterricht, éducation visuelle,* visual education) some critical thoughts in line with his critical position[38] in relation to Ušinskij, which, he held, was too tied to liberal bourgeois individualism[39] and therefore not enough "of the people," even for a convinced "Rousseauan" like himself.

The polemic of the PSM on "demonstrative education" (in the opposite sense however to that of L. Tolstoj: the *nagljadnoe obučenie* was denounced by the forger for its unacceptability as a maieutic system or Socratic dialogue potentially capable of subverting the edifice of social hierarchy) therefore unloosed a debate throughout Russia, and found an "external" term of reference in the name of Bourgeois.[40]

Why Bourgeois? His name had come to the notice of liberal journalists like V. Gol'cev[41] and soon he appeared in the encyclopedias.[42] However, at the time of the PSM's compilation, this would not have been sufficient to credit him with the role they conferred on him.

During the Paris Universal Exhibition (1900), a group of Russians affiliated with French Freemasonry organized, at M. Kovalevskij's initiative, a "Russian School of the Social Sciences" (active from November 14, 1901) which was meant to "prepare the future activists of the liberal movement."[43] Among the academic staff was "the ex-President of the French government Léon Bourgeois"[44] (ibid.), who we find therefore participating in a Masonic initiative intended to combat Russian autocracy. Little more than a year later, a prestigious review (*Russkaja mysl'*) dedicated an essay to him,[45] and these two thing could have been a compelling motive to indicate him as the agent of the "Jewish-Masonic" plot.

The other controversial subject, connected to classical education (which in the 1st Protocol is significantly connected with "early debauchery" according to the opening pages of the *Kreutzer Sonata* by L. Tostoj[46]) is the teaching of Ancient History, which conforms with Tolstoj's hostility to the teaching of history in general as expressed in the 1901 letter to Birjukov, which here, however, is connected to the examples "more bad than good." This is to say, therefore, in the view of the forger, to those examples of Pericles and Augustus who, according to Leont'ev, characterised the fatal "democratic involution" of the ancient societies.

In this case, too, the sense is distorted by that Tolstojan thought, and is strongly ambiguous. "The Sages of Zion" (like Tolstoj) wished to expunge Ancient History from the curriculum, but only because it could inculcate the "germs" of democratic ideas.

More generally, the "Sages," like Russian liberal circles, opposed the imposition of the reforms of Dm. Tolstoj which were then, at the beginning of the century, beginning to come apart (the reader was led to believe, therefore, that the Jews had a hand in this). However, together they add up to the values of those reactionary reforms for their future projects, which thus coincide with the aspirations of the writer of the PSM. In the same way, they adopt some of L. Tolstoj's points of view, but for opposing reasons, which also end up coinciding with those of the radical Russian Right.

7. THE SYMBOLIC SERPENT

Here is a design in which one sees the road we have followed and the little distance which remains to undertake to close the cycle of the symbolic snake, which for us symbolised our people. When this cycle is finally closed, all the European states will be caught in its vice-like grip.... (3rd)

These sages decided to pacifically conquer the world for Zion, with the wisdom of the symbolic serpent whose head constituted the Government of the Jews...and the body — the Jewish people (Translator's Note)

What does that serpent mean? Men'šikov attributes to the "refined lady" an explanation based on Apocalypse 12.9 ("The great dragon, the primeval serpent, known as the devil or Satan, who had led all the world astray...."). Butmi (1906, 29) gives the following explanation for it:

There exists a doctrine which explains the origins of the race of Israel collocated from Chapter IV and V of Genesis.[47] According to another doctrine, it would appear that Israel, descendant of Noah, came from

Cain, and Cain from the sin of Eve with the Devil, who had assumed the form of the Serpent.

An Italian publisher of the PSM, more aware of the esoteric tradition than philological research, proposes that:

> The serpent that bites its tail—the dragon Uroboros—is...the traditional symbol of matter without form" (Mutti 1976, 77),

which recurs especially in writings on alchemy.[48] On the other hand, the *velikij zmej* that encircles Babylon (according to a legend connected with the ritual of the Imperial coronation[49]), or the *zmeja lunnyj* (the cycle of the Moon when it appears like a serpent biting its tail[50]), have a deep-seated tradition in Russia, but have nothing to do with the symbolism employed here. More recently, G. E. Sarfati (in Targuieff 1992, 2:150) has confirmed the idea that

> The myth of the "Symbolic Serpent" *is the* anti-Jewish projection of the "Serpent" of Genesis,

which is then the same as that of the Apocalypse[51] which speaks of the mysterious lady of Men'šikov and from which Butmi believes the people of Israel derive. Dudakov, attributing to Nilus the image of the "Symbolic Serpent," holds that it comes from the Qabalah (1993, 166–67):

> The cabalistic treatise *The mystery of the serpent and the judgment on him* contains the myth of the origin of evil.... The ring formed by the body did not close the "sacred circumference of the wall," but defined the "internal" and the "external." Transforming the cabalistic image of the Serpent (probably known from Blavatskaja[52]) into the "Symbolic Serpent,..." Nilus founded a myth that in fact was neither linked to the Bible nor to Orthodoxy.

One must pose the question *ex novo* as to what the image in the PSM might be referring to, and what is its authentic meaning. In fact, it does not appear to me that sufficient attention has been paid to the fact that, while in Men'šikov 1902 and the *Note,* the definition of the Jewish people as the "serpent" is objective, in the text of the PSM (3rd) it is subjective.[53] Now, if it is likely that others indicate Israel as the serpent of the Apocalypse (or of Genesis), it is much less likely, indeed it is not at all likely, that the Jews would indicate it thus themselves.

In modern Russian, "serpent" (even in the sense of somebody "malignant, cunning, or untrustworthy") is *zmeja*. The lemmas or headwords used here, *zmej* and *zmij* are both old-fashioned, and alongside the general meaning of "serpent" there is the mythological one of "dragon" (e.g., in the icon of St. George[54]). The only "serpent" which lends itself to an auto-referential definition is the brass serpent of Numbers 21.9–11, which is the totemic symbol of Israel which was so threatening to Israel's monotheism that it was destroyed by Hezekiah, King of Judah (II Kings 18.4). It could have been included in the PSM by way of the Bible or through the Gnostic sect of late Judaism from which it takes the name of the Ophits.[55] However, neither one nor the other help us explain the passage in question. One is dealing with a serpent which wraps itself around a staff and whose head does not reach its tail. Furthermore, the Ophits represent a marginal phenomenon, of little use for designating the Jewish people in their entirety.

It has already been seen (Chap. 5) that the use of the metaphor of the "serpent" to indicate Judaism was present in Butmi before the creation of the PSM because a passage in A. Chabry (the boa constrictor of high finance), and if, as I think, Butmi took part in the creation of the forgery, one needs to look there for the first evidence of the images concerning the serpent in the PSM. One is dealing therefore with a metaphor which still savors of "accusation," and it must be allowed to reveal its own definition; one must suppose its contamination to have come through second referent, which in my opinion is to be identified in a passage of the *Non Divine Comedy* by Z. Krasiński:

> Our lord is Jehovah and none other. He has scattered us everywhere.
> He has encircled the world of the adorers of the Cross with us, as with
> the coils [*splotami*] of an immense reptile [*gadzina*].

This image of the reptile which encircles "the world of the Christians" (in the PSM this refers to the European states) is convincingly explained by Ju. Kleiner[56] on the basis of the mention in the *Talmud* of the Old Testament figure of *liwyāthān* (cf., e.g., Isaiah 27.1).[57] In the Note of the first edition of the PSM (1903), the "serpent" is indicated as blessed with "wisdom" *(s mudrost'ju),* while in the succeeding editions (1905–1906) it appears as possessing "cunning" *(s xitrost'ju).* Now, while in Krasiński's text one finds it implicitly matching the Jewish self-qualification of "the wise" (they are "the adorers of the Cross" and are indicated as "ignoramuses" [*niepiśmienny*] in Holy Scripture), the more banal diabolic image (in Russian, the Devil is also *Lukavyj,* the Maligned One, and as such the maker of *xitrosti*) brings us to an "objective" definition.

To sum up, Krasiński has provided the forgery with an auto-referential model of Judaism as "serpent/dragon" (objectified by Men'šikov using the mouthpiece of the lady, and from the "translator" in the *Note*), in a metaphor with political overtones (the Leviathan). Taken together, the circular image has overtones of the "suffocation" of Christianity (the "*sploty*" of Krasiński, coincides with the "*anneaux*" — lambs — of Chabry, becoming the "*tiskī*" of the PSM), and of the return to Jerusalem (the "cycle").

Tazbir (1992, 22) had already maintained some role for the dramatic poem of Krasiński in the creation of the PSM, but as a subtext of *The Rabbi's Discourse* (the *Non Divine Comedy* had been translated into German since 1841, and could therefore have fallen into the hands of Goedsche), which in turn provided the subtext for the PSM. Thus was confirmed in other ways the idea (of Dudakov) that Russian Judeo-phobia traced its origins principally back to the mythology of Polish version. It remains, however, for us to understand the historical/philosophical sense of the route of the "Symbolic Serpent."

We can compare the information of Men'šikov with that of the five editions of the PSM:

	M	K	A1	A2	N	B
	(1902)	(1903)	(1905)	(1905)	(1905)	(1906)
1. Jerusalem	929 BC	929 BC	929 BC	929 BC	929 BC	929 BC
2. Greece[58]	—	429 BC	429 BC	429 BC	429 BC	469-429 BC
3. Rome[59]	[up to 476 BC]	69 BC	69 BC	69 BC	69 BC	63 BC- 14 AD
4. Spain[60]	—	from 1558	from 1558	1552	1552	1500- 1558
5. France[61]	[1790?]	1700	1700	1700	1700	1638- 1715
6. England	[1649?]	from 1814	from 1814	from 1814	from 1814	from 1814
7. Germany	[1517?]	from 1871	from 1871	from 1871	from 1871	from 1871
8. St. Petersburg	1880-1902	1880	1880	1881	1881	from 1880
9. Moscow	—	—	—	—	—	—
10. Kiev	—	—	—	—	—	—
11. Odessa	—	—	—	—	—	—
12. Constanti- nople	—	—	—	—	—	—
13. Jerusalem[62]	—	1999	1999	2005	2005	1999

From this one can see that regarding the origins of the plan referred to in 929 BC, there is no date which recurs, nor an appreciable logic. To understand the meaning of the stages of the "Symbolic Serpent," which together form a sort of parody of the succession of kingdoms according to the dream of the King of Babylon (Daniel 2), one must distinguish between the age of "antiquity" (Athens and Rome), the "modern" one (from Spain to St. Petersburg), the "future" one (Moscow-Kiev-Odessa-Constantinople-Jerusalem).

We shall not spend time over this last one, which, conceived in 1902–1903, was only reported on following the events which validated the prophetic nature of the PSM (Moscow: the 1905 Revolution, then that of 1917; Constantinople/Istanbul: the revolt of the "Young Turks" [1909],[63] Zion/Jerusalem: the Balfour Declaration [1917], then even the Six-Day War [1967]; and why not the halting places or staging posts of Kiev and Odessa?).

As far as the first phase goes, the source (and therefore the implicit "idea" of the text) has to be sought in K. Leont'ev who, in the context of a philosophic history of civilization which ascribes the "decadence" of state structures to the progressive "disintegration" of authority, to "levelling" and therefore, in a word, to the "democratic process", indicates in *Vizantizm i slavjanstvo* (1875)[64] the fatal halting places or staging posts of Athens and Rome respectively governed by Pericles and Augustus:

> The autonomous Athenian State was carried to perdition by the demagogues.... The rule of Athens, not too aristocratic since the times of Solon, *after* (my italics) Pericles took on an egalitarian and liberal character.[65]

> And speaking of Rome? Her progressive democratisation is well known.... Caesar and Augustus democratized the state even more. They were constrained to it by the process of development, and one cannot condemn them for this.

Assuming that the "guilty one" is Judaism, and not (as in Leont'ev) the anonymous "development process," the forger squares the "history" with the plan of the "Sages of Zion." This is the reason for the "true" dates: 429 BC (the year of Pericles's death[66]) and 63 BC–14 AD (Augustus's dates as given in B, which covered in part the age of Caesar), generating as they do an ambiguous intersection with the beginning of the Christian era.[67]

As regards the "second phase," in the primitive form (Men'šikov) Spain was absent, and were cited (in order) "France, Germany, and England" were cited (in that order), not "France, England, and Germany." In reality, the central route of the "Symbolic Serpent" has never been very established. Nilus, in the Postscript (Optina Pustyn', October 22–24, 1905) proposes a fairly different line, even from the steps indicated in "his" text:

Here in brief are the more evident traces left by the Symbolic Serpent
in the history of European existence (1905, 410):

a proud Rome "fallen not without the influence of the Jews" (though
admittedly we are in 476 AD so what has Augustus got to do with it?
however we are following Men'šikov's directions), has transmitted to the
Papacy "the anti-Christian idea of Caesaro-Papalism." On this terrain, the
Papacy comes into conflict with Israel, who first robes itself as the Templars
who "not by chance" had chosen the symbol of the Temple of Solomon.
However, thanks to Philip the Fair, they managed to have the best of it
(1307–1314). The Synedrion, however, was powerful, and the "root of evil"
was transferred from France to Scotland.[68] From then on it did not cease to
promote "a war to the death with the Papacy." However the Papacy was
"Antichrist," thus Nilus would have approved of the war. But why in
England? "Perhaps for the close relationship between the English and the
Jewish races."[69] The weapons, as one knows, were the Masonic Lodges ("the
symbol of the Temple of Solomon is also used by them") which gave life to
the French Revolution and Napoleon.[70] Even the attempt by Leo XIII to
counterbalance the Synedrion with the Banque Catholique de France failed
miserably.

> The mass of Catholic capital flowed into the coffers of the Synedrion,
> and so causing the fall of the last defense in Western Europe against
> Jewish world conquest.

However

> in the midst of the victorious way of the Symbolic Serpent and its
> head, the Synedrion, the Lord has placed Russia, strong in its
> Orthodoxy and its Autocracy,

and it is for this that the forces of the Synedrion are concentrated against her
(ibid, 413): "the fire of internal revolution, defeat after defeat in the Far
East", strikes, disorders, apostasy from the faith of the fathers, in short
everything seems to be going from bad to worse here as well. However,
"Russia was bowed, lamenting, trembling, but not divided" (ibid, 414–15),
while "Israel, hidden in the so-called movement of Zionism, was on the road
to Palestine," and had succeeded in arriving there. Here, then, is "the king of
blood of Zion, the false messiah, the Antichrist and…the end of everything"
(ibid, 416). One seems to hear echoes of the prophecy of Filofej (1523):
"Two Romes have fallen, but the third [*Moscow*] holds [firm] and there will
not be a fourth."[71]

In October 1905, a picture of this type was certainly suggestive for the "Black One Hundred"; but, in this picture, where is there a place for Spain[72] and Germany? And how do they fit in with the dates?

Four years later, the map published by *Russkoe znamja* (organ of the *Sojuz Russkogo naroda,* July 1909)[73] proposed the following list:

1. Zion 2. Athens 3. Rome (Augustus) 4. Madrid 1552 5. London 1648 6. Paris 1789–1801 7. Berlin 1871 8. St. Petersburg 1881 9. Moscow 1905 10. Kiev 11. Odessa 12. Constantinople 1909 13. Zion.

This thus indicates the two central staging posts to be the English Revolution and that in France, instead of the time of Louis XIV and on the fall of Napoleon. (Here there is some significant similarity with the indications of Nilus). Even Bostunič (1921, 9–10) held that the London and Paris stages were wrong, and proposed to restore the text in this manner:

IV stage: I maintain [*that it is*] 1648, when the fanatic Cromwell...made that revolution which brought advantages only to the Jews....

V stage: I maintain [*that it is*] the age of the "great French Revolution" (1789–1801), and the place Paris, when the Judeo-Masons...obtained equal rights.

For Ževaxov (1939, 16–17), the route of the "serpent" is that indicated in the *Translator's Note* (in the N variant), but with the modification of the mentioning of Moscow referring to the October Revolution, and not that of 1905:

Athens 429 BC 2. Rome *up to* Augustus 3. Madrid *up to* Charles V 4. Paris 1700 *until* Louis XIV 5. London 1814—after the fall of Napoleon 6. Berlin 1871—Franco-Prussian War 7. St. Petersburg 1881 8. Moscow 1917 (Revolution).

According to the Arab edition by Nuwaihid (Beirut 1967)[74] the path should be instead:

1. Babylon (exile: 6th century BC) 2. Greece 429 BC 3. Rome 69 AD [*sic!*] 4. Madrid 1552 ("after the expulsion of the Jews from Spain and Portugal") [*?!*] 5. Paris 1790 6. London 1814 7. Germany 1871 8. St. Petersburg 1881 9. Russia 1917;

Evidently, for the Arab reader the term *ad quem* must be "Jerusalem 1967" (The Six-Day War). However also in this case the French staging post is connected with the 1789 Revolution.

The original sequence, (that is to say the one confusingly mentioned by Men'šikov and later variously guessed at, even if modified in all the sources noted, and therefore already in the protograph), must foresee in the central part not "France, Germany, and England," nor even "France, England, and Germany," but on the contrary "Germany, England, and France," according to the "classic" view of the order of the revolutions in Europe. That is, it refers to the Protestant Reformation (Germany 1517), the English Revolution (1648), and lastly to the French Revolution (1789).

However, in the visualization of the "cycle" or coil, on the one hand, the western extremity of Europe was lacking (and so Spain was inserted), and on the other hand, the route of the Serpent, after Rome (and Madrid) would have been forced into undertaking too pernickety circumlocutions (Germany-England-France-Russia) to have been planned *ab antiquo* and to be immediate evidence for contemporaries. Not being able to change the geographic maps, they resorted to a change in the historical terms of reference. No longer was it Jacobin France, therefore, but that of the Sun King, no longer the England of Cromwell, but that of the ringmaster of the Congress of Vienna, no longer the Germany of Luther, but that of Bismarck. The establishment of these last two stages derives from a passage in Chamberlain ([1889] 1913, 453), the antisemitic text used by Men'šikov, which highlights "the operations of Jewish finance" in recent European history, as witnessed by "the presence of Nathan Rothschild at the Battle of Waterloo" and "the participation at the 1871 peace negotiations of [*Gerson*] Bleichroder on the German side and Alphonse Rothschild on the French side."[75]

As regards Spain, Charles V was chosen (A2, N, and B: shades of the age of the Reformation?) or even Philip II (K and A1), concerning whom however the allusion to "marranos" appears out of context.

However the "memory" of the original draft has survived in the same edition of the PSM, as a constituent element of the myth of the "Jewish Plot."

NOTES

1. Research by *Vestnik znanija* (1910) found that among the best-known authors in Russia, only three were foreign: Darwin, Hegel, and Marx; cf. J. Brooks, *When Russia Learned to Read* (1985; Italian trans., Bologna 1992), 469.

2. Cf. A. Vucinich, *Darwin in Russian Thought (*Berkeley 1988).

3. Dudakov 1993, 256.

4. B. Lazare, *L'antisémitisme. Son histoire et ses causes* (Paris 1934), 2:73.

5. From here comes the reluctance of antisemites to accept the image of "Jewish Agent": "The thesis does not hold whereby the work of destruction achieved by Nietzsche can be connected to Jewish subversive design" (Mutti 1976, 75).

6. Cf. B. Glatzer Rosenthal, "Introduction" to AA.VV., *Nietzsche in Russia* (Princeton 1986), 47.

7. In R the word *(staćki)* is expressed by the equivalent *"tresty"* (trusts).

8. R1 states that "the agreements of the cartel" *"take away* [and not "give," as in the PSM] from the worker the guarantee of a regular and secure salary"; R2 even says they take it "as much from the workers as the capitalists."

9. Trans. Komrska 1926: "lock-outs and organized strikes by the entrepreneurs and from their associates."

10. Trans. Lamberlin 1921.

11. Trans. Preziosi 1921.

12. Trans. Rudzki 1937: "from the agreement between the entrepreneurs or the fellow workers."

13. M. C. Kaser, "L'imprenditorialità russa," in AA.VV. *Storia economica di Cambridge,* 7 (It. trans. Turin 1980), 2:600: "The industrial depression of 1900 accelerated the tendency towards the cartelization of industry."

14. Also producing the sliding of the meaning of *terror*; no longer the "terrorism" of the anarchists, but the "red terror" of Soviet power.

15. The other cases (Carnot, Gambetta, and Faure) all concerned France, which in the PSM represents something more than *one of* the European countries. The series becomes canonical in "conspiratorial" writings (cf. Šmakov 1912, 250).

16. Cf. *Luč sveta* (1920): 161.

17. 10 August 1900; cf. De Felice 1961, 46.

18. L. Tolstoj, "Ne ubij" (8 August 1900), published in England in *Svobodnoe slovo* (Free speech), No. 17.

19. The interpretation *"koznjami"* in A2 is much more singular. Here one is dealing with the stemmatic conservation of the original interpretation, from the correction *ad sensum* of the publisher, or of a mere printing error, equal to and the contrary to that which created the variant?

20. Elsewhere (12th, 13th) one certainly speaks of *executions,* but in situations in which the "bosses" of the Jewish plot *already* hold or will be in power.

21. *"Le moment est venu* [but *after* the success of the coup d'état, author's note] d'imprimer une terreur qui frappe la cité entière, et fasse defaillir les âmes les plus intrepides."

22. Lit.: "capitals"; the plural, which implies an international political plan, could have been dictated by the fact that, traditionally, Russia had *two* capitals, St. Petersburg and Moscow (cf. 10th: "the aspirations which...we must *launch in the capitals.*")

23. Although Rollin had understood the correspondence (1991, 241) between the passage of the PSM with this of Joly, he was seduced by the "subway" and immediately afterwards (269) he interprets it in the light of the *"haussmannisation de*

Paris," that is, the ripping apart of the city for political motives, referring to another passage from Joly, 200 pages later.

24. Joly referred to an obscure threat extended by Machiavelli-Napoleon III, which Montesquieu interprets as an allusion to the "*the sinister execution of Borgia in Cesène,*" with reference to Chap. 7 of *The Prince.*

25. The second "mysterious interlocutor" became, however, Frenchified into "d'A."

26. *Memorie per servire alla storia del giacobinismo scritte dal'abate Barruel* (Italian trans. 1800), vol. 3, part 1, iii.

27. In 1889, at the time in which he had taken part in the drafting of the PSM in the "Memphis and Mizraïm" lodge (cf. Chap. 7), Doinel published *The Glorious Anniversary* in which he debated on Celestial Androgyne, the Virgin Mother, Sophia of the Theosophites, and the esoteric Christ.

28. Masanov (1956, 1:314) reports six "D. Ž."

29. Who had recently come to public attention with the essay "Nemnožečko v storonu," *Russkoe bogatstvo* 5 (1901).

30. In the text: *narodnye školy* (lit. "popular schools"), a term for indicating primary schools dependent both on the *zemstva (zemskie)* and on the parishes *(prixodskie).*

31. At the time (1902–1903) the term *kollektivizm* was a neologism (the Russian trans. from J. Guesde, *Kollektivizm,* with reference to "Scientific Socialism," which came out in 1905). It was then used in the generic sense of "principle of solidarity, of collaboration between comrades," not without the political inflexion which, however, inclined more towards the "co-operativism" of the anarchists rather than towards the Marxist "collectivism" of the II International.

32. Léon Bourgeois (1851–1925), Minister of Education (1892 and 1898), of Justice (1893), Prime Minister and Foreign and Interior Minister (1895–1896), President of the Chamber (1902); Later Nobel Peace Laureate (1920) and author of *L'éducation de la démocratie française* (1897).

33. Already Osman Bey (1901) had accused L. Tolstoj of being a "Judeo-phile," and of being, so to speak, sponsored by the Jews: "who have put the trombones and clarinets of international publicity at his disposal to make Tolstoj a celebrity."

34. Cf. "Bor'ba za školu i prosveščenie pri starom režime," in Miljukov, vol. 2, 2 (1931), 808–42.

35. "I shall try everything," wrote Dm. Tolstoj in 1867, "so that those who leave the gymnasiums will not be presumptuous superficialities who know everything and nothing, but modest and solidly prepared youths" (cf. Miljukov cit., 808).

36. Dm. Tolstoj's expression (in Miljukov, 826) harks back to 1876.

37. "This type of education was so widespread in Russia at the end of the last century that the word *frejbelička* was created to indicate a teacher who had followed

the preparatory teacher training courses following the Frœbel system" (Rollin 1991, 341).

38. In the essay "Ob obščestvennoj dejatel'nosti na poprišče narodnogo obrazovanija" (1862), in PSS (Moscow 1936), 7:267f.

39. Cf. D. Maroger, *Les idées pédagogiques de Tolstoi* (Lausanne 1974), 243.

40. While the German and Polish translations give "Bourgeois," the English translation gives "Bouroy," from whence comes the note in the Fascist ed. of the PSM who proposed to read it "borghese" (It. for "bourgeois") *(buržua)* in the sociological sense, as was probably understood by the Censor, and keeping it also in N.

41. "L. Buržua o solidarnosti," in AA.VV., *Bratskaja pomošč', postradavšim v Turcii Armjanam,* (Moscow 1897).

42. *Bol'šaja Enciklopedija* (St. Petersburg 1903), 4:102 and *Novyj Enciklopedičeskij Slovar'* (Brokgauz-Efron), (St. Petersburg n.d. [but:1913]), 7: coll. 639–40.

43. Starcev 1996, 42.

44. Member of the *Sincerité* Lodge of Rheims.

45. A liberal-inclined monthly founded in 1880 (after the Revolution of 1905, it was the organ of the *Kadety* party): X. G. Insarov, *Sovremennye francuzskie dejateli. L. Buržua,* 2–3 (1903): it spoke, among other things, of the "solidarity" of Bourgeois ("La solidarité" and "La philosophe de la solidarité").

46. "[*The Government*] controls the smooth running of the brothels and assures the depravation of the Lyceum students" ("*Krejcerova sonata* [1889]," in SS, 12 (Moscow 1964): 145.

47. Respectively, on the descendants of Cain and on the posterity of Adam down to Noah by the line of Seth. According to the Bible, this second is the origin of Israel, via Abraham.

48. It represents the cyclical process of matter starting with "fire," derived from Heraclitus among the Stoics, which the Rosicrucians made theirs. One does not see what it had to do with Judaism, even in the imagination of a Russian Judeophobe at the beginning of the century, if not for the fact (very vague) that "the image of the serpent which bites its tail had the meaning of Eternity, of Wisdom, both for Masons and the non-initiated" (D. Lotareva, *Znaki masonskix lož rossijskoj imperii* [Moscow 1994], 45).

49. Cf. E. Barsov, "Drevne-russkie pamjatniki svjaščennogo venčanija carej na carstvo," ČOIDR, 1 (1883): 5, 24 (I thank S. Schwarzband for pointing this out).

50. Cf. A. Černecov, "Illjustracija k Šestokrylu," in AA.VV. *Vzaimodejstvie drevne- russkoj literatury i izobrazitel'nogo iskusstva*, TODRL, 38, 50 (1985).

51. Genesis 3.1 and Apocalypse 12.9.

52. Dudakov cites in comparison A. Bosman, *Mysteries of the Qabalah* (1916).

53. "The symbolic [*zméj*] serpent, which *we use to illustrate our* people."

54. The difference between *zmejà* and *zméj* is fundamental. Many languages conserve it: in German *die Schlangel/der Drache,* in English *snake/serpent,* in Italian *serpente/drago,* etc." (S. Senderovič, *Georgij Pobedonosec v russkoj kul'ture* [Bern 1994], 227).

55. Cf. M. Craveri, *L'eresia (*Milan 1996), 22: "The doctrine of the Ophits...recalls the Biblical image of the serpent raised on Moses's staff." Of the Ophits, Butmi speaks (N. 1914), but as one of the sects which would have served the plot.

56. Z. Krasiński, *Nie-boska komedia* (Wrocław 1962), 63. I thank J. Ślaski for pointing this out.

57. On the "antisemitism" of Krasiński, cf. L. Sofronova, *Tema bogoizbrannogo naroda v pol'skom messianizme,* in *Slavjane i ix sosedi,* 1994.

58. Pericles (495?–429 BC): "429" means "from the death of Pericles," while "469–429" means "at the time of Pericles."

59. Augustus (63 BC–14 AD): The Nilus ed. 1911 says: "Not much before the Birth of Christ": and *almost* the same thing, but while the first wording refers to the Roman Empire (as in Men'šikov), the second refers to the Incarnation.

60. Charles V (1500–1558): 1552 because for him it was a particularly unfortunate year. He nearly became a prisoner and he abdicated in 1556. "From 1558" means "after Charles V" and "1500–1558" means "with Charles V."

61. Louis XIV (1638–1715); but the Marsden Ed. (cf. Taguieff 1992, 2:393) writes: "1790, at the time of Louis XVI" and comments: " It seems to me that Lambelin, speaking of Louis XIV, was the victim of a printing error in one of his sources, where Louis XVI became Louis XIV." A bad transcription, "1700" for "1790," is also probable here.

62. In the 12th Protocol, it says that the plan will take place "towards the end of the century" from which we usually see 1999 as "the return to Jerusalem" (in K, A1, and B). A2 and N modify it into "another century on," which, from the date of publication, 1905, carries the date to 2005. From here we find the *vulgate* according to which "it is well known that the Zionist conquest of the whole world is planned for the year 2000" (V. Emel'janov [1973], cited in Janov 1981, 294).

63. Chayla 1921 (in Taguieff 1992, 1:57–58) maintains that when the newspapers reported news of the Turkish Revolution, Nilus was shocked and had said to him: "The serpent's head is nearing Constantinople." There is no evidence that the two met in the days immediately following April 27, 1909.

64. The text which demonstrates the incompatibility of Leont'ev with the "too liberal" Slavophilism (G. Kologrivoff, *Costantino Leontjev* (Bergamo 1949), 209–10).

65. Cf. 1st protocol: "At the time of the greatness of Greece, we have shouted the word liberty for the first time." The 16th Protocol paraphrases a passage of Joly which quotes Pericles: "*Il est au moins essential de connaître son temps que celui de Péricles,* " which became "We shall substitute...for the study of Ancient History *in*

which there are more bad examples than good examples [my italics; author's note], learning...from the present."

66. The only Biblical passages which draw attention to any contact between the Jewish and Greek worlds are in two apocryphas in the Old Testament, I Macc. 12.21 and II Macc. 5.9 (a legend of which it is not possible to trace the origins). They are, however, relative to the second and not the fifth century BC, and they concern Sparta, not Athens. The death of Pericles (which took place during the reign of Artaxers, 465–424 BC) coincides with the time of the prophet called Malachi, the anonymous post-exile author of the last book of the Old Testament (436–420 BC), when there is no evidence of any Jewish trade with Athens.

67. In 69 BC (K, A1, A2, and N) Pompey and Crassus began democratic reforms, which Caesar also favored. The date does not seem to have any logic, and is the fruit of the corruption of "63 BC," the date of the *birth* of Augustus.

68. The idea of the derivation of "Scottish" Masonry with "French" Templars is widespread also in Russia in the literature on secret societies; cf. the Russian trans. of Ch. W. Heckerthorn, *The Secret Societies of all Ages and Countries* (1875; *Tajnye obščestva vsex vekov i vsex stran* [1876]).

69. "As one knows, a whole "scientific" theory exists intended to demonstrate that the English are the descendants of one of the ten lost tribes of Israel." The idea, born with J. Sadler in the 17th century, spread with J. Wilson (*Our Israelitish Origin* [1850]) and was taken from the "British Israelites" by R. Brothers (*The Lost Ten Tribes of Israel* [1877]).

70. Cf. Chap. 1, n. 59. In Fry 1931, 141 the "fourth coil" of the serpent is indicated as referred to by N "to 1790, in the reign of Louis XIV."

71. AA.VV., *L'idea di Roma a Mosca. Secoli XV–XVI* (Rome 1993), 357.

72. G. Butmi ("Spravka o Iudejax," *Zarja,* 9 July 1905), republished with an introduction to B), mentions the influence of the Jews in Spain (16) *before* they were driven out (1492) and speaks of the role assigned by Charles V to the Jews (17) *well before* the fateful 1552. One has the impression of a tardy justification of the "coil of the symbolic serpent" already established from the text in which it is submerged.

73. Cf. Chayla, in Taguieff 1992, 1:57–58.

74. Cf. Taguieff 1992, 2:393f.

75. The same indication in B3 (29), while Fry (1931, 130) indicates the couple of Jews who would have influenced the treaty of Ludwig Bamberger and Jacques Rothschild ("in this way it assures us that the treaty gave full satisfaction to the Alliance Israélite Universelle").

CHAPTER 7

Mystification, Narration, and Verisimilitude

Apocrypha means, etymologically, "hidden writing, something secret," but it has come to mean "a text falsely attributed to a period or an author." The PSM appears to be an "apocrypha" in the first sense of the word, but, in fact, turns out to be one in the second sense.

It is a "forgery" therefore, but compared with its antecedents (from the *Donation of Constantine* to the *Monita secreta;* from the *Testament of Peter the Great* to the *Polish Catechism*) it is special, being conceived in such a way as to regain its condition of "apocrypha" in the first meaning even beyond the usual opposition of "genuine/fake." This process was put into effect as a result of imponderable circumstances at the moment of the drafting, especially with its fruition on a worldwide scale at a distance of more than fifteen years with a war and a devastating revolution in between.

How were the PSM intended to be read when they were composed between 1902 and 1903 in *Russkoe sobranie* circles which included people such as Men'šikov, Kruševan, Butmi, Šarapov, and Mordvinov? Their origins were intentionally wrapped in ambiguity, which, therefore, is not a discovery of later commentators, like Msgr. Jouin (1920, 1:190) in France, G. Preziosi (1921, 6), and J. Evola (in Preziosi 1938, 13) in Italy, who undertook to split hairs between "authenticity" and "truthfulness," arriving in effect at a tautology. The PSM were "truthful" over and above their "authenticity," because they mirrored the true nature of Judaism and its ends which, *Protocols* or no *Protocols,* were truly what was shown in the PSM.

The first news of the PSM (Men'šikov 1902) already revealed a mystification or hoax, even if it had been already finalized at the conception of the text in the variant we have defined the "true forgery." Therefore, the "truthfulness" of the PSM was guaranteed by the fact that one was dealing with a forgery, thought up, however, in truth by modern Jews. Producing the pamphlet as a "forged truth" [a forgery that has been passed off as genuine], the preliminary discussion of its authenticity continues. Kruševan maintained in fact that it was the truthfulness that guaranteed the authenticity of the PSM:

We are unconditionally convinced of their authenticity...: their tone is too characteristic,... for us to doubt their authenticity.

Butmi (1906a, v), who seems to unreservedly assert the authenticity, also puts forward possible doubts:

This circumstance [*the fact that it is not possible to indicate with accuracy* "the place, day, year, and where and when they were written" — author's note] could give rise to a doubt as to the authenticity of these protocols,

but resolving it in turn with the truthfulness argument:

But the impudent bragging that every line breathes forth, the contempt for all mankind...convince every attentive reader the [PSM] are really the authentic fruit of Jewish thought,

and adds the argument that the *Rabbi's Discourse* ("whose authenticity is firmly established") confirms the PSM's content.

The anonymous Muscovite (1905, 1) follows a similar line:

Let us not enter into a discussion of their authenticity...but let us present to the attention of Russian readers that...comparing [the theories of the PSM] with the present confused disturbances at all levels of society in the Russian Empire.

Nilus also touches on the argument, and resolves it with a curious truism:

If it were possible with documentary evidence to demonstrate its authenticity,... it would destroy the "mystery of iniquity."

In recent years, an "explanation" has been developed which seeks to combine all the available evidence. Sooner or later the Jewish hegemony over the world of finance and manufacturing at the end of the nineteenth century would have become clear, and that would have induced the non-Jewish world to draw an unpleasant conclusion. The "Zionist" authors of the PSM would thus have given a hypertrophied picture of the Jewish predominance, attaching to the PSM all the possible considerations on the matter. From then on, every form of antisemitism would be able to declare itself as inspired by this provocative document. However, so that it might be possible in every instance to render the consequences harmless, "delayed action mines" were introduced into the text in the form of extracts from Joly's book, destined— where necessary—to bear witness to the plagiarism characteristic of the text.[1] The origin of such an explanation of the use of Joly's book harks back to General Nečvolodov (1924, 372) who owed it to Gincberg. In this way, one had a variant of the "true forgery," capable of transforming itself on command into a "forged forgery."

In myth, to narrate is already to set in motion. The persuasive potential of the PSM, which has survived dozens of confutations, is based in reality on a typical mechanism of mythologems; that of finding in its own interior systematic auto-referentiality. And this shifts the attention to the literary construction of the text, which not by chance the zealots reject as a dangerous blunder.[2]

This, too, has been the subject for reflection regarding the characteristics peculiar to the PSM. Dudakov writes (1933, 134):

> Undoubtedly in this question the fiction of invention [*belletristika*] was not only the "midwife" but also the "wet nurse." This is why in the myth of the "world conspiracy" of the Jews the principal writers of belle lettres occupy with reason the dominant position.

Another critic specifies:

> The idea of the "secret Jewish government, which takes part, usually together with other callow forces, in the conspiracy against all mankind"…already appears in Russian prose in the 1820s; the theme is taken from the nihilistic novel and brought to completion in the PSM.[3]

U. Eco (1994, 171–72) also considers the question, and after having proposed a midway between the literature of invention and conspiracy theory journalism, concludes:

> Reflecting on the complex relationships between the reader and history, fiction and reality, can prove a form of therapy against all those dreams of reason which generate monsters.

In such a context, it seems significant that some among the more recent studies on the PSM (Tazbir [1991, 5], Hagemeister [1996, 127]) turn to quotations from U. Eco's novel (*Foucault's Pendulum*) which uses the story of the PSM as a story-telling device.

To fully examine the relationship "truth-forgery" in the conception of the PSM one needs also to run through the history of the stories and their presumed authors. The "semiophere"[4] within which they should be read is defined by the "question of authorship" as the decisive nexus between the universe of reality and that of *fiction (belletristika)*. Reconstructing who has been mentioned as authors of the PSM means following the paths of the narratologic potentiality of the PSM and therefore the understanding of the anomalous duration of its fruition.

1. THEODOR HERZL

The attribution goes back to Nilus who, after having first given other versions, wrote (1917, 88):

Only now have I learnt from authoritative Jewish sources that these *Protocols* are none other than the strategic plan for conquering the world and placing it under the yoke of Israel,... worked out by the leaders of the Jewish people over many centuries of diaspora,[5] and in the end presented to the Council of Sages of the "Prince of Exile," Theodor Herzl, at the time of the First Zionist Congress convened by him at Basle in August 1897.

The attribution to Herzl was again proposed by Müller von Hausen[6] in an alternative reading which slightly differs from that of Nilus, but in compensation is richer in fictional invention:

When it appeared in the papers that the Zionists had decided to convene a Congress at Basle in the Autumn of 1897, the Russian Government (as we have been informed by a personage who for many years held an important post in a Ministry at St. Petersburg) sent a secret agent. He corrupted a Jew who was in the confidence of the leaders of Freemasonry and who at the end of the Congress was charged with procuring at Frankfurt on Main the report of the secret sittings of which, naturally, nothing became public.... This trip represented an extraordinary occasion for the realization of the project. The messenger slept overnight along the road where the Russian agent was waiting for him with a group of copyists who in the course of one night copied the whole document.[7] Therefore it may be possible that the report of the sittings were not complete since they transcribed what they could from the original French text in one night. The copies were carried in secret to Russia to the right people, among whom was an academic, A. Nilus, who in December 1901 translated these reports into Russian.

The Preface to the Polish edition (1919) asserted that the PSM were stolen in Vienna from Herzl's apartment. B. Engel'gardt in his evidence at the Bern Trial,[8] claimed that an elderly civil servant at the Ministry of the Interior had told him that he had found in his time there, among the papers of his boss, the *Documents du sujet autrichien Dr. T. Herzl*. It was a document in Hebrew taken from a Russian agent who was operating under the cover names of "Johnson" and "Kahn," along with French and German translations, and a handwritten note by Herzl: *"faire rapport aux anciens[9] de Zion."* The text had been translated into Russian by the Academy of Theology, and

Pobedonoscev had recognised Joly's pamphlet. This translation was then passed on via Suxotin and Nilus, who used it as the basis for "their" PSM, without suspecting the real origins of the document.

Although it was soon discarded (except for the late revival of 1935), the attribution to Herzl reflects the connection between the PSM and Zionism. L published the 1st Protocol in the section dedicated to *Zionism;* B advances a parallel between the PSM and the Herzl texts, R proposes the text as one read at a meeting of "the leaders of Zionism," and I presents it as a lecture by Herzl.

The attribution has therefore two faces. One is "ideological" with the similarity between the *content* of the PSM and the writings of Herzl while the other is "narratologic" with the circumstances, already noted above, with which in 1897, there were, alongside the public sittings of the First Zionist Congress, other "secret ones," in which Herzl had read the text of the PSM to an inner group of delegates. Obviously the second depends on the first. It has already been said that at the roots of the "similarity" between the PSM and the *Judenstaat* there does not lie a generalized distorted idea of Zionism but a "parodying" of Herzl's manifesto in the compilation of the PSM.

This version attributes to Nilus, therefore, two different possible roles: that of translator of the PSM,[10] which he himself denies, or a genuinely unaware reviser, as General Krasnov was later to say. However, in this latter case, the "finished product" would be the archetype of the PSM, something which is denied by an analysis of the textual tradition.

2. Ašer Gincberg

This second attribution was advanced by L. Fry (1921),[11] who in the interwar years put herself forward as the "expert" on the PSM.[12] It was then taken up by Russian (Nečvolodov, Bostunič, Ževaxov) and foreign antisemitic propaganda, until it was revived, if not as "certain" then at least as "plausible" by Vol'skij (1993). However, it was taken seriously even by historians such as F. Koneczny,[13] something which conferred on it a certain measure of plausibility.

This, too, has a double face: an ideological one based on the "Zionist" interpretation of Nietzsche's superman, and the documentary one of the opposition between the "political" Zionism of Herzl and the "spiritual" version of Gincberg, who, as an authoritative and mysterious figure in Russian Judaism, offered cross-checking evidence not to be despised. Indeed, having disappeared in 1927, *without* having ruled out his involvement, the attribution held the fascination of an implicit confirmation.

Furthermore, it implied a "history" of the text which harked back to the years immediately after the assassination of Alexander II (1881),[14] as a text written first in Hebrew and as such circulated in the "soft underbelly" of Judaism (Odessa), to be then translated into Russian, and finally into French for the members of the *Alliance Israélite Universelle*. This edition would have been read "by a handful of Zionists at the Zionist Congress at Basle in 1897,"[15] and from there it would have been again retranslated into Russian in the version that circulated in the early years of the twentieth century.

The purpose of the attribution to Gincberg is similar to that of the attribution to Herzl; the falling back on the history of the PSM, which thus validates their existence at least from 1897, and as such provides yet more pseudo evidence:

> Right at the end of the Basle 1897 Congress, the Jew Alfred Nossig, a furious Zionist,[16] who was working on the libretto of an opera of which Paderewski was composing the music (*Mauru* [*sic!*]),[17] spoke of the Protocols to his collaborator. I. Paderewski immediately communicated this to many Poles (Fry 1921, 230).[18]

This story was re-proposed by Begunov (referring it, however, to Herzl; 1996, 62),[19] who not only moved the year of this confidence to 1901, but also specified the circumstances in which the plan of the PSM had been read to the "Council of Elders," which was between the 32nd and the 33rd public sittings of the 1897 Congress.[20]

3. PAPUS

The first version of a history that attributed the fake to a non-Jewish author was published in 1920 by a Warsaw newspaper, and Rollin commented (1991, 453):

> As regards the assertion in the *Varšavskoe slovo,* which in its July 17, 1920 edition presented Papus as the author of the PSM, it is not a priori unlikely.

Thus conferring a patina of plausibility on the story, which does not explicitly confirm the paternity of Papus even if the allusion was fairly evident, but on the other hand it was connected with the Račkovskij.

At the time of the Russian offensive on Warsaw,[21] the Russian language daily, the *Organ of the Democratic Idea,* published an article signed by a certain "Axeron," "Očerki iz Rossijskogo Dekamerona. Kolduny i kudesniki pri carskom dvore," with the following story:

Papus[22] undertook a special tour through Europe and collected information on magic and Masonic circles of all kinds. From this he made a very detailed report, which showed precisely that Philippe belonged to a secret Masonic Lodge and, gaining the confidence of Nicholas II, he aimed to destroy him and all his family. Papus managed to insert into his report a series of *Protocols of the sittings of the secret Masonic Lodges* [*scil.:* The PSM; my italics] which had been held in different parts of Europe. According to Papus, the participants at these meetings had sworn on iron, blood, and fire to use all their might to destroy the entire Russian Imperial family. P. I. Račkovskij, who well understood influential circles at court, spiced up this sensational report so as to guarantee the desired effect. The report, along with the necessary instructions, was sent with special precautions to St. Petersburg to the Intendent of the Imperial Palace General Gesse. The Dowager Empress, Marija Fëdorovna, also gave her help in this affair to the enemies of Philippe, who, to better compromise the protégé of the Empress, Aleksandra Fëdorovna, made every effort to launch the Papus-Račkovskij-Gesse Report.[23]

Assuming that the "Protocols of the sittings of the secret Masonic Lodges" to be the PSM, Rollin judged the story "in principle likely" because starting from October 24, 1901, *L'Écho de Paris* published a series of articles, "La Russie d'aujourd'hui" under the byline of "Niet," to support the theory that the secret engine behind the tribulations of contemporary Russia were the "great financial syndicates," which closely accorded with some of the theses of the PSM; and

> a manuscript note found among the papers of Papus after his death establish that [*that series*] was due to Papus's collaboration with Jean Carrère, journalist on *Le Temps* (Rollin 1991, 442–43).

Taking account of the fact that Papus criticized the materialism of the dominant Freemasonry and that his collaborator was linked to Drumont's *La libre parole,* and could therefore be considered a militant antisemite, in itself it is plausible that Papus might also be the author of the PSM. It was, however, the reason indicated by the *Varšavskoe slovo* which gives rise to suspicions that Papus had written the PSM to "combat the influence of Philippe at the Russian Court," which is, on the contrary, an "a priori unlikely hypothesis" because "the loyalty [*of Papus*] to his 'spiritual master' was never in question," and "every time Philippe was attacked, Papus rose, fighting and fiery, to his defense." This was particularly so at the time at which the PSM (1902) were being composed, when it was rather the Russian

Secret Police in Paris who were doing everything possible to "discredit the Lyonese faith-healer" (Rollin 1991, 453–54).

Chronologically, the attribution to Papus (1920) is the first after that of Herzl advanced by Nilus, and certainly the first to attribute the PSM to non-Jewish circles. However, the interest here lies not only in this, but also in the fact that it connects it with the attempt to set up in Russia a "Martinist" Lodge and therefore, in one way or another, to the presence at Court of Mr. Philippe. This "Papus-thesis" was to be taken up anew a year later by Princess Radziwiłłowa and Count Chayla.

Simply ignored by the zealots, rapidly dropped by the critics, the attribution to Papus soon vanished from the scene; but not completely. Since a fascination with the occult heavily outweighs that for historical and philological enquiry, another version of the origin of the PSM has come into being.

4. THE PRIORATE OF ZION

In a successful book on the *The Holy Blood and the Holy Grail,* the anglophone[24] journalists connected the PSM to the presumed "Priorate of Zion" which, from the times of the First Crusade pursued the aim of replacing on the throne (possibly a universal one) the Merovingian dynasty, which in turn descended from none other than Jesus of Nazareth. And where might the connection be? The three "independent researchers" write:

> It is known that a copy of the PSM was already in circulation in 1884, a good thirteen years before the [Zionist] Congress at Basle. The 1884 copy came into the hands of a member of the Masonic Lodge [*Memphis and Mizraïm*], the same one Papus was a member of, and of which he was to become Grand Master....[25] (p. 201).

Now, Papus was a friend of Philippe and, according to Cohn's[26] reconstruction, the appearance of Nilus at Court was motivated by the intention

> to discredit the esoteric group at the Imperial Court; the group of Papus, Monsieur Philippe and other members of the secret society in question (1969, 204).

According to the three journalists, Nilus had done none other than modify the "original text" of the PSM (that of 1884, which appeared in "Papus's Lodge"), which

> was not a fake. On the contrary, it was authentic. But it had nothing to do with Judaism.... Rather, it came from a Masonic organization or a

secret society of Masonic leanings which incorporated the word "Zion" (p. 203),

in other words, the Priorate of Zion. Naturally, this does not mean that Papus was the author of the PSM, but only that they were in some way connected with his name. The signature of the "representatives of the 33rd degree" being accepted as valid, the authors indicate them as "unknown superiors." We are dealing therefore with a later version of the PSM, a "true forged-truth," and this has given rise to another theory which foresees instead a "true truth."

5. THE "MEMPHIS AND MIZRAÏM" LODGE

Coming into circulation a decade later for obvious political-cultural reasons, in Russia the book on the Grail had engaged the imagination of readers more than elsewhere as a result of the long abstinence from Western cultural outpourings, added to the foreignness in the Slav-Orthodox world of a Celtic tradition like that of the Grail.[27] Thus an academic like Ju. Begunov[28] was able to convince himself that the key for discovering the origins of the PSM should be sought in the fantastic inventions of three journalists:

> The most probable thing is that the PSM were really composed in the heart of that Lodge [*"Memphis and Mizraïm"*][29] which aimed at the hegemony over Judaism and Masonry.... Nilus in his book says precisely that the PSM were signed by members of that Lodge who were shown in the title as the "Sages of Zion...."[30] The definitive edition of the PSM...was created at the end of the 1880s, but not after 1892...at the time of the composer Claude Debussy....[31] Justina Glinka bribed a member of the Lodge, Joseph Schorst-Shapiro...who offered to acquire an important document for him...and when he obtained the money he gave it to Glinka...: it was the PSM in French. However the Sages of Zion knew of this and suspected Schorst. They had to flee, but the Masons found him in Egypt and killed him (Begunov 1996, 85–90).

"False mysteries abound around Memphis-Mizraïm,"[32] and that which is renewed by Begunov was put forward by Butmi in 1906:

> the aforementioned Protocols were taken from the acts of the Masonic Lodge of the Egyptian or "Mizraïm" rite, into which above all the Jews enter,[33]

to which Bostunič (1928, 35) ascribes even L. Trockij, which L. Fry takes up in 1931as the "second version" of the origins of the PSM:

In 1884...Miss Justina Glinka sought to serve her country in Paris by providing political information which she sent to General Orževskij at St. Petersburg. To this end a Jew, Joseph Schorst,[34] member of the Mizraïm Lodge at Paris was necessary. One day, Schorst promised to procure for her for the sum of 2500fr a document of great importance for Russia. Having received the money from St. Petersburg and having given it to Schorst, the document was consigned to Miss Glinka. She sent the original in French to General Orževskij accompanied by a Russian translation. He gave it to his head of department, General Čerevin, to be forwarded to the Tzar. However, Čerevin, who was under obligation to certain rich Jews, refused to forward the document and merely filed it....[35] Miss Glinka gave a copy of the PSM to Alekeej Suxotin, District Governor General [*of Orël*],[36] pointing out to him that Sipjagin had been assassinated for being favorable to strong measures to repress revolutionary threats. Suxotin showed the document to two of his friends: Stepanov and Nilus, the first of whom had it printed and circulated among his close acquaintants in 1897; the second...published it for the first time at Carskoe Selo in 1901 in a book entitled *Velikoe v malom*.[37]

Thanks to Glinka, the story of Schorst and of the "Mizraïm" Lodge is connected to that of Suxotin and Stepanov. However, Fry reconnects it also to that which she had attributed ten years in reference to Gincberg and the first Zionist Congress at Basle:

Finally, still in the same period, by the means of a few Jewish [E. Azef[38] and S. Efron] Russian Secret Police agents, it was possible to have the minutes of the meetings of the Zionist Congress held at Basle in 1897, and check that they corresponded with the PSM (ibid.).

It appears that the ingenious Mrs Fry-Šišmareva had succeeded in squaring the circle, and therefore Bugunov has accepted the validity of the "framework." However, some details do not square, and highlight the intentionally confusing character of the whole construct. First of all, there is the confusion between the Paris agent, Akim Efron, and the writer Savelij Efron-Litvin. Moreover, there is the presumed role of Azef, which is without foundation. However, above all, there is the fact that Ju. Glinka could not have consigned the PSM to Suxotin in 1895 with the abovementioned grave warnings because Dimtrij Sipjagin, the Minister of the Interior, was killed on April 2, 1902.

It remains to note that while Rollin held the role of Papus in the creation of the PSM to be plausible because of his antisemitic propensities, Butmi's version, reworked by Fry and accepted by Begunov, proves exactly the opposite, which is that the Lodge of which he was a member had strong "Jewish" connotations.

6. SERGEJ NILUS

The idea that Nilus was not simply the "best" publisher (or perhaps the translator), but the author of the PSM was fairly widely accepted in Russia around 1905. After the Revolution, S. Reinach took this up again in 1920, while in 1921, A. Kuprin sought documentary proof on a stylistic level and to a certain degree subsumed the first English edition, by publishing the translation of the PSM under the name of Nilus. In 1934 even General Krasnov was in agreement, even if he rejected the "Jewish" nature of the material used (Cohn 1969, 179).

It is the easiest thesis, and finds confirmation in the confused and discordant versions he himself offered about the date of the origin of the text, which in such a case would only be awkward attempts to entrench himself behind useful fairy tales. However, it has already been seen that they are without foundation, because from them it would appear that the text edited by him would be "the best," even the protograph itself, while the examination of the textual tradition indicates that it is a later editing of the archetype. Yet such an hypothesis has left not-to-be-undervalued traces in one of the most lucid studies of the PSM, that of Dudakov (1993, 142), when he claims that they "should be seen in the context of S. A. Nilus's book and not as autonomous newspaper editing," which is the opposite of what has been sought to be argued so far.

7. PËTR RAČKOVSKIJ

The direct or indirect attribution of the PSM to the Head of the Foreign Section of the Russian Secret Police resident at Paris is at the moment the most widely accredited.[39] It is not therefore another reading of the "novel" of the PSM, but a strong hypothesis based on factual reconstruction. I have already said (Chap. 4) that I believe it to be without foundation, and I shall not repeat myself. I shall rather concentrate on the modalities with which such an indication came to be formed and diffused.

The name of Račkovskij was mentioned by H. Bint to S. Svatikov in 1917, but this only became known in 1934.[40] After the allusion in *Varšavskoe slovo* (1920) to the role of "editor and dispatcher," the first mention of his name as the author of the PSM (with the assistance of Golovinskij and Manasevič-Manuilov) harks back to the Princess Radziwiłłowa (February 25, 1921), who placed the undertaking to 1904–1905. Previously L. Wolf[41] had instead alluded to a possible origin of the PSM in *Oxrana* circles, but without involving Račkovskij and the "Paris Section," but rather (not knowing the 1903 edition) placing it in relation to the *pogromy* of 1905.

The Princess Radziwiłłowa, who continued to ignore the 1903 edition, has the origins of the PSM harking back to 1884–1885 when General Orževskij had commissioned it from Russian agents sent to that end to Paris who had made use of "old books, quotations from Jewish philosophers, annals of the French Revolution."[42] Twenty years later, that manuscript, forgotten in the archives of the St. Petersburg Police (but according to her, were inserted into *Memoirs* of General Čerevin[43]), was exhumed and entrusted to other agents to be once more carried to Paris, and there "reworked to give it a more modern form" (ibid., 278).[44] What was necessary was carried out by Račkovskij with his agents. His friend, Mrs. Hurlbut, was specific that Golovinskij "came on the Champs Elysées from the Princess Radziwiłłowa, directly from the National Library where the compilation was carried out" (ibid, 280: there is still no allusion to Joly's *Dialogue*). According to a novel by J. Kessel about Rasputin, the sole compiler was Manasevič-Munuilov. One character in the novel, Pëtr Lavrent'ev-Bel'skij, confides to another, Elizaveta Dmitrievna:

> Some years later [*around 1904–1905*], a traveling companion to Paris told me that he had met Manuilov at the National Library. He was taking notes on Judaism for his own edification, he said. I have good reason to believe that he was forging a fake on the orders of the *Oxrana* on behalf of the antisemitic government of the time.[45]

The Polish Princess completes her story of *Oxrana* being the commissioners of the PSM with three precise names, among which emerges that of Račkovskij. The name, that is, relaunched shortly afterwards (May 1921) by Count Chayla, on the basis of his presumed conversation with Nilus (in 1909) which went as follows:

> Yes, — said Nilus, Madame K. has lived much abroad, including France. And there, in Paris, she received the manuscript from a Russian general, and passed it on to me. That general had managed to steal it from the archives of the Masons.
>
> I shall find out if the name of the general is a secret.
>
> No — replied Nilus, it is General[46] Račkovskij, a marvelous man, very active, who in his time has done much to draw the sting of the enemies of Christ."[47]

Chayla, too, had "squared the circle" by putting the name of Račkovskij into the mouth of Nilus (who could not deny it, and who for his part had distributed the Suxotin version, now indicated as acting as a windbreak for Mme K.), thus giving him greater credibility than the botched version of the Polish Princess. Moreover, he had completed the square with a reference to Mr. Philippe, whose claims had already been put forward the previous year in *Varšavskoe slovo* but was now "purged" of the role of Papus:

> It is very possible—continued Chayla—that Račkovskij, who at that time, it is said, was exercising himself to negate the influence of Philippe over the Tsar, having been informed of the role that was predestined to S. Nilus,[48] wished to profit from the chance to finally eliminate Philippe and ensure the good will of the new favorite. Be that as it may, when Nilus arrived at Carskoe [Selo] in 1901, he was already in possession of the PSM.[49]

It is true that Račkovskij plotted against Philippe, but Nilus was introduced at Court in 1905 (not in 1901), and could not have had the PSM in 1901 for the good reason that they were compiled between 1902 and 1903. Chayla did not know the 1903 edition, or of its use in the compilation of Joly, and is mistaken on the date of the first edition of Nilus. Despite this, his thesis, which proves therefore an able montage of what was said in *Varšavskoe slovo* in 1920 and by Princess Radziwiłłowa in 1921, has served as a basis for reconstructing the history of the PSM and, via first Rollin and then Cohn, is even now accredited as the most acceptable account of the origins of the text.

H. Arendt (1996, 337) has published another reading, according to which the PSM were

> forged around 1900 in Paris by agents of the Russian Secret Police [scil.: Račkovskij] under the orders of Pobedonoscev, the Councillor of Nicholas II, the only Pan-Slavist who had reached a position of influence.

The thesis demonstrates a most summary knowledge of the workings of the Russian Government. Pobedonoscev had been Nicholas II's tutor, in whose reign, however, he lost some of the influence he had wielded under Alexander III. He was Procurator of the Holy Synod from 1880 to 1905, but the *Oxrana* was responsible to the Police Department, and Račkovskij was "a man of Vitte." Pobedonoscev belonged, with Leont'ev and Katkov, to that extreme Right which was critical of the philo-Slav tradition, which for them was too "liberal," but leaned towards a form of reactionary Pan-Russianism. However, despite being imbued with Judeo-phobic sentiments, they

> were averse to every form of *pogrom*.... They were opposed also to the rising of a...formation that wanted to combat the revolutionaries with

revolutionary methods. Their mentality, fundamentally conservative, typical of "men of order," fled from violence.... In such movements, they recognized a threat to order and to the State, whatever might be the banner under which they intended to agitate and fight.[50]

It appears absurd that someone of this type should promote an operation such as the PSM for "subversive," even if reactionary, ends. The evidence gathered by H. Arendt[51] remains, therefore, only another piece in the mosaic of the history of the histories of the PSM.

The name of Račkovskij, endorsed like those whom Nilus (according to Chayla) had indicated as "discoverers" of the PSM, recurs in another reading which seeks to square up the data that emerged in various ways in yet another way:

> The secret documents of that first Zionist Congress [the PSM, Author's note] were consigned to the Russian Government, an agent called Račkovskij procured them by paying two Jews who betrayed their race. They were called Azev [*sic!*] and *rabbi* Efrom [*sic!*]. The latter took refuge in a Serbian monastery, where he died in 1925.[52]

The misinformation has thus produced a life of its own, which proves valid however, for those who wish to give credit to the PSM.

8. JUSTINA GLINKA

Here we are dealing with another reading of the "French" origins of the PSM as a work of Russian antisemites. First suggested with many reservations by J. Webb (1976, 247), recorded as merely a hypothesis of P. Barrucand,[53] it was upheld by V. Skurativs'kyj with a broad cultural/biographical[54] reconstruction in which Glinka was not the "go-between" between Račkovskij (or Schorst-Shapiro) and the Russian Secret Services, but the author of the document.

She was recalled to Russia in 1895 following the scandal caused by "Comte Paul Wassili"'s book, and the "exile" to the family estates in the Province of Orel made contact with Suxotin[55] plausible. Returning home to Russia, she could also have brought the PSM with her, which she would have passed on to Suxotin, and the latter first to Stepanov and then on to Nilus.

However, leaving aside the likelihood of the thing (such as explaining the errors in French and Russian and the Ukrainianisms by a person like Glinka), the effective compilation date of the PSM (1902–1903) is an insurmountable obstacle to collocating the fake to the middle of the 1890s, which the Glinka hypothesis would require.

9. FRENCH PRIESTS

At the beginning of the 1920s, rumor had it that the writer A. Amfiteatrov had involved the Roman Catholic church in some way in the PSM[56] affair. However, if this had any foundation,[57] one is dealing with an imaginative invention. P. Barrucand, however, has put forward the hypothesis that the PSM might have been forged by some French priests at the time of Leo XIII (1878–1903), that is to say, at the time of the "intense anti-Semitic campaign conducted...by the Assumptionists in *La Croix* (Moro 1988, 1033). The go-between would have been the same Glinka, who was supposed to have sent the text to St. Petersburg, to the *Oxrana* and Suxotin.

While aware that "it is difficult to study conspiracy theories without coming under their influence, even unconsciously," Barrucand was convinced that under Leo XIII ("a Pope, who I do not know why, has a reputation for liberalism"), there existed "in the precincts of the Vatican an anti-Jewish archive and research center," whose members "would have been a source of inspiration for the PSM [*to the French priests*], by abandoning the theory of ritual murder."

The thesis, which leads decisively to the "French" but with relevant "Italian"[58] implications, and is an alternative to that of the (Russian) Police origins of the PSM, has been embraced, as has been seen, by the majority of academics. It is based on arguments—negative ones—which are not to be despised. These are the links between Račkovskij and Vitte which would exclude the participation of those in an attack on these, and the modality of the Russian first edition, of Stepanov (whom Barrucand trusted[59]) and of the "half-mad mystic" Nilus, effectively extraneous to an operation conducted by the Secret Police.

Even Tazbir's counter objections are not without weight. However, neither the one nor the other suspected the real linguistic and cultural genesis of the PSM, which excludes both Račkovskij's paternity as well as that of the "French antisemitic priests," if for no other reason than because the PSM were written in Russian, *and not* in French. There exists, however, another variant of the history of the PSM, which ends by ascribing it more to the needs of late nineteenth-century Catholic antisemitism.

So many names, so many stories; but, in essence, two opposing theses (apart from that extravagant one of the Priorate of Zion[60]).

Herzl, Gincberg, the "Sages" of the "Memphis and Mizraïm Lodge": the PSM as a product of evil Judaism which reclaims a "national homeland" but in reality intends to dominate the world. Nilus, Račkovskij, Glinka, Papus, the "antisemitic priests": the PSM as a fake thought up by Judeo-phobic circles (Russian, in the first three cases; French in the other two) to give substance to the anti-Jewish struggle, connecting it along the way with secondary but no less substantial objectives (the influence of Mr. Philippe, the policies of Vitte, Liberal Catholicism, and so on).

The PSM are largely silent on their origins. The surprising thing is that the text (initially referring, at its more ancient levels, to Solomon and the "heads of Israel") has managed to pass undamaged (or almost) from one attribution to another, maintaining in some way "credibility" even in the face of the most fantastic reconstructions of their origins.

Evidently this is due in good measure to the impermeability of the creators to every form of critical approach to a "literary" product with a high degree of ideological involvement. The strange thing is that that impermeability has been so effective against the asserters of the "truthfulness" (if not of the "authenticity") of the PSM but, at least in part, also against on the critics, as is shown by the story of the claimed writing in French and of the Court conspiracy on which is grafted the attribution to Račkovskij.

I do not believe that all this is sufficient to explain the "longevity" of the PSM. A no less relevant reason may be sought in the very nature of the text itself, which was the (perhaps not unintended) fruit of an interweaving of fiction and reality, of myth and emotiveness, which allowed the crystallization in a form which is both confused and clear-cut, of a fairly sophisticated product which could still be used twenty years after its creation in cultural and political conditions totally different from those for which it had been planned. One is even more surprised by their lasting "success," nearly a hundred years after their drafting, in a world that has known the most devastating effects of them.

The PSM are not only "the most important forgery of the century," they are also one of the most ambiguous, and thus, one of the most dangerous.

NOTES

1. S. Putilov, "'Dymovaja zavesa' nad tajnoj kagala," *Naš sovremennik,* 3 (1994).

2. Cf. Ford 1939, 89.

3. M. Vajskopf, "Sem'ja bez uroda (obraz evreja v literature russkogo romantizma)," *Okna* suppl. to *Vesti* (Jerusalem), 14 May 1998.

4. "That semiotic space outside which the existence of the semiosis is impossible" (Ju. Lotman, *La semiosfera,* It. trans. [Venice 1985], 58).

5. The primitive version is thus attributed no longer to Solomon, but to the Jewish diaspora.

6. Preface to the German ed. (1919); Russ. trans. In *Luč sveta* (1920), 102.

7. A does not hide that the 1911 ed. of Nilus, which he had before him, is different. However, he has us to understand that it had been invented to distract attention away from the tracks left by the traitor (ibid, 104).

8. In *Berner Prozess,* 21:39 (13 May 1935).

9. This already indicates the spurious nature of the information: in French the *mudrecy* are always called "sages," and "anciens" is the translation from the English "Elders" introduced in 1919.

10. The idea had been taken from Begunov 1996. It denies already only the fact that N inserted into the text a "Translator's Note."

11. Ževaxov (1939, 48) refers it to Count Reventlow, dating it back to 1920.

12. Leslie (or Lydia) Fry, (alias P. A. Šišmareva, Lidija Svečina, Princess Golicyna: cf. Hagemeister 1996, 142) is not registered in the *Index notorum hominum.* In 1922, she was editor of the *Gentile Tribune* of Scranton, Pennsylvania (Jouin 1922, 4:199), and in 1935 founded the Movement of Christian Patriots (Taguieff 1992, 2:214). Her last book is from after the Second World War (*Is the University of California To Be Seized by Communists?* 1952).

13. J. Tazbir 1922a, 48: cf. J. Mitkowski, "Koneczny Feliks Karol," in PSB, vol. 13 (1967–1968).

14. Fry knew of the interview with Radziwiłłowa which re-dated the first draft of the PSM to 1884-5.

15. Fry 1921, 23.

16. Cf. *Die Bilanz des Sionismus* (Basle 1903).

17. The opera is *Manru,* performed in 1901; the libretto is taken from a Gypsy novel, *Chata za wsią* (1857) by Jósef Ignacy Kraszewski.

18. The name of the pianist Ignacy Jan Paderewski (1860–1941), Prime Minister and Foreign Minister in 1919, was associated with the "Jewish Question" also by H. Ford (1939, 120). Ževaxov (1939, 184) takes the story from Fry, keeping even the printing errors (*Mauru*).

19. Who even sustains another thesis about the origins of the PSM. He distorts even the name of the librettist: *A. Nossige.*

20. The matter was repeated at the beginning of the 1920s by S. Efron-Litvin, who even ("Testimony of A. Šatilova," in Begunov 1996, ibid.) had ascribed to the shocking discovery of the decision to become a Christian. However, Efron was baptized at the beginning of the 1880s, and his antisemitic novel *Sredi evreev* came out in *Istoričeskij vestnik* already in 1896 (Dudakov 1993, 135).

21. Stopped August 16, 1920 by Piłsudski's counter-offensive.

22. Pseud. of Gérard Encausse (1865–1916).

23. The article concludes: "Philippe had to retire and in fact make himself scarce from Russia, but immediately after Gesse and Račkovskij were forced to retire." The

story (based on the fact that Račkovskij compiled a report attacking Mr. Philippe at the request of Gesse: cf. Vitte 1923, 1:246) should therefore refer to 1902.

24. M. Baigent, R. Leigh, and H. Lincoln, *The Holy Blood and the Holy Grail* (1982; Russ. trans. from Fr. *Svjaščennaja zagadka* [St. Petersburg 1993]).

25. In 1884, Papus was an "isolated occultist" just initiated by the "friends" of Saint Martin (G. Ventura, *Tutti gli uomini del Martinismo* [Rome 1978], 33) and his candidature for the Mizraïm Lodge was blackballed in 1896 and 1897 (S. Caillet, *La Franc-Maçonnerie égyptienne de Memphis-Misraïm* [Paris 1988], 22). Later in 1906 he had a patent from the Ancient and Primitive Order of Memphis and Misraïm (G. Ventura, *I riti massonici di Misraïm e Memphis* [Rome 1980], 91), but he never became Grand Master of such a Lodge. The "news" is dealt with by Fry 1931, and the anonymous "member" is therefore Schorst-Schapiro (cf. others).

26. Which depends on that of Rollin, which in turn elaborated a deduction by Chayla.

27. The only (possible) connection is the identification of the Grail with the "Chalice of Solomon" (cf. Capaldo 1990b, 561). Bostunič (1928, 259) has endorsed the version that one is dealing with the emerald cup donated to Solomon by the Queen of Sheba.

28. Previously author of a research paper, "Slovo o pogibeli Russkoj zemli" (1965) and the essay "Kozma Presviter v slavjanskix literaturax" (1973); more recently (1993) he published a surprising *Legenda o Guse* in Southern Russian at the end of the 15th century.

29. The Memphis rite (which appeared in France in 1838, but "in dream" from 1869) was "traditionalist and Christian" like that of Mizraïm (1815) of which it was a rival, and in the 1880s no Lodge of this sort existed in France. In England, J. Yarker was just preparing the fusion of the two Rites (cf. G. Ventura, *I riti massonici di Misraïm e Memphis,* 93 and A. Comba, *Le Rite de Memphis au XIXème siècle,* in AA.VV. [G. M. Cazzaniga ed.], *Symboles, signes, languages sacrés. Pour un sémiologie de la franc-maçonnerie* (Pisa 1995), 90).

30. Apart from the fact that the signature of the "representatives of Zion of the 33rd degree" is a variant of the third editing. The rite of Mizraïm had 90 degrees and that of Memphis 95 (then 97).

31. Who, according to the *Secret Dossiers* of H. Lobineau (on which are based the story of the "Priorate"; cf. Baigent, Leigh, and Lincoln, *The Holy Blood, and the Holy Grail,* 135, 464), had been Grand Master from 1885 until 1918.

32. S. Caillet, *La Franc-Maçonnerie,* 13.

33. B3, pp. v, 107. Butmi claimed to be an expert on secret societies, and in 1914 edited a booklet written by one of his relations, N. Butmi.

34. Alias Schapiro; according to Fry, he was killed in Egypt by the French police.

35. The story repeats that of the *Secret of Judaism.* Fry adds that Čerevin, on his death (1896), had left a copy of his *Memoirs,* with the PSM, in the hands of Nicholas II, who however only read it in print in 1906.

36. According to Nilus (1917), the "Marshal of the Nobility of the District of Čern' [*between Orël and Tula*], then Vice-Governor of Stavropol."

37. Fry 1931, 93f.; this explains the "first edition of Nilus of 1901."

38. Evno Azef, (1869–1918) leader of the Revolutionary Socialists and police informer unmasked by V. Burcev in 1908.

39. More than being reported in encyclopedias and manuals, it was rather given as bibliographical information in the catalogue of the British Library (filed under: Nilus, S. *Velikoe v malom* Carskoe Selo 1905).

40. *Berner Prozess* (1:444; 30 October 1934). Declarations of the same tenor from Lopuxin to Burcev and from "a French personage" to Harting (around 1920) were published in 1938–1939 (Rollin 1991, 482).

41. *The Jewish Bogey* (London 1920).

42. Cited in Nečvolodov 1924, 277.

43. Here one is dealing with the same story of Fry, but with opposite aims.

44. The conviction that the text had been written in French forces the "non-existent manuscript" to make repeated trips from Paris to St. Petersburg and vice versa.

45. J. Kessel (with Elena Izvol'skaja), *Les rois aveugles* (Paris 1925), 55. The detail of the "note on Judaism" indicates that such a version was created *before* the discovery of the use of M. Joly, even if the novel is later.

46. In reality, effective Councillor of State, a civil rank on a par with a General.

47. In Taguieff 1992, 1:54.

48. To become ordained a priest so as to take up the position of the Tsar's confessor. This refers to 1906, and foresaw the exercise of his priestly duties not at Court but "in Volynije" (N. Koncevič, in Nilus 1995, 1:10).

49. In Taguieff 1992, 1:60.

50. W. Giusti, *L'ultimo controrivoluzionario russo* (Rome 1974), 107.

51. I would not say it was born spontaneously, or with some relationship with the deposition of B. Engel'gardt at the Bern Trial.

52. Creutz 1934, 13. S. Efron was converted at the beginning of the 1880 and A. Efron died in 1909.

53. Barrucand expressed his theses in a typed letter sent to Taguieff and to Tazbir (cf. Tazbir 1992b, 72–73 and 1996, 44) who has kindly sent me a copy. Miss Glinka could have reworked Joly's text as an "authenticated forgery", but Barrucand (1992, 2) discards such an eventuality because "it does not explain her constant later activity."

54. Presented at the conference "Jerusalem in Slavic Culture," Jerusalem , 11 December 1996; cf. ID, "Protokoly sionskix mudrecov"—k anatomii odnogo mifa.

Predvaritel'nye zametki," *Egupec'. Xudožno-publicističnij al'manx institutu judaiki* (Kiev), 3 (1997).

55. Cohn, 1969, 72.

56. "In a novel by A. V. Amfiteatrov, there is reference to the question of the origin of these *Protocols,* to which end a whole story is told according to which they had been presented by a certain fervent Catholic to the Pope of Rome" ("Kem i kogda byli sfabrikovany t. n. 'Sionskie Protokoly,'" by "a well known Russian jurist," *Obščee delo*, 6 May 1921).

57. "As a novelist I very much like A. V. Amfiteatrov very much, in particular as the author of *Vos'midesjatniki,* but I am unable to remember one (of his) novels with a passage of this sort" (Bostunič 1921, 35).

58. According to Barrucand 1992, the first text on which a similar manoeuvre might have been carried out was *L'Église et la Synagogue* (Paris-Tournai 1859) under the signature of L. Rupert. However Rupert declared himself to be only the translator of the work of "a learned foreigner" who wished to preserve his anonymity. This would have been an Italian (perhaps a priest) who intended to "refute the philo-Jewish theories of Gioberti and D'Azeglio." This is an extremely plausible hypothesis, given the considerable amount of Italian publicity.

59. Even if through a simple error he indicates him as "Suxotin."

60. And still others, which are not worth discussing, e.g., the attribution to G. B. Shaw (cf. S. Igra, *The "Doctor's Plot" in Moscow and the Protocols* [1960], and idem., *G. B. Shaw on Success* [1972]).

CHAPTER 8

Theology and Anti-theology

The PSM are based on pseudo-theologems, that is to say, on expressions and concepts taken from the Judeo-Christian religious culture, without, however, any intention of genuine theological meditation. This also refers to their "framework" (Men'šikov's introduction or the commentaries of Nilus and Butmi), rather than the writings dedicated to them.

On the other hand, the "religious" aspect of the PSM is often promoted to uphold their trustworthy provenance[1] as if their publishers' (or the "translators'") declared fidelity to Orthodoxy guaranteed their genuineness. It is also true that Ževaxov (1939, 68) imputed the limited success of the PSM in Russian society at the beginning of the century to precisely the reverse; to the fact that "the majority of the Church Hierarchy gave it an unfavorable reception," even if "it is not exaggerated to say that the greatest responsibility [of the "conquest of Russia by the Jews"] falls on the official Russian church" (ibid., 71). However this involves a very different and more radical argument, which we shall touch on later.

The nature of the cultural referent of the PSM is therefore historical-theological, or better, of a special theology of history; indeed almost a parodied re-reading of the "succession of the kingdoms" in the second chapter of Daniel,[2] with an implicit reference to the "third Rome." This has to be studied, therefore, in terms of critical theology, for at least two reasons:

a) because the semiotic horizon within which the supposed plan of the Jewish conspiracy is situated is that of the Old Testament "Chosen People"; and

b) because the viewpoint from which the forger observed this horizon is that of "Christian Civilization," which would be threatened by the plan in action.

The PSM may not be a "Concise Bible,"[3] but they certainly have many of the characteristics, also of structure, to be taken as "duplicates" of books of the Bible, beginning with the number of chapters. K proposes, even if confusedly, a segmentation in 22 chapters similar to that the Apocalypse; the second edition reorganized the material according to the divisions of Leviticus 27; while the third turns to that of the book of Joshua—24, taking on the connotations of the book of the effective conquest of the "Promised Land."

Examining the text in its original form, the apocalyptic aspects (confusingly overshadowed in the first edition), the concern for the coming advent of Christ "as a political possibility" (from which comes Nilus's subtitle), are less marked than they may seem. Rather, the "king of the line of David" is normally taken to be the messiah; the explicit reference to it belongs almost exclusively to Nilus, who combines it together with the "medieval ghost" of the Antichrist,[4] and the recent (for his times) "vision" of the Antichrist in the story of Vl. Solov'ëv[5]:

> At present, the voice of Orthodoxy has become the voice of the Universal Church. The Lutheran heresy is a case apart, in that it is not only without the grace of the Sacraments, but also because in it the question of the Anti-Christ is evidently placed in the category of the most burning and urgent questions (Nilus 1905, 315).

Solov'ëv's position on the Jewish problem was of solidarity with a discriminated and oppressed minority in the Russian Empire,[6] and therefore far from Nilus's "point of view." However, that contact proved particularly insidious. It induced potential readers of the PSM, in all likelihood a not very sophisticated public, to believe that the authority of Solov'ëv validated the arguments of the PSM (Nilus 1905, 322: "Solov'ëv provided the canvas, the embroidery of the arabesque belongs entirely to the manuscript proposed here").

In reality, the Antichrist was never mentioned in the PSM (not even in N), and Nilus inserted the Apocalyptic motif in its essence in the commentary. It is difficult, therefore, to share the assumption of Dudakov (1993, 144) according to which the PSM should be "considered in the *mystic-religious context* of the conception of the "academic of Optina Pustyn'." They instead, also from a "theological" point of view, should be read in their original form, leaving the ravings of Nilus to the *history* of their creation.

We turn thus to the two points mentioned. As regards the first, from the "Jewish point of view" represented in the apocrypha of the "sages," we are struck not so much by the repeated and distorted value attributed to the concept of the "Chosen People" (which it was considered was destined to rule over all the people of the Earth and not just a single "Promised Land"), but rather by the absence of any reference to the Messiah,[7] who was the sovereign (*car'* in the Russian text) of the line of David who was mentioned with many attributes such as Patriarch, Pontiff, even Protector (like Cromwell[8]), but never as messiah.

As regards the second, one registers a "totalitarian" vision of Christianity which a close-up view alone is sufficient to show it to be riddled with contradictions at an ecclesiastical level.

So, two other questions are revealed to be decisive so as to read the PSM "from the theological point of view." The first is of an *ecclesialogical* (confessional) nature, while the other is more properly *dogmatic.*

The PSM describes a *Jewish* plot at the expense of a *Christian* world, which according to Nilus (1905, 323) could find salvation only in unity, and this could be achieved only by convoking the exponents "of all the confessions" in the Eighth Ecumenical Council, which obviously should take place in Moscow— the Third Rome (ibid., 406[9]). One is dealing therefore with a "point of view" which is not generically "Christian" but specifically "Orthodox," and the vision which the PSM gives of the two other great branches of Christianity—Catholicism and Protestantism—is in no way irrelevant.

As regards the "Catholic Question," the Solov'ëvian viewpoint of Nilus (Solov'ëv was notorious as a champion of union with Rome) has greatly diminished the latent polemical contrast in relation to "Jesuitism." In fact, the text does not raise the question of the Jesuits, but of the Papacy; the phrase:

> In this, only the **Jesuits** would have been able to take us on, but we
> have known how to discredit them (4th)

appears only in N, is not in a note on Joly's text, and therefore is to be considered his addition, in the same way that the "threat" Russian autocracy would have represented for the Jews was compared with that of the papacy (12th). However, elsewhere the discourse on the papacy keeps to the original text:

> When the time comes to destroy the **Papal** court, the finger of an
> invisible hand will indicate to the nations the direction of that Court....
> The king of Judah will be the one who had at one time had been the
> **Pope** (17th).

While the second phrase appears conditioned by the "Porta Pia Syndrome," the first comes from a passage in Joly on the policy of Napoleon III on the "Roman Question," with the variant of a certain significance: the expression *"indiquer du doigt"* has been substituted by "the finger *of an invisible hand* will indicate," obviously referring to Daniel 2.24, and perhaps via the *Balthasar* of H. Heine. However referring the passage from Daniel (the mysterious hand that wrote *"Mene, Techel, Peres"*) to the Vatican is a *topos* of Italian Protestantism of the Risorgimento,[10] which—however it managed to reach the Russian forger[11]—is here attributed to Jewish conspirators.

The text therefore expresses a sort of "solidarity" with Catholicism, if for nothing else as the common enemy of the "Sages," reinforced in the third edition by the addition which denounces the anti-Catholic line of the French Government as the workings of the "Zionist" plans:

> France has asked for help from Turkey for the schools and religious organizations of all confessions.... This point, obviously, does not concern the Catholic organizations...and only shows that the Dreyfusard diplomacy defends the interests of Zion and opens the door to the colonization of Asia Minor by the French Jews *(Translator's Note).*

This does not involve the idea, however, "of the Jesuits" as appears, leaving apart the additions, the comments of the publishers of the PSM, which cannot be made to agree with that "of the Papacy"; rather the very reverse.

Men'šikov (1902) wrote:

> The Jews, with a more than **Jesuitical** simply devilish cunning, have undermined the foundations of order and Christianity with the propaganda of liberalism, of cosmopolitanism, of anarchy.

Kruševan (1903) for his part confirmed it:

> Today...to achieve this aim they have at their disposition a weapon as powerful as Zionism, which has the vocation to reunite all the Jews on Earth in an alliance even more compact and dangerous than the **Jesuit** Order.[12]

The reference to "Jesuitism" is a decidedly negative sign. Nilus adds to the text the insertion on the wise black propaganda used to draw the talons of the Jesuits, but in his second comment he explains thus his attitude towards them:

> The Papacy threw the Jesuit Order into the struggle; they have slowed down the devilish work of Freemasonry for a long time. But **Jesuitism**, which served a human and not a divine principle...was destined to be discredited and fall (1905, 412).

The ambiguity, or rather the contradiction, is evident. On the one hand, Nilus has the "Sages" say that Jesuitism was a potential enemy of their plans, and therefore *they* had been obliged to discredit and thus "destroy" them. On the other, he asserted that the end was understandable since the untrustworthy nature of Jesuitism could not but lead the noble undertaking to ruin, even if the discredit was due not the Jews but to the *Jesuits themselves.*

Here one puts a finger on the dual nature in Nilus's attitude toward Roman Catholicism, which highlights that of the PSM. It was a potential ally in the struggle against the Antichrist (one hears echoes of Solov'ëv), but at the same time, it was an incurable deviation from Orthodoxy, and therefore by its nature unacceptable even if fascinating:

> But the idea of world domination has not been foreign even to Christianity...and it manifested itself with particular clarity in the Catholic world, creating and working for the enthroning of a Pope-King, as sole sovereign of all the races and peoples of the world (1905, 408)

and so much more in the threatening form of Jesuitism (and here we discover the harmony with the comments of Men'šikov and Kruševan).

This second idea recurs in Russian Orthodox culture, and depends not so much on the anti-Jesuit writings of Western Europe (*The Wandering Jew* of E. Sue[13]) as from the perverse image of Jesuitism (protected by Catherine the Great at the time of the disbanding of the Society,[14] then later banned by Alexander I[15]) which became rooted in Russia for confessional reasons, and was sharpened by the Jesuit's role in the Polish Revolt of 1863 which reactivated the historic memory of the *Monita Secreta* in its modern variant the *Polish Catechism*[16] to such an extent that Russian law forbade at that time the entry into Russia of both Jesuit and secular priests (Rollin 1991, 451).

Šmakov (1912, 37) could baldly say that "the Jew is a natural Jesuit, and the Jesuit is only an artificial Jew," and Bostunič (1928, 146) took his views to their extreme: "In the Jesuit Order there is much that is similar to Freemasonry, and also to the secret Jewish government."

Taking the variations (and the commentaries) of the publishers as a "second" framework, one could well say that the PSM are part and parcel of such an aversion, being at odds with a considerable philo-Catholic inclination implicit in the text. This, however, does not remain without comparison. Three of the first translations of the PSM were made by Catholic priests: the first Polish one by Father Joseph Evrard (1919),[17] the second, French, one by Msgr. Jouin (1920) and the third, Italian, one by Msgr. Benigni (1921).

If the PSM show some ambiguity towards Catholicism, the "Protestant Question" is explicitly raised in the passage in the 12th Protocol which speaks of countries

in which we have planted deep roots of discord and of **Protestantism**.

That this reference is intentional is underlined by the fact that it is added to a phrase copied from Joly which does not contain it (*Dans les pays incessamment troublés par les discordes* [in the countries incessantly troubled because of discord]), and its "extraneousness" (the concept is not be immediately grasped) to the fact that A1, for *lectior facilior* reads *protesta* instead of *protestantizma*. However, there is a passage in the same Protocol in which one can discern a "cryptic" allusion to Protestantism. The Russian text of the PSM is fairly sibylline[18] but, if one decodifies it on the basis of that of Joly from which it derives (1864, 154)

> En matière de religion, la doctrine du **libre examen** est devenue une sorte de monomanie. Il ne faut pas contrarier cette tendance [In matters of religion, the doctrine of **free examination** has become a sort of monomania. It is not necessary to oppose this tendency]

One notices that the *Jewish* criticism of Christianity is stamped with the *Protestant* principle of "free examination," which Butmi will take to heart in his reprint of the PSM (B3, 95).

The warhorse of liberal Protestantism at the time of Napoleon III and of the PSM, free examination, is in reality one of the fundamental concepts of the Reformation and one of the major contributors to the formation of the modern world itself. The same is said of "freedom of conscience" and all that flows from it and which is equally indicated (17th) as the precursor of nothing but disintegration.[19]

The passages cited offer us a simplistic and vulgar interpretation, which is a summary which could have emanated only from circles, such as those of Russian Orthodoxy, which rejected on principle "free examination" even in its most serious and correct uses, because it was in radical opposition to the doctrine of "tradition."

Toward Protestantism, therefore, there was not the slightest sign of ecumenism; not even in the distorted and minor form which is seen in the *Brief Story of the Anti-Christ* by Vl. Solov'ëv. Fear of the spread of Protestantism in Russia was highlighted by the 1903 measures, and even more by the decree of 1905 on the freedom of religious confessions, which led to the paroxysms of feeling that had already been expressed by Dostoevskij thirty years before:

> In a corner of Russia a very strange phenomenon has been spotted: Protestantism...in Orthodox circles.... It is an almost monstrous phenomenon, but it appears to feel itself in some way prophetic.[20]

Butmi (B3, 105) introduces the PSM with an explicit denunciation of the Reformation, both of the "First" and that of the sixteenth century ("under the same influx [*of the Jews*] in the XIV (?) century the heresy of Jan Hus was born, which is fundamental to the Reformation to which Luther and Calvin gave birth"). He involves even the contemporary Russian offshoots ("the sect of Paškov," ibid., 95) and elsewhere (Butmi 1906e, 95) "Albigensians, Templars and *Waldensians.*"

More generally one is dealing with a *topos* of antisemitism that E. Małyński, a Polish nobleman from Voylnja who emigrated to France[21] and whose Catholic antisemitism had great success between the wars, formulated thus: "the Reform Movement was imbued, from its birth, with a Jewish spirit."[22]

The idea, which derives from nineteenth-century[23] "anti-conspiratorial" and Legitimist Catholicism and which is found also among Jews,[24] refers to the series of events "Reformation/English Revolution/French Revolution/ Russian Revolution." There is also the idea that "The Reformation was the first revolutionary offensive"[25]), which in Russia had been expressed by O. Pr>eclavskij (1799–1879) ("Only in this [*fomenting the masses in revolt against the authorities*; editor's note] lies the mechanism of all revolutions, beginning with Luther's Reformation"[26]). We also see this in B3.

In the PSM, this explains both the original route of the "Symbolic Serpent," and the Cromwellian connotations ("Protector") which are applied to the "King of the line of David." One understands, therefore, how, in the tradition flowing from the PSM, there is a rooted antipathy for Cromwell and the English 17th-century Puritans. Dudakov (1893, 217) records that Bostuni> (1922, 109) had already denounced that

> by the hand of the fanatic Cromwell they grafted themselves onto the
> English Revolution of 1648, the result of which was that the Jews,
> having obtained equal rights in England, made the country their base
> for subsequent Jewish offensives.

The question of the relations between the Jewish tradition and that of the churches which sprang from the Reformation is not so linear. As is known, in his old age Luther also held anti-Jewish feelings.[27] German antisemitism down to the 19th century had roots also in the Lutheran world,[28] and on their appearance, the PSM also found echoes among Protestants.[29] However, this does not alter the historical philosophical mytholem which has come into being. Evola, for example, remains convinced that the Reformation had "constituted the incentive for a later spiritual involution [*of Europe*] and for its relevant Semitization."[30] On the other hand, more than the senile antisemitism of Luther, in Russia what counted was the memory of the Lutheran Church of St. Petersburg which had undertaken protection of the Jewish community[31]:

> In 1802, the Evangelical Lutheran community of St. Peter had donated
> a part of their own cemetery to the Jews,... and the first Jews could
> now rest legally in the damp earth of the Russian Imperial capital.[32]

Protestantism also enters the PSM's sights by way of Freemasonry. As Dudakov reminds us, many members of the "Bible Society" were Protestants and Masons, and the Secretary, V. M. Popov (1771–1842), "together with other adepts, aspired to substitute "Authentic Orthodoxy" with English Protestantism (Methodism)" (ibid., 580).

Since Protestantism is invariably linked with the figure of St. Paul, among the supporters of the PSM there was a latent aversion towards him since as a Pharisee he would have known about the plan of the "Sages of Zion":

> The Apostle Paul, as one of the most gifted students of the Pharisee's School, could not but have been privy to this "mystery of the iniquity *which was* taking place" [cf. II Thessalonians 2.7] even in his times (Nilus 1905, 395).

However for Ževaxov (1939, 68) another aspect prevails. In fact, he intended

> to destroy the dependence of the New Testament on the Old, artfully created by the Apostle Paul who allows the Jews to affirm that "the Word of God is entrusted to them" (Romans 3.2).

With Ževaxov's thesis of the opposition of the New Testament to the heritage of the Old Testament, we have reached the heart of the *theological* question, or rather more properly the *dogmatic* one.

The theme of the "election of Israel" appears in the PSM with the citing of Nehemiah 9.22–25[33] to test the Jewish vocation for world domination. However, the theme runs through the whole text with references to an Old Testament God presented as exclusively for the Jews and *therefore* in contrast with the God of the New Testament, the God of the Christians.

Our "councilors of genius" have "studied in the Temple of *our* God", "every victim of *ours* "is worth a thousand "gojim" to *our* God" (2nd). "*Our* prophets have said that "we were elected by God to reign over the Earth" (4th). "There must be no other religion than *ours,* that of the God to whom our destiny is linked" (11th). "Our" Government "has been predestined for the world by God" (21st). The Jews are convinced that "only *they* are sons of God" (*Translator's Note*).

From the PSM emerge two different visions of Judaism. One, implicitly present in the *Translator's Note,* contrasts, according to a classic scheme,[34] the Mosaic Law with the Talmud, in the sense that the former would be basically acceptable, but in reality has been substituted among the Jews by the latter,[35] intrinsically in agreement with the desire for dominion expressed in the PSM. The other is more radical. As opposed to the God of the New Testament, the God of the Old Testament was "malign."[36] Such an idea, if it is not explicitly enunciated in the PSM, is in reality implied by the text ("*our*" God is not "*your*" God). To follow it to its natural conclusion, the defense of Orthodoxy touches on heresy. So much so that, even in a hagiographic context, Striž ěv (1993, 331) distances himself from it: "Naturally for us this point of view of Ževaxov is unacceptable."

Taken to its extremes, the logic of the PSM leads us to a radical contrast between the God of the Jews[37] and the God of the Christians, and has a very precise matrix, which is the thought of the Gnostics, the Paulicians, the Bogomils, and before them, even the Marcionite heresy.[38] To my knowledge, the only person to refer to this heterodox theme in relation to the PSM has been U. Eco, even if only in a fictional form, which does not require proof but only enunciation: "*The Protocols* appeared in the Russian environment. Therefore they are a Paulician initiative."[39]

Does this perhaps mean that those who copied the PSM were of Bogomil (or Paulician, or Gnostic, or Marcionite) inclinations? Certainly not. *To use* a model does not in fact mean to agree with it. Rather, it means that the Bogomils (even in their heterodoxy) were "true believers," while the creators of the PSM, despite their proclaimed "defense of Christianity," reveal themselves to have been in the end misbelievers. "Your inquisitor," says Alěša to Ivan, "does not believe in God. There is his secret!"[40] The same words could be repeated of the PSM.

The antisemitic envy does not only appear tempered by expressions of Jesuitical moderation which distinguish it from that of its Catholic contemporaries ("discriminating, not persecuting"); not only are Jesus of Nazareth and his message (the *foedus gratiae*) never mentioned, but the fact is that the "God of Mercy" of the New Testament faced with the "malign God" of the Old Testament has no role in the PSM. Their drafter reduces Joly's "*Providence*" to "destiny" (*sud'ba;* 22nd), and formulates the idea (attributed to the "Sages") that Christianity is "our most dangerous adversary *in the doctrines of the world of the spirit and the future life*" (17th), which reveals his misbelief, not his orthodoxy.

Rather, the PSM uphold the idea that religion is an optimum social drug (4th: "the people who go with submission and mildness under the leadership of the spiritual pastors"), even if its most instrumental formulation (the people "will be guided by the cure of their parish priests") is an addition in the third edition to a phrase taken from Joly.[41]

It could be said that the PSM represents the nexus between the "religious" anti-Judaism of Orthodox origins, of which it keeps the vocabulary (even if it is a hybrid with a smattering of French and Italian Catholic vocabulary, and in part that of German Lutheran), and modern, biological, and "pagan" antisemitism. However, the categories developed to analyze that antisemitism of the Romano-Germanic tradition are not very evident in the Slav-Orthodox one. Thus, we have the contrast between the two varieties of "infected Christianity" (Catholic antisemitism born of a rejection of "revolutionary modernity," and the Protestant variety of "romantic nationalism"),[42] as well as that other contrast typical only of the Catholic world between "traditional" and "ideological"[43] antisemitism. Neither does the distinction between a *racial* antisemitism, divided into *political* and *irrational,* developed by the same Russian Judeo-phobia[44] seem more appropriate.

The relatively recent epoch (i.e., the end of the eighteenth century) in which *Russian* Orthodoxy has made contact with the Jewish world, has produced a sort of short circuit between the anti-Jewishness of the theological tradition[45] and the Jew-phobia of secular society, which is expressed in the accusatory interpretation of *qahal* (Brafman 1869).

In reality, the dominant theme of the PSM is radically conspiratorial, and if the story is governed by a great plot (almost three thousand years old, and with its origins recalling the Temple of Solomon), that is the same as saying it is dominated neither by God, nor the Old nor New Testaments. Both Taguieff (1992, 1:23: "the fake reduces the complexity of modern history to a single but not transcendent fortuitous principle") and Zolotonosov come to analogous conclusions. The latter who (1995, 162), in relation to that which he calls the "third characteristic" of the "subculture of Russian anti-Semitism" says that the "Superior Will" which rules the world is not identified in God, but in "his secularized substitutes like the "Jewish World Government," "the Sages of Zion," and the "Black Cabinet." One notices here the greatest distance between the PSM and the *Secret of Judaism,* which instead recalls the "deicide" and defines the Jewish Plot as thought up by the Essenes with the end of speeding up the return to the Jews of God's grace.

Despite the anomalous dating of the reign of Solomon, the PSM show a clear familiarity with the Old Testament.[46] Here I am not referring only to the passage from Nehemiah as a "thematic key,"[47] which implies a certain familiarity with the history of post-exilic Israel, nor to the similar use of the universal vocation of the Messianic Kingdom,[48] so much as to the question of the "succession to the throne" in the Kingdom to come. In the 1st Protocol, it is said that:

> For this very reason the dynastic government of the Jewish sovereigns was established, so that the son might learn from the father knowledge of the political plan,

while in the 22nd it is claimed:

> Some members of the seed of David were prepared to reign...not according to the law of direct succession. The direct heirs were often

excluded from the...throne if in the period of study they showed...qualities which rendered them inept at government.

The apparent contradiction is explained by the fact that the dynastic principle, always observed in the Kingdom of Judah but not in that of Israel,

> did not necessarily include that of primogeniture.... One is King by Grace of God, not only because God has made a pact with the Davidic dynasty, but because his choice is exercised in every succession to the throne.[49]

From the original draft of the PSM, one gathers that the effective choice was undertaken by the "sages" as the holders of "the system which has permitted them to retain the knowledge of all the world's affairs." However, an addition to the second edition already speaks of "masters who have initiated him [*the king*]," and the variant of this addition, present in the third edition, speaks of "the three who have initiated him," according to a ritual that has something of the Masonic. Such a procedure is only a secularized variation of the principle in operation in the Kingdom of Judah, in which, however, God (no less than the God of Abraham, Isaac, and Jacob) undertakes no role. He has been completely substituted for secular ends by the conspiracy and by the means to put it in action. The addition of pantheistic characteristics of A2 (1st: "nature is only a synonym for God") only serves to reinforce a constant theme of all the PSM.[50]

To use another expression of Dostoevskij, what the PSM defends is a "church of atheists,"[51] a completely political Christianity (Throne and Altar: Tsar and Priests) to which the Jew, Jesus of Nazareth, has nothing to say.

In their depths, and in any case in their potential, "the PSM are a book which is anti-Christian, anti-Jewish, and atheist,"[52] even if strangely, "the anti-Christian essence (in general) and anti-Orthodox (in particular) of the Protocols has in fact been hardly studied" (Dudakov 1993, 162). From this angle, they appear to be the prototype of that "pseudo-theology" which "has maintained a considerable influence on the development of modern totalitarian movements" (Arendt 1996, 326).

NOTES

1. Cf. again Vol'skij 1993, 30.

2. On this biblical passage in the reflections on history, cf. M. Miegge, *Il sogno del re di Bibilonia* (Milan 1995).

3. Zapponi 1984, 90.

4. Cf. Beljakov-Beljakova, "O peresmotre esxatologičeskix koncepcij na Rusi v konce XV veka," *Arkiv russkoj istorii,* 1 (1992).

5. "Kratkaja povest' ob Antixriste" [1900], in *Tri razgovora o vojne, progresse i konce vsemirnoj istorii* (now in *Sočinenija v dvux tomax,* vol. 2 [Moscow 1990]).

6. W. Giusti (*L'ultimo controrivoluzionario russo,* 106) records how much K. Pobedonoscev wrote about it: "The madman of Solov'ev had the idea of gathering at Moscow a species of *meeting* to protest against the trend of the measures taken against the Jews." Cf. *Solov'ev, Vl. S.* in AA. VV., *Tajna Izrailja. Evrejskij vopros v russkoj religioznoj mysli konca XIX-pervoj poloviny XX vv.* (St. Petersburg 1993). Cf. also N. Minskij, "Vladimir Solovief et les juifs," *La Tribune Juive,* 20 August 1920, and Dudakov 1989.

7. And no less the presence of New Testament expressions such as "the blind leading the blind," "they know not what they do," "not an iota," etc.

8. Cf. 19th Protocol: "the role of father and *Protector* of the Jewish Patriarch." L. Fry (*The Jews and the British Empire,* s.d., 3) makes explicit this role of Cromwell in the sense that, having readmitted the Jews into England, he had been the *"Protector"* of the Jews themselves in the first place.

9. In the 1911 edition (*Luč sveta* 1920), Nilus reconsiders and locates the site of the Council at Jerusalem rather than Moscow.

10. Cf. P. Bassanesi, *L'infallibilità del papa! Mene techel, peres* (manifesto, Padua 1870).

11. News of contemporary Italian Protestantism was propagated in Russia in the second half of the 19th century. In particular, the fame spread of L. Desanctis, one of the most lively anti-Catholic polemicists. At the end of the century, the leader of a branch of Russian evangelicalism (Paškov) attended the Baptist church in a piazza in Lucina while an emigrant in Rome.

12. In the reprint of Nilus 1995, 2:474, one reads (is it the result of poor deciphering or of intentional mystification?) *"Genuitskij"* rather than *"Iezuitskij."*

13. The figure of the "wandering Jew" (Russ. trans: *Stranstvujuščij u žid* [Moscow 1845–1846] and *Večnyj žid* [Moscow 1846]) comes to be used, however, in Russian antisemitic writings. (Šmakov 1912, 257).

14. Cf. *La compagnie de Jésus conservée en Russie* (Paris 1872).

15. With the *ukaz* of March 23, 1820; cf. I. Čurkina, "Iezuity v Rossii (1772–1820)," *Voprosy Istorii,* 10 (1996).

16. A copious anti-Catholic and specifically "anti-Jesuit" body of writing developed then in Russia (Ju. Samarin, *Iezuity ix otnošenie k Rossii,* 1868).

17. Joseph Evrard, an Assumptionist (1878–1960); cf. Jouin 1920, 1:2, 189, with the warning that it is was convenient to keep his name quiet so as not to harm him (elsewhere, 1921, 2:69, that "the translator must keep his name quiet to protect his life") in *Fede e Ragione* (Faith and Reason), 13 (27 March 1921).

18. "Our philosophers will examine and criticize all the defects in the beliefs of the *gojim,* and they will not be able to reply when faced with our faith."

19. "The influence of the priests over the population declines day by day, everywhere liberty of conscience is proclaimed."

20. F. Dostoevskij, *Dnevnik pisatelja za 1873g.*

21. Cf. R. Aftanazy, *Matyński Emanuel,* in PSB 19 (1974): 457.

22. Małyński 1928, 6:227: and on the radical Reformation: "the Anabaptists, led by a Jew under the pseudonym of John of Leyden" (ibid., 313).

23. Cf. G.-L. Ségur, *La Rivoluzione* (It. trans. Naples 1862), 29: "The Revolution [*was*] prepared by Protestantism...; the secret societies presided over its birth."

24. Cf. B. Lazare, *L'antisémitisme* (1894; [Paris 1934], 1:225: "The Reformation, in Germany as in England, was one of those moments in which Christianity refreshes itself at the Jewish source. It was the Jewish spirit which triumphed, with Protestantism."

25. Małyński 1928, 46.

26. *Razoblačenie velikoj tajny frankmasonstva: Iz bumag pokojnogo Prže- clavskogo* (Moscow 1909), 87. Cited in Stepanov 1992, 29.

27. Especially in the book *I giudei e le loro menzogne* (The Jews and their lies) (1543). Butmi 1906e, to reduce the weight, adds paradoxically to gather its true origin: "Luther became anti-Semitic when he had the delusion that the Jews were not being converted." The senile anti-Judaism of Luther was naturally used by modern antisemitism, as much German as Russian (Ževaxov 1939, 120).

28. I am referring in particular to Pastor A. Stöcker.

29. For example, Rev. Bendor Samuel (*The Jewish Peril and World Unrest* [London 1921]); on Rev. Samuel, cf. Ford 1939.

30. J. Evola, *Sintesi di dottrina della razza* (Milan 1941), 206. One of the first racist formulations was expressed in polemic with the Italian neo-Calvinists ("Spiritualità imperiale e retorica neoprotestante," *Critica fascista* 20 (15 October 1926): 393).

31. It appears paradoxical that Nilus came from a Lutheran family (only the father had converted to Orthodoxy; cf. Hagemeister [1991; Fr. trans. 1995], 143).

32. V. Toporov, in *Slavjane i ix sosedi* 1994, 186.

33. In the 2nd Protocol; having been expunged from the third edition, it has passed unnoticed.

34. Cf. A. Rohling, *Talmud-Jude* (1871).

35. Cf. Ževaxov 1939, 100: "From that moment [scil.; after the destruction of the Temple], the Talmud substituted the Bible and the Jews were educated in a fanatical hatred of Christ."

36. An analogous thesis had been put forward in Italy twenty years before by D. Pergola, an apostate Jew who distinguished himself in antisemitic publishing at the end of the 19th century: "Jehova-Ham, or Jove Mammon, confused by the Jews with

the Supreme Being, represents the genius of evil" (*L'antisemitismo questione religiosa e morale* [Turin 1885], 7).

37. Ževaxov 1939, 16: "The Russian academics…and…Germans…have unmasked the true essence of the Jewish God Jehovah."

38. Cf. Miccoli 1997, 1435. This does not take away the fact that in antisemitic writings (Šmakov 1912, 41) "Gnosticism, Arianism, Manicheism" are seen as similar to the *Qabalah* that is to the "spirit of Judaism."

39. *Il Pendolo di Foucault* (Foucault's pendulum) (Milan 1988), 377.

40. F. Dostoevskij, *Brat'ja Karamazovy,* 1880.

41. *"La religion…où le peuple…marchait sous la main de ses pasteurs"*; the "government of the parishes" was effectively a dream a the time of the 1905 Revolution, and that can date the addition.

42. Cf. Moro 1988, 1020.

43. Ibid., 1023.

44. V. Šul'gin, *Čto nam ne nravitsja* (Paris 1929), cited in I. Levin, *L'antisemitismo russo* (It. trans., *Sisfo* 26 (October 1993).

45. Which had generated the *topos* of the Jewish or Judaized nature of the "heresy." "Ritual murder" is only a by-product, and is mostly imported. Of the 203 cases categorised by Brant 1926, 1, only a few concern territory then in the Russian Empire, concentrated in the eighteenth century and relating mostly to the Polish ex-*Rzeczpospolita.*

46. Which comes probably from Chamberlain via Men'šikov: "Read the Bible," we repeat behind to M. O. Men'šikov" (Butmi N. 1914, 25).

47. G. Butmi (one of the possible "authors" of the PSM) often used Biblical quotations in a similar way: cf. for example Deut. 15.6 (in Butmi 1898, 1), or Deut. 7.22–24 (in Butmi [1899] 1904, 222).

48. Cf. 4th: our prophets have told us that "we have been elected by God himself to rule over the whole world," paraphrases of the Apc. of Baruch (72.4–6).

49. De Vaux 1964, 107–108.

50. Cf. 14th: "nature herself has predestined us…to rule the world."

51. Cf. *Dnevnik pisatelja za 1876g.*

52. M. Volina, *Tajnye sily. Masonstvo i "židomasony"* (Moscow 1991), 27.

CHAPTER 9

The "Judaic-Masonic" Plot

To preface the section dedicated to the "plot" in an imposing bibliographical repertory of Freemasonry, G. M. Cazzaniga writes:

> The historiography of the question of the "Masonic Plot" has still not been satisfactorily ordered. Without harking back to the medieval premises and those of the first period of the Reformation, it should be revealed that as already in the *querelle* on *Unigenitus* the question of the plot had already taken form in the version of the "Jansenist Plot," which was a version which, in the thirties and forties [*of the seventeenth century*] became intertwined with the first appearance of the "Masonic Plot." This *romance* forcefully presents itself in the eighties in Germany in the *querelle* on crypto-Catholicism, assuming now the form of the "Jesuitical Plot," not without an admixture of both,... until the Barberi version of the trial of Cagliostro (1790) determined the success of the "Masonic Plot" version.[1]

The picture is completed by Ja. Tazbir revealing the role of the *Monita Secreta* in the "historiography of plots" (thus, "Jesuit Plot" already in 1614). On the other hand, S. Markiš has shown in Erasmus's polemic against Pfefferkon in 1517 the traces of the popular myth of the "Jewish Plot":

> Erasmus alluded to a Jewish Plot and claimed that Pfefferkon had been baptised only *pro forma,* so as to more effectively serve his people.... In the eyes of Erasmus,... membership of the Jewish nation is not cancelled out by baptism. And this, therefore, in fact follows when he speaks of the services Pfefferkon has rendered to "his people.[2]

To sum up, the myth of the Masonic Plot and that of the Jewish one have a long history prior to the PSM. The lowest common denominator of the two terms is naturally the formation of the idea of a "Judaic-Masonic" synergy. However, also in this case "it needs to be shown how the 'Judaic-Masonic' version of the plot is already present in these years [*the end of the eighteenth century*]" (Cazzaniga, ibid.), as is shown by specific studies.[3] That is to say, not only was the formation of the myth moved much back in time in relation to its "French" manifestation in the second half of the nineteenth century (by many held to be archetypal), but it further precedes the first "Russian" formulation, which in his turn, Dudakov holds to be the "original," maintaining that the primacy in the denunciation of a Judaic-Masonic Plot was held by a Russian:

> Contrary to Ju. Delevskij and many others who maintain that the legend of the "Judaic-Masonic" Plot originated in France in the 1860s, from where it was taken up by Russian anti-Semitism, in our opinion the history of social ideas in Russia contains a sufficient quantity of facts and documents to demonstrate that this "discovery" was strictly Russian (Dudakov 1993, 60).

A dubious merit goes to Mixail Magnickij[4] (1778–1844), a minor writer from the beginning of the nineteenth century who was, however, a civil servant of some importance under Alexander I. He was a reactionary stickler who upheld the providential blessing of the "Tartar yoke" for having saved Russia from the contagion of European culture.[5] He first worked in the Foreign Ministry in Paris (1801–1803), and then became the trusted confidante of A. Arakčeev, then Deputy Governor of Voronež (1816), and lastly (from 1825), Inspector of the University of Kazan. His career was interrupted in 1826 by the accusation of wasting public money, and he retired into private life. Magnickij, already a Freemason, though he left in 1811, and a member of the Bible Society,[6] on February 1, 1831 sent Nicholas I a note, *Obličenie vsemirnogo dogovora protiv oltarej i tronov,*[7] which accused the "enlightened" of having prepared a plan to set up a universal tyranny. The epicenter of this plot was London; the infiltration of the Jews had been decisive, and the possibility of taking action in Russia would have been suddenly increased with the birth of the Bible Society. Consequently, says Dudakov (1993, 59), "the primacy for the "discovery" of the links between the Masons and the Jews should really go to Magnickij."

The very fact that he speaks of the "enlightened" indicates that Magnickij's idea was in some way indebted to the previous tradition cited by Cazzaniga, the most notable fruits of which are the pamphlet of the Abbé Barruel and the "letter of Captain Simonini." From a Russian viewpoint, this does not matter as much as the fact that he adds the Bible Society, which had been active in Russia in the time of Alexander I from 1812–1826, and which, as Magnickij well knew, contained many Masons (the Masonic Review of the time was called *Sionskij vestnik*). So much so that

> The possibility of a Masonic agitation was born at the moment of the creation of the "Bible Society," indicating by this same fact the

appearance in Russia of "Spiritual Enlightenment" (Dudakov 1993b, 58).

The Protestant-Masonic synergy was denounced by Šmakov (1912, 493). However, in the course of the nineteenth century, many other sources also validating also the idea of the "Judaic-Masonic" Plot also reached Russia, and at the beginning of the twentieth century the compiler of the PSM had at his disposition a vast repertory, in which were found traditions, of which Ljutostanskij (1902, 1:188f.) offers a detailed map of the most disparate. Such themes, which have the fascination of being the knowledge of the initiated, are then used by those implicated in the compilation of the PSM or those close to them (Butmi 1906e, Šmakov 1912, Butmi N. 1914, Nilus 1917), and will find maniacal interpretations in Bostunič (1922 and 1928) and in Čerep-Spiridovič (1926).

Not only this, but from the logic of the plot, the nexus between the "plan of the Sages" and Freemasonry (the secret societies) is transformed into motivation to explain the origins of the PSM itself, both in the "apologetic" variant (the "Memphis and Mizraïm" Lodge) and the "critical" one (the relationships between Račkovskij and French occultism, of Glinka with Blavatskaja, and the Martinism of Papus and Philippe). This finds its most articulate exposition in Webb 1976.

What is the incidence of such a mythological complexity in the conception of the PSM? And, in particular, is it possible to identify at a textual level which specific traditions fit?

If one compares the titles of the first editions of the PSM, one notes that, in the syntagma "Judaic-Masonic," the *Masonic* element disappears from the titles of the PSM:

(K, 1903) *"...vsemirnogo sojuza franmasonov i sionskix mudrecov"*

(L, 1904) *"...iz massonsko-sionistskix protokolov"*

(A1, 1905) *"...Sionskix mudrecov Vsemirnogo obščestva Fran-Masonov"*

(R, 1905) *"...odnogo iz rukovoditelej Sionizma"*

(A2, 1905) *"...sionskix mudrecov"*

(N, 1905) *"...sionskix mudrecov"*

(B, 1905–1906) *"...iz tajnyx xranilišč Sionskoj Glavnoj Kanceljarii"*

K speaks of a "world alliance" which reunited Masons and the Sages of Zion, while A1 maintains that the "sages of Zion" are part of the "world society" of the Masons. In the title of A2, N, and B (but in reality already in Men'šikov 1902) the Masons make their exit from the Jewish Plot. The instability is evident, as is also the subordination of the "Masonic" to the "Jewish" component.

G. Butmi intervenes in the argument with a paper (1906f) which proves to be a mere disquisition on the libel of A. Rive *Les Juifs dans la Franc-Maçonnerie* (Paris 1895), but *in* the text of the PSM it speaks of Freemasonry essentially as a metaphor for a form of occult connivance, close to the notion of *solidarnost'* (as in the case of "the freemasonry of journalism" and of "our social freemasonry"), or as an instrument entirely in the hands of "unknown superiors", obviously Jews:

> However we have organized façade institutions, the Masonic Lodges, which make a show with their fine words of their worthy progressiveness (4th).

The "sages of Zion," as is indicated in the 12th Protocol, repeat the promise not to allow the Masonic organizations to survive the installation of the "Kingdom of the line of David." Its separate use of the "Jewish central command" is therefore instrumental and transitory:

> Until the moment we ascend our throne, we shall multiply and create **Masonic** Lodges in all the countries of the world," *but* "all these Lodges will be centralized under an unknown single directorate which will be constituted of our sages."

The 13th Protocol goes further, saying that Freemasonry could prove dangerous for the realisation of the "plan":

> But let us turn to **Freemasonry**. We have now already punished them for disobedience.... In this way, we have torn from **Masonic circles** the roots of any protest against our plans.

These statements (and it is completely irrelevant that they largely depend on Joly's text, that is—historically—to the attitude of Napoleon III toward secret societies) are substantially incompatible with K's title, according to which the "sages of Zion" would sit together with Freemasons in the same organization. The Protocols being the fruit of their joint meetings, there is little probability that the sages would let the Masons know of their intention to use and then eliminate them (Reznik [1988] puts the same thought into Men'šikov's mouth). However, this is also very unlikely as regards A1's title (in which Freemasonry was the water in which the fish-"sages" swam), because in an internal discourse (between "fish") it does not make sense to reveal their cover, which has been adopted for the outside world (the water). To substantiate this, one can cite a passage in the *Secret of Judaism,* which the writer of the PSM certainly did *not* know, dedicated to the "structure of the Jewish organisation":

> Freemasonry, seen in its visible entirety, represents only the army of the secret society; there is also a sort of general staff which operates in

the secret society a similar role to that of the central nervous system in the human body. In every Masonic Lodge...there are some capable and influential Masons who are at the same time members of a special secret confraternity, exclusively Jewish,"[9]

whose members (in the version of the PSM) were of course the "sages of Zion."

However, the third edition (1905) modified the first sentence of the *Translator's Note* by having the text signed by "Representatives of Zion of the 33rd degree," and with this introduced a strong "Masonic" connotation into the Myth of the Jewish Plot. The mention of the "33rd degree" comes from Msgr. Meurin (*La Franc-Maçonnerie, Synagogue de Satan* [Paris 1893], who was in turn indebted to Leo Taxil[10]), who not only holds that

everything in Freemasonry is fundamentally Jewish, exclusively Jewish, passionately Jewish from beginning to end; (p. 260; cited in Cohn 1969, 26),

but also advances the existence of mysterious "behind-the-scenes lodges" (undercover, or secret) who are responsible for all the revolutions that break out in the world, and asserts that such lodges "consist of Masons and Jews *"of the 33rd degree"* [my italics; ed.].

Naturally the problem is not to establish how the highest grade of the "Scottish ancient and accepted rite" has come in Meurin to designate the "nomenclature" of the Judaic-Masonic Plot, but rather to ascertain how such an idea was transmitted from the Archbishop of Port Louis to the editor of the third edition of the PSM.[11] It is even more difficult to understand how and why the Masonic component, which was about to withdraw from the idea of the Judaic-*Masonic* Plot, was then exhumed. Nilus reinforces the concept of another addition to the 9th Protocol, which takes up again the theme of the "secret lodges":

Our organization of a secret Freemasonry, unknown to [those] *beasts of "gojim" (of which they did not suspect even the purposes) which we have attracted into the frontline army of the Masonic Lodges to hypnotize their co-nationals.*

All this indulgence in fantasies about Freemasonry, both openly and secretly, on the part of the Russians at the beginning of the twentieth century, is anything but obvious. Russian Freemasonry had been banned in 1822 by Alexander I, and even down to 1905 (when the PSM appeared in its second and third edition) there was not even one Masonic Lodge in Russia.[12] This obviously does not mean that there were no Russian Masons, but as members however of foreign lodges, above all the *Grand Orient de France*. However, out of over four hundred Deputies at the 1st State Duma, there were in all three (!) Russian subjects already members of French Freemasonry. Two of these joined the *ka-dety* group, where there were more than one hundred Deputies, and one, M. M. Kovalevskij, formed a separate group, "The Party of Democratic Reforms."[13]

The "Judaic-*Masonic*" nature of the PSM was therefore thought up in a country where Freemasonry did not exist. When, in 1917, the "Judaic-Masonic" thesis was re-proposed in the *Extract* of the PSM attributed to Herzl, nothing better could be found than to attribute it to a supposed *American* Masonic document of 46 years earlier.[14] This could have led to the conclusion that the entire mythological system had been imported from abroad (as, in effect, various fragments had been imported: Msgr. Meurin, A. De La Rive, A. Chabry, etc.[15]

The rejection both of Freemasonry and of other confessions (especially if of Protestant origin[16]) than Orthodoxy was a trait typical of more conservative Russian circles from the seventeenth century onwards, as is shown in a brilliant pamphlet in verse which Count Adam Olsuf'ev (one of the principal aides to Catherine the Great) put into the mouth of the "old-believer" Ivan Danylič,[17] who admonishes those who seek salvation (among other things) from:

Those who sprawl down on seeing a *popizon*,[18]

A pastor, a *pater*,[19] a Waldensian or a Freemason,....

thus lumping together with Masons and Protestants (and "Papists") the priest of the "official" Orthodox Church. Olsuf'ev is joking, but a few decades earlier, Magnickij (it is difficult to say whether more from conviction or calculation) had treated the matter as extremely serious.

Magnickij's denunciation of the "Judaic-Masonic" Plot against altar and throne dates from 1831, the year of the first Polish Revolt.[20] Two years later, F. Bulgarin in *Mazepa* named it as "Jesuitical-Judaic-Gynecratic," attaching to it the maledictions of "Ivan Danylič" of fifty to sixty years before, and comparing it with the *Polish Catechism* of thirty years later, at the time of the second Polish Revolt. The diachronic conspiracy of a radically hybrid conception is revealed in the sense that "Masonic" can tranquilly pass for (or be substituted for) "Jesuitical"; "Jewish" for "Protestant" (and even for "Catholic"); and all is held together by an evident xenophobic glue.

It is no great discovery that at the basis of the Judeo-phobic fantasies there lies a xenophobic propensity, even if it is inappropriate to reduce antisemitism to xenophobia. Yet explaining this fact within a concrete Russian referent allows us to better read some elements of the PSM, which otherwise can seem only "foreign." I refer in particular to the connotations, which are both "Pontifical" and "Puritan," of the future King of the line of David which, if they can (partially) be matched with Joly's plagiarized text, diverge from the figure of Napoleon III especially for the accentuated syncretism which conditions the image of the "King of the line of David."[21]

It is useless then to say that the "Masonic" variant put forward by Butmi in 1906, followed by Fry in 1931, and re-proposed by Begunov in 1996, is so improbable at the level of Masonic history to prove how still today references to Masonry remain in Russia an esoteric *topos*.

The "Judaic-Masonic" Plot as we find it in the PSM, which they would wish to be the most evident factual testimony of it, reveals itself to be therefore a ideologeme of a specifically Russian nature and validity, which dilutes its eccentricity in a conceptual mixture of connotations which are both more threatening to, and distant from, the actual historical reality of the phenomenon to which they are referring.

The writers of the PSM want us to believe that they constitute a self evident testimony to the existence of a "Judaic-Masonic" Plot. The PSM reveal themselves however to be an ideologeme of a specifically "Russian" nature and validity, whose eccentricity is watered down with a conceptual mix of connotations which are even more threatening to humanity than they are distant from any historical reality of the plot they claim to refer to.

NOTES

1. G. M. Cazzaniga, *Massoneria, sette segrete politiche e origine del socialismo. Rassegna bibliografica universale ragionata* (unpl. ms. 1996).

2. S. Markish, *Erasme et les Juifs* (Lausanne 1979), 94.

3. J. Katz, *Jews and Freemasons in Europe, 1723–1939* (Cambridge, Mass. 1970).

4. Cf. A. Černov, "Magnickij M. L.," RP 3 (1994): 448–49.

5. *Sud'ba Rossii*; cf. F. Dostoevskij, *Dnevnik pisatelja* (June 1876); PSS, 23:33: "Despite Magnickij and Liprandi, already in the last century every European movement had become immediately known to us."

6. T. Bakounine, *Répetoire biographique des Francs-Maçons russes (XVIII & XIX siècles)* (Paris 1967), 318. For the history of the Bible Society in Russia, cf. V. Ovčinnikov, *Britanskoe i inostrannoe biblejskoe obščestvo v Rossii*, in AA. VV., *Rossija i Evropa. Diplomatija i kul'tura* (Moscow 1995).

7. Cf. N. Šil'der, "Dva donosa v 1831 g.," *Russkaja starina*, January–March 1899.

8. Reznik 1988 puts the same thought into Men'šikov's mouth.

9. In Delevskij 1923, 153. The image of the "army" and the "general staff" comes from Osman Bey 1891, 6 (who spoke however of Nihilism, not Freemasonry).

10. Who was very popular in the USSR thanks to his anti-religious writings: *La bible amusante* (1882) was translated in 1926 *(Zabavnaja Biblija)* and republished several times through 1961.

11. Meurin's book appears in Šmakov's 1897 *Bibliografija.*

12. Avrex 1990, 234. The first Russian lodges were reconstituted towards the end of 1906.

13. Starcev 1996, 47–48.

14. The "Pike Document" *(How to Annihilate Russia)* of 1871; cf. Chap. 1, n. 76.

15. Even Wolski 1887 turns out to be a pastiche of Brafman 1869, of the "Rabbi's Discourse" and of *Les Juifs rois de l'époque,* by A. Toussenel (Paris 1845; cf. Klier 1995, 499).

16. "Masonry went had in hand with Protestantism" (Šmakov 1912, 493); cf. also "Russkoe masontsvo i sektantstvo," in Dudakov 1993.

17. "Simvol very Ivana Daniliča," in *Devič'ja igruška, ili Sočinenija gospodina Barkova* (Moscow 1992), and S. Garzonio, 'Cikl ob Ivane Daniloviče' v issledovanii M. M. Nikitina," *Study Group on Eighteenth Century Russia. Newsletter* 20 (1992). I am citing the text from the second edition.

18. A slang term for "a pop (pope) of the official "nikonian" Russian Orthodox Church

19. Obviously "Catholic priest."

20. The demonstration in Warsaw on January 25, 1831 for the Decabrists had provoked the decision of the Polish Sejm to depose Nicholas I from the Polish Throne. This was enough to generate the suspicion of a vast plot.

21. In their own way, also Baigent, Leigh, and Lincoln are right when they ask (Italian trans., *Il Santo Graal,* 203): "When someone forges a document so as to attribute it to a Jewish plot, why include echoes that are so avidly Christian? Why speak of a specifically and unequivocally Christian like a Pope?" Only that, not being able to give the question a textually based reply, they go off on a tangent about the "Priorate of Zion."

CHAPTER 10

Russian Judeo-phobia and Italian Antisemitism

"It is often asked whether an unknown orchestral conductor did not direct the tumult provoked...by the simultaneous appearance of the PSM in the principal countries of the world."[1] In the fifteen years after they appeared in Russia (between the end of 1918[2] and 1920), there were German,[3] Swedish,[4] Polish,[5] English,[6] American,[7] Hungarian,[8] and French[9] translations.

The PSM appeared immediately after the war in Italy too, but a little later and in secondary translations. We first hear of it in March 1920:

> No. VIII of the secret Zionist report or protocol of 1897 ended with the following words: "We must force the goy government to favor by their actions a vast plan of our conception.... We will manifest our power to some of these governments with assassinations and terror.[10]

In June, P. Misciattelli (of a Russian mother, Avrora Buturlinà[11]) introduced in *Il Resto del Carlino* the first English edition of the PSM.[12] He claimed not to be antisemitic, but—in his words—the Jewish manoeuvre explained what was going on in the world. Two months later, a Milan daily referred to the articles with which the *Morning Post* had exposed the thesis of a world conspiracy, with references to the PSM:

> In 1903 a Russian, Sergio Nilus, published a book entitled *The Great in the Small*; in the second edition of the book the text of 24 Protocols of the Elders of Zion is reported, which Nilus had purloined.[13]

L'Osservatore Romano took up the story of the PSM,[14] validating their "truthfulness" without supporting their authenticity:

> In our opinion *their* Jewish provenance remains doubtful.... It is possible that [*Nilus*] had invented them. However, what remains without doubt is that the subversive ideas which they express, are really the same as those that animate the Jews in Russia.... The Jewish danger is verily not a vain one.

Already the year before, however,

> typed copies [*of the PSM*] in various languages were beginning to circulate among the delegates at the Peace Conference [of Versailles],

and they even made their appearance on the desks of ministers and officials in London, Paris, **Rome**, and Washington (Cohn 1969, 93).

I have found no evidence of this information for that which regards Italy. However, the Foreign Minister followed the phenomenon of antisemitism throughout the civil war and one cannot exclude the possibility that, in some way, the PSM also passed through the hands of Italian diplomacy.

At the beginning of 1921, the PSM was advertised in a review by Preziosi[15] who was the first to publish them. This immediately gave rise to bitter polemic.[16] Since then there have been five Italian translations:

1. G. Preziosi (Rome 1921), from Nilus via G. Shanks's English trans.;

2. U. Benigni (Florence 1921) from Nilus via E. Jouin's French 1920 trans.[17];

3. Anon. I (Milan 1938), from the Russian of Nilus[18];

4. Anon. II (Florence 1943), from Nilus via H. Coston's French trans., in Creutz (1934);

5. Anon. III (Lucera 1972), from Nilus via R. Lambelin's French trans.[19]

Successive reprints all use the Preziosi translation,[20] so that in Italy the PSM have only been known through the Nilus edition, and even more through the English translation, illustrated by the following scheme[21]:

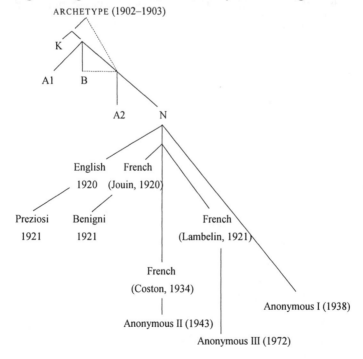

Their coming from a Russia rocked by revolution, conditioned from the beginning the interpretation of the PSM with its nexus between Bolshevism and "the Jewish Plot." Even though it was obscured by the story of its "Parisian" origin and by the trans-national idea of Judaism, the Russian connection remained determinant. The attribution to the Odessa Jew, A. Gincberg, put forward by L. Fry and spreading rapidly among the zealots, obviously reinforced such an approach.

The relationship of the PSM with the Russian world thus becomes decisive also in Italy. The question of the relationship between Russian and Italian Judeo-phobia is therefore essential to the understanding of the "soil" into which the PSM were transplanted, and the point of reference by which they are to be understood.

A systematic task of documentation in such a sense has never been undertaken, and here I shall restrict myself to some particularly significant cases.

The first is only tangentially "Russian" and predates the era of the PSM. Osman Bey (1836–1901?),[22] a character with a mania for self-promotion which bordered on the grotesque, is one of most malign figures in nineteenth century antisemitism. Considered by many to be a renegade Jew (according to some, from Serbia,[23] to others, Romania[24]), he has even been identified as the French student of Turkish antiquities, J. A. Decourdemanche.[25] In reality, he was Frederick, the second son of Julius Michael Millingen,[26] an English doctor who went to Greece to follow Byron and then settled in Constantinople,[27] and Marie Dejean (1816–1874), a French woman resident there. However, "it was in Russia, and via the Russian anti-Semitic movement, that [*Osman Bey*] sought to make his career."[28]

He was, therefore, an Englishman who, between the Ottoman Empire of his birth and the Russian one of his profession, was brought up in Rome, where his mother had sought refuge in 1837. His father had written a pamphlet claiming that his sons had been kidnapped by "papists."[29] In July 1838 he was

> solemnly admitted into the bosom of the Catholic Church and to this end, Cardinal [*Carlo*] Odescalchi [*1786–1841*], Vicar to His Holiness, was given the task of baptizing him according to the rites of the Roman Church. His godfather was Prince Pietro Odescalchi [*1789–1839*], the Cardinal's brother, and his godmother [*sic!*] was Princess Luigia de Bourbon, ex-Queen of Saxony.[30]

After his mother had left Rome (Osman Bey [1877a] 1882, 75),[31] he remained at his aunt's and studied at the Roman College until at the time of the Roman Republic, the father managed to reclaim his children.[32]

Frederick often returned to Italy, but soon began his peregrinations around the globe. Upon reaching adulthood, he made for the Ottoman Empire to stay with Kibrizli-Pasha,[33] where he took up a military career and the Muslim faith with the name of Osman-Seify-Bey.[34]

His Turkish experience did not last long. In 1864[35] he headed for New York, and the following year, Paris. In 1871 he was in Romania to sing the praises of Hellenism,[36] while in 1872 he was in Venice and Trieste. After having published an essay in Russia on the female condition in Turkey (1873a), he moved there in 1874 thanks to the refuge offered him by Alexander II whom he had contacted from Ems, the same year in which his pamphlet on "The Jews' plan to conquer the world"[37] appeared. Here, with a new baptism (Orthodox), he took the name of Vladimir Andreevič and became completely Russian in everything. During the Russian-Turkish war, he put all his "Ottoman" military experience at the disposition of the Russians.[38]

His antisemitism was unleashed by anti-English resentment which had had its roots in his bad relationship with his father, and was then reinforced in the years of the Disraeli[39] government, which he saw as evidence of a submerged Anglo-Jewish synergy. The 1873 pamphlet is the most celebrated contribution to the "cause" which earned him fame as a paranoid hoaxer[40] but also a certain credit from the police. Arriving at St. Petersburg in June 1881, three months after the assassination of Alexander II, he was taken on by Pleve to track down the sources of the nihilist plot which he did triumphantly in Paris at the headquarters of the *Alliance Israélite Universelle*. He gave an account of this in a memoir which appeared in serial form in 1883 in an Italian paper[41] and then in volume form in German and French.

On his peregrinations, in search of money as much as Jews, he often returned to Italy. In Venice, where we find him once again in 1880, his booklet went through two editions. In 1883, he was in Rome, then in Florence staying with P. Demidov,[42] then in Salerno, where he returned in 1885.[43] In Milan, during the visit of the Russian Foreign Minister,[44] accused by him of every baseness and moreover of being a Jew,[45] he published another booklet in which he prophesied that

> a daughter will come into the world and she will be called *War*....
> Hostilities will break out with a massacre of the Jews, with a
> catastrophe that will strike humanity with horror.[46]

He finally settled in France and lastly in Nice where he published some monographs, the last of which applauded the excommunication of Tolstoj, who is indicated as the *"true Lucifer"* as opposed to that *"Jewish Satan"* that Lord Beaconsfield had been. When almost seventy (1901), he represented himself as *"L'Éteigneur sur les Judéo-nichilistes"* and *"the Savior of Alexander III."* The first version of the "discovery" of the PSM (that it had been stolen in Nice "which at that time had been chosen as the secret capital of Judaism"; Men'šikov 1902) is probably connected with his presence in the city. The story of the theft twenty years earlier in Paris in the headquarters of the *Alliance Israélite Universelle* was the prototype for that of the theft at Nice in 1901.

The Italian edition of his pamphlet did not pass unnoticed. *Il Tempo* of Venice wrote that the material was a pamphlet ("or rather *with an aggression*")

> of which we do not know the motivation, nor understand the aim, nor find the justification,[47]

S. Beruatto, a philo-Jewish evangelical, argues:

> if Osman Bey's pamphlet...wants to proclaim a veritable crusade against [the Jews], we, on the other hand, want...to return their land and nationality to this people,[48]

while an activist of early Italian socialism, one "Spartaco," replied with a salacious pamphlet.[49]

His writings had, therefore, a certain effect. His "revelations" on Nihilism were taken up by an ex-combatant of the Crimea in a booklet on Russia,[50] and in the years of the Racial Laws *Gli ebrei alla conquista del mondo* was exhumed under the editorship of "an Italian lady patrician of distinction," who proposed it as the forerunner of the cause.[51] The *Preface* said that "many of the ideas in this booklet fermented later...in the vigorous anti-Jewish pages of our Pietro Ellero"; and he was not alone, because in 1914 Francesco Gaeta also took advantage of them in his book on "Jewish-Masonry."[52]

Russian antisemitism was followed with attention. In 1891 an anonymous *Letter from an Italian citizen to His Majesty the Tsar Alexander III...to implore clemency for Russian Jewry* was published in Florence. When at the dawn of the new century the *pogromy* recurred (and the PSM appeared), many condemned the anti-Jewish fury. In 1903, two booklets came out in Rome: *I massacri di Kiscineff* (The massacres of Kiscineff), by R. Prato, and a pamphlet, *La Russia e i fatti di Kicheneff* (Russia and the facts about Kicheneff), by Rossana (Z. Centi-Tartarini). In Turin, there appeared in a single issue, *La protesta civile contro le stragi di Kiscinew* (The civil protest against the massacres at Kiscinew) with articles by various writers (including C. Lombroso, A. Graf, and A. Fogazzaro). *Nuova Antologia* (16 December

1903) published one of the stories Tolstoj had written for the victims of the *pogrom.*[53]

The concern for the Russian Jews grew in 1905. The rabbi S. Margulies gave a lecture (later printed) on *I nostri martiri di Russia* (Our martyrs in Russia) and the Treves publishing house published a miscellany on the "Russian Question"[54] with a lengthy essay by M. Virtus (*Gli ebrei* [The Jews]) which underlined the role of *Novoe vremja* (in which Men'šikov had "introduced" the PSM)[55] in the antisemitic campaign and referred to the activities of Kruševan who "over many years preached in the newspaper *Bessarabetz* a crusade against the Jews."

During the First World War, the Hoepli publishing house published *La Russia d'oggi* (The Russia of today) by F. Livchiz (Milan 1916) which spoke of the "radicals and revolutionaries of reaction,... the organizers of *pogroms* against the Jews" (p. 196), and also of the "moderate" right of Stolypin, who promoted a "purely "zoological" nationalism, a nationalism which is basěd on the concept of race" (p. 199). However, the PSM gave rise to some comment despite the fact that their many editions and reprints had given rise to little interest in a Russia where in 1906 they had been recognized as apocryphal.

Even the Italian government was on the alert. In 1892, the ambassador at St. Petersburg wrote to the Foreign Ministry (MAE) to keep him informed on "the Israelites in Russia."[56] Some ten years later, the Vice Consul at Odessa informed the government of the *pogrom* of Kišiněv (April 25, 1903 and May 3, 1903), revealing the role of Kruševan:

> Nothing, however, was said (*in the Police Circular*) about the insinuating action by the anti-Semitic journalist Kruscevan, whose paper [*Bessarabec*] for a long time did nothing but seek to foment hatred against the Jews.[57]

During the Civil War, Italy kept an agent in the territory of Denikin, from whom often came news of anti-Jewish persecutions.[58] F. Medici di Marignano sent (November 21, 1919) some information on "Antisemitism in Russia," appending an article from *Večernee Vremja* (4/17 November 1919) by B. Suvorin. Other news on the subject arrived from "the Committee of the Jewish Delegations" at the Versailles Peace Conference.[59]

Between 1919 and 1922, the question of the "Jewish role" in the Bolshevik Revolution was raised by several parties, among them also B. Mussolini,[60] while a pamphlet of the "Pro-Israele"[61] and the book by a naval commander of Jewish origin[62] denounced the persecutions in the Ukraine.

Very soon the echoes of those events came close to home. After the revolution and the civil war, emigration also touched Italy.[63] Some of the

158 Cesare G. De Michelis

Russians who settled in Italy shared the positions on emigration of the extreme right. Such was A. Amfiteatrov,[64] who adhered to the *Bratstvo russkoj pravdy,* an organization which was "a secret terrorist one, completely imbued with the psychosis of the PSM" (Rollin 1991, 88), with General Pëtr Krasnov (who himself would also be in Italy towards the end of the Second World War and who fought against the Partisans with his "Cossacks of Friuli"), along with many others blessed by Bishop Antonij, already Metropolitan of Kiev (and also already a member of the *Sojuz russkogo naroda*).

It is disconcerting to find, behind that good-natured epitome of Russian humour (*Intorno al Samovar* [Around the samovar] [Milan 1931]), the shadow of the Black Hundred,[65] or better, of those para-Fascist emigrant circles which, in the mortal combat with Soviet power, adopted the means once attributed to the supposed "sages of Zion."[66]

However, significant active Russian antisemitism in Italy has passed almost unnoticed. Introducing the essay of R. De Felice on the Jews in the Fascist era, D. Cantimori wrote that

> In 1939, under the authorship of a Prince N. Gewakhow,... there appeared in Rome a slim volume on the *Background of the "Protocols."*... The author...tells that in 1920...only Pantaleoni shared his opinions.... Pantaleoni had introduced the Russian to Preziosi, who however attributed to the *Protocols*..."only scientific and not political importance."[67] (De Felice 1961, xvii).

The episode recorded by Cantmori was taken up by M. T. Pichetto (1983, 43) with the addition, however, that

> Preziosi...holds that Pantaleoni never knew Gevakhow and that he gave these directly to him.

And in effect, in an insertion of 1942, Preziosi accused the Prince of "bad faith and impudence," of "suffering from fantasies," and concluded that "the Italians have nothing to learn from the said Russian prince."

Nikolaj Davidovič Ževaxov (1874–1947)[68] is undoubtedly an interesting character, today exhumed by the Russian Right,[69] and if his Russian writings were not of note in Italy, abroad his book on the PSM has been ignored above all just because it appeared in Italian. As for Preziosi's accusations, they merit separate examination.

Already substituted by the penultimate Procurator of the Holy Synod, N. Raev,[70] his presence in Italy at Bari had been originally the result of the building of an Orthodox Church beside a hostel for pilgrims, organized by the Imperial Orthodox Society of Palestine presided over by Elizaveta

Fedorovna, widow of the Grand Duke Sergej Aleksandrovič: General M. Stepanov, brother of the eponymous first publisher of the PSM was an assistant of the presidency.[71]

Ževaxov undertook to carry out the project himself (to the displeasure of the Archbishop of Bari, who perceived "schismatic" competition[72]), and presided over the laying of the foundation stone.[73] The architect of the project was A. Ščusev, the future constructor of Lenin's Mausoleum.[74]

In February 1920, Ževaxov took refuge in Serbia where he established close relations with monarchist emigrants, even if he met with many reservations regarding his conviction that the Russian tragedy was caused by the Jews.[75] After several months, on September 13, he reappeared in Bari where he settled.

During his stay in Italy, he occupied himself with the long dispute with the Soviet Government over the ownership of the Bari site. From an internal dispute within the small Russian community (begun before the Fascist coup d'état), it became, over the years, an "affaire" of great significance. It involved not only the Soviet Embassy in Rome and the Italian one in Moscow, but the Foreign Ministries of both countries, as well as the Italian Government at the highest level (Mussolini), the official institutions (the King and Queen), and King Boris of Bulgaria. Even the British Foreign Office interested itself in the matter.

According to Ževaxov and his supporters, they were attempting to save the Bari church from the clutches of an atheist Government, but the question gave rise to a serious rift inside the Russian Orthodox Church itself.[76] For the Soviet authorities, on the other hand, their credibility in international relations was in question. An acceptable solution was reached for both parties: an Italian citizen, F. Rodriguez, would advance credit to the Soviet Government.[77] Litvinov made the settling of the indemnity (with the eventual ceding of "all or part of the valuables...situated in Italy") conditional on the recognition of the

> legitimate possession of the Church of Bari and its property by the Soviet Society for Palestine, that is to say the Government of the USSR.[78]

The idea of an exchange was then proposed. Once the courts had decided to assign the property to the Russian Society for Palestine (November 13, 1936), the dispute ended with the purchase of the church by the Comune (City Council) of Bari.

The affair placed the fascist regime in an uncomfortable position. Ideally, it was completely on the side of the interests represented by Ževaxov, but it was also most careful not to damage the excellent relations it enjoyed with the USSR (which in fact in 1933–1934 reached their apex). Ževaxov, on the other hand, lived out his battle against the "Bolsheviks" amid internal disputes within the Russian emigrant community and difficult relations with the Italian Government, which in his eyes represented the final bulwark against the Bolsheviks themselves.

The role he carried out in validating the PSM has to be seen against this background. More than occupying himself with the Russian church, he sought to gain credit in the higher spheres of the regime for political ends. These usually rejected him, however. This had something to do with the fact that while he defended Orthodoxy in the case of Bari and proclaimed to Mussolini his commitment to "moral and state obligations,"[79] Ževaxov was called into court with the following charges:

> This day 30 January [1931], you are summoned to appear before the Pretore (judge) of Foggia at the hearing of 11th next to face charges of gross indecency committed at Foggia on 6 November 1930 with a minor: a sixteen year old boy.[80]

He was acquitted due to insufficient evidence, but the Foggia affair cost him dear, affecting the success of his requests for financial assistance and his "political" ambitions.

His book on the PSM remains, however, one of the few texts of Russian antisemitism which appeared in Italy and, despite his fruitless attempts to make contact with Mussolini, one still finds the PSM among the books the Fascist dictator had with him at the time of the Republic of Salò.[81] Apart from the books of Ževaxov and the pages of Nilus published by Preziosi, it is only possible to find the translation of General Nečvolodov,[82] which we also find, in the original edition, among Mussolini's books.[83]

This is the version of the booklet *Sergej Aleksandrovič Nilus* which appeared three years earlier at Novi Sad,[84] however, to which had been added a second part (*I "Protocolli dei savi anziani di Sion" e il loro significato* (The "Protocols of the Learned Elders of Zion" and their meaning), the summary of which corresponds to the second part found in the Russian edition (*"Sionskie protokoly" i ix značenie*). This appears only in Italian and, even though it is mostly made up of material taken from L. Fry, as Preziosi will reveal, it merits greater attention. As regards the last two parts (*Podlinnost' "Sionskix protokolov" i Popytki ix opreverženija* and *Bernskij process*[85]), it does not appear that they were ever published; that is, if they were ever written.

Nikolaj Ževaxov was not only a friend[86] and correspondent of Nilus, he was also the brother of Vladimir (1874–1938)[87] on whose estate of Linovica (Ukraine) Nilus settled with his wife from the summer of 1917 until April

1923, and where he continued to make visits as long as it was still possible. (Ževaxov 1939, 52).

Even allowing that he was "a sinister character at the confines between religious mania and witchcraft" (Laqueur 1991, 139), Ževaxov had every right to express his opinions on the PSM, as the reviewer of the magazine *Tempo di Mussolini* (7–12, 1939)[88] pointed out. His firm opinion that the PSM should be attributed to Ašer Gincberg appears however not so much the candid conviction, or the tardy discovery, of a "religious maniac" as the "last resort" of one who, aware of the forgery, kept to the most suitable thesis that would defend the authenticity of the PSM.[89]

Before settling in Italy, Ževaxov was in Germany. In Berlin in November 1928 he came into contact with Ernst zu Reventlow, Ludwig Müller von Hausen, Max Erwin von Scheubner-Richter[90] and Arno Schickedanz (ibid. 83–84). On January 16, 1922, he moved to Munich (ibid., 86), got to know Marshal Ludendorff and socialised with Russian emigrants, in particular Colonel F. Vinberg and his lieutenant P. Šabel'skij-Bork,[91] the publishers of the magazine which reprinted the PSM. Vinberg published the first volume of his *Vospominanija* (1923).[92] Šabel'skij-Bork remained in correspondence with him and in 1925 he contacted Mussolini (together with S. Taborickij, from the prison in which he was held for the assassination of Vl. Nabokov) to support the case of the church in Bari.[93]

In October 1926 he moved to New York (Ževaxov 1939, 154). Here he met Artur Čerep-Spiridovič (promoter of the campaign of the PSM in the United States [Rollin 1991, 611] and a "clinical case."[94] In March 1931, he moved to Paris over the question of the Bari church.[95] Then he made a trip to the Trans-Carpathians, and published a slim volume at Chișineu (Ževaxov 1934c), which in some ways was the "birthplace" of the PSM[96] and which at that time belonged to Romania, where antisemitism was deeply rooted.

Therefore in the 1920s and 1930s, Gewakhow represented in Italy a direct intermediary between Black Hundred circles dispersed in the various centers of emigration and rising National Socialism.

In Italy he was in contact with certain nationalists later to be fascist personalities in sympathy with his anti-Jewish beliefs:

> The first of these—he wrote twenty years later (Ževaxov 1942, 21)— was Senator Maffeo Pantaleoni[97].... The second...was...Alfredo Rocco[98].... The minister Arrigo Solmi[99] *was* a third dignitary"

to believe him, and so much that he wrote the *Preface* to the Italian Edition of a part of his *Memorie* (Memoirs) (1942). Obviously, besides these, G. Preziosi (1881–1945) should be remembered, to whose accusations against Ževaxov it is now time to return. The gravest thing referred to by Preziosi to the detriment to the credibility of the Prince is the fantastic story concerning the reason for his having been in America:

Where he had gone to accompany the Tsar....

—The Tsar?!!!

The Prince took both my hands and, with much widening of the eyes:

—Yes the Tsar. No one else but you knows. The Tsar is alive!....

—But, and the tragedy at Ekaterinburg?...

—All a trick prepared by us, rather prepared by me, with the help of a faithful few. The night before the carrying out of the sentence, the Tsar and his family were substituted and carried into safety. And to avoid recognition of the assassinated, the corpses were burned and in their ashes were put the jewels that the Tsar and the Tsarina habitually wore.

Preziosi remembers on the contrary "the news that the American press had published at the time about the Grand Duchess Anastasia," but while having his leg pulled by the "fairy tales" of the Prince, he did not take into account the Russian tradition of "false-Tsars" and of fabulous stories about them,[100] nor the fact that at that time such beliefs were fairly widely held.[101] Naturally all this does not mean that, if Ževaxov's tale was not quite like this that it was not a "piece of fantasy" but was systematic, and certainly was less dangerous than his hallucinatory denunciations of the "invisible government" (of the Jews, naturally) which would have eliminated, one after the other, the Russian Emperors from Paul I (1801) onwards.[102] It is, therefore, not so different from the ideas of the same PSM, in which, on the other hand, the Italian racists made a good show of believing. In conclusion, the accusations made against him are not the *cause* of the attack, but the instruments of the denigration.

What drove Preziosi, in June 1942, to attack Ževaxov? In that insertion he said:

Prince N. Gevakhow...in his book *Il Retroscena dei Protocolli* (The background to the Protocols)...(Rome 1939-XVII) **which only recently has come to my notice...."**

Yet how could this be? Could the publisher of the PSM, the editor of the review which—well before the Racial Laws—had conducted a long anti-Jewish campaign, have become aware *only in 1942* of a book on the PSM written by an acquaintance of Nilus, printed three years earlier in Rome and reviewed by his colleague J. Evola? And why wait fifteen years (1927–1942) to denounce the author as an untrustworthy charlatan rather than one who was healthily antisemitic?

In 1942 the political activities of Preziosi were becoming more influential,[103] thanks to his "distinguished" anti-Jewishness, and suddenly a stateless alien with a murky past appears, and has the temerity to claim that he, Preziosi, had once said that

> *For us the Jewish Question does not exist,* our Jews are patriots like all other Italians...and nothing gives us any occasion *to suspect them of betraying our national interests* (Preziosi 1942, 592; my italics, C.D.M.)

However, in another moment (August 1920), to parry the reactions created by the article *L'Internazionale Ebraica* (The Jewish International), he had freely asserted that

> Anti-Semitism is repugnant to our Italian liberal conscience [?!], to the Jews we do not ever deny the right of political liberty *until they reach the point of becoming an instrument* of the dissolution of Italy *in the service of* foreign political and economic *interests and anti-nationalism.* (my italics, C.D.M.)[104]

One should not be surprised that in those later years he referred in these terms to the Russian prince, who in his ingenuous attempt to offer to the Italian state his experience as a Russian antisemite, pure and simple, had got everything wrong. After having first reproved Mussolini for his excessive openness towards Soviet Russia, now, to show off his own anti-Jewish convictions, he put those of Preziosi[105] in doubt, at that very moment when the Italian was beginning to become someone, and when, vice versa, the Russian's own image was coming under a cloud both for the Foggian incident and his lunatic words on the "tsar who is not dead."

The truth is the contrary of what Preziosi wrote. In fact, concerning antisemitism Italy would have had much "to learn from that Russian prince," who, not by chance, was involved in the most bitter exchange on the PSM, the Bern Process. Or at least, using his own fanatical availability, they would have been able to have from him a direct translation of the PSM, without having to trust to the double errors of a second hand version.

But perhaps they did have it, but were unaware of this.

There exists an Italian translation of the PSM made directly from the text of *Luč sveta* 1920, which is "still wrapped in mystery as regards its editors": *Chi sono questi ebrei! I protocolli dei saggi di Sion. Sensazionale documentario* (Who are these Jews! The Protocols of the Sages of Zion. Sensational documentary) (Milan 1938).[106] This version, very free, almost a summary, is preceded by a note (*Che cosa sono I "Protocolli" dei saggi di Sion* [What are the "Protocols" of the sages of Zion]) which does not appear to have been written by an Italian and such a slip appears more typically Russian than Italian. Some French borrowings (*demoralizovannyj,* from *démoraliser* [to demoralize]) are rendered with incorrect notes, which make a not inconsiderable shift of meaning ("[*a society*] rendered immoral," rather than "demoralized"). Therefore, instead of being fairly free flowing, the version confirms the impression of the introductory note, that it cannot be by an Italian.

Ževaxov obviously knew the *Luč sveta* edition.[107] The note to the text repeats common passages, but in a form that is very similar to that that one finds in Ževaxov 1939. It is very possible that in a difficult moment of his life (the final loss of the church at Bari) but one extraordinarily propitious for the diffusion of the PSM, he had agreed to edit anonymously a new translation directly from the Russian. For the rest, he gained the merit of having agreed to let the Italian public know the "most important extracts" of Russian antisemitic writing ("This work has been entrusted to me," Ževaxov 1939, 17), and they knew no other contributions of the genre.

The Italian social circles in which the Russian Judeo-phobes moved (from Vladimir Andreevič Osman Bey, with his thesis of "the Jewish world conquest", to Nikolaj Davidovič Ževaxov, with his guaranteeing of the PSM) intersects with the antisemitic activities of Italians who had special contacts with the Russian world[108] The two were in conjunction at the darkest moment of antisemitism in Italy: the time of the Racial Laws in 1938.

NOTES

1. Rollin 1991, 604.

2. "In October 1918 a German who had lived in Russia brought quite by chance these notes [scil.: the PSM] from Moscow" (*Luč sveta* 1920, 100).

3. *Die Geheimnisse der Weisen von Zion* (Charlottemburg 1919).

4. *Sions vises hemliga protokoll* (Helsingfors 1919).

5. *Protokuly posiedzen mędrców Sjonu* (Warsaw (n.d., ?December 1919).

6. *Protocols of the Learned Elders of Zion* (London, (n.d., ?2 December 1919).

7. *Protocols of the Meetings of the Zionist Men of Wisdom* (Boston 1920). The *Public Ledger* (Philadelphia), 27–28 October 1919, had already published lengthy extracts.

8. *Cion Bölcseinek Jegyzökönyvei* (Vienna 1920).

9. *"Protocols." Procès-verbaux des réunions secrètes des Sages d'Israël* (Paris 1920); *L'Opinion* (5, 12, and 19 June 1920) had already published an abridged version

entitled *Les origines du bolchevisme: procès-verbaux des sages de Zion* (cf. Rollin 1991, 39).

10. "Spectator," "Sinedrio e Triangolo o sia la grande congiura ebraico-massonica internazionale," *Fede e Ragione* (March 1920): 279. The news came from the report by B. Brazol' (from which it repeats the title; cf. Chap. 11, No. 13) which U. Benigni incudes among *I documenti della conquista ebraica del mondo.*

11. A branch of the ancient family who had established themselves in Florence, where the poet Pëtr Buturlin (1859–1895) was born.

12. *Imperialismo massimalista,* 12 June 1920, which reworks G. Preziosi ("the only one who in Italy was interested" [in the PSM] was Piero Misciatelli in *Resto del Carlino*; *La Vita Italiana,* 15 August 1920).

13. G. Agnino, "Una trama infernale," *La Perseveranza* 15 August 1920).

14. *Un pericolo,* 15 October 1920.

15. "Il pericolo ebraico. I protocolli dei 'Savi Anziani di Sion,'" *La Vita Italiana,* 15 February 1921).

16. G. Prezzolini, *Un romanzo storico antisemita;* and "L'autenticità dei 'Protocolli dei Savi Anziani di Sion' e il plagio di Giuseppe Prezzolini," *La Vita Italiana,* 15 June 1921.

17. It appeared in serial form edited by *Fede e Ragione* (Faith and reason) in the review's supplement between 27 March 1921 and 12 June 1921. The editor stated that "the original French edition was that of Msgr. Jouin," adding that in making "his translation" he chose from among the various editions which had appeared (Polish, English, cited by Jouin) "that which seemed *to him* best suited to the style" (ibid, n. 13, 27 March 1921).

18. From the reprint in *Luč sveta* 1920.

19. From the Beirut reprint 1967.

20. I have not tracked down the 1972 Brescia edition which, however, from the quotatons in V. Mattioli, *Gli ebrei e la Chiesa* (Milan 1997), one would say also depended on Preziosi.

21. We shall indicate the "Eng. 1920" translation by G. Shanks, the "French 1920" translation by E. Jouin, the "French 1921" translation by R. Lambelin, and "Fr. 1934" translation by H. Coston.

22. For more details, see De Michelis 1997a.

23. Cohn 1969, 33.

24. Laqueur 1991, 441; Klier 1995, 499.

25. J. Richardot, *Decourdemanche J.-A.,* in DBF 10 (1965).

26. Son of James (1774–1845), an archaeologist ("Dutch in origin, Londoner by birth and Italian by choice." P. Pirri, *Vita sel servo di Dio Carlo Odescalchi* (Isola del Liri 1935), 8.

27. J. Millingen, *Memoirs of the Affairs of Greece* (London 1831); cf. S. Mavrongény, *Notice biographique sur Jules van Millingen in Id., Les bains orientaux* (Strasbourg 1891).

28. Cohn 1969, 33f.

29. J. Millingen, *Arbitrary detention by the Inquisition at Rome of Three Protestant Children* (London 1842).

30. Osman Bey (1877a, It. trans. 1882), 72. Cardinal Odescalchi knew his paternal aunt, Cornelia, a Catholic and resident of Rome together with the grandmother Elizabeth and the uncle Augustus (who instead "was a supporter of rabid republicans" who, being "in contact with Mazzini and his faction," at the time of the Republic helped the brother [Osman Bey, ibid., 127]). The Cardinal "loved to give [*to neophytes*] godfathers and godmothers from the highest Roman nobility." Maria Louisa Carlotta de Bourbon, Infanta of Spain and Dowager Duchess of Saxony, arrived in Rome on June 9, 1838 (cf. *Notizie del giorno,* 13 June 1838) and could thus have taken part in the service.

31. M. Dejean returned to Constantinople to divorce and remarry Kibrizli-Mehemet-Pasha. She passed most of her life in the harem and committed suicide in Paris.

32. The sister Evelina (1834–1900) settled in Venice and married (1853) Count Almorò Pisani (cf. V. Spreti, *Enciclopedia storico-nobile italiana* [Milano 1932], 395). Given his character it is permissible to be dubious about his writings. However, comparisons apart, (DNB, vol. 37 and P. Pirri, *Vita sel servo di Dio Carlo Odescalchi*) the book in question (Osman Bey 1877a) is in the possession of the Marciana of Venice as a copy (Rari Tursi, 157) with autograph notes by the stepson, Alexander van Millingen (1840–1915), Professor of History at Robert College in Constantinople, who confirms the information here referred to.

33. By whom "he was treated as a son" (Osman Bey, 1877a, 171), and effectively became such by adding his surname "Kibrizli."

34. "The surname Seify means *Sabreur*—swordsman, and was given to me because of my leanings towards a military career" (Osman Bey 1877a, 171–72). In 1862 he had "the command of the 4th Regiment of the Army of Asia, garrisoning Van" (ibid. 192) and in 1864 he saw service on the Turkish Persian frontier.

35. He later claimed to have been forced to leave Turkey for having defended the Jews oppressed by the Kurds.

36. Osman Bey 1871.

37. Cf. rec. in *Kievljanin,* 6 July 1874.

38. Osman Bey 1877b. He boasted of having been solely responsible for victory over the Turks at the Battle of Kars (6[18]. XI. 1877) and to have saved Russia.

39. Cf. Chap. 3, n. 12.

40. Cf. O. Lerner, *Major Osman Bej pered sudom zdravogo smysla* (Odessa 1874).

41. The *Gazzetta d'Italia*; publication began on 4 September 1883 and was interrupted at Chapter 19 on 18 January 1884. According to Laqueur (1991, 134) it is "one of the most notable books written outside the walls of a madhouse."

42. Pavel Demidov, Prince of San Donato (1839–1885), author of a report on the condition of the Jews: *Evrejskij vopros v Rossii* (St. Petersburg 1883).

43. *Lettera a S. E. il signor de Giers, Ministro degli Affari esteri di Russia in Mosca* (31 May 1883, in Osman Bey 1873; It. trans., 1883) was datelined Salerno as also was another letter to Girs (10 June 1885, in Osman Bey 1883, Fr. transl. 1886, 3).

44. The meeting of Girs with Di Rudiní took place on October 13, 1891.

45. "We therefore are prepared to announce *urbi et orbi* that Mr [*Nikolaj Karlovič*] de Giers ["this name is none other than the alteration of the surname Hirsch, which is held by thousands of Jewish families"], Foreign Minister of all the Russias is a Jew!" (Osman Bey 1891, 29–30).

46. Ibid., 28.

47. "Un opuscolo sugli israeliti," *Il Tempo,* 29 January 1880.

48. *Britannia-Israel,* 23, 141.

49. *Gli usurai alla conquista del mondo. Risposta al libro di Osman-Bey "Gli ebrei alla conquista del mondo"* (Mantova-Cremona 1880).

50. P. L. Perdomo, *La Russia. Studio storico sul progresso ed avvenire degli Slavi* (Brescia 1887), 104.

51. Cappelli, Bologna 1939; in the Milanese edition of the PSM (1938) *Gli ebrei alla conquista del mondo* (The Jewish conquest of the world) was claimed to be imminent.

52. Gaeta 1945, 73 and passim.

53. Cf. A. Salomoni, *Il pensiero religioso e politico di L. Tolstoj in Italia.* (The religious and political thought of L. Tolstoy in Italy [1886–1910]) (Florence 1996).

54. J. Melnik, ed., *I russi sulla Russia* (The Russians on Russia), 2 vols. (Milan 1906).

55. "No calumny against the Jews it too atrocious for it not to have appeared in the columns of *Novoje Wremia.*"

56. AS MAE AP (Russia 1891–1895), 341.

57. AS MAE AP (Russia 1899–1905), 343.

58. Cf. telegram from G. C. Majoni from Odessa (29 January 1919, in AS MAE AP [Russia 1919–1930], b. 1521).

59. Communiqués of 21 July and 14 August 1919, in AS MAE, Peace Conference, b. 58, *Palestine and Zionism.*

60. "I complici" (The accomplices), *Il popolo d'Italia,* 4 June 1919.

61. *I pogrom contro gli Ebrei in Russia e in Ungheria nell'anno 1919* (The pogroms against the Jews in Russia and Hungary in the year 1919) (Rome 1920).

62. G. Forte, *"Abbasso gli ebrei." Echi degli avvenimenti degli ultimi anni di Russia e impressioni sul movimento nazionale semita* ("Down with the Jews." Comments on the events of recent years in Russia and impressions on the Jewish national movement) (Rome 1923).

63. Cf. C. Scandura, "L'emigrazione russa in Italia 1917–1940," *Europa Orientalis* (1995): 2.

64. Once full of revolutionary ideas and philosemitic (cf. Amfiteatrov 1906), he positioned himself against Soviet power from an extreme Right position and was openly philo-Fascist; cf. L. Spiridonova, "Amfiteatrov A. V.," in *Russkoe zarubež'e. Zolotaja kniga emigracii. Pervaja tret' XX veka* (Moscow 1997), 28.

65. Amfiteatrov asserted that tales of his antisemitism were unfounded, but when Vl. Burcev invited him to provide him with evidence for the Bern Trial, he refused saying that "that trial did not seem to *him* a very astute or necessary enterprise" (letter to Mil'rud of 14 September 1934, in *Amfiteatrov mss.*)

66. Among the attached papers to the *Berner Prozess* one finds the leaflet: *"Communism will die—Russia will not die* RUSSIAN TERROR AND THE SWORD OF GOD! In the name of God and of Russia, the Confraternity of Russian Justice, flesh of the flesh of the people and bone of the bone of the people, declares the power of the Commissars of the Kremlin and all their knavish activities to be outside of divine and human law and calls on all Russian citizens to be ready to sacrifice themselves for Christ and for Russia, and to initiate against the representatives of Red Power a pitiless and ferocious terror. We do not serve men, we serve God and the Fatherland! *Directive of the Confraternity of Russian Justice."*

67. Ževaxov 1939, 15.

68. For further details, see De Michelis 1996.

69. Cf. the reprints of some of his works (Ževaxov 1992, 1993a and b).

70. Therefore, he was right to present himself as "ex-Secretary of the Russian Imperial Government." This was doubted by both the Fascist authorities and Preziosi.

71. A. Dmitrievskij-V. Jušmanov, *Svjataja Rus' i Italija u mirotočivoj grobnicy Svjatitelja Nikolaja Mirlikijskogo v Bare-grade,* 1915.

72. Cf. the letter of G. Vaccaro, Archbishop of Bari, to the Papal Secretary of State Cardinal Merry del Val (23 May 1913) in ASV, Segr. Di Stato, 1913, rubr. 3, prot. 64530.

73. On 9 May 1913; cf. *Il Giornale delle Puglie,* 23 May 1913.

74. Cf. Ževaxov 1910.

75. Ževaxov 1939, 7.

76. Arising at the end of 1921. The Russian Palestine Society had the intention of sending a priest to Bari nominated by the Metropolitan Evlogij of Paris, with the agreement of the Patriarch of Moscow, against whom was ranged Antonij (who even

appealed to King Victor Emanuel III [S MAE, AP Russia 1927]; cf. *Russica Romana* 4 [1997]).

77. Cf. G. Petracchi, *Da San Pietroburgo a Mosca* (Rome 1933), 303.

78. Telegram n. 1288/513 of the Soviet Embassy in Italy, of 7 May 1930. In AS MAE, AP (Russia 1929) b. 1557.

79. Cf. letter of 27 September 1930, in De Michelis 1996.

80. *Riservatissima* (Top Secret) of the Prefecture of Bari, 1 February 1931, in MAE, AP (USSR 1933), b. 11.

81. Biblioteca ACS, Coll. Mussolini 99.

82. *Giuda senza maschera* (Judah unmasked) (part of Nečvolodov 1924, La stirpe ariana [The Arian breed] edition, Florence 1927).

83. Biblioteca ACS, Coll. Musolini 99.

84. After a first partial and serialized publication in the newspaper *Novoe slovo* in Berlin (from 15 August 1934). Ževaxov attributed great importance to his book on Nilus on the aims of the Bern Trial: cf. letter of 14/27 December 1934 to B. Todtli, in the attachments (papers of advocate Livšic) at the *Bernes Prozess*.

85. Ževaxov was nominated one of the "experts" by the defence.

86. "I must have known him not later than 1900" (Ževaxov 1939, 22).

87. Took orders under the name of Ioasaf, was Bishop of Mogilëv between 1934 and 1936. He died a victim of Stalinist purges.

88. Who three years later published another installment of his *Memorie* (Memoirs) (Ževaxov 1942).

89. He gave expression to a similar ploy in a letter to Todtli (in *Berner Prozess,* 17 February/2 March 1935): "Make known to your advocate that one must establish ONLY the two following facts: 1. That the text published with the title PSM is the work of Ul'šer Ginzberg for the Odessa secret organisation "Bne-Mojše" and 2. That a whole series of historical events are the putting into execution of the pre-ordered plan of the text."

90. Author of the novel *Korni zla,* in which appears a thinly veiled portrait of E. A. Šabel'skaja as the one who announces to Rasputin (16 December 1916, i.e., the day before his assassination) his imminent punishment for the services he has rendered to the Jewish-Masonic forces; cf. Dudakov 1992.

91. Son of the antisemitic actress and writer E. A. Šabel'skaja (see n. 90). In September 1918, she was in Ekaterinburg when a copy of the PSM came to light in Ipat'ev's house.

92. After his death, Ževaxov dedicated a pamphlet to his memory (1928).

93. Letter dated 4 September 1925 in AS MAE, AP (Russia 1925), b. 1545; in *Russica Romana,* 4 (1997).

94. Laqueur 1991,160; at his death he dedicated a pamphlet to him (Ževaxov).

95. Ževaxov 1934b, 32.

96. Cf. Chap. 5.

97. Economist (1857–1924), first Deputy (MP) with the Radical Group (1901), nationalist, Rector of Finances with D'Annunzio at Fiume, later as Senator of the Kingdom (Life Peer), he sided with Fascism.

98. Fascist who was originally a nationalist (1875–1935), Minister of Justice 1925–1932, and Rector of the University of Rome 1932–1935.

99. Fascist historian of Law (1873–1941), Minister of Justice from 1935.

100. Cf. B. Uspenskij, *Lo zar e l'impostore* (The Tsar and the impostor), in idem., *Storia e semiotica,* Ital. transl. (Milan 1988).

101. For example, Prince Golicyn-Muravlin, formerly President of *Russkoe Sobranie,* wrote the preface to the second volume of the *Vospominanija* of Ževaxov (1928) in which he claims that: "I affirm that the death of His Majesty is not proved."

102. Cf. Ganelin 1992, 138.

103. De Felice 1990, 1342.

104. G. Preziosi, "Ancora l'Internazionale," *La Vita Italiana,* September 1920, 197.

105. As Laqueur records (1991, 161), "he had accused of insufficient anti-Semitic passion even Markov II," leader of the "Union of the Russian People."

106. Cf. *La Menzogna* (The Lie) 1994, 264. The only copy identified is in the Consorzio Instituto Storico resistenza in Cuneo and Provincia.

107. Which is cited in Ževaxov 1936, 22 [1939, 39].

108. Cf. the Chap. "I "Protocolli" e l'anti-semitismo italiano" in C. G. De Michelis, *Il manoscritto inesistente* (Venice 1998), the Italian edition of this book.

Note on the Edition

The PSM have been handed down to us from three types of text (respectively of 22, 27, and 24 chapters), which place side by side two revisions in a single "discourse." There are five redactions[1] with three full ones (represented respectively by [K], [A1 and B] and [A2 and N]) and two shortened or concise ones ([R1, R2, R3 and R4] and [I]).

The edition may be limited to any one of these. From this point of view, the first full edition (K, 1903) and the last short one (I, 1917) create no problems as representing a single source each. This is not so with the edition of R (1905). R3 and R4 are *descriptae* of R2, of which, however, the latter is not of R1 because one notes expressions in it which are absent, but vouched for by the rest of the tradition.[2] R should contain both of them, and to restore them one must assume that R1 is the base-text, integrating it with the passages from R2 which compare with the rest of the tradition.[2]

The major problem concerns the other two "full" redactions. The one that is divided into 27 Protocols (the "second," which we shall call X), is identified by a high number of significant variants in relation to the "first" (K) and to the "third" (which we shall call Y). Among the two sources that they represent, A1 occupies a position closer than B to their common antigraph, conserving readings close to, or identical to K, in respect of which B distances itself adopting such a course to contaminate readings from A2 and/or N.

As regards Y, subdivided into 24 "Protocols," it could even give rise to the suspicion that N might be a descripta of A2, and the question would then be closed. However, this is not so, as a small number of cases show, and they are sufficient, however, to suppose that also in this case there is a common antigraph. This does not remove the fact that the hierarchic position of N is lower than that of A2 [cf. Chap. 1], readings of which would therefore be in the last resort privileged.

Setting off in search of the archetype of the PSM, we come across five redactions, of which one can only say that the first (K) represents the state of development of the PSM at the time of the pogrom of Gomel' (1903), while the other two show the development of the text for its use in 1905; X from a more "Russian" perspective and Y more "European." As regards the two "short" compilations, I is dependent on N (cf. Chap. 1), and R on the antigraph of K. In fact, R follows K and X where they diverge from Y,[3] K and A1 where they diverge from B,[4] and K where it diverges from A1.[5] However, there are also phrases missing in K, but present in the rest of the tradition (cf. infra).

Can one can go further and, despite the situation of the "open tradition," seek to restore the PSM as it was originally conceived and drafted, and therefore reach in some way the archetype? The combined errors in respect of the text used for the compilation of the PSM (the *Dialogue* of Joly)[6] show that all of the ten sources noted come from a single text and the variants are often represented as transformations (or degradations) of the same protograph.

To restore the primitive text, one needs, therefore, to refer to the individual sources which would usually be assumed to be those of a sole tradition. Obviously this will first of all be based on the three full redactions. K has a distinct identity and keeps (at times in opposition to the rest of the tradition) readings which adhere to Joly's text.[7] A1 and B, even though very similar, above all for the dividing up of the material and for many additions and minor variants, are clearly distinguishable one from the other with A1 more similar to K,[8] and B to A2 and/or N.[9] The last of these are very similar to each other, even if A2 is more conservative, and therefore in various places closer to N than to the rest of the tradition.

Joly's *Dialogue* as a subtext is central to the restoration of the text. In each of the editions passages are missing (sometimes also fairly consistently) which are present in the others, and which contain quotations from Joly. For example:

In K, XIX a long passage (34 lines), concerning financial questions (inc. «Этот бюджет, видите ли, дотягивается...» expl. «...остается все таким непокрытым долгом»;

In A1, (12 [IX] a short passage (3 lines), concerning parliamentary diversionary tactics (inc. «эту роль...»; expl. «Министров»);

In A2 (10 [XII] a short passage (6 lines), concerning the servility of journalists (inc: «Пока эти раны...» expl. «...не попали. Ныне»);

In A2 and N,[10] (2 [11]) a substantial passage (44 lines) concerning the subdivision of power in constitutional states (inc. «Такими путями мы приведем...» expl. «...к вечному отдыху»);

In B, (17 [XII]) a fairly long passage (23 lines) concerning internal dissent and the example of Sylla (inc. «В гоевских странах...» expl. «...своею силою и храбростью»).

Moreover, each of the five editions, in the part of the text which it has in common with the others, distorts and modifies quotations from Joly which are maintained correctly elsewhere. These two observations together are indicative of the fact that, after it had been used in the drafting of the archetype, Joly's text was no longer recognizable, and probably not even obtainable for any of the five publishers.

Thus we have the textual material revealed by K, A1, A2, N, and K and a certain indicator to trace back to the archetype: the quotations from Joly. The textual transmission should be studied on this basis.

There are, however, a good number of significant variants which separate K from the other four sources, let alone entire phrases which do not contain quotations from Joly absent in K and which (though with variations) are found in A1, A2, N and B.[11] This proves the individuality of the "first redaction."

Some interpretations (and some additions) are found only in A1 and B, and derive therefore from their common antigraph. They are therefore really from the "second redaction" (X).[12] Other interpretations, on the other hand, are common only to A2 and N and are not characteristic of the "third redaction" (Y).[13]

We therefore have confirmation that the three redactions are not differentiated only for external data such as the different segmentation, but also by their textual structure.

The singularity of the three redactions (K, X and Y) is rendered less evident, however, by "transversal" phenomena which the individual witnesses variously take up. One encounters, for example, additions which (with some modifications) B has in common with A2 and N, which both come from the development of phrases present in K and A1,[14] and from how the phrases are integrated (containing quotations from Joly), but which are, however, absent in them.[15]

Many innovations were introduced into Y (some are already met with in A2, but the majority in N) which one finds however contrary to those in K and X, Čerikover 1934, Rollin 1939, and others had already guessed, with the exception, one knows not why, of Dudakov 1993.

I end by maintaining that K, despite the declared omissions, is the witness text nearest to the archetype; that A2 is that which contains the greater part of the textual material, and that A2 and above all N are the most developed, and one comes to the conclusion that none of the published witnesses can be assumed to be more authoritative than the others.

In A1, both in the omissions and in the additions in respect of K, one notes phrases taken from Joly. Therefore, A1 is not the "complete" version, nor a free remake. On the other hand, B is not a mere *descripta* of A1, nor N or A2. We need, therefore, the following diagram:

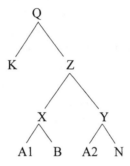

This is confirmed by variants such as the following:

Joly: *le journalisme est une sorte de francmaçonnerie*

K: в журналистике существует масонская...

A1, A2, B: в *формах журналистики* существует масонская

N: в *формах* **хотя бы французской** *журналистики* существует масонская...

K ("there exists in journalism") shows the form closest to the French text, coinciding with the archetype of the PSM. Z, the text on which the other four depend, has modified with the interpretations that we find in A1, A2, and B ("in the forms of journalism") and N has added a French flourish ("at least that French one").

Again (VII, 87):

Joly: *je les toucherai une à une par un trait de main inaperçu qui en dérangera le mécanisme*

K: мы коснулись их осторожно, умелой рукой избрали концы пружин их механизма

A1, B: мы коснулись их осторожно умелой рукой **и забрали** концы пружин их механизма

A2: мы коснулись их умелой рукой **и забрали** концы пружин их механизма

N: мы коснулись их умелой рукой **и забрали в свои руки** концы пружин их механизма

The meaning of the phrase is not modified very much (from K: "we have touched them with care, we have tested with a wise hand the limits of the springs of their mechanism," to N: "We have touched with a wise hand and we have grasped in our hands the limits of the springs of their mechanism"), but the passage is no less significant. K shows an original reading closer to Joly. Z corrupts "izbrali" into "i zabrali." Such a reading is maintained in X, while Y, as A2 proves, leaves out "ostorožno" (with care, which becomes the "une à une" of Joly) and N adds "v svoi ruki."

Once more, but without the subtext of Joly (XII):

K:	Бесполезные	дефекты	перемены	правлений
B:	Бесполезные	де факто	перемены	правлений
A1:	фактически	бесполезные	перемены	направлений
A2, N:	Бесполезные		перемены	правлений

The change in meaning (from K: "The useless defect of the change of government" to N: "The useless changes of governments") indicates that the original reading attests that K ("defekty") was corrupted in Z into the form one finds in B ("de facto"), again modified in A1 ("faktičeski") and omitted in Y (A2 and N).

In XIII, 70:

K:	Наибольшие	жертвы...
A1, A2, B:	*Небольшие*	жертвы...
N:	*Сравнительно **немногочисленные***	жертвы...

The *lectio facilior* leads to a radical distortion of the meaning. K says the "the majority [*the greatest number of*] victims" whom we have been obliged to make among "our people" have still served,… etc. Z modifies this into "nebol'šie" in the sense of "insignificant, very few," and the same goes for X, the antigraph of A1 and B and for Y. A2 maintains this already secondary reading while N corrects the already corrupted text with the more fluent Russian ("relatively few").

Over and above the many variants and individual additions, X and Y contain, even if with some deformities, the passages absent in K which contain quotations from Joly, and hark back to the archetype (Q), and thus conserved in Z. For example, in the 3rd, 24:

K: omitted

A1, A2, N, B: **Царствующие заслонены своими представителями**...

Joly: *Le prince...souverain...qui acceptera...le rôle passif auquel vous l'aurez condamné...*

However, some of the readings taken from Joly are found *only* in Y (A2 and N):

IV:

K, A1, B:	Второе		средство...
A2, N:	Вторая		**тайна,** потребная...
Joly:	*Un des...secrets...*		

K, A1, B:	которое все		будет считать
A2, N:	которое		будет **называться**
Joly:	*qui*		*s'appelle*

VI:

K, A1, B: защищать наши интересы как свои собственные

A2, N: защищать   наши   интересы   **до   последнего**   своего **издыхания**

Joly: *défendre jusqu'au dernier souffle*

VII:

K, A1, B:	люди		всех доктрин
A2, N:	люди	всех мнений,	всех доктрин
Joly:	*hommes de toute opinion et de toute doctrine*		

VIII:

K, A1, B:	идеи о скрытом налоге	
A2, N:	идея о скрытом налоге, **обратной силы законов**	
Joly:	*de la non*	*rétroactivité des lois*

In other cases, the readings derived from Joly are omitted in the first two redactions (K and X) but are present in the third.

V:

K, A1, B: omitted

A2, N: **Одним словом, чтобы резюмировать** нашу **систему**

Joly: *Pour resumer d'un mot   tout le système*

VIII:

K, A1, B: omitted

A2, N: что **принципы современного права** признаются нами

Joly: *je confirme les grands principes du droit moderne*

IX:

K, A1, B: omitted

A2, N: **Государственный совет**...как бы **комитетом редакции**

Joly: *Le Conseil d'État?... Ce n'est qu'un Comité de Rédaction*

K, A1, B: omitted

A2, N: **не станет относиться с бдагодарностью, считая должными**

Joly: *vos sujets ne vous sauront aucun gré...qu'ils jugeront être forcé*

In one case only A2 maintains the original reading:

VIII:

K, A1, N, B: неприкосновенности собственности [и] жилища

A2: неприкосновенности собственности, жилища, **потиционного** [*sic!*]
    права

Joly: *de l'inviolabilité de la propriété et du domicile, du droit de pétition*

and in another only N does:

III:

K, A1, A2, B: на борьбу против всяких сил

N: на борьбу против всяких сил, **против всякой власти**

Joly: *en guerre   ...   coutre tous les pouvoirs*[16]

Study of the variants offers an intricate picture. The readings common to A2 and N largely prevail over K, A1, and B, followed by those common to A1, A2, N, and B over K, those common to A1 and B over A2 and N, and lastly those of A2 and/or N, and B, over A1. Part of these phenomena can be explained by the interference of the texts already published on successive editions (all evidently would have known K, and B certainly knew of N). However not everything can be explained on the basis of interference.

Therefore, the interrelations between the various texts are different from those implied by the vulgate, but also from the hypothesis summarized above. To explain the modality of the tradition which results from the texts at our disposition, one must suppose that the original text comes from an unknown W, from which derives K with its 22 chapters, R in a single "discourse" and the unknown Z, from which in turn came the unknown X (in 27 chapters) and Y (in 24), which however keep textual material which derives directly from Q of which we find traces in A2 and N. In turn, B shows traces of contamination with the third redaction. All this may be represented by the following diagram:

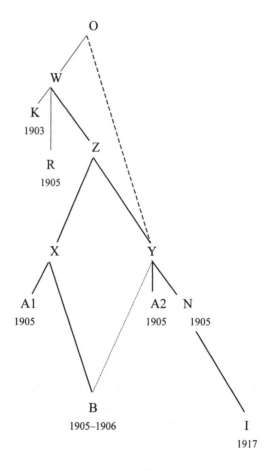

At the basis of the restored text, therefore, must be placed the material in common (choosing the readings closest to Joly), integrated with that in each text, even if absent in the others. This guarantees that it belongs to the first draft of the PSM because of the citations from Joly.

The question remains of the extracts which do not come from Joly, which appear in A1, A2, N, and B (that is to say, common to X and Y) but not in K, for which one must ask whether one is dealing with material present in the original text which had been omitted from K, or rather with additions inserted in the antigraph in common with the other redactions (Z).

Overall, one is dealing with fewer than four sheets, which do not offer evidence for dating them. But perhaps a sentence from the Note (273) will serve:

> The attribution to various theories under the heading of "scientific" has guaranteed and guarantees to Zion services of no little value.... For example: the economic theory of the system of balloting [?] has given [Y: *the systems of balloting has given*] the possibility to carry on all that was auspicious for the growth of Zion [Y: *wished the chiefs of staff of Zion*].

The reading of X is not evident: the "systems of balloting" concern electoral procedure and not "economic theories," even if Y eliminates reference to this last phrase giving place to a discussion on universal suffrage, in congruity with the next sentence which is common to all the witnesses. The primitive diction, shown by X, arises probably from interference between the Russian meaning of the verb *ballotter*[17] which has generated an improper use of the derivative adjective (*баллотировочный*). The phrase is intended to be, however:

> The economic theory of systems of **fluctuation** [*of currencies*] has offered the possibility to carry forward all that is auspicious for the growth of Zion.

And this could relate to the difficulties experienced by the rouble following the Russian Japanese War, and therefore not hark back to before the summer of 1905.

A later dating of the other extracts leads also to the thought that the other variants of A1, A2, N, and B against K (when these keep to the original reading) lead us to suppose, already in their common antigraph, divergences from the original text, and therefore likewise that many phrases (without calques from Joly) found only in X and Y go back to an unknown witness (Z).

Many, however, but not all. One must take into account also the short redaction R which, as has been said, derives from the antigraph of K. In R, one finds (even if with variations) passages absent in K and as attested by X and Y evidently present in the common antigraph of K and the rest of the tradition (W). For example, 19th, 174:

R: Every new loan demonstrates the insolvency of the state in the payment of past loans, and in the meantime these last hang like a sword of Damocles over the heads of the governments of the *gojim* who deserve to be put on trial because, rather than taking money from the real capitalists for special needs, they go with cap in hand to our bankers.

A1, A2, N, B: Every loan shows the impotence of the state and the lack of understanding of the state laws, and in the meantime the loans, like a sword of Damocles, hang over the heads of the governors who, rather than raise a temporary tax for special needs from their own subjects, go with hands outstretched to ask charity of our bankers.

Therefore to the material in common in the three redactions, integrated as far as they contain quotations from Joly, there should be added that which finds correspondence in R. The rest should rather be consigned to the apparatus, as additions of Z[18] or of X and Y, two redactions from 1905.

One takes K as the base text therefore, not only because it is the oldest (1903), but because—through its Ukrainianisms, its uncertainties of exposition, its linguistic anomalies, and uncertain segmentation of chapters—it testifies to the primitive state of the compilation, which is nearest to Q. It went on to be integrated and corrected[19] with what had been taken from A1, A2, N, and B following the criteria shown above. Likewise, its division into 22 chapters follows. This must be since they were at the beginning of the tradition. In fact, while the division of X (into 27) and of Y (into 24) is explained by that of K,[20] the reverse is not possible to explain.

NOTES

1. "One may call 'redaction' the revising of a text that has been produced for a specific end, resulting from some social event or from purely literary intentions" (V. Istrin, *Očerk istorii drevnerusskoj literary* [Petrograd 1922], 59).

2. E.g., R1 «Взгляните на наспиртованных, оживотелых, **одурманенных** наркотами, **классицизмом** и гипнозом **гоев. Они развращаются** чуть не с детства **нашими агентами**»; R2 «Взгляните на наспиртованных, озверелых, **одурманенных** наркотами **гоев. Они развращаются** чуть не с детства **нами**, примером товарищей, дрессированными на то **женщинами** и **нашими агентами**».

PSM: «*Народы* **гоев** *одурманены спиртными напитками, а их молодежь одурела* **от классицизма** *и раннего* **разврата**, *на который их подбивали* **наши агенты** *гувернеры, лакеи, приказчики и пр., в богатых классах наши* **женщины**».

3. 7th: K, X: «осколки когда то **сильных партий, разбитых** нами»

Y: «осколки когда то сильной партии, ныне покоренной нами»

R: «осколки когда-то **сильных партий, разбитых** нашими незримыми ударами»

cf. Joly: *"des tronçons de partis autrefois victorieux, aujourd'hui vaincus."*

4. 2nd: K, A1: «Карно—ножем, Мак Кинлея—пулею, **Гамбеты,** Феликса Фора—ядом»

B: «Карно—ножем, Мак Кинлея—пуею, Феликса Фора—ядом»

R: «Карно—ножем, **Гамбетта** и Фелилс Фор—ядом, Мак-Кинлей...—пулею»

5. 3rd: K: «Республиканские права для **труженика суть** горькая ирония»

A1: Республиканские права для тружеников есть горькая ирония»

R: Республиканские права для **труженика суть** горькая ирония»

cf. Joly: *"Ces droits...ne sont pour lui qu'une ironie amère."*

6. Cf. the errors in translation from the French (Chap. 3).

7. E.g., 1st, K: «Отбросив лишние фразы», cf. Joly: *"laissons...les mots"* (A1, A2, N, B: «Отложив фразерство»); K: «их правители», cf. Joly: *"ceux qui les gouvernent"* (A1, B: «правительства», A2, N: «правительство»), etc.

8. Cf. the retention of «борятся» for «бор**ю**тся» (3rd).

9. E.g., 1st, K, A1: «должен умело прибегать» vs. A2, B: «должен уметь [N omits] прибегать»; K, A1: «планы могут выработаться ясными» vs. A2, N, B: «планы могут выработаться обширно ясными»; K, A1 «обладания» vs. A2, N, B: «преобладания».

10. There are no significant omissions in N apart from those in common with A2, which shows the accuracy of this edition, but also its subordination to Y.

11. I draw attention to all the following cases (3rd): «Царствующие не могут уже сговориться с народом A2: ними; N: ним] как в былые времена [A2, N omit: как...], и укрепиться против властолюбцев. Разделенная нами, зрячая Царская сила и слепая сила народа, потеряли всякое значение, ибо отдельно друг от друга, как слепец без палки [B adds: и обратно], они немощны»

12. E.g. 16th, «Знание якобы политики толпою сильнее всего замутило [A1: замутили] этот строй»

13. E.g., 1st, «Было время когда [N omits] правила вера»; or 7th: «метрополитэновые подземные ходы-корридоры будут к тому времени проведены во всех столоцах».

14. E.g., 13th, «**Вы не можете себе представить,**...как легко обезкуражить [B adds: самообольщенных простачков малейшей неудачей; N, B add: хотя бы] прекращением апплодисментов и [B adds: каждения их авторитету; как легко] привести [B adds: их] к рабскому [N: рабьему; B adds: уже почти сознательному] повиновению ради возобновления силы успеха.... Насколько наши пренебрегают успехом, лишь бы провести свои планы, настолько гои готовы

жертвовать всякими планами лишь бы получить успех [B add: ради личного успеха].... Это [N: Эта их психология] значительно облегчает нам задачу их направления [B: руководства ими]».

15. E.g., 13th: «**Мы посадили их теперь** [A2, N omit] **на конька мечты о поглощении** [B: превращении] **человеческой индивуальности в символиче-скую единицу** [N: символической единицей] **коллективизма** [cf. Joly: "*Leur rêve est l'absorption des individus dans une unité symbolique*"]. Они еще не разобрались и [B: Можно наверняка рассчитывать, что они] не разберутся, что в этой мысли — [N: этот конек есть явное; B adds: им нами навеянной, зиждится] нарушение главнейшего закона природы, создавшей [B add: которая создала] единицу, непохожую на лругие [B: всякого вида,] с самого [B omits] сотворения мира, именно, в целях индивидуальности.... Если мы могли их привести [B: довести гоев] к такому [N adds: безумному] ослеплению [B: до такого ослепления], это [N adds: то не] доказывает [N adds: ли это с поразительной ясностью], до какой степени ум гоев не развит человечески по сравнению с нашим умом [B: значит степень их ума в сравнении с нашим умом недоразвита человечески], что [N adds: ?! Это то, главным образом,] и гарантирует наш успех [B: а стоит на степени животного, что доказывает наше избрание и дает нам гарантию успеха]».

16. Being isolated cases, it is more economical to maintain that such expressions that one finds in Y, and N and A2 were omitted in each case rather than consider their direct relationship with the archetype.

17. Respectively *баллотировать, качать, колебать* (Makarov 1884), 10, 257, 267 and (idem 1887), 103).

18. Except in the cases in which such passages are datable after 1903, there remains the doubt that some may be present in W, but have been omitted from K and from R and kept only in the other two redactions. The reconstruction seems to propose, however, the reading of the PSM according to a text *certainly* referable to the protograph.

19. So as to have a "normalized" edition. The anomalies of the highest level of the text (attested to by K) maintain all their value in relation to the problem of the origin of the document.

20. The last section of the 11th Protocol was inserted from Y at the beginning of the next, which consolidates with a variant the beginning of the 12th, while X, even with a different numeration, follows also here the segmentation of K.

[1]ПРОТОКОЛЫ[2] СИОНСКИХ МУДРЕЦОВ[3]

I [4]

Отбросив лишние **фразы**[5] **будем говорить** только[6] о значении каждой **мысли** (a). **Сравнениями** и **выводами** осветим обстоятельства. **И так, я формулирую**[7] **нашу систему** (b) разглядывая[8] факты[9] с нашей и с[10] гоевской стороны[11]. Надо заметить, что **люди с дурными инстинктами**[12] **многочисленнее добрых** (c); поэтому можно большего результата достичь[13] **насилием и устрашением, чем разумными** и убедительными[14] **рассуждениями** (d): ведь[15] **каждый человек стремится к**[16] **власти и мало кто не**[17] **сделался бы**[18] **диктатором, если бы**[19] **мог,** [20]при этом **редкий не**[21] **готов жертвовать благами всех ради достижения благ своих** (e).

---

[1]   A2 add.: **Древние и современные**

[2]   K add.: **заседаний всемирного союза Франмасонов и**; A1: **Выдержки из древних и современных протоколов**; A2, N add.: **собраний**

[3]   A1 add.: **Всемирного общества Фран-Масонов**; B: **извлеченные из тайных хранилищ Сионской Главной Канцелярии**

[4]   K, A1, N omitt.; B: **Протокол (1)**

[5]   A1, A2, N, B: Отложив фразерство

[6]   N omitt.

[7]   K omitt.: будем говорить... & add.: постараемся формулировать; A1: формируем; B: формулируем

[8]   A2: разбирая

[9]   N omitt.: разглядывая факты

[10]   K omitt.

[11]   A2, N: точки [N: точек] зреня

[12]   A2: дурным инстинктом

[13]   N: лучшие результаты в управлении достигаются ими

[14]   A2: рассудительными; N: а не академическими

[15]   N omitt.

[16]   A2, B: ко

[17]   N: каждому хотелось

[18]   N: сделаться

[19]   N add.: только он

[20]   N add.: но

[21]   N add.: был бы

Что сдерживало и руководило **этими**[22] **хищными животными, которых зовут людьми** (f)[23]**? В начале общественного строя** они подчинялись **грубой и слепой силе, потом закону, который есть тоже**[24] **сила, но**[25] **замаскированная.** Вывожу заключение, что по закону естества **право в силе** (g). **Политическая свобода есть идея**, а не факт: ее[26] надо уметь применять, когда является **нужным** (h), идейной[27] приманкой привлечь народные силы к своей партии, если таковая задумала сломить другую, у власти находящуюся. Эта задача облегчается, если и сам[28] противник заразился[29] идеей свободы ([30]либерализмом) и поступится ради этой[31] идеи своею мощью, в чем[32] и проявится торжество нашей теории. Ведь[33] по закону бытия[34] распущенные бразды правления тотчас[35] подхватываются и подбираются новой рукой[36], потому что слепая сила народа не может пробыть одного[37] дня без руководителя, следовательно, лишь новая[38] заступает место[39] ослабевшей от собственного[40] либерализма власти[41]. В данное[42] время

22	N omitt.: и...
23	N add.: Что ими руководило до сего времени?
24	A2, N: та же
25	A2 omitt: и; N: только
26	N: эту идею
27	В: идейною
28	N omitt.: и...
29	A2, N, В: заразится
30	N add.: так называемым
31	A2, N omitt.
32	N: Тут-то
33	N omitt.
34	A2 omitt.: Ведь по закону...
35	A2, N add.: же
36	A2 add.: по закону бытия; N, В: рукою
37	N omitt.
38	N, В add.: власть
39	N add.: старой
40	N omitt.
41	N omitt.
42	N: наше

заместительницей власти[43] (либералов) правителей явилась власть золота, т.е. наша.[44] Идея свободы неосуществима, **потому что никто не умеет пользоваться ею в меру. Стоит только на некоторое время предоставить народ самоуправлению, как оно**[45] **превращается в распущенность.** С этого момента **рождаются**[46] **междоусобицы**[47], скоро **переходящие в социальные битвы**, в которых государства горят, [48]их значение превращается в пепел. **Истощается ли государство в собственных конвульсиях, или же внутренние распри отдают его во власть внешним врагам, во всяком случае оно может считаться** безвозвратно **погибшим** (i): оно[49] в нашей власти. Деспотизм нашего[50] капитала[51] протягивает ему соломинку, за которую ему[52] приходится держаться, или[53] в противном случае, катиться[54] в пропасть. Того, который мне[55] скажет[56], что мои[57] рассуждения безнравственны, я спрошу: если у[58] **государства два врага и если по отношению к внешнему** врагу ему[59] дозволено[60] **употреблять всякие** стратегические[61] **меры** борьбы, как, например, **не ознокомлять врага с планами нападения**[62] **или**[63] **защиты, нападать на него ночью или не равным**

---

43   A2, N omitt.

44   A2, N omitt.: т. е. .., & add.: Было время когда [N omitt.] правила вера

45   N, B: свобода

46   N: возникают

47   K: междоусобищи; A1, A2: междуусобицы

48   N add.: и

49   B omitt.

50   A2, N omitt.

51   N add.: который весь в наших руках

52   N: государству

53   N: поневоле

54   N: оно катится

55   N omitt.

56   A2, N: от либерализма души сказал бы

57   A2: такие; N: такого рода

58   A2, N add.: каждого

59   K omitt.

60   N add.: и не почитается безнравственным

61   N omitt.

62   N: или нападениями

количеством[64] людей, то почему же такие меры могут называться **безнравственными в отношении худшего врага** (j), нарушителя нашего[65] благоденствия, нашего конкурента[66] на власть[67]. **Может ли здравый логический ум** надеяться постоянно[68] **руководить**[69] **разумными увещаниями**[70] или уговорами[71], при возможном, хотя бы и бессмысленном, противоречии[72], могущем[73] показаться **народу**, поверхностно разумеющему, более справедливым[74], ибо[75], **руководствуясь**[76] исключительно мелкими **страстями**, **повериями**, обычаями, традициями и **сантиментальными теориями** (k), люди в толпе[77] поддаются партийному расколу, мешающему всякому соглашению даже на почве[78] разумного увещевания. Всякое решение толпы зависит от случайного или подстроенного большинства, которое в неведении[79] политических тайн произносит абсурдное решение, кладущее зародыш анархическому периоду управления[80]. Из всего вышесказанного[81] выходит, что[82] **политика не имеет ничего общего с моралью** (л). Правитель, руководящийся[83] ею[84], неполитичен, а потому

63   N omitt.

64   N: числом

65   A2, N: общественного строя и

66   B: конкуррента

67   A2, N omitt.: нашего....

68   N add.: успешно

69   A1, A2, N, B add.: толпами

70   A1, B: увещеваниями; N: при помощи разумных увещаний

71   N: уговоров

72   N: возможности противоречия, хотя бы и бссмысленного

73   N: но которое может

74   A2, N: принятым

75   N omitt.

76   N: Руководясь

77   N add.: и люди толпы

78   N add.: вполне

79   A2, N: по неведению

80   N: анархии в управлении

81   K: сказанного

82   N omitt.: Из всего...

83   A2: руководящий

и[85] не прочен на своем престоле. Кто хочет править, должен умело[86] прибегать[87] к хитрости и[88] лицемерию: **великие** народные **качества**, откровенность и честность, **суть порохи в политике**,[89] они свергают с престолов лучше и вернее сильнейшего врага. Эти качества должны быть атрибутами гоевских царств; **мы же**[90] **не должны ими руководиться** (m). Наше право в силе. **Слово право есть отвлеченная,**[91] ничем не доказанная **мысль** (n), оно[92] означает как бы[93]: «дайте мне того[94], что я хочу, чтобы[95] тем самым доказать мне[96], что я сильнее вас». **Где начинается право, где оно кончается** (o), в чем оно состоит[97]? **В государствах, в которых**[98] плохая организация общественной[99] власти (p), **бессилие**[100] законов и правителя, обезличенных либерализмом и его мнимыми[101] правами, я вижу[102] наше[103] право **броситься** с правом[104] сильного и **разнести все существующие порядки и установления, наложить руки на законы, перестроить все учреждения** (q) и сделаться владыками[105] тех, которые предоставили

---

84   N: моралью

85   N omitt.

86   N omitt.; A2, B: уметь

87   N add.: и

88   N add.: к

89   A2, N add.: потому что

90   A1, A2, N, B add.: отнюдь

91   N add.: и

92   N: Слово это

93   A2, N: не более, как

94   A1 omitt.; N: то

95   A2 add.: я

96   A2, N: получил доказательство

97   A2, N omitt.: в чем...

98   A2, N: в государстве в котором

99   N omitt.

100   N: безличие

101   A2, N omitt.: либерализмом... & add.: размножившимися от либерализма

102   A2, N: черпаю

103   A2, N: новое

104   A1, A2 omitt.: c; N, B: по праву

105   N: владыкою

нам свою мощь[106], добровольно, либерально отказавшись от нее[107]. Наша власть[108] непоборимее других[109], потому что она незрима[110], каковой и останется[111] пока[112] укрепится настолько, что никакая хитрость, ни сила[113] не подточит ее. **Из** временного **зла**, которое[114] мы вынуждены совершать[115], **произойдет добро** (r) непоколебимого правления, которое восстановит правильный ход механизма народного бытия, нарушенного либерализмом, **результат оправдает средства** (s). **Обратим же внимание**[116] **не столько на доброе и нравственное, сколько на нужное и полезное** (t). Перед нами план; в нем[117] стратегически указана[118] линия, от которой нам отступить[119] нельзя без риска видеть разрушение многовековых работ[120]. Чтобы выработать целесообразные действия, надо принять во внимание подлость, **неустойчивость**[121], **непостоянство толпы, неспособность ее понимать и уважать условия собственной жизни** (u), собственного благополучия, надо понять, что **мощь толпы слепая** (v), неразумная[122], нерассуждающая, прислуживающая[123] направо и налево. Слепой не может водить слепых без того, чтобы их не довести до пропасти,[124] следовательно члены толпы- выскочки из народа, хотя бы и гениально умные, но в политике неразумеющие, не могут

---

[106] A2, N: права своей силы
[107] A2, N: них
[108] N add.: при современном шатании всех властей, будет
[109] N: необоримее всякой другой
[110] A2, N: будет незримой
[111] A2, N omitt.: каковой... & add.: до тех пор
[112] A2 add.: не
[113] A2, N omitt.: ни сила; N add.: уже; B: или
[114] A2: который
[115] A1: совершить
[116] A2, N add.: в наших планах
[117] A2, N: котором
[118] A2, N: изложена
[119] A1, N: отступать
[120] A1: забот
[121] K: неусточивость
[122] A2: неразумна
[123] N: прислушивающаяся
[124] A2 add.: точно так

выступать в качестве руководителей толпы без того, чтобы не погубить свое стадо[125]. Только с детства подготовленные лица могут[126] ведать слова, составляемые политическими буквами. **Народ предоставленный самому себе**, т. е. выскочкам из его же[127] среды, **саморазрушается** (w) партийными раздорами, возбуждаемыми погоней[128] за властью и почестями и происходящими от сего[129] беспорядками. **Возможно ли** народным массам[130] спокойно, без соревнования рассудить[131] и **управиться**[132] **с делами страны**[133], которые[134] нельзя безнаказанно смешивать[135] с личными интересами; соревнование мешает[136] **защититься**[137] **от внешних врагов** (x) и даже увидеть[138] их[139]. План, разбитый на несколько частей, на несколько[140] голов в толпе, теряет цельность, а потому становится непонятным и неисполнимым от разных[141] пониманий его[142]. Только у одного[143] лица планы могут выработаться[144] ясными, в порядке, распределяющем[145] все в механизме государственной машины, из чего надо заключить, что целесообразное

[125]   A2, N: всю нацию

[126]   A2, N: подготовляемое к Самодержавию лицо может

[127]   A2, N omitt.

[128]   N: погонею

[129]   N: этого

[130]   K: масам

[131]   N, B: рассуждать

[132]   N, B: управляться

[133]   N, B: государственными

[134]   N, B: которых

[135]   A2, N omitt.: нельзя... & add.: не могут смешиваться

[136]   A2, N omitt.: соревнование...

[137]   N: защищаться

[138]   K: удивить

[139]   A2, N omitt.: и даже... & add.: Это немыслимо, ибо

[140]   A1, A2, N: сколько

[141]   A1: разнородных; B: вследствие разнородных

[142]   A2, N omitt.: от разных...

[143]   A2, N: Самодержавного

[144]   A2, N, B add.: обширно

[145]   A2: распределящем

для пользы страны управление должно сосредоточиться[146] в руках одного ответственного лица. **Без** абсолютного **деспотизма не может существовать цивилизация** (у), проводимая не массами, а руководителями[147] их, кто бы они не были[148]. Толпа есть[149] варвар, проявляющийся таковым[150] при каждом случае. Как только толпа захватит[151] свободу (идею свободы)[152] она ее тотчас[153] превращает в анархию, которая[154] есть высшее[155] из варварств[156]. Взгляните на наспиртованных, оживотелых[157], одурманенных вином, право на безмерное употребление которого дано со свободою гоям (наши ведь свободно не пользуются, памятуя херемы)[158]... Не допускать же[159] во время нашего открытого, а потому и ответственного[160] правления, что либо подобное[161]. Народы гоев одурманены спиртными напитками, а их молодежь одурела от классицизма и раннего разврата, на который их подбивали наши агенты[162]-гувернеры, лакеи,[163] приказчики[164] и пр., в богатых классах[165] наши женщины[166], в числе которых много[167] их[168]

---

[146] A1: сосредоточиваться

[147] A2, N: руководителем

[148] A2, N: он ни был

[149] N omitt.

[150] N: проявляющий свое варварство

[151] N: захватывает в свои руки

[152] A2, N omitt.

[153] A2 omitt; N: вскоре

[154] N add.: сама по себе

[155] A2, N: высшая

[156] N: степень варварства

[157] N: животных

[158] A2, N omitt.: гоям...

[159] A2, B add.: нам

[160] A1 omitt.: а потому...

[161] A2, N omitt.: во время... & add. и наших дойти до того же ...

[162] N omitt.: на которые... & add.: на который ее подбивала наша агентура

[163] N add.: гувернантки

[164] B: прикащики

[165] A1, A2, N, B: домах; A1 add.: а также; B add.: тоже

[166] A2: нашими женщинами

последовательниц по разврату и роскоши. И так[169] **наш пароль сила и лицемерие** (z), только **сила побеждает в делах политических**, особенно если она **скрыта в талантах, необходимых правительственным[170] людям** (aa). **Насилие должно быть принципом,[171] хитрость и лицемерие правилом для правительства** (ab), которое не желает[172] сложить свою власть[173] к ногам[174] какой нибудь[175] новой мощи[176]... Это **зло помогает[177] добраться до добра[178]**(ac), поэтому мы не должны останавливаться перед **подкупом, обманом, и[179] предательством, когда они должны послужить к достижению нашей цели**: в политике надо уметь **брать чужое добро[180]**(ad) без колебания[181], чтобы добиться[182] покорности и власти, наше правление[183], шествуя мирным[184] путем завоевания, **имеет право** заменить ужасы войны менее заметными, но[185] более целесообразными кознями[186], которыми мы поддерживаем[187] террор,

---

[167] A1, B: считаю [B add.: также]; N omitt.: в числе... & add.: в местах гоевских увеселений. К числу этих последних я причисляю и так называемых дам из общества, добровольных

[168] A2: и

[169] N omitt.

[170] A2, N: государственным

[171] A2, N add.: а

[172] A2, N: правительств, которые не желают

[173] A2, N: корону

[174] A2, N add.: агентов

[175] A2, N, B: либо

[176] A2, N: силы

[177] A2, N: есть единственное средство

[178] K, A2: цели доброй [A2: добра]

[179] K omitt.

[180] A2, N: чужую собственность

[181] A2, N: колебаний

[182] A2, N omitt.: чтобы... & add.: если ею мы добьемся

[183] A2, N: государство

[184] N: мирного

[185] A2, N: и

[186] A1, N, B: казнями

[187] A2, N: надо поддерживать

распологающий гоев[188] к **слепому послушанию** (ae) или к[189] бездействию[190]. Справедливая, но и[191] неумолимая строгость есть величайший фактор правительственной[192] силы: не только ради выгоды, но и во имя долга[193] победы нам нужно[194] держаться программы[195] насилия и лицемерия. **Доктрина расчета настолько же сильна насколько и средства ею употребляемые** (af), поэтому не столько самой строгостью[196], сколько доктриной ее[197] мы восторжествуем и закрепостим все правительства своему сверхправительству. Достаточно, чтобы знали, что мы неумолимы, чтобы прекратилось ослушание[198]. **Во**[199] **времена** величия Греции[200] мы[201] впервые крикнули слово[202] **свобода** (ag)[203], столь много[204] повторенное[205] с тех пор бессознательными попугаями, [206]налетевшими на эту приманку, с которой[207] они унесли[208] благосостояние мира, истинную свободу личности, находящуюся в ограждении ее[209] от давления толпы. Якобы

---

[188] A2, N omitt.

[189] K omitt.

[190] A2, N omitt.: или...

[191] N omitt.

[192] A2, N: государственной

[193] A2 add.: ради

[194] A2: надо

[195] K: програмы

[196] A2, N: самими средствами

[197] A2, N: строгости

[198] N: прекратились ослушания

[199] N: Еще в древние

[200] N omitt.: величия...

[201] A2, N add.: среди народа [N: народов]

[202] A2, N: слова

[203] A2, N add.: равенство, братство [N add.: слова]

[204] A2 add.: раз

[205] A2, N: повторенные

[206] N add.: отовсюду

[207] A2, N: эти приманки, с которыми

[208] A1: потеряли

[209] N omitt.: находяшуюся... & add.: прежде так огражденную

умные интеллигентные[210] гои не разобрались в отвлеченности произносимых[211] слов, не заметили[212], что в природе нет свободы, не может быть и равенства, ибо[213] сама природа установила неравенство умов, характеров и способностей, равно и подвластность ее законам отношений[214]; не узрели[215], что наша политика выбила их из жизненной колеи на путь, ведущий к нашему правлению[216]. Ознакомленный с политикой[217], хоть[218] и дурак, а[219] может править, а не ознакомленный с нею[220], будь он[221] гений, запутается в указанных[222] нами путях[223]. Поэтому[224] и было установлено[225] династическое правление еврейских[226] царей, чтобы[227] сын узнавал от отца[228] знание политического плана[229],

[210] К: интелигентные

[211] N: произнесенных

[212] А2, N add.: противоречия их значения и несоответствия [N: соответствия] их между собою, не увидели

[213] А2: и что; N: что

[214] А1 add.: и; N omitt.

[215] А2 omitt. отношений... & add.: (каковы суть законы Творца ибо природа есть только синоним Бога), слабейшего сильнейшему, слепого зрячему; N: рассудили

[216] А2, N omitt.: наша... & add.: толпа есть [N omitt.] сила слепая, что выскочки, выбранные [N: избранные] из нее для управлениа, в отношении политики суть столь же слепые [N omitt.: суть... & add.: такие же слепцы], как и она сама, что

[217] А2 omitt.: с политикой; N: посвященный

[218] N: хотя бы

[219] А2, N: да

[220] А2 omitt.: с нею; N: непосвященный

[221] А2, N add.: даже и

[222] В: указываемых

[223] А2, N omitt.: запутается... & add.: ничего не поймет в политике [N add: - все это гоям было упущено из виду]

[224] N omitt.; А2, В: Почему

[225] N: а между тем на этом зиждилось

[226] В: наших

[227] А2, N omitt.: еврейских...

[228] А2, N: отец передавал сыну

[229] К: права; А2, N omitt.: политического... & add.: хода политических дел

для того[230], чтобы никто не знал последнего[231]. Гои утратили этот смысл династического правления, что и[232] послужило к успеху нашего дела. Во всех концах мира слова **«свобода»**, **«равенство»**, **«братство»** ставили[233] в наши ряды через[234] наших слепых агентов целые легионы, которые с восторгом несли наши знамена. Между тем, эти слова были червями[235], которые подтачивали благосостояние гоев, уничтожали[236] всюду мир, спокойствие, солидарность с законом[237], разрушая все основы их государства[238]. Вы увидите в последствии, что это и[239] послужило[240] торжеству нашей системы завоевания мира мирным путем[241]. Это дало нам возможность[242] добиться[243] **уничтожения привилегий,**[244] самую сущность[245] **аристократии** (ah) гоев, которая была естественной защитою[246] народов и стран против наших действий[247]. На этих[248] развалинах[249] мы поставили аристократию выскочек[250], ценз ее[251] мы

---

230 A2 omitt.; N: так
231 A2, N: ведал их [N: его], кроме членов династии, и не мог бы выдать тайны сей [N: его тайны управляемому народу]; B: узнал
232 A2, N omitt.: Гои... & add: Со временем смысл династической передачи истинного положения вещей [N: дел] был утерян [N: утрачен], что
233 A1, A2, N: становили
234 K: чрез
235 A2, N: червяками
236 A2, N: уничтожая
237 A2, N omitt.; B: в повиновении законам
238 A1, A2, N, B: государств
239 N omitt.
240 A2, N add.: к нашему
241 A2, N omitt.: нашей системы...
242 N add.: между прочим
243 N add.: важнейшего козыря в наши руки-
244 A1: привиллегий; N add.: иначе говоря
245 A1, N: самой сущности
246 K: защита; A1: защитницей; A2: единственная защита; N add.: против нас
247 A2: нас; N omitt.: против...
248 N omitt.
249 N add.: природной и родовой аристократии
250 A2, N: нашей интеллигенции во главе всего, денежной
251 N: этой новой аристократии

установили в науке и[252] богатстве[253]. Наше торжество облегчалось[254] тем, что в сношениях с нужными нам людьми мы всегда действовали на самые чувствительные стороны[255] человеческого ума, на[256] рассчет, на алчность, на материальные потребности людей[257], а каждая из перечисленных человеческих слабостей отдельно уже[258] способна убить личную[259] инициативу, отдавая волю людей в распоряжение покупателя их деятельности. Абстракция свободы дала возможность убедить толпы, что **их правители**[260] **ничто иное, как управляющие собственников**[261] **страны** (ai)- народов[262], и что эти правительства[263] можно менять[264], как изношенные перчатки. Сменяемость администраторов[265] отдавала их в наше распоряжение и как бы[266] нашему назначению.

QUOTATIONS FROM JOLY'S *DIALOGUE*

a   «laissons (...) les mots (...) pour nous en tenir aux idées»

b   «...comparaisons... Voici comment je formule mon système... déductions...»

c   «L'instinct mauvais chez l'homme est plus puissant que le bon»

d   «la crainte et la force ont sur lui plus d'empire que la raison»

252   N omitt.: в науке и

253   N add.: от нас зависимом и в науке, двигаемой нашими мудрецами

254   A2, N: облегчилось еще

255   A2, N: струны

256   A2: в

257   A2: его; N omitt.: матеряльные... & add.: ненасытность материальных потребностей человека

258   A2 omitt.: уже; N omitt.: отдельно & add.: взятая в отдельности

259   N omitt.

260   A2, N: правительство; B: правительства

261   A2, N: управляющий собственника

262   A2, N: народа

263   A2 omitt.: и что... & add.: которое; N: omitt.: эти... & add.: его

264   A2, N: сменять

265   A2, N: представителей народа; A2 add.: нации

266   A1 add.: подчинила

e   «Les hommes aspirent tous à la domination, et il n'en est point qui ne fût oppresseur, s'il le pouvait; tous ou presque tous sont prêts à sacrifier les droits d'autrui à leur intérêts»

f   «Qui contient entre eux ces animaux dévorants qu'on appelle les hommes?»

g   «À l'origine des sociétés, c'est la force brutale et sans frein; plus tard, c'est la loi, c'est à dire encore la force, réglée par des formes (...) la force apparaît avant le droit»

h   «La libérté politique n'est qu'une idée relative; la nécessité»

i   «il y a des peuples incapables de modération dans l'exercice de la libérté. Si la libérté s'y prolonge, elle se transforme en licence; la guerre civile ou sociale arrive, et l'Etat est perdu, soit qu'il se fractionne et se démembre par l'effet de ses propres convultions, soit que ses divisions le rendent la proie de l'étranger»

j   «Les Etats (...) ont deux sortes d'ennemis (...). Quelles armes emploieront-ils en guerre contre les étrangers? Les deux généraux se communiqueront-ils réciproquement leurs plans de campagne pour se mettre mutuellement en état de se défendre? S'interdiront-ils les attaques nocturnes (...), les batailles en nombre de troupes inégal? (...) vous ne voulez pas qu'on l'emploie contre les ennemis du dédans, contre les factieux?»

k   «Est-il possible de conduire par la raison (...) des masses (...) qui ne se meuvent que par des sentiments, des passions et des préjugés?»

l   «Est-ce que la politique a rien à démêler avec la morale?»

m   «Avez vous jamais vu un seul Etat se conduire d'après les principes qui régissent la morale privée?»

n   «Ce mot de droit (...) est d'un vague infini»

o   «Où commence-t-il, où finit-il?»

p   «...un Etat: la mauvaise organisation des pouvoirs publics (...) l'impuissance des lois»

q   «...s'élance (...) il brise tous les pouvoirs constitués; il met la main sur les lois, il remanie toutes les institutions»

r   «le bien peut sortir du mal»

s   «le fin justifie les moyens»

t   «Je me suis moins préoccupé de ce qui est bon et moral que de ce qui est utile et nécessaire»

u   «...l'inconstance (...) la lâcheté de la populace (...) son incapacité à concevoir et à respecter les conditions de la vie libre»

v   «une force aveugle»

w   «le peuple, livré à lui-même, ne saura que se détruire»

x   «il ne saura (...) administrer (...) ni faire la guerre» y   «sans le despotisme (...) l'éclatante civilisation (...) ne se fût jamais développée»

z   «vous n'avez à la bouche que deux mots: la force et l'astuce»

aa   «la force joue un grand rôle dans les affaires humaines (...) l'habilité est une qualité nécessaire à l'homme d'Etat»

ab   «la violence en principe, l'astuce en maxime de gouvernement»

ac   «il est permis de faire le mal quand il en peut résulter un bien»

ad   «...trahir sa parole (...) user la corruption (...) quand cela est nécessaire, prendre le bien d'autrui quand cela est avantageux»

ae   «... a le droit (...) une obéissance aveugle»

af   «la doctrine de l'intérêt est donc aussi impuissante à elle seule que les moyens qu'elle emploi»

ag   «L'antiquité nous a montré (...) gouvernement libre»

ah   «ils ont (...) détruit les privilèges (...) l'aristocratie»

ai   «ils ne voient plus dans ceux qui les gouvernent que des mandataires»

II [267]

Нам необходимо, **чтобы войны**[268] **не давали территориальных**[269] **выгод** (а). Это перенесет войну на экономическую почву, в которой нации с[270] нашей[271] помощью[272] усмотрят силу[273] обладания[274], а такое положение вещей отдаст обе стороны в распоряжение нашей интернациональной[275] агентуры, обладающей миллионами[276] глаз, взоров, непреграждённых никакими границами. Тогда наши **интернациональные права** сотрут[277] все народные права и **будут ими**[278] **править так**[279], как **гражданское**[280] **право** государств **правит отношениями** своих **подданных** (b) между собою.

[281]Такими путями мы приведем наших сынов к тем результатам, которые были[282] теми же путями достигнуты еще в древние времена, что описано в Библии, в книге Неемии, глава 9, 22-25. Государственные законы, измененные **конституциями**, были внушены в самых либеральных формах для того, **чтобы народы привыкли к познанию своей силы** (с), вздумали бы[283] посчитаться с царствующими... Вы знаете, чем это кончилось. Конституция **разделила государственную мощь на три части: законодательную, исполнительную и**[284] **судебную,**

---

[267] K omitt.; A1, N, B: **Еще** [N: **Следующий**] **протокол** [B add.: **(2)**]

[268] N add.: по возможности

[269] К: териториальных

[270] N: в

[271] В: нашею

[272] N: помощи

[273] N add.: нашего

[274] А2, N, B: преобладания

[275] К: интернационной

[276] К: милионами

[277] А2: сожрут

[278] N: народами

[279] А2 add.: же

[280] К: гражданскее

[281] А2, N omitt.: Такими..... отдыху.

[282] А1 add.: бы

[283] K omitt.

[284] B: omitt.

с определенными границами, которые нельзя переступить без того, чтобы весь политический корпус не дрогнул (d) до основания. При таких условиях **царствующее лицо уже не вмешало в себе и не олицетворяло государства** (e)[285]. Весь народ мог распределять власть царствующих, как равно и **политических учреждений, независимых друг от друга** (f), тем, что жалоба, поданная на одно из них в другие[286], пересылается[287] на рассмотрение обвиняемого, под предлогом дачи объяснений... Это их поставило в положение неуязвимости, всемогущества и независимости, почему мы могли им внушить, что они служат уже не царствующему, раз они и он зависят от народа, но еще[288] и не народу, пока существует контроль царствующего, направляемый им к собственному интересу. Чтобы сильнее воздействовать на них, мы обещали многим администраторам, что они будут бесконтрольно, в коллективности[289], править странами, если своими действиями[290] помогут нам создать предлоги к неудовольствиям на их правления и подстроить[291] через[292] это республики и в их странах; республики же дадут нам престол мира. Пока мы только заменили своей[293] властью (золотом) влияние либеральных правительств.[294] **Самодержавное ли, республиканское ли правительство, одинаково руководствуются** для объявления своих постановлений **законами** (g), **поэтому** наши заботы должны быть обращены **на то, каким направлением изменить их** (h), замаскировать или прикрыть. Либеральное изменение законов ведет к привычке все новых требований, потом к неисполнению их, к распущенности, а там и к анархии. Когда наступит[295] коронованный царь

---

[285] A1: Государство

[286] B: другое

[287] A1: пересылаются

[288] K omitt.

[289] K: колективности

[290] B: действами

[291] K: построить

[292] K: чрез

[293] B: своею

[294] A1, B add.: [B add.: Ныне ни один Министр не может продержаться у власти, если мы не поддерживаем его рекомендацией из за спины или народа...] **Еще протокол** [B add.: **(3)**].

[295] B add.: последний период, то мы как фактический, хотя и не

вселенной, можем усилить свой деспотизм, могущественный тем, что он незрим, а потому и не ответствен. За нас отвечают те представители народов, которые исполнят[296] нашу программу[297], часто незаметно для себя и, конечно, не ведая ее цели. Но так как мы им покровительствуем за послушание нашим советам, то их ответственность, в сущности, сводится в перемене рода деятельности в администрации, или ко[298] временному отдыху от таковой, и[299] лишь в случае их[300] протеста против наших распоряжений, к вечному отдыху...(*)

Администраторы, выбираемые нами из публики, смотря по их рабским способностям[301], -не подготовленные[302] для управления лица[303]: они легко делаются[304] пешками нашей игры[305]... наших ученых и гениальных советчиков, специалистов с раннего детства воспитанных для управления делами всего мира. [306]Вам известно, что эти последние учились в храме Бога нашего, что они[307] черпали[308] нужные сведения из наших политических планов, из опыта[309] истории, из наблюдений за[310] каждым отдельным[311] моментом. Гои же руководятся теорией[312] и[313] рутиной без всяких наблюдений за результатами их[314], поэтому нам

---

[296] В: исполняют

[297] К: програму

[298] К omitt.

[299] А1 omitt.: в администрации...; В: а

[300] А omitt.

[301] N omitt: смотря... & add.: в зависимости от их рабских способностей

[302] А1, В: приготовленные; А2, N: будут [N add.: лицами,] приготовленными

[303] А2: лицами; N omitt. & add.: и потому

[304] А2, N: сделаются

[305] N: в нашей игре, в руках

[306] А2, N add.: Как

[307] А2, N omitt.: что; N: специалисты наши

[308] N add.: для управления

[309] А1, А2, N, В: опытов

[310] N: над

[311] А1, А2, N, В: текущим

[312] В: теориями

[313] N: практикой беспристрастных исторических наблюдений а теоретической

[314] N: всякого критичрского отношения к ее результатам

нечего с ними считаться: [315]они веселятся[316]. Для них веления научных теорий играют[317] сильнейшую роль[318], для чего[319] мы возбудили[320] слепое доверие к ним[321]. Интеллигенты[322] их[323] кичатся[324] знаниями, [325]без логической проверки их[326], и приводят[327] в действие[328] все почерпнутые из науки сведения, написанные[329] нашими агентами, с целью воспитания умов в нужном нам[330] направлении (**)[331]. Нам необходимо считаться с современными мыслями, характерами, тенденциями народов, чтобы не делать промахов в политике[332] административных дел[333]. Торжество нашей системы, механизм которой можно комбинировать разно, смотря по темпераменту народов,

[315]   N: пусть себе до времени

[316]   A2, N add.: или живут надеждой [N: надеждами] или воспоминаниями новых и пройденных веселий [N: на новые увеселения, или воспоминаниями о прежных. Пусть]

[317]   A2: науку (теории) должны играть

[318]   N omitt.: веления... & add.: играет главнейшую роль то, что мы внушили им признавать за великие науки (теории)

[319]   A2: сего

[320]   A2: возбудим; N: этой цели мы постоянно, путем нашей прессы, возбуждаем

[321]   A1: ней; B: науке

[322]   K: Интелигенты

[323]   N: гоев

[324]   A2, N: будут кичиться

[325]   A2 add.: и
[326]A2 omitt.

[327]   A2, N: проведут

[328]   A2: действия

[329]   N: скомбинированные

[330]   N: для нас

[331]   N add.: Вы не думайте, что утверждения наши голословны: обратите внимание на подстроенные нами успехи Дарвинизма, Марксизма, Нитшеизма. Растлевающее значение для гоевских умов этих направлений науки нам то, по крайней мере, должно быть очевидно.

[332]   N add.: и в управлении

[333]   N: административными делами

встречаемых нами по[334] пути, не может иметь успеха, если практическое применение ее не будет основываться на итогах прошлого и настоящего[335]. **В руках современных государств имеется великая сила, соединяющая**[336] **движение мысли в народе, это- пресса** (i): ее роль[337], якобы, **указывает**[338] **необходимые требования, передавать жалобы народного голоса, выражать**[339] **неудовольствия** (j), в ней выражается[340] торжество свободоговорения; но, кроме нас, никто не умеет[341] организовать эту силу в свою пользу,[342] через нее мы добились влияния[343], благодаря ей- мы собрали[344] золото, не взирая на то, что[345] приходилось его брать из потоков крови и слез. Но ведь[346] **цель оправдывает средства** (k), да[347] мы откупились, жертвуя многими из нашего народа, из коих[348] каждая жертва[349] стоит тысячи гоев перед Богом нашим[350].

(*) *Переводчик напоминает: на успокоение*[351] *Карно- ножем, Мак Кинлея- пулею, Гамбеты*[352], *Феликса Фора- ядом, и многих известных и не известных*[353] *деятелей не еврейского*[354] *лагеря*[355].

334   N: на

335   N: в связи с настоящим

336   N: создающая

337   N: роль прессы

338   A2: указывать яко-бы

339   A2, N, B add.: и создавать

340   N: прессе воплощается

341   A1: умел

342   A2, N omitt.: кроме...; N add.: государства не умели воспользоваться етой силой, и она очутилась в наших руках.

343   N add.: сами оставаясь в тени

344   A2: собирали; N add.: в свои руки

345   N add.: нам

346   A2, B omitt.

347   A2, N omitt.: ведь цель...

348   N omitt.

349   N add.: с нашей стороны

350   A2, N omitt.

351   B: об упокоении

352   A1: Гамбету; B omitt.

(**) *Переводчик напоминает*[356] *успехи дарвинизма, марксизма, ницшеизма*[357] *и других недоказанных теорий.*[358]

QUOTATIONS FROM JOLY'S *DIALOGUE*

a   «...guerres...qu'elles ne donnent plus (...) la proprété des Etats vaincus»

b   «le droit international régit (...) comme le droit civil régit les rapports des sujets dans chaque nation.»

c   «ils ont assuré leurs droits politiques par des constitutions»

d   «ils on séparé les trois pouvoirs, législatif, exécutif et judiciaire, par des lignes constitutionelles qui ne peuvent être franchies sans que l'alarme soit donné à tout le corps politique.»

e   «La personne du prince cesse d'être confondue avec celle de l'État»

f   «des corps politiques indépendents les uns des autres.»

g   «...sous le règne de la liberté comme sous celui de la tyrannie, on n'a pu gouverner que par des lois.»

h   «C'est donc sur la manière don't les lois sont faites...»

i   «...les Etats modernes (...) Une puissance (...) est venue leur donner (...) C'est la presse»

j   «...une voie publique (...) se manifeste tout le mouvement des idées chez les peuples (...) elle exprime les besoins, traduit les plaintes, dénonce les abus»

k   «le fin justifie les moyens»

---

[353]   A1 omitt.: и не известных

[354]   B: противуеврейского

[355]   A2, N omitt.: Переводчик...

[356]   A2: переводчиком указываются

[357]   A2 add. и т. д.; K: нитшейзма

[358]   A2 omitt.: и других...; N omitt.: Переводчик...

III [359]

Сегодня хочу сказать[360] вам[361], что наша цель уже в нескольких шагах от нас. Вот рисунок, на котором изображен весь пройденный нами путь и намечено[362] небольшое пространство, которое нам осталось пройти[363], чтобы[364] сомкнуть[365] цикл символического змия, каковым мы изображаем наш народ. Когда этот цикл[366] окончательно[367] сомкнется, то[368] им будут замкнуты все европейские государства[369] крепкими тисками... Современные **конституционные весы** скоро опрокинутся, потому что мы их установили не с точностью для того, чтобы они не переставали колебаться, пока не перетрется их держатель. А[370] гои **предполагали, что они так**[371] **крепко сковали его** (а)[372], и все ожидали, что весы придут[373] в равновесие[374]. Но[375] **Царствующие заслонены своими представителями** (b), которые дурят, увлекаясь своею[376] бесконтрольной и безответственною[377] властью, сознавая, что[378] они обязаны ею[379] навеянному на[380] дворцы террору. Не имея доступа к

---

[359]   K omitt.; A1, N, B: **Еще** [N: **Следующий**] **протокол** [B add.: **(4)**]

[360]   A2, N: могу сообщить

[361]   A2 omitt.

[362]   N omitt.: Вот рисунок... & add.: Остается

[363]   B: пройдти

[364]   N omitt.: которое... & add.: и весь пройденный нами путь готов уже

[365]   N add.: свой

[366]   N: круг

[367]   N omitt.

[368]   N omitt.

[369]   N add.: как

[370]   A2, N omitt.

[371]   N: достаточно

[372]   B: их

[373]   A: прийдут

[374]   A2: к разновесию

[375]   A2 omitt.; N add.: держатель-

[376]   A1, N: своей

[377]   A1, A2: безответственной

[378]   A2, N omitt.: сознавая, что; A2 add.: которой; N add.: Властью же этой

[379]   N omitt.

своему народу, в самую его среду, благодаря страху своему,[381] Царствующие не могут уже сговориться с народом[382] как в былые времена[383], и укрепиться против властолюбцев[384]. Чтобы побудить властолюбцев к злоупотреблению властью, **мы противопоставили**[385] **друг другу все силы** (c), развив их либеральные тенденции к независимости. Мы[386] **возбудили всякую предприимчивость,**[387] **мы вооружили все партии, мы поставили власть мишенью**[388] **всех амбиций. Из государств мы сделали арены, на которых разыгрываются смуты** (d); **еще немного- и беспорядки,** банкротства[389] **появятся всюду** (e)[390]... **Неистощимые говоруны превратили в ораторские состязания заседания парламентов** и административных собраний. **Смелые журналисты, бесцеремонные памфлетисты**[391] **ежедневно нападают** на административный **персонал** (f). Злоупотребления властью[392] окончательно подорвут[393] учреждения[394] и все полетит вверх ногами под ударами обезумевшей от либерализма[395] толпы... [396]**Народы прикованы**[397] к тяжелому **труду- бедностью**

---

[380]   A2, N: во

[381]   A2, N omitt.: благодаря...

[382]   A2: ними; N: ним

[383]   A2, N omitt.: как...

[384]   K omitt.: Но Царствующие.... против властолюбцев; A1, A2, N, B add.: Разделенная нами, зрячая Царская сила и слепая сила народа, потеряли всякое значение, ибо отдельно друг от друга, как слепец без палки [B add.: и обратно], они немощны.

[385]   A2: противупоставили

[386]   N add.: в этом направлении

[387]   A1 omitt.: Мы возбудили...

[388]   A2, N add.: для

[389]   B: банкротство

[390]   K, B: подорвут все существующие установления

[391]   B: панфлетисты

[392]   A1: властей

[393]   K: подорвет; A2, N: подготовят

[394]   N add.: к падению

[395]   A2, N omitt.: от либерализма

[396]   K, A1, B add.: мы приковали

[397]   K, A1, B omitt.

сильнее, чем их[398] приковывало крепостное право и[399] рабство (g); от последних[400] они освободились[401], от нужды и горя[402] они не оторвутся. Мы включили в конституцию[403] такие права, которые для масс являются фиктивными (h), а не действительными правами, [404]эти права[405] выражали неосуществимую на практике идею[406]. Какая нужда[407] для пролетария[408]-труженика, согнутого[409] под[410] тяжелым трудом, пролетария[411], придавленного[412] своею участью, что говоруны получили право[413] болтать, журналисты право[414] писать (i) всякую чепуху наравне[415] с делом, раз пролетариат[416] не имеет[417] иной выгоды от конституции, как те крохи[418] которые мы им бросаем с нашего стола, за подачу ими[419] голосов в пользу наших предписаний и[420] агентов.

---

[398] K omitt.

[399] B: или

[400] N: них

[401] A2, N: [N add.: так или иначе] могли они освобождаться, могли с ними считаться [N omitt.: они... & add.: освободиться], а

[402] A2, N, B omitt.: и горя

[403] A2, N: конституции

[404] N add.: все

[405] N: так называемые права народа

[406] A2 omitt.: эти права...; N omitt.: выражали...; A2 & N add.: они [N omitt:] могут быть [N: существовать] только идеей [N: в идее, никогда] неосуществимой на практике

[407] A2, N: Что

[408] K, A1, B omitt.

[409] B: труженику согбенному

[410] A1, A2: над; N: в дугу над

[411] A1: для пролетария; A2, N omitt.

[412] B: пролетарию придавленному

[413] A2, N omitt.: что... & add.: получение говорунами права

[414] A2, N: журналистами права

[415] A2, N: наряду

[416] B: пролетарии

[417] B: имеют

[418] N, B: кроме тех жалких [B omitt.] крох

[419] K omitt.

[420] N add.: ставленников наших, наших

Республиканские **права** для труженика[421] **суть**[422] **горькая ирония** (j), ибо необходимость чуть ли[423] не поденного[424] труда не дает ему[425] настоящего пользования ими, но зато отнимает у него[426] гарантию постоянного и верного заработка, зависяшего[427] от стачек хозяев или товарищей, возбуждаемых нами по мере надобности, чтобы отвлечь умы от текущих дел и провести незаметно нам потребное[428]. Народы и правительства гоев уничтожили[429] под нашим руководством аристократию, которая была их опорой,[430] защитой и кормилицей ради ее[431] собственных интересов[432]; зато ныне они попали[433] под гнет кулачества разжившихся пройдох[434], насевших[435] на рабочих безжалостным ярмом. Мы явимся[436] спасителями для[437] рабочего[438], когда предложим ему[439] вступить в ряды нашего войска социалистов, анархистов, коммунаров[440], для которых[441] мы всегда имеем[442]

421 A1: тружников; N: бедняка
422 A1: есть; N omitt.
423 A2, N omitt.
424 A1: подденного
425 A1, A2, N, B: им
426 A1, A2, N, B: них
427 N: ставя его в зависимости
428 A2, N omitt.: возбуждаемых...
429 A2, N: Народ уничтожил
430 A1 add.: и; A2 omitt.: их опорой & add. его; N omitt.: их... & add.: его
     естественной
431 A2, N omitt.; B: своих
432 A2: выгод; N omitt. & add.: выгод, неразрывно связанных с народным
     благосостоянием
433 A2: Ныне он подпал; N: Теперь же, с уничтожением аристократии, он
     попал
434 A1 omitt.: разжившихся...
435 A1: насевшего
436 N add.: якобы
437 A2, N omitt.
438 N add.: от этого гнета
439 К, B: им
440 A1: комунаров
441 N: которым

поддержку из якобы брасткого и солидарного[443] правила[444] нашего социального масонства[445]. Аристократия, пользовавшаяся по праву трудом рабочих, была заинтересована[446], чтобы они[447] были сыты, здоровы и крепки, мы же заинтересованы[448] в вырождении гоев, а[449] наша власть заинтересована[450] в голодности, в[451] слабости своего[452] рабочего, потому что недостатками[453] он закрепощается по[454] нашей воле, а в слабости[455] он не найдет ни сил[456] ни энергии, чтобы нам противодействовать[457]: голод создает[458] права капитала[459] вернее, чем давала аристократии это право царствующая[460] власть над рабочими[461]. Нуждою[462] и происходящею от нее завистливой[463] ненавистью мы двигаем толпами[464] и стираем их[465] руками тех, которые[466] нам

442   N: оказываем

443   N omitt.: и ...

444   N: общечеловеческой солидарности

445   A1: массонства

446   N add.: в том

447   A2: те; N: рабочие

448   N add.: в обратном,

449   N omitt.

450   B omitt.: в вырождениии ... заинтересована

451   A2 omitt.; N omitt.: заинтересована в голодности в & add.: в хроническом недоедании и

452   A1: всего; N omitt.

453   N: всем этим

454   A2, N, B omitt.

455   N: области своей

456   A1 add.: ни желания,

457   A2, N: для противодействия ей

458   N: создаст

459   A1: Капиталу; A2, N add.: на рабочего; B add.: над рабочими

460   N: законная Царская

461   A2, N omitt.: над ...; B omitt.: давала аристократии... & add.: царствующая власть могла укрепить над нами права аристократии

462   A1: нуждой

463   N: завистливою

464   B: толпою

465   A2, B: ее

мешают[467]. Когда прийдет время нашему всемирному владыке из дома Давидова[468], короноваться, то те же руки сметут все могущее быть сему препятствием. Гои отвыкли думать без наших[469] советов; поэтому и[470] не думаются до того, что в период нашего управления[471] поставим на первый план преподавания[472] в народных школах важнейшую из всех наук[473] - науку о строе человеческого бытия, социальной жизни, требующей[474] разделения труда, а следовательно разделения людей на классы[475] и сословия. Это преподавание мы установим[476], чтобы все знали, что равенства в правах[477] не может быть, вследствие различия назначения в[478] деятельности,[479] что места[480] и труд должны сохраняться в определенном круге[481], чтобы не быть источником[482] мук,

---

467 N: мешает на пути нашем

468 A2, N omitt.: из дома...

469 A2, N: научных; B: научных или умных

470 N, B: они

471 N omitt.: думаются.. & add.: видят настоятельной необходимости в том, чего мы, когда наступит наше царство

472 A2 omitt.: думаются до того...; N omitt.: поставим...; A2, N add.: видят того, чего мы будем [N add: неукоснительно] придерживаться, а именно, что надо преподавать

473 A2, N omitt.: важнейшую из всех наук & add.: истинную [N add: единую] науку, первую из всех

474 A2, N: человеческой жизни, социального быта, требующего

475 K: класы

476 A2, N omitt. Это преподавание...; N add.: Необходимо

477 A2, N omitt.: в правах

478 A2, N omitt.

479 A2, N add.: что не могут одинаково отвечать перед законом тот, который своим поступком компрометтирует [N: компрометирует] целое сословие и тот, который не затрогивает им никого [N add: кроме своей чести. Правильная] наука социального строя [N add: в тайны которой мы не допускаем гоев] показала бы всем,

480 A1, A2, N: место

481 A2, N: кругу

482 A2: источниками; A2, N add.: человеческих

от несоответствия воспитания с предназначенной от природы[483] работой; это мы тогда должны внушать из чувства самосохранения[484], чтобы никто не оспаривал наши[485] положения[486]. При изучении этой науки люди[487] станут[488] повиноваться властям и распределенному ими строю в государстве нашем[489], иначе народы[490], в[491] неведении требований природы, лезут из своих мест, питая[492] вражду ко всем сословиям, которые считают[493] выше своего[494], ибо не понимают[495] значения[496] каждого сословия. Сказанная[497] вражда еще больше[498] увеличится[499] на почве экономического кризиса, который скоро[500] остановит биржевые сделки и ход промышленности. Такая мера бросит[501] на улицу целые толпы рабочих во всех странах Европы одновременно... Вы понимаете, с каким[502] наслаждением они[503] бросятся проливать кровь тех, кому они[504]

---

[483] A2, N omitt.: предзначенной...

[484] K: самоохранения

[485] B: нашего

[486] A2, N omitt.: это мы тогда должны... положения

[487] A2: народы

[488] N add.: добровольно

[489] A2 omitt.

[490] A2: народ

[491] A2 add.: своем

[492] A2 omitt.: народы ... питая; N omitt.: нашем... питая; A2, N add.: [N add: При теперешнем же состояния науки и нами созданном ее направлении,] народ. [N add.: слепо верящий печатному слову,] питает [N add.: во внушенных ему заблюждениах,] в невидении своем

[493] A2, N: [N add: он] считает

[494] N: себя

[495] A2, N: понимает

[496] A2: назначения

[497] N: Указанная

[498] A2: более

[499] A2, N: увеличивается

[500] A2, N omitt.

[501] N omitt.: Такая.. бросит & add.: Создав всеми доступными нам подпольными путями с помощью золота, которое все в наших руках, общий экономический кризис, мы бросим

[502] A2, N omitt.: Вы... & add.: Эти толпы с

завидуют с детства[505]. Наших они не тронут, потому, что момент нападения нам будет известен и нами будут приняты меры к ограждению своих, как это было сделано нами во время коммуны[506] в Париже[507]. Мы убедили гоев[508], что прогресс[509] **приведет** людей[510] **к царству разума** (k); наш деспотизм и будет таковым, ибо он сумеет разумными строгостями замирить все волнения, вытравить[511] либерализм из всех учреждений. Когда мы прививали либерализм гоям, их[512] **народ** увидел[513], что во имя свободы ему делают[514] уступки и послабления в сказанных учреждениях; из этого[515] он **понял**[516], **что** он **представляет**[517] **из себя силу**, с которой[518] считаются, вообразил[519] равноправность[520] и **ринулся ко власти**[521], но тут то[522], как и всякий слепец, наткнулся[523] на массу[524] препятствий, **бросился**[525] искать

---

503   A2, N omitt.

504   N add.: в простоте своего неведения

505   A2, N add.: [N add: и] чьи имущества им можно будет [N add: тогда] грабить

506   К: комуны

507   A2, N omitt.: как это было... Париже.

508   A2, N omitt.

509   К: прогрес

510   A2, N: всех гоев

511   В: вытравив

512   A2, N omitt.: мы прививали...

513   В: народы увидели

514   N add.: всякие

515   A2, N omitt.: в сказанных...

516   N: вообразил себе; В: они поняли

517   В: они представляют

518   В: которою

519   В: вообразили

520   A2, N omitt.: представляет... & add.: владыка

521   A2: во власть; В: ринулись во Власть

522   A2, N: конечно

523   В: наткнулись

524   К: масу

525   В: бросились

руководителя, попал[526] к нам в руки[527] **и сложил**[528] **полномочия у ног** (l) наших агентов[529]. С тех пор мы водим его[530] от[531] одного разочарования к другому[532], для того, чтобы он[533], в конце концов, от всех[534] отказался[535] в пользу того царя-деспота сионской крови, которого мы готовим для мира. В настоящее время мы, как интернациональная сила, неуязвимы, потому что при нападении на нас одних, нас поддерживают другие государства гоев[536]. **Неистощимая подлость** гоевских **народов, ползающих**[537] **перед**[538] **силой, безжалостных к слабости, беспощадных для проступков**[539] **и снисходительных для преступлений**[540], **не желающих выносить противоречий**[541] свободного строя, терпеливых до мученичества перед[542] насилием[543] смелого деспотизма (m),- вот что способствует нашей неуязвимости[544]. От современных премьеров[545]- диктаторов, нами воспитанных[546], они **терпят** и выносят **такие злоупотребления, за меньшее из которых они бы обезглавили двадцать**

---

[526]   В: попали

[527]   A2, N omitt.: попал... & add.: не догадался вернуться к прежнему

[528]   A2, N add.: свои; В: сложили

[529]   A2, N omitt.: агентов; N add.: Вспомните французскую революцию, которой мы дали имя «великой» тайны ее подготовления нам хорошо известны, ибо она вся- дело рук наших.

[530]   N: народы; В: их

[531]   A, В: из

[532]   В: в другое

[533]   В: они

[534]   A2, N omitt.: в конце... & add.: и от нас; В: всего

[535]   В: отказались

[536]   A2, N omitt.

[537]   К: полающих

[538]   К: пред

[539]   N: к проступкам

[540]   N: к преступлениям

[541]   A2, К, В: противоречия

[542]   К: пред

[543]   A2: насилиями

[544]   К: неузвимости; N: независимости

[545]   К: примьеров

[546]   A2, N omitt.: нами...

королей[547] (n), но это потому, что наши агенты им[548] шепчут[549], что[550] ущерб государству[551] делается с целью[552] привести к интернациональному благу, к братству народов, к[553] солидарности и[554] равноправию[555]. Конечно, им не говорят, что такое соединение всех народов под интернациональным правлением совершится[556] нашей державой. И вот народ осуждает[557] правых и оправдывает[558] виновных, чтобы убедиться[559], что он владыка положения[560]: этим они разрушают[561] всякую устойчивость и создают[562] беспорядки на каждом шагу. Слово «свобода» **выставляет** человеческие[563] **общества на борьбу** против всяких сил, **против всякой власти**[564] даже **Божеской** (o)[565] и

---

547   К: властителей

548   A2, N omitt.: но ... им & add.: [N add.: Чем же объяснить такое явление, такую нелогичность в реагировании народных масс на события, казалось бы, одного порядка? Объясняется это явление тем,] что деспоты эти

549   A2, N add.: им [N: народу] через своих агентов

550   A2 add.: они делают; N add.: они злоупотреблениями теми наносят

551   A2, N, B: государствам

552   A2, N omitt.: делается... ; A2 add.: чтобы; N add.: для высшей цели

553   A2, N omitt.: привести... к & add.: добиться [N: достижения] блага народов их интернационального братства

554   B add.: к

555   A2, N: равноправия

556   A2, N omitt.: всех ... & add.: [N add: должно] совершиться [N add: только] под одно [N omitt.]

557   A1: народы осуждают

558   A1: оправдывают

559   A2: только убедить себя; N: все более и более убеждаясь

560   A1 omitt.: чтобы убедиться, что он владыка положения; A2, N omitt.: владыка.. & add.: он [N omitt.] может творить все, чего [N add.: ни] пожелает; B: положение

561   A2, N: Благодаря такому положению [N add.: вещей,] народ разрушает; B: он разрушает

562   A2, N, B: создает

563   A2, N: людские

564   К, A1, A2, B omitt.

565   К, A1, A2, B: Божеских

природной[566], вот почему при нашем (правлении)[567] воцарении мы должны будем исключить его[568] из человеческого лексикона, как принцип животной силы, **превращающей толпы в** кровожадных **зверей.** Правда, **эти звери засыпают** всякий раз, **как они**[569] напьются крови, и в **это время их легко заковать в цепи** (р), но если им не дать крови, они не спят а[570] борются[571].

QUOTATIONS FROM JOLY'S *DIALOGUE*

a   «…cette bascule constitutionelle! (…) fonctionnait avec précision (…) à la première occasion le mouvement se produira par la rupture d'un des ressorts que vous avez si soigneusement forgés.»

b   «…le prince (…), souverain (…) qui acceptera (…) le rôle passif auquel vous l'aurez condamné»

c   «vous aurez mis aux prises toutes le forces contraires»

d   «Vous aurez (…) suscité toutes les enterprises, donné des armes à tous le partis. Vous aurez livré le pouvoir à l'assaut de toutes les ambitions, et fait de l'État une arène où se déchaineront les factions.»

e   «Dans peu de temps, ce sera le désordre partout»

f   «d'intarissables rhéteurs transformeront en joutes oratoires les assemblées délibérantes; d'audacieux journalistes, d'effrénés pamphlétaires attaqueront tous les jours la personne (…) les hommes en place.»

g   «Il y a des populations (…) rivées au travail par la pauvreté, comme elles l'étaient autrefois par l'esclavage.»

h   «Vous avez créé des droits qui resteront (…) pour la masse (…) à l'état de pure faculté»

i   «Qu'importe au prolétaire courbé sur son labeur, accablé sous le poids de sa destinée, que quelques orateurs aient le droit de parler, que quelques journalistes aient le droit d'écrire?»

j   «Ces droits (…) ne sont pour lui qu'une ironie amère»

k   «…qu'ils conduisent au règne de la raison»

---

[566] K, A1, A2: природных; B: сил природы
[567] A2, N, B omitt.
[568] K: ee; N: это слово; B: самое слово Свобода
[569] N omitt.
[570] N: и
[571] K, A1: борятся

l   «Le peuple (…) s'emparera (…) de tous les pouvoirs dont on a reconnu que le principe était en lui (…) Il les jettera (…) au premier soldat de fortune»

m   «…l'inépuisable lacheté des peuples (…) rampants devant la force, sans pitié devant la faiblesse, implacables pour des fautes, indulgents pour des crimes, incapables de supporter les contrariétés d'un régime libre, et patients jusq'au martyre pour toutes les violences du despotisme audacieux»

n   «des maîtres (…) pardonnent des attentats pour le moindre desquels ils auraient décapité vingt rois»

o   «Il met les sociétés en guerre ouverte contre tous les pouvoirs humains et même contre Dieu»

p   «Il fait du peuple une brute féroce qui s'endort quand elle est repue de sang, et qu'on enchaine»

IV [572]

Всякая республика проходит несколько стадий: первая из них находится[573] в первых днях безумствования слепца, мечущегося[574] направо и налево, вторая в **демагогии, от которой**[575] **родится анархия, приводящая** неизбежно **к деспотизму** (a), но уже не[576] легальному, открытому, а потому ответственному[577], но[578] к невидимому и неведомому, не[579] чувствительному деспотизму[580], тем бесцеремоннее действующему[581] под прикрытием[582] разных агентов, что[583] смена их[584] не[585] задевает[586], а[587] воспособляет тайной силе, избавляя ее[588] от необходимости награждать[589] долгосрочно прислужавших[590]. Правда[591], и **свобода могла**[592] **бы быть безвредной**[593] и просуществовать[594], **если**

---

[572] K omitt.; A1, N, B: **Еще** [N: **Следующий**] **протокол** [B add.: **(5)**]

[573] N: заключена

[574] N, B: мятущегося

[575] A2: нее

[576] A2, B add.: к

[577] A1 omitt.: но уже не...

[578] N: а

[579] A2: но; N: и тем не менее

[580] N add.: какой бы то ни было тайной организациии,

[581] N: дейсвтующей

[582] N: что она действует прикрыто, за спиной

[583] A2, N omitt.

[584] A2, N: которых

[585] N add.: только

[586] N: вредит

[587] N: но

[588] A2, N: избавляющейся; N add.: благодаря этой смене

[589] N: тратить свои средства на вознаграждение

[590] A2, N, B: прослуживших; A2, N, B add.: Кто и что может свергнуть незримую силу?!; N, B add.: А сила наша именно такова. Внешнее масонство служит слепым прикрытием ей и ее целям, но план действий этой силы, даже самое ее местопребывание для народа всегда останется неизвестным.

[591] A2, N: Но

[592] K, A1: могли

бы она держалась[595] **на принципах веры в Бога**, на братстве человечества вне мысли о равенстве, которому противоречат[596] законы творения, установившие подвластность. При такой вере **народ**[597] **шел бы** смирно[598] и **кротко под руководством**[599] духовных **пастырей** (b)[600], повинуясь распределению Божьему на земле; вот почему нам необходимо подорвать веру, вырвать из ума гоев принцип Божества и Духа, и все это[601] заменить арифметическими рассчетами и материальными потрбностями и интересами[602]... Чтобы умы гоев не переставали[603] думать и замечать, надо их отвлечь на алчную добычу промышленности и торговли[604]. Таким образом лица и[605] нации будут искать свою выгоду[606], и в борьбе[607] за нее не заметят своего общего врага- наш интерес, а[608] чтобы свобода окончательно разложила и разорила гоевские общества, надо поставить промышленность на спекулятивную почву; это послужит к[609] тому, что отнятое промышленностью от земли не удержится в ее[610] руках, а[611] перейдет к спекуляции, то есть в наши кассы[612], так как- нити от последней будут

---

[593]   K, A1: безвредными

[594]   N add.: в государственном обиходе без ущерба для благоденствия народов

[595]   K, A1: они держались

[596]   N add.: сами

[597]   A2, N add.: был бы управляем опекой приходов и

[598]   A2, N, B: смиренно

[599]   A2, N: рукой

[600]   A2, N: своего духовного пастыря

[601]   A2, N omitt.

[602]   A2, N omitt.: и интересами

[603]   A2, N, B: успевали

[604]   A2, N omitt.: алчную ... & add.: промышленность и торговлю

[605]   A2, N omitt.: лица и & add.: все

[606]   N: своей выгоды

[607]   B add.: из

[608]   A2, N omitt.: наш ... a; N add.: Но для того

[609]   A2, B omitt.

[610]   A2, N omitt.

[611]   A2: и

[612]   K, A1: классы

исходить от нашего клубка[613]. Напряженная **борьба за превосходство и**[614] толчки экономического характера[615] **создадут**[616] **разочарованные, холодные**[617] **общества, безсердечные, получившие**[618] **полное отвращение**[619] **политике и**[620] **религии. Руководителем их будет только разсчет;**[621] **они будут иметь настоящий культ золота**[622], **за**[623] **материальные наслаждения** (c), которые оно могло бы им дать, и этим[624] попадут[625] в наше полное рабство...[626] Тогда[627] из одной[628] **ненависти к привилегированным**[629], **низшие классы** гоев **пойдут**[630] против наших конкурентов[631] **на власть** (d), интеллигентов[632]- гоев чуть нам понадобится их двинуть[633].

[634]**Какую форму**[635] правления можно дать обществам, в которых подкупность проникла всюду, где богатства достигаются[636] только

---

613   A2, N omitt.: так как ... клубка.

614   A2, B, N omitt.

615   N: в экономической жизни; A2, B: рода

616   N add.: да и создали уже

617   A2, N add.: и

618   N: Эти общества получат

619   A2, N, B add.: к; N add.: высшей

620   A2, N, B add.: к

621   A2, N add.: т.е. золото, к которому

622   A2, N omitt.; B: к золоту

623   N add.: те

624   B add.: путем

625   A1: падут

626   A2, N omitt.: и этим ... рабство

627   A2, N add.: [N add.: то] не для служения добру и богатству [N: даже не ради богатства] а

628   A2 omitt.

629   K, A1, B omitt.: из одной ненависти к привилегированным; N: привиллегированным

630   A2, N add.: за нами

631   A2, B: конкуррентов

632   K: интелигентов

633   A1 add.: на них; A2, N omitt.: чуть..... двинуть; B: когда нам понадобится создать решительный переворот

634   A1, N, B add.: **Еще** [N: **Следующий**] **протокол** [B add.: **(6)**]; A2 add.: V

ловкими   проделками[637],   где   царствует   распущенность,   **где**
нравственность   поддерживается   карательными   мерами[638], а не[639]
воспринятыми принципами, **где чувства к родине** и к религии **затерты**
космополитическими принципами (e)[640]; какую форму правления дать
таким обществам, как не ту изрядно[641] деспотическую, которую[642]
опишу вам далее?

Для   чего[643]   мы   должны   **создать**[644]   **усиленную централизацию**
управления, **чтобы все общественные силы забрать в руки.** Затем,[645]
урегулируем   механически   все   действия политической   жизни   наших
подданных новыми законами, **законы** эти **устрашат**[646] все послабления и
вольности[647] и наше царство ознаменуется **таким величественным**
деспотизмом, что он[648] **будет в состоянии во всякое время** и во всяком
месте **прихлопнуть противодействующих или недовольных** (f)[649]. Д. Ж.
говорит[650], что[651] **деспотизм** о котором я говорю, **не согласуется с**
современным прогрессом (g)[652], но я[653] докажу обратное. **В те времена,**
когда народы глядели на царствующих[654]**, как на чистое проявление**

---

637   A2, N add.: административного

636   N: достигают

637   A1, A2, N, B: сюрпризами [N add.: полумошеннических;] проделок [B:
         сюрпризами ловких проделок]

638   N add.: и суровыми законами

639   A2, N add.: добровольно

640   N: убеждениями

641   N omitt.

642   N add.: я

643   A1, N, B omitt.; A2: Для них

644   A2, N: создадим

645   N omitt. Затем; A2, N, B add.: мы

646   A1, A2, N, B: отберут [A1: оберут] один [N: одно] за другим

647   A2, N add.: которые были допущены гоями

648   A1: оно

649   A2, N add.: гоев

650   N: Нам скажут

651   N add.: тот

652   K: прогресом

653   A2, N add.: вам

654   A2, N: царствовавших

Божьей воли, они покорялись безропотно их воле[655]. **Но с того дня**[656], **как** мы их навели на[657] **мысль о собственных правах,** они стали считать царствующих[658] простыми смертными, **помазание Божиим**[659] **избранием ниспало с главы их** (h)[660] в глазах народов[661], а когда мы[662] отняли[663], подорвали[664] веру в Бога, то мощь[665] была выброшена на улицу, в место публичной собственности, которая[666] захвачена[667] нами. Кроме того, **искусство**[668] **управлять массами** и лицами посредством теорий[669], фразеологии, правилами якобы[670] общежития, этикета[671] и всякими[672] уловками в которых гои ничего не смыслят и разобраться в цели их установления не могут[673], **принадлежит** тоже[674] **к специальностям** нашего **административного ума** (i), воспитанного на анализе, на[675] наблюдении, на таких тонкостях соображений, в которых у нас соперников нет, как их[676] нет и в составлении планов политического

655   A2, N, B: самодержавию Царей
656   K: врсмсни
657   A2: им дали; N: им внушили
658   A2, N add.: лиц
659   A2, B: Божеским; N: Божественным
660   A2, N, B: царей
661   A2, N, B: народа
662   A2, N add.: у него
663   A1 omitt.
664   A2, N omitt.
665   N add.: власти
666   N: и
667   A2, B: которое захвачено
668   K: искуство
669   A2 add.: и; N: ловко подстроенной теории и
670   N omitt.
671   N omitt.
672   A2, N add.: другими
673   N omitt.: и разобраться ... могут
674   N: также
675   N omitt.
676   N omitt.

действия и солидарности.[677] Временно с нами могли[678] бы еще[679] справиться современные коалиции[680] гоев, но с этой стороны мы обезпечены теми глубокими корнями разлада[681], которые[682] вырвать нельзя. Мы противопоставили[683] друг другу их[684] личные и национальные разчеты[685], религиозные и племенные ненависти, выращенные[686] нами в их сердцах в течение[687] многих[688] веков. Благодаря всему этому, ни одно государство не встретит ответа[689] своей протянутой руке для солидарного против нас действия[690], ибо каждое подумает[691], что соглашение против нас невыгодно ему самому. Мы слишком сильны, с нами приходится считаться. Державы не могут даже небольшого, частичного[692] соглашения[693] составить без того, чтобы не были к тому[694] тайно причастны мы. **Господь сказал:**[695] *«Per Me reges*

---

[677]   N add.: Одни Иезуиты могли бы в этом с нами сравняться, но мы их съумели дискредитировать в глазах бессмысленной толпы, как организацию явную, сами со своей тайной организацией оставшись в тени. Впрочем, не все ли равно для мира, кто будет его владыкой- глава ли католичества, или наш деспот Сионской крови?! Нам то, избранному народу, это далеко не все равно.

[678]   A1, A2, N, B: могла

[679]   N omitt.

[680]   A2, N, B: всемирная коалиция

[681]   N add.: между ними

[682]   N, B: которых

[683]   B: противупоставили

[684]   N omitt.

[685]   N add.: гоев

[686]   N: вырощенные

[687]   A2: продолжение; N: продолжении; B: течении

[688]   A2, N: двадцати

[689]   N: ни откуда поддержки

[690]   A2, N omitt.: для солидарного....

[691]   A2, N: каждый должен думать

[692]   N: частного

[693]   A2 add.: (концерта)

[694]   N: нему

[695]   A2, N omitt.

regnant» (j)[696] - через Меня царствуют цари-, а наши пророки сказали[697] нам[698] что «мы избраны самим Богом на царство по всей земле[699]». Для этого[700] Господь[701] нас наградил гением, чтобы мы могли справляться со своей задачей[702] покорения мира мирным путем. Ныне[703] все колеса государственных **механизмов** ходят воздействием двигателя, находящегося в наших руках,- золота[704]. Измышленная нашими мудрецами наука **политико**[705]-**экономия**[706] давно установила[707] **престиж**[708] за капиталом. Последний[709] для действий без стеснений должен создать **свободу** (k)[710] для монополий[711] промышленности[712], а[713] это послужит к стеснению народа. **Ныне важнее обезоруживать**[714]

---

[696] N: regnat; A1, B omitt.: Per Me...

[697] A2, N: пророками сказано

[698] K omitt.

[699] N: над всею землею

[700] K: того

[701] A2, N omitt: Для... & add.: Бог

[702] A2: своею; N: свою задачею

[703] A2, N omitt.: покорения мира мирным путем. Ныне & add.: Будь гений у противоположного [N: противного] лагеря, он бы еще поборолся с нами, но пришлец не стоит старого обывателя: борьба была бы между нами не на живот, а на смерт [N omitt.: не на живот, а на смерть] безпощадно [N: безпощадной] какой не видывал еще свет. Да и опоздал бы гений их: цари не царствуют уже de facto, а лишь de jure, террор их обезличил [N omitt.: цари не царствуют...]

[704] N: а двигатель этот- золото

[705] N: политической

[706] A2, B: экономии

[707] A1, A2, N: указывает [N add.: царский]; B: воздает

[708] A1 omitt. престиж & add.: Царский престол; B: царские почести Капиталу

[709] A2, N: Капитал

[710] A2, N: добиться свободы

[711] A1, A2: монополии

[712] A2, N add.: и торговли; [N add.: что уже и приводится в исполнение незримой рукой во всех частях света] такая свобода даст политическую силу промышленникам

[713] K, A1, A2 omitt.

[714] K: обезкураживать

народы от всяких средств[715], **чем вести их на**[716] **войну**; важнее **пользоваться** разгоревшимися **страстями** в нашу пользу, **чем их заливать**; важнее **захватить** и толковать **чужие мысли** по своему[717], **чем их изгонять. Главная тайная**[718] **задача** нашего **правления состоит в том, чтобы ослабить**[719] общественный **ум критикой, отучить** его[720] **от размышлений, вызывающих отпор** (l), отвлечь силы ума на перестрелку пустого красноречия. **Во все времена народы, как и отдельные лица, принимали слово за дело.**[721] Они удовлетворяются показным (m), редко замечая, последовало ли точное[722] исполнение за обещанием на общественной почве. Поэтому мы учредили[723] показные учреждения, франмасонские ложи[724], которые красноречиво доказывают[725] свои благодеяния для прогресса[726]. Мы **присвоили**[727] себе **либеральную**[728] **физиономию всех партий** (n), всех направлений[729] и снабдили[730] их ораторами[731], которые[732] столько говорили, что переутомили слушателей[733] получивших отвращение к ораторам[734]. Чтобы[735] взять

[715] A2, N omitt.: от...

[716] A1 omitt.: их на

[717] K omitt.

[718] N omitt.

[719] K: ославить

[720] A2, N omitt.

[721] A2, N add.: ибо

[722] A2, N omitt.; A2 add.: и

[723] A2: учредимь N: установим

[724] A2, N omitt.

[725] A2, N: будут доказывать

[726] K: бладеяния для прогреса; A2, N, B: прогрессу

[727] A2, N: присвоим

[728] K, A1, B omitt.

[729] K, A1, A2, B: либерального [A2: этого] направления

[730] A2, N: снабдим

[731] A2, N: ими [N: ею] же ораторов

[732] A2, N add.: бы

[733] A1: слишателей

[734] A2, N omitt.: переутомили... & add.: привели бы людей к переутомлению от речей, к отвращению к ораторам [N: от ораторов]

[735] A1: чтоб

общественное мнение в руки, **надо** его **поставить в недоумение, высказывая с разных сторон столько противоречивых мнений** и до тех пор, **пока** непосвященные[736] гои **не затеряются в лабиринте** (o) их и не придут к заключению[737], что лучше всего не иметь[738] мнения в вопросах политики, которых обществу не дается[739] ведать[740] в их[741] настоящем виде[742], потому что ведает их лишь тот, который[743] ими[744] руководит.[745] **Вторая тайна,** потребная[746] для успеха управления **заключается в том, чтобы настолько размножить**[747] народные обычаи[748], **привычки, страсти,** правила общежития, **чтобы никто в этом хаосе не мог разобраться и**[749] **вследствие**[750] этого перестали бы понимать друг друга (p), видя все в разумном свете и все толкуя и растолковывая различно. На такой почве вражда гоев заставит их предать друг друга нам. Различия[751] взглядов лучше всего создают[752] недоразумения и вражду. Этой[753] мерой мы посеем[754] разлад[755] во всех партиях, разнесем[756] все

---

[736] A2, N omitt.

[737] A2, N: поймут

[738] A2, N add.: никакого

[739] A2, N: дано

[740] A: знать

[741] A1 omitt.

[742] A2, N omitt.: в их...

[743] N: кто

[744] N: обществом

[745] N add.: Это первая тайна.

[746] K, A1, B: Второе средство; A2 omitt..: потребная

[747] K: размножили

[748] N: недостатки

[749] A2, N add.: люди

[750] B: вследствии

[751] B: Различие

[752] B: создает

[753] B: Этою

[754] A2, N: omitt.: видя все... посеем & add.: Эта мера нам] N add: еще] послужит к тому, чтобы посеять

[755] N: раздор

[756] A2: разнести; N: разобщить

коллективные[757] силы, которые[758] не хотят нам повиноваться и[759] покориться[760], обезкуражим[761] всякую личную инициативу, могущую сколько нибудь мешать нашему делу. Нет, ничего[762] опаснее[763] личной инициативы; если она гениальна, она может сделать больше того, что могут сделать миллионы[764] людей, среди которых мы посеяли раздор. Нам нужно[765] воспитать[766] гоев[767] так, чтобы[768] **перед**[769] **каждым делом, где нужна личная**[770] **инициатива, у них опускались**[771] **руки** (q) безнадежно[772]. Свобода[773] действий, какую мы привили гоям,[774] разслабляет силы, встречаясь с чужой[775] свободой, отчего являются[776] неудачи, разочарования, нравственные толчки; всем этим мы так переутомим[777] гоев, что вынудим их, в конце-концов[778], предложить нам интернациональную власть, по своему расположению и подготовлению[779] могущую без ломки всосать в себя все

757   К: колективные

758   N add.: еще

759   A2 omitt.: нам... и & add.: нам; N omitt.: повиноваться...

760   В: покоряться

761   A2, N: обезкуражить

762   A2, В omitt.

763   A2: опасней

764   К: милионы

765   N: надо

766   N: направить воспитание

767   N: гоевских обществ

768   A1: чтоб

769   К: пред

770   A2 omitt.

771   A, N add.: бы

772   N: в безнадежном безсилии

773   A2, N: Напряжение, происходящее от свободы

774   A2 omitt.: какую ... гоям

775   В: чужою

776   N: происходят тяжелые

777   A2, N: утомим

778   A2, N omitt.: в конце-концов

779   A2, N omitt.: и...

государственные силы мира и образовать сверхправительство. Тогда[780] **на место царствующих**[781] **мы поставим страшилище, которое будет называться**[782] сверх**правительственной**[783] администрацией: **руки его будут протянуты во все стороны**, как клещи, при такой **колоссальной**[784] **организации** (r), что она не может не покорить[785] народы.

[786]**Скоро мы начнем учреждать громадные монополии, резервуары** колоссальных[787] **богатств, от которых будут зависеть**[788] даже крупные гоевсие **состояния настолько, что они потонут вместе с кредитом государства**[789], **на другой день после политической катастрофы. Вы все,**[790] господа, здесь присутствующие, **экономисты взвесьте-ка значение этой комбинации** (s). **Преобладание** нашего сверх правительства будет развиваться[791], **представляясь**[792] **покровителем, проводителем**[793] **и вознаградителем** (t) либерализма[794]. **Как политическая сила, аристократия**[795] **скончалась,** с нею нам считаться нечего: **но как территориальная**[796] **владелица**, она для нас **вредна тем, что может быть самостоятельна** (u)[797] в источниках своей жизни, может задержать в своих руках земельную собственность, которую нам

---

[780] A2, N omitt.

[781] A2, N: [N add.: современных] правителей

[782] K, A1, B: все будут считать

[783] B: сверхправительственною

[784] K, A2: колосальной

[785] A2, N add.: все

[786] A1, N, B add.: **Еще** [N: **Следующий**] **протокол** [B add.: **(7)**]; A2 add.: VI

[787] K: колосальных

[788] K: зависить

[789] A2: государств

[790] N omitt.: Вы...

[791] A2, N omitt.:. Преобладание... & add.: Всеми путями нам надо непомерно [N omitt.] развивать [N: развить] преобладание [N: значение] нашего сверхправительства

[792] A2, N: представляя его

[793] A2: праводателем; N omitt.

[794] A2 omitt.; N: всех нам добровольно покоряющихся

[795] N add.: гоев

[796] K: териториальная

[797] B: самостоятельною

нужно[798] передать в руки нашего народа, которого[799] мы теперь станем обучать земледелию, к которому он неспособен[800], потому что нам[801] потребны были все его силы в торговле, посредничестве, т. е. спекуляции, и во всех тех трудах, которые разоряли[802] гоев для того, чтобы их превратить в батраков. Когда с помощью земельных банков все дворянские[803] земли перейдут в наши руки, тогда они будут работать, чтобы мы их кормили, потому что земледельческие продукты[804] им продавать никто не будет, как это было во времена Соломона. Как животных и рабочий скот, мы будем их[805] беречь для работы: человеческих прав купли-продажи для гоев дано не будет во дни нашего царства. Для этого, чем скорее, тем лучше,[806] **нам надо**[807] **обеземелить** их аристократию, а там будет возможно то же действие обратить и[808] на крестьян.[809] **Для достижения этого плана**[810] **лучший способ заключается в увеличении земельных повинностей** (v), в задолжности земли. Эти повинности[811] **задержат землевладения**[812] гоев[813] **в состоянии** безделовой[814] **приниженности** (w). Не умея пользоваться[815] малым, аристократия[816] быстро прогорит[817] и бросится

---

798 В: надо всцело

799 А1: который

800 В add.: ныне

801 К omitt.

802 А1: раззорили

803 В add.: и крестьянские

804 В: земледельческих продуктов

805 В add.: кормить и

806 А2, N omitt.: может задержать...тем лучше

807 А2, N add.: поэтому ее во что бы то ни стало

808 К omitt.

809 А2, N omitt.: их аристократию...крестьян

810 А2, N omitt.

811 А2: которые; N: меры

812 А2, N, В: землевладение

813 А2, N omitt.

814 А2, N, В: безусловной

815 А2, N: [N add:. Наследственно] не умеющие довольствоваться

816 А2, N: аристократы гоев

817 А2, N: прогорят

бежать с земли, которую мы с торгов[818] скупим, если не лично, то чрез подставных лиц, пока...[819] В то же[820] время надо **покровительствовать сильно**[821] **торговле и промышленности, а главное спекуляции**, роль которой заключается в противовесе промышленности: **без спекуляции промышленность умножает**[822] **частные капиталы** (x) и может послужить[823] к поднятию земледелия, освободив земли[824] от их[825] задолженности, установленной ссудами земельных банков, а нам[826] надо, чтобы промышленность высосала земледелие и через спекуляцию[827] передала[828] в наши руки все мировые деньги, и тем самым выбросила[829] всех гоев в ряды пролетариата[830]; тогда гои преклонятся перед нами, чтобы только получить право на существование. Для разорения гоевской промышленности в подмогу спекуляции **мы введем** в обычай[831] **сильную потребность к**[832] **роскоши, всепоглощающей** роскоши... **поднимем заработную плату**, которая, однако, не принесет никакой пользы рабочим, ибо одновременно мы произведем вздорожание припасов[833], якобы от причины[834] падения земледелия и скотоводства, да, кроме того, мы искусно[835] **и глубоко подкопаем источники производства** (y), приучив рабочих к[836] спиртным напиткам, а[837]

---

[818] B add.: и

[819] A2, N omitt.: и бросится бежать...

[820] N add.: самое

[821] A2, N, B: усиленно

[822] A2, N: умножит

[823] A2, N: послужит

[824] N: землю

[825] N omitt.

[826] A2, N omitt.: а нам

[827] A2: спекуляции

[828] N, B add.: бы

[829] N, B add.: бы

[830] A2, N, B: пролетариев

[831] A2, N omitt.: введем... & add.: пустим [N add.: развитую нами среди гоев]

[832] A2, N, B: в

[833] N: предметов первой необходимости

[834] A2, N omitt.

[835] N, B: искуссно

[836] N add.: анархии и

интеллигентных[838] гоев, кроме того, еще оторвем от земли[839]. Чтобы истинная подкладка[840] не стала заметна гоям раньше времени, **мы ее прикроем** якобы **старанием**[841] **послужить рабочим классам, и великим экономическим принципам** (z), о которых гласят[842] наши экономические теории.

QUOTATIONS FROM JOLY'S *DIALOGUE*

a   «...la démagogie engendre l'anarchie, l'anarchie ramène au despotisme.»

b   «...la liberté (...) eût été (...) inoffensive dans le temps où le principe (...) la religion (...) où le peuple (...) marchait sous la main de ses pasteurs.»

c   «...révolutions (...) des sociétés froides et désabuséss, qui sont arrivées à l'indifference en politique comme en religion, qui n'ont plus d'autre stimulant que les jouissances matérielles, qui ne vivent plus que par l'intérêt, qui n'ont d'autre culte que l'or»

d   «Les classes inférieures essayent de monter à l'assaut du pouvoir (...) par haine de ceux qui possèdent»

e   «Quelles formes de gouvernement voulez vous appliquer à des sociétés où la corruption s'est glissée partout, où la fortune ne s'acquiert que par les surprises de la fraude, où la morale n'a plus de garantie que dans les lois répressives, où le sentiment de la patrie (...) s'est éteint dans (...) cosmopolitisme universel?»

f   «...l'institution d'une centralisation (...) qui mette toute la force publique à la disposition (...) qui règle mécaniquement tous les mouvements des individue (...) un système de législation qui reprenne (...) toutes les libertés (...) un despotisme gigantesque (...) qui puisse frapper immédiatement et à toute heure tout ce qui résiste, tout ce qui se plaint.»

g   «comment vous vous prendriez pour organiser le despotisme chez les peuples dont le droit public repose (...) sur la liberté»

h   «Tant que les peuples ont regardé la souveraineté comme une émanation pure de la volonté divine, ils se sont soumis sans murmure au pouvoir absolu (...)

---

837   A2, N: и удалением [N: приняв вместе с этим все меры к изгнани] с земли всех сил

838   K: интелегентных

839   A2, N omitt.: кроме того...

840   A2, N, B add.: вещей

841   N: стремлением

842   N: ведут деятельную пропаганду

Mais du jour où leurs droits ont été reconnus (...) la politique à l'usage des princes est tombée de son haut.»

i   «l'art du gouvernement s'est changé en un affaire d'administration»

j   «Il est écrit: *Per me reges regnant.*»

k   «L'économie politique [*est*] un mécanisme nécessaire [*pour*] détruire le prestige (...) Elle ne peut se passer de liberté»

l   «Il s'agit moins aujourd'hui de violenter les hommes que de les désarmer, de comprimer leurs passions politiques que de les effacer, de combattre leurs instincts que de les tromper, de proscrire leurs idées que de leur donner le change en se les appropriant. (...) Le principal secret de gouvernement consiste à affaiblir l'esprit public, au point de la désintéresser (...) des idées (...) avec lesquels on fait (...) les révolutions.»

m   «Dans tous les temps, les peuples comme les hommes se sont payés de mots. Les apparences leur suffisent»

n   «il faut avoir le talent de ravir aux partis cette phraséologie libérale»

o   «avant de songer à la diriger, il faut l'étourdir, la frapper d'incertitude par d'étonnantes contradictions (...), l'égarer insensiblement dans ses voies.»

p   «Un des (...) secrets (...) est de savoir s'emparer des préjugés et des passions populaires, de manière à intriduire une confusion de principes qui rende impossible toute entente entre ceux qui parlent la même langue»

q   «à paralyser dans toutes ses manifestations l'initiative individuelle»

r   «à la place des monarques (...) vous avez mis un monstre qui s'appelle l'Etat (...) dont les bras s'étendent partout (...) organisme colossal»

s   «j'instituerais (...) d'immenses monopoles (...), réservoirs de la fortune (...) dont dépendrait le sort de toutes les fortunes privées, qu'elles s'engloutiraient avec le crédit de l'Etat le landemain de toute catastrophe politique. Vous êtes un économiste (...), pesez la valeur de cette combinaison»

t   «développer démesurément la préponderance de l'Etat, en (...) protecteur, promoteur et rémunérateur»

u   «l'aristocratie, en tant que force politique, a disparu; mais la bourgeoisie territoriale est (...) dangereux (...), parce qu'elle est d'elle-même indépendante»

v   «il peut être nécessaire de l'appauvrir (...). Il suffit, pour cela, d'aggraver les charges (...) sur la propriété foncière»

w   «mantenir l'agriculture dans un état d'infériorité relative»

x   «favoriser à outrance le commerce et l'industrie, mais principalement la spéculation; car la trop grande prospérité de l'industrie peut elle-même (...) en créant (...) de fortunes indépendantes»

y   «l'excitation à un luxe disproportionné (...) l'élévation des salaires (...) des atteintes profondes habilement portées aux sources de la production» z   «L'intéret du peuple, et même une sorte de zèle pour (...) les grands principes économiques»

V [843]

Напряженное вооружение (a)[844], увеличение полицейского штата, **суть**[845] **необходимые пополнения**[846] вышесказанных[847] **планов** (b). **Необходимо достичь**[848] того, чтобы все[849], кроме нас, **во всех государствах** в конце концов[850] **были только массами**[851] **пролетариата, несколько** преданных нам **миллионеров,** полицейские и **солдаты** (c)[852]. Для достижения этого по[853] всей Европе, а с помощью ее отнощений- и в[854] других континентах, мы **должны создать брожения** (d), пререкания[855], раздоры и вражду. **В этом двоякая**[856] польза (e): во первых,[857] **мы держим в решпекте**[858] все страны, хорошо ведающие, что **мы властны по желанию произвести безпорядки, или водворить порядок в**[859] **них** (f)[860]. Они[861] привыкли видеть в нас необходимое давление; во вторых- **интригами**[862] мы **запутали**[863] **все нити,**

---

[843] К omitt.; А1, N, В: **Еще** [N: **Следующий**] **протокол** [В add.: **(8)**]; А2: VII

[844] А2, N: напряжение вооружения [N: вооружений]

[845] А2, N omitt.

[846] В: дополнения

[847] А2, N: вышеуказанных

[848] В: достигнуть

[849] А2, В omitt.

[850] В: концев; А2, N omitt.: в конце....

[851] А2, N, В: массы

[852] К omitt.: несколько преданных нам миллионеров, полицейские и солдаты;
А1, В add.: да правительство нашей формации [В: фабрикации]

[853] А2, N omitt.: Для... & add.: Во; В: во

[854] N, В: на

[855] N omitt.

[856] К: двоякова

[857] А2, N add.: этим

[858] К, А1, В: страхе

[859] К, А1: у

[860] А2, N omitt. в них

[861] N: Все эти страны

[862] К, А1, В omitt.: во вторых...

[863] А2, N: запутаем

протянутые[864] в[865] государственные **кабинеты всемирной**[866] **политикой** (g), экономическими договорами и[867] долговыми обязательствами. Для достижения этого[868] нам надо было[869] вооружиться большою[870] **хитростью** и даже[871] пронырливостью **во времена**[872] переговоров (h) и соглашений, **но в том, что называется официальным**[873] языком, мы **должны** были[874] **держаться противоположной тактики** и[875] казаться[876] **сговорчивыми и правдивыми** (i)[877]. Таким образом **народы**[878] и правительства гоев[879], которых мы приучили **смотреть только на показную сторону** (j) того, что мы им представляем, приняли[880] нас еще за благодеятелей и спасителей рода человеческого. **На каждое противодействие мы готовы**[881] **ответить войной**[882] противодействующей **стране**- (k) с соседями, а[883] если многие[884] думают[885] коллективно[886]

---

[864] N add.: нами

[865] N: во все

[866] N omitt.

[867] A2, N, B: или

[868] A1, A2, B add.: последнего обстоятельства

[869] A2, N omitt.

[870] A2: большой

[871] A2, N omitt.

[872] A2, N: время

[873] A1, A2, B: оффициальным

[874] A2, N: будем

[875] K, A1, B omitt.: держаться противоположной тактики и; A2, N add.: с этой
      стороны мы [N omitt.] будем

[876] A2, N add.: честными и

[877] A2, N omitt.: и правдивыми

[878] K, A1, B: гои

[879] K, B omitt.: и....

[880] A2, N: примут; B: принимают

[881] A2, N: должны быть в состоянии

[882] B: войною

[883] A2, N omitt.: Противодействующей... a & add.: той страны [N: стране]
      которая противодействует [N: осмелится нам противодействовать] с
      соседями, но

[884] A2: эти последние; N: и соседи эти

[885] A2, N, B: задумают

действовать[887] против нас[888], то мы завяжем узел **всеобщей войны** (l),[889] не заметно для них[890] подобьем[891] их на[892] это...[893] Главный успех в политике заключается в тайне ее предприятий: **слова не должны[894] согласоваться с действиями** (m) дипломатов[895]... Мы успешно не раз вынуждали к войне[896] гоевские правительства якобы общественным мнением, в тайне подстроенным нами[897]. **Одним словом, чтобы резюмировать нашу систему** (n) обуздания этих[898] правительств в Европе,[899] одному из них мы доказывали[900] свои силы[901] в покушениях- в терроре[902], а всем, если допустить их восстание[903], мы ответим американскими,[904] китайскими или японскими пушками[905].

[886]   K: колективно

[887]   N: стать

[888]   A2 omitt.: действовать... & add.: нам противодействовать

[889]   B add.: и

[890]   A1 add.: и

[891]   A1: побьем

[892]   A1: за

[893]   A2, N omitt.: завяжем... на это & add.: должны дать ответ [N: отпор] всеобщей войной.

[894]   A2, N: слово не должно

[895]   A2, N: дипломата

[896]   A2, N omitt.: Мы... & add.: Вынуждать мы должны [N add.: К действиям в пользу широко задуманного нами плана, уже близящегося к вожделенному концу,]

[897]   N add.: при помощи так называемой «великой державы»- печати, которая, за немногими исключениями, с которыми считаться не стоит,- вся уже в руках наших

[898]   N: гоевских

[899]   K, A1, B omitt.: Одним словом... в Европе,

[900]   A2, N: покажем

[901]   A2: свою силу

[902]   K: тероре; A2, N omitt.: в покушениях... & add.: покушениями, т. е. в терроре [N: террором]

[903]   N add.: против нас

[904]   A2, N add.: или

[905]   A1, B add.: которые всецело в нашем распоряжении

QUOTATIONS FROM JOLY'S *DIALOGUE*

a   «...l'entretien (...) d'une armée formidable»

b   «doit être le complément (...) de ce système»

c   «il faut arriver à ce qu'il n'y ait plus, dans l'Etat, que de prolétaires, quelques millionaires et des soldats»

d   «il faut exciter, d'un bout de l'Europe à l'autre, la fermentation...»

e   «Il en résulte deux avantages»

f   «on tient par là en respect toutes les puissances, chez lesquelles on peut à son gré faire de l'ordre ou du désordre»

g   «enchevétrer par des intrigues de cabinet tous les fils de la politique européenne»

h   «...tromper dans ses négociations (...) l'astuce»

i   «Mais dans ce que vous appelez (...) le langage officiel, il faut un contrast frappant (...) loyauté et conciliation»

j   «les peuples qui ne voient que l'apparence»

k   «A toute agitation (...) il doit pouvoir répondre par une guerre extérieure»

l   «...par la guerre générale»

m   «... les paroles ne doivent jamais être d'accord avec les actes»

n   «Pour résumer d'un mot tout le système, la révolution se trouve contenue dans l'Etat, d'un côté par la terreur de l'anarchie, de l'autre, par (...) la guerre générale.»

VI [906]

Мы должны[907] **заручиться для себя всеми орудиями, которыми наши противники могли бы[908] пользоваться против нас** (a). Мы должны будем выискивать[909] **в самых тонких выражениях** и загвоздках **правового словаря** (b) оправдания, если[910] нам придется произносить **решения, могущие показаться** неимоверно[911] **смелыми и несправедливыми**: такие[912] решения **важно высказать**[913] **в таких выражениях, в которых бы казались**[914] высшие нравственные правила (c)[915]. **Наше правление окружит**[916] себя всеми силами цивилизации, **среди которой**[917] **ему**[918] **придется действовать. Оно окружит себя публицистами, юристами, практиками, администраторами** (d), дипломатами,[919] подготовленными сверхобразовательным воспитанием в наших особых школах: **они**[920] **будут ведать**[921] **все**[922] **тайны социального быта, они будут знать все языки** (e), составляемые политическими буквами и словами. Они будут ознакомлены, если можно так выразиться, с[923] подкладочной стороной человеческой натуры, то есть с[924] чувствительными струнами человеческого ума,[925] на которых

---

[906]   K omitt.; A1, N, B: **Еще** [N: **Следующий**] **протокол** [B add.: **(9)**]; A2: **VIII**.

[907]   A1: должно

[908]   A2 omitt.

[909]   K, A1: выискать

[910]   N: для тех случаев, когда

[911]   A2, N: непомерно

[912]   A2, N: ибо эти

[913]   A2, N: выразить

[914]   N, B: выставлялись

[915]   N: высшими нравственными правилами; A2, N add.: правового характера

[916]   A2, N: должно окружить [N.: окружать]

[917]   A2, N: которых

[918]   A2: им

[919]   A2, N add.: [N add.: и, наконец,] людьми

[920]   N: Эти люди

[921]   A1, B: знать

[922]   K omitt.

[923]   N: со всей

[924]   N: со всеми

им придется разыграть[926]. Понятно, что эти гениальные сотрудники нашей власти[927] **будут взяты** (f) не из числа гоев, которые привыкли исполнять свою административную работу, не задаваясь мыслью, чего ею надо достигнуть, не думая о том, что ею можно сделать[928]: они действуют по шаблону заведенной регламентной машины,[929] подписывают бумаги не читая их, служат из корысти или из[930] честолюбия... Мы окружим свое правительство **целым миром экономистов** (поэтому[931] экономические науки составляют главный предмет преподавания[932] евреям),[933] **банкиров, промышленников, капиталистов, прожектеров,** а главное **миллионеров**[934], **потому что в сущности все будет решено**[935] **вопросом цифр** (g)...

На время, пока еще[936] не безопасно вручить **ответственные места**[937] в государствах нашим братьям евреям, **мы их будем поручать лицам, которых прошлое и характер таковы, что между ними и народом лежит**[938] **пропасть**: таким лицам[939], **которым** в случае непослушания

[925]   A2 omitt.: человеческого ума

[926]   A1, B: разыгрывать- на тенденциях [B: с тенденциями, недостатками, пороками и качествами гоев... им будут выяснены особенные черты] всех их классов; A2, N omitt.: придется & add.: надо будет уметь играть, на [N: Струны эти:] строение ума [N: умов] гоев, на [N omitt.] их тенденциях, недостатках, пороках и качествам [N: тенденции, недостатки, пороки и качества], им будут известны [N omitt.] особенности всех классов [N omitt.: всех & add.: И сословий].

[927]   N add.: о которых я веду речь

[928]   A2, N: на что она нужна

[929]   A2 omitt.: действуют ... машины; N add.: Администраторы гоев

[930]   A1 omitt.

[931]   N: Вот отчего

[932]   A2: главное преподавание

[933]   N add.: Нас будет окружать целая плеяда

[934]   K: милионеров

[935]   A2: разрешено; B: решаемо

[936]   A2, N add.: будет

[937]   N: посты

[938]   N: легла

[939]   A1, B: такими людьми; A2, N: людям

нашим же интересам и[940] предписаниям, **остается ждать**[941] **суда или ссылки** за открывшиеся злоупотребления; таким образом, **они станут защищать**[942] наши интересы, **до последнего своего издыхания** (h)[943].

QUOTATIONS FROM JOLY'S *DIALOGUE*

a   «...employer contre ses adversaires toutes les armes qu'ils pourraient employer contre vous.»

b   «...aux subtilités du droit»

c   «décisions qui peuvent paraître injustes ou téméraires, il est essentiel (...) les énoncer en de bons termes, de les appuyer des raisons les plus élevées de la morale et du droit.»

d   «Le pouvoir (...) doit attirer à lui toutes les forces (...) de la civilisation au sein de laquelle il vit. Il devra s'entourer de publicistes, (...) de juriconsultes, d'homme de pratique et d'administration.»

e   «de gens qui connaissent (...) tous les secrets (...) de la vie sociale, qui parlent tous les langages»

f   «Il faut les prendre»

g   «tout un monde d'économistes, de banquiers, d'industriels, de capitalistes, d'hommes à projets, d'hommes à millions, car tout au fond se résoudra par une question de chiffres»

h   «principales dignités (...) on doit les donner à des hommes dont les antécédents et le caractère mettent un abîme entre eux et les autres hommes, dont chacun n'ait à attendre que la mort ou l'exil (...) et soit dans la nécessité de défendre jusqu'au dernier souffle.»

---

[940]   A2 omitt.: же интересам и

[941]   A2, N add.: или

[942]   A2, N omitt.: за открывшиеся... & add.: сие для того, чтобы эти последние [N: они] защищали

[943]   K, A1, B omitt.: до последнего... & add.: как свои собственные

VII [944]

Применяя законы наших теорий[945], обращайте внимание на **характер народа**, в стране которого вы будете[946] действовать[947]: общее, одинаковое применение их[948], ранее перевоспитания народа этого[949], не может иметь успеха. [950]Шествуя же[951] в применениях[952] постепенно и осторожно, вы увидите, что **не пройдет и десяти**[953] **лет, как самый упорный характер народа**[954] **изменится и мы зачислим** еще[955] народ **в ряды уже покорившихся** (а) нам[956] -идее интернационализма- людей[957]. Слова либерального[958] пароля ісвобода, равенство и братство», когда мы воцаримся мы заменим словами их[959] идейности и скажем[960]: право свободы, долг равенства, идеал братства,[961] и поймаем еще раз того же[962] козла за рога. Фактически[963], мы уже стерли всякое правление своим[964], хотя по виду их[965] еще много. Ныне **если** какие либо

---

[944]   К omitt.; А1, N, В: **Еще** [N: **Следующий**] **протокол** [В add.: **(10)**]; А2: **IX**

[945]   А2 omitt.: наших теорий; N: omitt.: законы наших теорий & add.: наши принципы

[946]   N add.: находиться и

[947]   А2: находиться

[948]   А2: его

[949]   А2 omitt.; N: на наш лад

[950]   А2, N add.: Но,

[951]   А2, N omitt.

[952]   А2 add.: его; N: применении

[953]   N: десятка

[954]   А2, N omitt.

[955]   А2, N: новый

[956]   В: нашей

[957]   А2, N omitt.: идее интернационализма- людей

[958]   N add.: в сушности, нашего масонского

[959]   А2, N: не пароля [N add.: уже] а лишь

[960]   А2, N omitt.

[961]   А2, N add.: скажем мы

[962]   А2, N omitt.: еще раз того же

[963]   А2, N: De facto

[964]   А2, N: кроме нашего

[965]   А2, N omitt. хотя по виду их & add.: de jure таковых

государства **поднимают протест против нас, то это только**[966] **для формы** (b) и по нашему научению[967], ибо их антисемитизм нам нужен для управления нашими меньшими братьями. Не буду вам излагать подробности этого факта, потому что[968] это[969] было предметом наших неоднократных бесед, укажу вам только, что действительно правлению нашего сверхправительства[970] нет препятствий со стороны гоевских администраций[971], наше сверхправительство **находится в таких экстралегальных условиях, которые принято называть энергичным и сильным словом- диктатуры** (c) [972]. По совести могу вам сказать, что **ныне**[973] **мы законодатели, мы творим суд и расправу** над гоевскими правлениями[974], мы их[975] казним и милуем, мы, **как шеф**[976] наших **войск- либералов**[977], **сидим на** предводительском **коне** (d). Мы правим сильной[978] рукой[979], потому что в этой руке[980] **осколки когда то сильных партий, разбитых** нами, в этой руке[981] **неудержимые честолюбия, жгучие жадности, безпощадные ненависти**, злобные мести; от нас[982] **все охватающий**[983] **террор**[984](e). У нас среди агентов

---

[966]   A2, N omitt.

[967]   A2: распоряжению; N: усмотрению и распоряжению

[968]   A2, N omitt.: вам излагать подробности этого факта, потому что & add.: этого разъяснять, ибо

[969]   A2 add.: уже

[970]   A2, N omitt.: укажу... сверхправительства & add.: В действительности для нас

[971]   A2, N omitt.: со стороны...администраций

[972]   A2, N, B: Диктатура; A2, N add.: Я

[973]   A2, N: в данное время

[974]   A2, N omitt.: над гоевскими правлениями

[975]   A2, N omitt.

[976]   A2, B add.: всех

[977]   A2, N omitt.

[978]   B: сильною

[979]   A2, N: волей [N.: волею]

[980]   A2, N: у нас в руках

[981]   A2, N omitt.: сильных партий ... руке & add.: сильной партии, ныне покоренной нами; в наших же [N omitt. руках]

[982]   A2, N, B add.: исходит

[983]   A2: схвативший; N, B: охвативший

сознательных и бессознательных[985] **люди всех мнений,**[986] **всех доктрин, реставраторы монархий**[987], **демагоги,** социалисты, **анархисты,** коммунары[988] и всякие **утописты, всех мы запрягли в**[989] **работу**; каждый из них **с**[990] **своей стороны** подтачивает[991], старается **свергнуть все установленные порядки** (f). Этими действиями все государства замучены,[992] **взывают к покою, готовы ради мира жертвовать всем** (g), но мы не дадим им ни[993] мира, ни покоя[994]; пока они не признают нашего интернационального сверхправительства открыто, с покорностью. Народы уже завопили[995] о необходимости разрешить социальный вопрос интернационализмом. Раздробление партий предоставило всех[996] в наше распоряжение[997], потому что[998] для того, чтобы вести соревновательную (войну) борьбу[999], надо иметь деньги, а они все у нас. Мы могли бы[1000] бояться соединения гоевской, зрячей более или менее[1001], силы царствующих со слепой силой народной[1002], но мы приняли[1003] все меры против такой возможности, воздвигли между ними крепкую стену[1004]-

[984]   К: терор

[985]   А2, N omitt.: среди...бессознательных & add.: в услужении

[986]   К, А1, В omitt.: всех мнений

[987]   А2, N: монархии

[988]   К: комунары

[989]   А1: за

[990]   В: со

[991]   N add.: последние остатки власти

[992]   А2, N add.: они

[993]   А2, N omitt.

[994]   А2, N omitt.: ни покоя

[995]   А2, N: Народ завопил

[996]   А2, В: все таковые; N: их все

[997]   К: враспоряжение

[998]   А2: ибо; N: так как

[999]   К, А1 omitt.: борьбу; N, В omitt: войну

[1000]   В omitt.

[1001]   А2, N omitt.: более или менее

[1002]   В: народною

[1003]   А2 add.: так как; А2, N: нами приняты

[1004]   А2: стеной

террор[1005], с обеих сторон,[1006] поэтому[1007] **слепая сила**[1008] останется[1009] нашей **опорой** (h), и[1010] мы[1011] будем служить ей руководителем и[1012] будем направлять[1013] ее к нашей цели, для этого наши агенты проникают в самую среду народов[1014]. Когда[1015] мы уже[1016] будем признанною[1017] властью, то мы будем открыто на площадях учить народ беседами[1018] по вопросам политики в том напрявлении, какое нам понадобится[1019], то[1020], что скажет[1021] сам правитель[1022], станет известным[1023] во всех концах земли в день, в который оно сказано...[1024] Чтобы **не преобразовать**[1025]

[1005] К: терор

[1006] A2, N omitt.: воздвигли... & add.: воздвигнутой между ними [N: тою и другой силой] стеной -террор обеих по отношению друг к другу [N: нами воздвигнута стена в виде взаимного между ними террора]

[1007] A2: то; N: Таким образом,

[1008] N add.: народа

[1009] A2, N: остается

[1010] A2: а

[1011] N add.: только мы,

[1012] N add.: конечно,

[1013] A2, N: направим

[1014] A2, N omitt.: для этого... & add.: Чтобы не могла рука слепого освободиться от нашего руководства, мы должны непременно [N omitt.] по временам находиться в его среде [N: в тесном общении с ним], если не лично, то через самых верных братьев наших.

[1015] B add.: же

[1016] A2, N, B omitt.

[1017] A1, N: признанной

[1018] A2, N omitt.: открыто... & add.: с народом лично беседовать на площадях и будем его учить сами [N omitt.]

[1019] A2, N add.: Трудно проверить то [N.: Как проверить] что преподается [N: ему преподают] в деревенских школах [N: ?]

[1020] A2, N: а

[1021] A2, N add.: посланник правительства, или; B: окажет

[1022] A2, N: царствующий

[1023] A1: будет известно

[1024] A2, N omitt.: станет... & add.: то не может быть неизвестным [N: не стать известным] тотчас всему государству, ибо быстро разнесется [N: будет разнесено] гласом [N: голосом] народа

гоевские **учреждения**[1026] раньше нужного нам[1027] времени, **мы коснулись их** осторожно[1028] **умелой**[1029] **рукой** избрали[1030] концы пружин их **механизма** (i). Эти пружины нужны[1031] были в строгом, но справедливом порядке,[1032] мы заменили их[1033] либеральным беспорядочным[1034] беспорядком и[1035] произволом. **Таким образом**[1036], **мы затронули юрисдикцию**[1037], **выборные порядки, печать, свободу личности**, а главное **образование** (j) и воспитание, как краеугольные камни общественного[1038] бытия. Мы одурачили, одурманили и развратили гоевскую молодежь посредством воспитания[1039]. **Сверх** существующих **законов**, не изменяя их сущности[1040], а лишь исковеркав их противоречивыми толкованиями, мы создали[1041] нечто грандиозное в смысле результатов; сначала они[1042] выразились в том, что толкования **замаскировали законы, а затем и совсем закрыли** (k)[1043] от взоров правительств[1044], вследствие невозможности[1045] ведать такое запутанное законодательство; отсюда теория суда совести. Вы говорите, что **на нас**

[1025] A2: уничтожить; N: уничтожать; B: переобразовались

[1026] A2, N: гоевских учреждений

[1027] A2, N omitt.: нужного...

[1028] A2, N omitt.

[1029] B: умелою

[1030] A1, A2, N, B: и забрали [N add.: в свои руки]

[1031] A2 omitt.; N omitt.: пружины нужны

[1032] A2, N add.: a

[1033] A2, N, B: его

[1034] B: бестолковым

[1035] A2, N omitt.: беспорядком и

[1036] A2, N omitt.: Таким образом

[1037] K, B: юристдикцию

[1038] A2, N: свободного

[1039] N add.: в заведомо для нас ложных, но нами внушенных, принципах и теориях

[1040] A2, N: существенно

[1041] A1 omitt.: мы создали & add.: дали

[1042] N: Эти результаты

[1043] A2, N, B add.: их

[1044] A2: правительства

[1045] A2, N: невозможностью

поднимутся с оружием в руках, если узнают[1046] в чем дело, раньше[1047] времени; но для этого **у нас** в запасе **такой терроризующий**[1048] **маневр, что самые храбрые души дрогнут:**[1049] от **столиц** ничего не останется, мы **взорвем**[1050] их (l)[1051] со всеми организациями и документами стран.

QUOTATIONS FROM JOLY'S *DIALOGUE*

a   «...le caractère d'une nation»

b   «...je ne vous demanderais pas vingt ans pour transformer (...) le caractère européen le plus indomptable et pour le rendre (...) docile à la tyrannie»

c   «...élever devant moi quelque obstacle (...) de pure forme»

d   «je suis dans cette condition extra-légale, que les Romains appallaient d'un mot si beau et si puissamment énergique: *la dictature*»

e   «je suis législateur, exécuteur, justicier, et à cheval comme chef d'armée»

f   «Il y aura là (...) des tronçons de partis autrefois victorieux, aujourd'hui vaincus, des ambitions effrénées, des convoitises ardentes, des haines implacables, de terreurs partout»

g   «des hommes de toute opinion et de toute doctrine, des restaurateurs d'anciens régimes, des démagogues, des anarchistes, des utopistes, tous à l'oeuvre, tous travaillant (...) de leur côté au renversement de l'ordre établi.»

h   «le pays a un grand besoin de repos et (...) ne refusera rien à qui pourra le lui donner»

i   «la puissance aveugle qui donnera le moyen»

j.   «Je ne détruirai donc pas directement les institutions, mais je les toucherai une à une par un trait de main inaperçu qui en dérangera le mécanisme»

k   «Je toucherai (...) à l'organisation judiciaire, au suffrage, à la presse, à la liberté individuelle, à l'enseignement.»

l   «une législation nouvelle qui, sans abroger expréssement l'ancienne, la masquera d'abord, puis bientôt l'effacera complétement»

[1046] A2, N: раскусят

[1047] A2, B: ранее

[1048] K, A1, B omitt.

[1049] K, A1, B omitt.

[1050] A1: изорвем

[1051] A2, N omitt.: от столиц... & add.: метрополитэновые подземные ходы-корридоры будут к тому времени проведены во всех столицах, откуда они будут взорваны

m   «on va se lever contre lui les armes à la main. Le moment est venu d'imprimer une terreur qui frappe la cité entière et fasse défaillir les âmes les plus intrépides».

VIII [1052]

Сегодня **начну**[1053] **с повторения уже сказанного**[1054]; прошу вас помнить[1055], что **правительства и народы** гоев[1056] **довольствуются показным** (a). Да и где им[1057] разглядывать подкладку вещей, когда их правителям[1058] стало[1059] важнее всего пользоваться благами жизни-[1060] веселиться... Для нас[1061] весьма важно принять это обстоятельство в соображение. **Перейдем же**[1062] к обсуждению[1063] **разделения**[1064] **власти, свободы**[1065] **слова, прессы, религии**[1066] (веры[1067]), **права ассоциации**[1068], **равенства перед законом, неприкосновенности собственности,**[1069] **жилища, потиционного** (sic!) **права**[1070], **налога,** идеи[1071] о скрытом налоге, **обратной силы законов** (b)[1072]; всех этих тем[1073] для народа не

1052   K omitt.; A1, N, B: **Еще** [N: **Следующий**] **протокол** [B add.: **(11)**]; A2: **X**

1053   A2, N: начинаю

1054   N add.: и

1055   A1: упомнить

1056   A2: правительство и народ & omitt. гоев; N: в политике

1057   A2: ему

1058   A2, N: представителям

1059   N omitt.

1060   A2, N omitt.: пользоваться...

1061   A2, N: нашей политики

1062   A2, N omitt.: принять... & add.: ведать эту подробность. Она нам поможет при переходе

1063   A1: суждению

1064   A1: о разделении; B omitt.

1065   A1: свободе

1066   K, A1, B omitt.

1067   A1: вере

1068   K, A1, A2, B: ассоциаций

1069   A1 add.: и

1070   K, A1, N, B omitt.

1071   A1 omitt.: налога & add.: и об идее; A2, N: идея

1072   K, A1, B omitt.: обратной силы...

1073   A1: тэм; A2, N: Все эти вопросы суть такие темы, которых никогда [N: таковы, что их, прямо и открыто] B add.: прямо

следует[1074] касаться, перечисляя свои намерения[1075], а заявлять без подробного изложения, что **принципы современного права признаются нами**[1076]; **значение этого умолчания заключается в том, что не названные принципы оставлят**[1077] **нам свободу действий, если понадобиться**[1078] **исключить**[1079] **то или другое из них** (c)[1080] непременно[1081], а раз они перечислены[1082], то они как бы[1083] дарованы[1084]. **Народы питают**[1085] **как бы особую любовь**[1086] **к гениям**[1087] **мощи**[1088]**, на все их насильственные поступки**[1089] **они восклицают**[1090]**, что, де**[1091]**, подло**[1092] **но ловко... фокус, но как сыгран**[1093]**, сколь**[1094] **величественно нахально!..** (d) **Мы рассчитываем**[1095] **привлечь все нации,** незаметно для них самих,[1096] **к работе возведения нового фундаментального здания,**

[1074] A2, N add.: никогда

[1075] A2, N omitt.: перечисляя... & add.: Надо в [N add.: тех] случаях необходимого касательства их [N: когда необходимо их коснуться,] не перечислять [N add.: их]

[1076] K, A1, B omitt.: а заявлять...

[1077] A2, N: неназванный принцип оставляет

[1078] A2, N omitt.: если...

[1079] K: осуществить; A1: включать; A2: исключать

[1080] N: него

[1081] A2, N, B: неприметно

[1082] A2: перечислить их

[1083] A2 add.: все

[1084] N: при перечислении же их, они являются все как бы уже дарованными

[1085] A2, N: народ питает

[1086] K, A1, B: особое уважение; A2 add.: и уважение

[1087] N add.: политической

[1088] N add.: и

[1089] N: действия

[1090] A2: отвечают; N: отвечает

[1091] N omitt.

[1092] N add.: то, подло

[1093] A2: сыграно

[1094] A omitt.

[1095] K: рассчитаем

[1096] A2, N omitt.: незаметно...

которое нами проектировано (e)[1097],- разложения всех существующих порядков и замены[1098] их нашим царством и его законами[1099]. Вот почему нам[1100] необходимо запастись,[1101] заручиться той[1102] бесшабашной[1103] мощью духа, которая в лице[1104] деятелей, современных премьеров всех стран и др.,[1105] сломит[1106] все препятствия на нашем пути. **Когда**[1107] мы **совершим наш государственный переворот**[1108], то[1109] мы скажем народам: «**Все шло** для вас[1110] ужасно **плохо**, все изстрадались, **мы разбиваем причину** всех[1111] ваших мук, народности, границы[1112], разномонетность: конечно, **вы можете осудить** (f), не поняв нас, наши действия; но, чтобы[1113] быть справедливыми[1114], приглядитесь сначала к тому,[1115] что мы вам дадим... С этим[1116] нас вознесут[1117] на руках в единогласной[1118] надежде[1119] и уповании[1120]... **Голосование, которое мы**

[1097]   N: проэктировано

[1098]   К: замену

[1099]   A2, N omitt.: разложения...

[1100]   A2, N add.: прежде всего

[1101]   A1 omitt.; N add.: и

[1102]   N add.: прямо

[1103]   N add.: удалью и; B: бесшабашною

[1104]   A2, N, B add.: наших

[1105]   A2, N omitt.: современных...; B omitt.: и др.

[1106]   A2: сложит

[1107]   A1, B add.: же

[1108]   A2 add.: (coup d'état)

[1109]   N: тогда

[1110]   A2, N omitt.: для вас

[1111]   A2, N: причины

[1112]   A2 add.: и

[1113]   A2, N omitt.: вы можете... & add.: вы свободны произнести над нами приговор, но разве токовой [N: он] может

[1114]   A2, N: справедливым

[1115]   A2, N omitt.: приглядитесь... & add.: если он вами будет издан [N: утвержден] прежде, чем вы [N omitt.] испытаете [N add.: то,]

[1116]   N: Тогда они

[1117]   A2, N add.: и понесут

[1118]   A1, A2, N, B: единогласном [N: единодушном] восторге

[1119]   A2, B: надежды; N: надежд

делаем[1121] **орудием нашего воцарения** (g), приучая[1122] к нему даже самых мелких[1123] членов человечества, составляя[1124], где только можно[1125], собрания и ассоциации[1126],- отслужит[1127] свою службу нам[1128]: оно подтвердит наши постановления[1129]... Но ранее этой последней его роли[1130] **нам**[1131] **надо подвести**[1132] **к голосованию всех, без различия ценза и классов, чтобы установить абсолютизм** (h) большинства, которого нельзя нам[1133] добиться с такой[1134] легкостью[1135] от интеллигентных[1136], цензовых классов. Таким порядком, приучив всех к мысли о самозначении[1137], **мы сломаем связь**[1138] гоевской **семьи**[1139], **устраним выделение** их[1140] индивидуальных **умов** (i), которым толпы, руководимые[1141] нами, не дадут[1142] высказаться; эти толпы

[1120]   А1: упоения; А2, В: упования; N: упований

[1121]   А2, N: сделали

[1122]   А2, N: приучив

[1123]   N: самые мелкие единицы из числа

[1124]   А2, N: составлением; В add.: всюду

[1125]   В: можем; А2, N omitt.: где только...

[1126]   К: асоциации; А2, N: собраний и соглашений

[1127]   К, А1, А2, В: отслужив

[1128]   А2, N, В omitt.; А2, N, В add.: [N add.: и] сыграет на сей [N: этот] раз свою последнюю роль [В add.: службу нам]

[1129]   А2, N omitt.: оно подведит... & add.: единогласием, в желании усмотреть [N: ознакомиться с нами поближе] прежде чем осудит

[1130]   А2, N omitt.: Но ранее... & add.: До [N: Для] этого

[1131]   К omitt.

[1132]   А1: довести; N: привести

[1133]   А2, N omitt.

[1134]   А1, В: такою

[1135]   А2, N omitt.: с такой...

[1136]   К: интелегентных

[1137]   А1: самознании

[1138]   А2: значение

[1139]   А2: силы, ее воспитательное назначение; N add.: и ее воспитательную цену

[1140]   А2, N omitt.

[1141]   А2, N: толпа, руководимая

[1142]   А2: дает; N: даст & add.: ни выдвинуться, ни даже

привыкнут[1143] слушать только нас, платящих им[1144] за внимание и послушание; это даст нам в руки[1145] **такую слепую мощь, которая**[1146] никуда **не двинется**[1147] **помимо руководства** (j) наших агентов, становащихся[1148] на места их[1149] лидеров:[1150] толпы[1151] будут ведать[1152] что от этих агентов[1153] зависит получение[1154] заработков, подачек и всяких получений[1155].

[1156]**План управления должен выйти готовым из**[1157] **одной головы** (k)[1158]: если его[1159] допустить к раздроблению[1160] на клочки[1161] многочисленных умов[1162], его уже не скрепить[1163]. Кроме правителя никто не должен его[1164] ведать[1165], администраторы же должны исполнять те части его, которые им постоянно[1166] сообщают без осуждения[1167], чтобы[1168] не

[1143] A2, N: она привыкнет [N: привыкла]

[1144] A2, N: ей

[1145] A2, N: Этим мы создадим

[1146] A2, N add.: никогда [N omitt.] не будет в состоянии

[1147] A2, N: двинуться

[1148] A2, N: поставленных нами

[1149] A2, N: место ее

[1150] A1, B add.: тем, что

[1151] A2: потому что народы; N: Народ подчинится этому режиму, потому что

[1152] N: будет знать

[1153] A2: них; N: лидеров

[1154] B: раздача

[1155] A2, N omitt.: зависит... & add.: будут зависеть заработки, подачки и всякое получение [N: получение всяких благ]

[1156] A1, B: **Еще протокол** [B add.: **(12)**]

[1157] K, A1, B: находиться в

[1158] K, A1, B: голове; A2, N add.: потому что его не скрепишь,

[1159] A2, N omitt.

[1160] A2, N: его раздробление

[1161] A2, N add.: в [N: во]

[1162] A2, N: умах

[1163] A2, N omitt.: его уже...; B: скрепишь

[1164] A2, N omitt.: Кроме... & add.: Поэтому нам можно

[1165] A2, N add.: план действий

[1166] B: постепенно

нарушить, не испортить[1169] его гениальности, связи его составных частей, а главное[1170] практической силы тайного значения каждого его пункта. Если осуждать[1171] или[1172] изменять подобную работу многочисленным голосованием, то она **понесет**[1173] **печать всех умственных**[1174] **недоразумений** (l)[1175]. Нам нужно, чтобы наши планы были сильно[1176] и целесообразно придуманы[1177], поэтому нам нельзя оповещать о них и[1178] бросать эту[1179] гениальную работу[1180] нашего руководителя на растерзание толпы или[1181] большого[1182] сборища[1183]. Пока мы[1184] воцаримся открыто, **мы не изменим вверх дном настоящие учреждения, а лишь изменим**[1185] **их экономию**[1186], следовательно всю **комбинацию** (m) их шествия, направляя ее к[1187] намеченному в наших

[1167] В: обсуждения; А2, N omitt.: администраторы... & add.: но не обсуждать его

[1168] А1: чтоб

[1169] А2, N omitt.

[1170] А2, N omitt.

[1171] А1, А2, N, В: обсуждать

[1172] А2, N: и

[1173] N add.: на себе

[1174] А1, В omitt.

[1175] К omitt.: понесет печать... & add.: внесет одни недоразумения; А1, А2, N, В add.: не узревших глубины и связи [N: не проникших в глубину и связь] ее замыслов

[1176] А2, N: сильны

[1177] А2, N, В: задуманы

[1178] А2, N omitt.: нельзя... & add.: не следует

[1179] А2 omitt.

[1180] N: гениальной работы

[1181] А1, В add.: хотя бы

[1182] А2: хотя бы

[1183] N omitt.: большого... & add.: даже ограниченного сообщества

[1184] А1, В add.: не

[1185] А2, N omitt.: Пока мы... & add.: Эти планы не перевернут [N add.: пока] вверх дном настоящие учреждения, [N.: современных учреждений.] они [N add.: только] заменят

[1186] К: физиономию; А2, N add.: а

[1187] А2, N: которое, таким образом, направится по

планах пути. **Под разными названиями, в разных**[1188] **странах существует приблизительно одно и то же:** представительство, **министерство**[1189], сенат, государственный совет, законодательный и исполнительный **корпус** (n). **Мне не нужно вам пояснять механизм**[1190] **отношений**[1191] **этих учреждений между собою, так как это вам хорошо известно; но я поставлю**[1192] **вам на вид,**[1193] **что каждое из них**[1194] **отвечает какой нибудь**[1195] **важной государственной функции; заметьте**[1196], **что слово ¡важный**[1197]**» я отношу не к учреждению, а к функции** (o)[1198], следовательно, не учреждения важны, а[1199] функции их. Учреждения поделили[1200] функции[1201] между собою: **административную,** исполнительную, **законодательную, мирительную,**[1202] **регулирующую** (p)[1203], поэтому они стали действовать в государственном организме[1204], **как органы в человеческом теле** (q), следовательно[1205], если повредить один орган[1206] в государственной машине, государство заболеет, как человеческое тело и... умрет. Когда мы заразили государственные тела

[1188] A2, N, B: во всех

[1189] A2, N: министерства

[1190] N: механизма

[1191] A2: отношения

[1192] A1, B: ставлю; A2: нотирую

[1193] A2 omitt.: на вид & add.: то; N omitt.: но я ... & add.: обратите только внимание на то

[1194] N: названных учреждений

[1195] A2, N, B: либо

[1196] A2, N: причем прошу [N add.: вас] заметить

[1197] A2: важной

[1198] A1 add.: их

[1199] N add.: важны

[1200] N add.: все

[1201] N add.: управления

[1202] K, A1, A2, B omitt.

[1203] A1, A2: урегулирующую; N omitt.

[1204] A2, B: государственной экономии

[1205] N omitt.

[1206] N: повредим одну часть

либерализмом, этим смертным ядом[1207], вся их[1208] политическая комплекция изменилась, они[1209] заболели смертельной болезнью-разложением крови; остается ожидать конца их агонии....

QUOTATIONS FROM JOLY'S *DIALOGUE*

a   «Je vous disais, il y a peu d'instants, que les peuples (...) comme les hommes (...) tenaient plus aux apparences».

b   «...ne manquierez (...) pas de me parler du principe de la séparation des pouvoirs, de la liberté de la parole et de la presse, de la liberté religieuse, de la liberté individuelle, du droit d'association, de l'égalité devant la loi, de l'inviolabilité de la propriété et du domicile, du droit de pétition, du libre consentement de l'impôt, de la proportionnalité des peines, de la non rétroactivité des lois».

c   «je confirme les grand principes du droit moderne (...) Si j'énumerais expréssement ces droits, ma liberté d'action serait enchainée vis-à-vis de ceux que j'aurais déclaré (...) en ne les nommant point, je parais les accorder tous et je n'en accorde spécialement aucun».

d   «les nations ont (...) secret amour pour les vigoreux génies de la force. A tous les actes violents marqués du talent de l'artifice, vous entendrez dire (...): Ce n'est pas bien, soit, mais c'est habile, c'est bien joué, c'est fort!»

e   «Vous comptez donc associer la nation au nouvel oeuvre fondamental que vous préparez?»

f   «...le coup de force que j'ai accompli contre l'Etat; je dirai au peuple (...): Tout marchait mal; j'ai tout brisé (...), vous êtes libres de me condamner».

g   «...le vote (...) dont j'ai fait l'instrument de mon pouvoir»

h   «J'établirai un suffrage sans distinction de classe ni de cens, avec lequel l'absolutisme sera organisé...»

i   «vous brisez (...) l'unité de la famille, vous (...) annulez la préponderance des lumières»

j   «une puissance aveugle qui se dirige à votre gré».

k   «Une constitution doit sortir tout armée de la tête d'un seul homme»

l   «elle portera (...) l'empreinte de toutes le faiblesses de vue»

[1207]   A2, N omitt.: заразили... & add.: ввели в государственные корпуса [N: государственный организм] яд либерализма

[1208]   N: его

[1209]   N: государства

m   «je n'ai pas besoin de détruire de fond en comble vos institutions (...). Il me suffira d'en modifier l'économie et (...) les combinaisons»

n   «dans les Etats (...) on retrouve partout, sous noms divers, mais avec des attributiorns à peu près uniformes, une organisation ministerielle, un sénat, un corps législatif, un conseil d'Etat»

o   «je dois vous faire grâce de tout développement inutile sur le mécanisme respectif de ces pouvoirs, dont vous connaissez mieux que moi le secret; il est évident que chacun d'eux répond à une fonction essentielle du gouvernement. Vous remarquez bien que c'est la fonction que j'appelle essentielle, ce n'est pas l'institution».

p   «...un pouvoir dirigeant, un pouvoir modérateur, un pouvoir législatif, un pouvoir règlementaire»

q   «comme de véritables organes dans le corps humain»

IX [1210]

От либерализма родились **конституционные государства**, заменившие самодержавные[1211], а конституция[1212] **ничто**[1213] **иное, как школа раздоров**, разлада, споров, несогласий, **безплодных**[1214] агитаций (a), партийных тенденций, одним словом,[1215] всего того, что обессиливает[1216] деятельность государств.[1217] **Трибуна не хуже прессы приговорила** правителей **к** бездеятельности[1218] (бездействию) и[1219] **безсилию** (b), после чего они стали не нужны[1220] и были во многих странах свергнуты. Тут настала пора[1221] республиканской эры, и[1222] мы заменили правительство нации[1223] карикатурой ее[1224]- президентом республики...[1225] взятым[1226] из толпы, из среды наших креатур,[1227] рабов. В этом состояла первая мина, подведенная[1228] нами[1229] под гоевские народы. В скором[1230] будущем **мы**

[1210]   K, A1, A2, N, B omitt.

[1211]   N: спасительное для гоев самодержавие

[1212]   N add.: как вам хорошо известно, есть; B: конституция

[1213]   A2: не что

[1214]   N add.: партийных

[1215]   N add.: школа

[1216]   N: обезличивает

[1217]   A2, N: государства

[1218]   K, A1, N, B omitt.

[1219]   A2: к; N add.: к

[1220]   N omitt.: после... & add.: и тем сделала их ненужными, лишними, отчего они

[1221]   A1, A2, N, B: [N: Тогда] стало возможно [N: возможным] восстановление [A2, N, B: возникновение]

[1222]   N add.: тогда

[1223]   A1, B: наций

[1224]   A2, N omitt.: правительство... & add.: представителя [N: правителя] карикатурой представительства [N: правительства]

[1225]   N omitt.

[1226]   A2: -президентами, взятыми

[1227]   N add.: наших

[1228]   A2, N: было основание мины подведенной

[1229]   A2, N add.: под гоевский народ, или вернее,

[1230]   N: близком

учредим ответственность президентов (c); тогда мы не станем уже церемониться в проведении того, за что будут[1231] отвечать эти президенты.[1232] Ответственность разделит[1233] ряды стремящихся к[1234] власти,[1235] наступит[1236] замешательство,[1237] дезорганизация страны[1238] от[1239] президентов,[1240] у которых в прошлом есть[1241] какая нибудь Панама; с этими пятнами в своем прошлом[1242] они будут верными исполнителями наших предписаний, боясь разоблачения[1243] их.[1244] **Палата** депутатов будет избирать, прикрывать, защищать президентов, но **мы отнимем**[1245] **у нее право предложения законов и**[1246] их изменения, ибо **это право будет**[1247] **предоставлено** ответственному **президенту** (d).[1248] Конечно, тогда его[1249] власть станет мишенью[1250] нападок[1251], но

[1231] A2, N: будет

[1232] A2: он; N: наша безличная креатура

[1233] A2, N omitt.: Ответственность... & add.:   Это [N.: Что нам] до того разредит [N: если разредеют]; В.: разредит

[1234] N, B: ко

[1235] A2: во власть, что

[1236] N: что наступят

[1237] N: замешательства и; B add.: и

[1238] A2, N omitt.: дезорганизация ...

[1239] A1, A2, N, B add.: ненахождения

[1240] B add.: Тогда мы выступим открыто в ряды правления. Ранее этого; A2, N add.: и [N: которые] окончательно дезорганизует [N: дезорганизуют] страну. Чтобы привести [N add.: наш план] к такому результату; A2, N, B add.: мы будем подстраивать выборы таких президентов

[1241] N add.: какое-нибудь не раскрытое темное дело,

[1242] A2, N omitt.: с этими... & add.: тогда

[1243] A2: разоблачений; N: из боязни разоблачений

[1244] A2, N omitt.: их; A1, A2, N, B add.: придерживаясь сохранения пользования привиллегиями [A2: привилегиями] и преимуществами [B: дорожа сохранением привилегий и преимуществ; N: и из свойственного всякому человеку, достигшему власти, стремления удержать за собою привиллегии, преимущества и почет, связанный со званием] президента

[1245] K: отнимим

[1246] B omitt.: и

[1247] N add.: нами

[1248] N add.: кукле в руках наших

мы ему дадим самозащиту **в праве обращения к народу** (e)[1252] (плебисцит)[1253], помимо[1254] представителей последнего, а народ[1255], т. е. большинство[1256] из толпы, это наш слепой прислушник[1257]. Еще[1258] мы ему[1259] дадим[1260] **право**[1261] **объявления военного положения**, это последнее право мы мотивируем[1262] тем, что **президент, как шеф всей армии** (f) страны, имеет ее в своем распоряжении на случай защиты[1263] республиканской конституции, [1264]которую ему подобает охранять, как ответственному представителю[1265] оной[1266]. Вы поймете, что при таком режиме[1267]- **ключ от святилища**[1268] будет[1269] **в наших руках** (g) и никто, кроме нас, не будет[1270] руководить законодательной силой. Кроме того, **у палаты будут отняты**[1271] **права**[1272] **допроса** (h)[1273] о замеченных[1274]

[1249] N: президента

[1250] N add.: для всевозможных

[1251] A2 omitt.

[1252] К, В: решению народа

[1253] К: плебесит; А1: плебесцит; А2, N omitt.; N add.: к его решению

[1254] А2, N add.: его

[1255] А2, N omitt.: последнего...

[1256] А2, N add.: к [N add: тому же] нашему слепому прислушнику [N: прислужанку-] большинству

[1257] А1: прислужник; В: послушник; А2, N omitt.: это..

[1258] B omitt.

[1259] В: президенту

[1260] N: Независимо от этого мы предоставим президенту

[1261] А2 omitt.: Еще мы ему дадим право & add.: а затем в праве

[1262] А2, N: будем мотовировать

[1263] А2, N add.: новой

[1264] А2 add.: на

[1265] А2 omitt.: ему подобает... & add.: он имеет право, как отвественный представитель

[1266] N: этой конституции

[1267] А2, N: Понятно, при таких обстоятельствах [N: условиях]

[1268] А1: святилищ

[1269] А2, N add.: находиться

[1270] А2, N add.: уже

[1271] N: мы отнимем со введением новой республиканской конституции

[1272] N: право

мероприятиях, под предлогом[1275] политической тайны[1276], за которую ответствен президент[1277]. **Число представителей** народа[1278] **будет сокращено**[1279] новой[1280] конституцией до возможного[1281] минимума, **чем сократятся**[1282] на столько же **политические страсти** (i)[1283]; если же таковые[1284] возгорятся и в этом минимуме, то мы обойдем[1285] их воззванием[1286] к всенародному большинству... **От президентов**[1287] республики[1288] **будет**[1289] **зависеть назначение**[1290] президентов и **вицепрезидентов** (j) палаты и сената. **Вместо постоянных сессий парламента**[1291]**, мы сократим**[1292] их[1293] на[1294] несколько[1295] месяцев (k); [1296]кроме того, президент республики[1297], **как начальник исполнительной власти, будет иметь право**[1298] собрать или распустить

[1273] N, B: запроса

[1274] A1: намеченных;A2 omitt.; N: правительственных

[1275] A2, N add.: сохранения

[1276] A2 add.: их

[1277] A2, N omitt.: за которую... & add.: да помимо этого [N: того]

[1278] A2, N omitt.

[1279] N: мы сократим

[1280] B: новою

[1281] N omitt.

[1282] N: сократим

[1283] N add.: и страсть к политике

[1284] N: они, паче чаяния

[1285] N: сведем на-нет

[1286] N add.: и обращением

[1287] A2, N: президента

[1288] A2, N omitt.

[1289] A2, B: будут

[1290] A2, B: назначения

[1291] N: парламентов

[1292] K, A1, A2, B: заставим сократить

[1293] N add.: заседания

[1294] N: до

[1295] A2 add.: лишь

[1296] A2 add.: и,

[1297] A2, N omitt.

[1298] K: в праве; A1, A2, B: всегда в праве

парламентское собрание[1299], и[1300] в случае роспуска[1301] его[1302] он может протянуть время до[1303] назначения нового[1304] собрания (l). [1305]**Чтобы не слышком отяготилась**[1306] от всего этого **ответственность президента**[1307], мы внушим **окружавщим его министрам** (m) и[1308] висшей администрации,[1309] обходить иногда[1310] его распоряжения[1311] собственными мерами[1312]. **Эту роль мы особенно рекомендуем**[1313] **сенату,**[1314] **государственному совету** (n) и комитету[1315] министров[1316]. Президент республики[1317] будет по нашему усмотрению толковать смысл тех из существующих законов, **которые можно**[1318] различно **толковать** (o)[1319], он будет[1320] их анулировать[1321], когда в этом

[1299] N: парламент

[1300] A2: а

[1301] K: распуска

[1302] A2, N omitt.

[1303] A1 omitt.

[1304] N add.: парламентского

[1305] A2 add.: A; N add.: Но,

[1306] A2, N omitt.: не слишком... & add.: не вступила не во-время [N: последствия от всех этих, по существу, беззаконных действий не пали на установленную нами преждевременно] для наших планов

[1307] A2: его

[1308] A2, N omitt.: внушим... & add.: дадим министрам и [N add.: другим] окружающим его [N: президента] чиновникам

[1309] A2, N add.: мысль

[1310] A2, N omitt.

[1311] A2 omitt.

[1312] A1, A2, N, B add.: за что и попадаться [N: подпадать под ответственность] иногда вместо него

[1313] N add.: давать для исполнения

[1314] A2 add.: и

[1315] A2, N: или собранию

[1316] A1 omitt.: Эту роль...; N add.: а не отдельному лицу

[1317] A2, N omitt.

[1318] A2 add.: будет

[1319] A2 add.: да еще; N: истолковать, к тому же

[1320] A1, B add.: и

[1321] K: окулировать; B: отменять

встретится[1322] надобность. [1323]**Он будет**[1324] **предлагать временные законы** (p) и[1325] изменение конституции[1326], мотивируя то[1327] и другое требованиями[1328] высшего блага государства. Такими мерами **мы уничтожим**[1329] мало по малу[1330] **все то, что пришлось учредить** (q)[1331] до сих пор и **придем**[1332] к незаметному **изъятию** из действия[1333] **всякой конституции** (r), когда наступит время превратить[1334] правление[1335] в наше самодержавие. **Признание нашего самодержца** правителем мира **наступит**[1336] **и ранее уничтожения конституции** (s). Оно может наступить[1337], когда народы, измученные[1338] несостоятельностью своих правлений[1339], какие[1340] они ни были бы[1341], воскликнут: уберите их всех[1342] и дайте нам одного всемирного царя, хотя бы из[1343] сионской

[1322] A2, N omitt.: в этом... & add.: ему [N add.: нами] будет указана в том

[1323] A2, N add.: кроме того

[1324] A2, N add.: иметь право

[1325] A2, N add.: даже новое

[1326] A2, N: правительственной конституционной работы

[1327] N: как то так

[1328] A2 add.: для

[1329] A2, N: получим возможность уничтожить

[1330] A2, N add.: шаг за шагом,

[1331] B: учреждать

[1332] B: перейдем; A2, N omitt.: пришлось... & add.: первоначально, при вступлении [N add.: нашем] в наши права, мы будем вынуждены ввести [N add.: в государственные конституции] для перехода

[1333] A2, N omitt.: из...

[1334] N add.: всякое

[1335] B: правления

[1336] A2, N omitt.: правителем... & add: может наступить

[1337] A2, N omitt.: Оно может... & add.: момент этого признания наступит

[1338] A2, N, B add.: неурядицами и

[1339] A2: правителей

[1340] B: каковы бы

[1341] A2 omitt.: какие они...; N omitt.: своих.... & add.: правителей, нами подстроенною; B omitt.

[1342] A2: последних; N omitt.: всех

[1343] B: и

крови[1344], который объединил бы нас и уничтожил бы[1345] причины наших[1346] раздоров- границы, национальности, религия[1347], государственные расчеты[1348], который наконец[1349] дал бы нам мир и покой, до какого[1350] мы никак[1351] не можем добраться[1352] с нашими правителями и представителями, которые жертвуют всегда нами ради своих личных выгод[1353]. Вы[1354] отлично понимаете[1355], что для того, чтобы подобные желания были высказаны[1356], надо не отступно[1357] мутить[1358] народные отношения между собою и по отношению к их начальству[1359], чтобы переутомить всех[1360] их[1361] разладом, враждою, борьбою, ненавистью и даже мученичеством, истребляя и терпеливцев, например русских, индейцев[1362] и др.[1363] голодом,[1364] привитыми заразными болезнями (от которых противоядия известны[1365] только

[1344] A2, N omitt.: хотя бы...

[1345] A2 omitt.

[1346] A2 omitt.

[1347] A1 omitt.: границы...; A1, A2, N, B: религии

[1348] K, A1, N: рассчеты

[1349] A2, N omitt.

[1350] A2: каковых; N: которых; B: какового

[1351] A2, N omitt.

[1352] A2, N: найти

[1353] A2, N omitt.: которые ... выгод & add.: Но

[1354] A2, N add.: сами

[1355] N: знаете

[1356] A2: выражены

[1357] A2: беспрестанно; N omitt.: того, чтобы... & add.: возможности всенародного выражения подобных желаний необходимо беспрестанно

[1358] A2, N add.: во всех странах

[1359] A1, B: начальствам; A2, N omitt.: между собою... & add.: или [N: и] правительства

[1360] K omitt.

[1361] A2, N omitt.

[1362] A1: китайцев

[1363] A2, N omitt.: истребляя...

[1364] A1 add.: и

[1365] A1, B: противоядие известно

нашим ученым)[1366], нуждою, чтобы гои сдались нашему денежному монопольному владычеству, не видя[1367] другого исхода[1368]. Нельзя давать передышки, а[1369] то результат наших бывших[1370] трудов затянется, а это не желательно[1371].

[1372]**Государственный совет** будет подчеркивать власть[1373] правителя: он, как показная часть законодательного корпуса, **будет**, как бы **комитетом редакций** (t) законов[1374] и указов правителя[1375].

И так, вот программа[1376] нашей переходной[1377] конституции: [1378]**мы будем творить закон**, право, и[1379] суд[1380], указами ответственного президента[1381]: **1)**[1382] **под видом предложений**[1383] **законодательному корпусу**[1384], **2)**[1385] **под видом постановлений сената и решений государственного совета, 3)**[1386] **под видом министерских**

[1366] A2, N omitt.: привитыми... & add.: прививкою болезней

[1367] A2, N omitt.: сдались... & add.: не видели

[1368] A2, N add.: как прибегнуть к нашему денежному но не [N: и] полному владычеству

[1369] A2, N omitt.: Нельзя... & add.: Коли [N: Если] же мы дадим передышку народам

[1370] A1 omitt.

[1371] A2, N omitt.: результат... не желательно & add.: желательный момент едва ли когда-либо [N.: нибудь] наступит

[1372] A2 add.: **XI**; N add.: **Следующий протокол**

[1373] N: явится, как подчеркиватель власти

[1374] A2 omitt.

[1375] K, A1, B omitt.: Государственный совет...; A1, B add.: **Еще протокол** [B add.: **(13)**]

[1376] K: програма

[1377] A2, N omitt.: нашей ... & add.: новой готовящейся

[1378] A1 add.: 1)

[1379] K, A1, B omitt.

[1380] B add.: :1)

[1381] A2, N omitt.: указами...

[1382] A1 omitt.; B: 2)

[1383] A2: предложения

[1384] K, A1, B: общих установлений

[1385] B: 3)

[1386] A1 omitt.; B: 4)

предписаний,[1387] 4)[1388] **указами** президента, 5)[1389] под видом общих установлений[1390], 6)[1391] а в случае[1392] наступления удобного момента,[1393] **в форме государственного переворота** (u)... Установив эти пункты[1394], займемся подробностями[1395] комбинаций, необходимых для переворота[1396] государственных машин в нужном[1397] направлении. Выясним вопросы о **свободе**[1398] прессы[1399], **праве**[1400] ассоциаций[1401], свободе[1402] совести,[1403] **выборных началах**[1404] и о[1405] **многом другом**[1406], **что должно будет исчезнуть** из человеческого репертуара **или быть**[1407] **в корне изменено** (v) на другой же день после[1408] провозглашения[1409]

[1387]   A2, N omitt.: под видом постановлений...

[1388]   K, A1, A2, N, B omitt.

[1389]   K, A1, A2, N, B omitt.

[1390]   K, A1, B omitt.; A2, N add.: постановлений сената и решений государственного совета, под видом министерских предписаний [N: постановлений]

[1391]   K, B omitt.; A1: 4); A2, N: 3)

[1392]   B: случаях

[1393]   K: 4)

[1394]   A2: этот пункт; N omitt.: эти... & add.: приблизительно *modus agendi*

[1395]   A2, N add.: тех

[1396]   A2, N omitt.: необходимых... & add.: которые [N: которыми] нам остается довершить для переворота [N: переворот] хода

[1397]   A2, N: вышесказанном

[1398]   A2, N omitt.: Выясним...; A2 add.: Я говорю о свободе; N add.: Под этими комбинациями я разумею свободу

[1399]   K: пресы; A2 add.: о

[1400]   N: право

[1401]   K: асоциаций; N: ассоциации; A2 add.: о

[1402]   N: свободу

[1403]   A2 add.: о

[1404]   N: выборное начало; B: выборном начале

[1405]   K omitt.

[1406]   N: многое другое

[1407]   A2, N: должно быть [N: будет]

[1408]   A1 omitt.

[1409]   K: превозглашения

интернационального владыки[1410]. **В этот момент надо**[1411] будет сразу **объявить все** наши **постановления** неукоснительно[1412], **ибо после всякое** [1413]**изменение будет не целесообразно**[1414]: **если**[1415] изменение поведет[1416] **к строгости**[1417], оно ожесточит[1418], **если же к послаблению**[1419], то[1420] скажут- познали[1421] свою неправоту, а это порвет[1422] ореол непогрешимости новой власти, **или** же скажут, что испугались и **вынуждены** идти на уступки,[1423] за которые никто **не станет относиться с благодарностью, считая их должными...** (w)[1424]; то и другое одинаково[1425] вредно для престижа новой силы[1426]. Нам нужно, чтобы в первый же момент ее возникновения,[1427] ее провозглашения,[1428] **народы, еще огорошенные**[1429] **переворотом, находясь в** недоумении и[1430] **терроре**

[1410] A2, N: новой конституции. [N add.: Только]

[1411] A2 add.: нам; N: нам возможно

[1412] A2, N omitt.

[1413] A2 add.: заметное

[1414] A2, N: опасно [N add.: и вот почему]

[1415] A2, N add.: это

[1416] A2, B: последует [B add.: после того]; N: проведено будет.

[1417] A2: в строгости; N: с суровой строгостью и в смысле строгости и ограничений, то

[1418] A2, N: приведет к большему отчаянию и к боязни [N: может довести до отчаяния, вызванного боязню] новых изменений в этом [N: том] же направлении

[1419] A2, N: оно произойдет [N: произведено будет] в послаблении [N: в смысле дальнейших послаблений]

[1420] A2 omitt.

[1421] A2, N: что [N: мы] сознали; B: сознали

[1422] A2, N, B: подорвет

[1423] A2 omitt.: идти... & add.: были делать послабления

[1424] K, A1, B omitt.: или же...благодарен; N: будет благодарен

[1425] A2, N omitt.

[1426] A2, N: конституции

[1427] A2, N omitt.: в первый... & add.: с первого момента ее провозглашения, когда

[1428] N add.: когда

[1429] A2, N: будут еще [N omitt.] огоршены [N: ошеломлены & add.: совершившимся]; B: ошеломленные

(x),[1431] сознали, что[1432] она с ними не будет[1433] считаться ни в каком случае; что мы[1434] не обратим внимания[1435] на их протесты, ни на мнения, а[1436] подавим[1437] то и другое, если они проявятся в[1438] деле[1439], в каждый момент и в[1440] каждом месте. Что **мы все сразу взяли** (у), что нам было нужно от власти[1441], и что мы не будем[1442] делиться ею ни с кем[1443]. Тогда от[1444] страха и недомумения,[1445] **они добровольно**[1446] **закроют глаза** (z)[1447] и станут ожидать, что из этого выйдет и не лучше ли будет. Тем более[1448], что **мы им обещаем**[1449] **вернуть все отнятые привилегии и**[1450] **свободы**[1451]**, после усмирения**[1452] **партий** (aa) и

1430   A2, N omitt.: находясь... & add.: будут еще находиться в

1431   K: тероре; A2: и недоумении, они; N add.: они

1432   A1, B add.: Наша Мощь так неуязвима, так сильна, что; A2, N add.: мы так сильны, так неуязвимы, так мощи [N: исполнены мощи], что

1433   A2, N: мы не будем с ними

1434   A2, N omitt.: что мы & add.: и не только

1435   B add.: ни

1436   A2, N omitt.: протесты ... & add.: мнения и желания, но

1437   N omitt.: подавим & add.: готовы и способны с непререкаемой властью подавить

1438   B: на

1439   A2, N omitt.: то и другое... & add.: их выражение и проявление

1440   A2 omitt.; N: на

1441   A2, N omitt.: от...

1442   A2, N: станем

1443   A2, N: с ними нашей властью

1444   N: из

1445   A2, N omitt.

1446   A2 add.: как бы; N omitt.

1447   A2, N add.: на все

1448   A2, N omitt.: и не лучше... ; N add.: Гои- баранье стадо, а мы для них волки. А вы знаете, что бывает с овцами, когда в овчарню забираются волки?.. Они закроют глаза на все еще и потому

1449   N: пообещаем

1450   A2, N omitt.: привилегии...

1451   K: свободу

1452   N add.: всех

укрощения врагов мира. [1453]**Сколько же**[1454] они этого[1455] **прождут**[1456] (ab) -это укажет будущее[1457]. Для **чего**[1458] мы **измыслили** для себя **Политику**[1459] и научили в нужных нам случаях гоев политике[1460]-**коль**[1461] **не для того, чтобы достигнуть обходом того, что не было**[1462] **достижимо**[1463] **прямым путем** (ab). Политика была[1464] основанием[1465] нашей организации, ныне[1466] нам[1467] остается ее[1468] достраивать и[1469] **поставить** наш трон[1470] **на этом** удобном и крепком[1471] **фундаменте** (ac).

[1453] N add.: Стоит ли говорить о том,

[1454] N: времени

[1455] A2, N add.: возврата

[1456] N: будут ожидать

[1457] A2: (если не всегда), уж ето будет задачей будущего; N omitt.: это....

[1458] N add.: же

[1459] K, A1 omitt.

[1460] A2, N omitt.: измыслили... & add.: придумали для себя [N omitt.] и внушили гоям [N add.: всю эту] политику [N add.: внушили, не дав им возможности разглядеть ее подкладку, для чего]; B: ей

[1461] A2: если; N: как

[1462] A2, N omitt.

[1463] N add.: для нашего разсеянного племени

[1464] A2: Это было [N: послужило]

[1465] N add.: для

[1466] A2 omitt.

[1467] N omitt.: ныне нам & add.: тайного масонства, которого не знают и целей которых даже и не подозревают скоты гои, привлеченные нами в показную армию масонских лож, для отвода глаз их соплеменникам. Бог даровал нам, Своему избранному народу, рассеяние, и в этой кажущейся для всех слабости нашей и сказалась вся наша сила, которая теперь привела нас к порогу всемирного владычества. Нам теперь немного уже

[1468] N omitt.

[1469] B: дабы

[1470] A2 omitt.: и поставить...

[1471] A2 omitt.; N omitt. и поставить... & add.: заложенном

QUOTATIONS FROM JOLY'S *DIALOGUE*

a   «Vos gouvernements parlementaires ne sont que des écoles de dispute, que de foyers d'agitations stériles»

b   «la tribune et la presse condamnent à l'impuissance.»

c   «le souverain que j'institue sera seul responsible»

d   «La Chambre (...) Je raye l'initiative parlementaire. La proposition des lois n'appartiendra qu'au souverain.»

e   «N'avez-vous pas pris le suffrage populaire pour base de vostre pouvoir?»

f   «L'appel au peuple, le droit de mettre le pays en état de siège; je suis chef d'armée»

g   «J'ai la clef du tabernacle.»

h   «je n'entends pas laisser à la Chambre ce que vous appelez le droit d'amendement.»

i   «Je réduirais (...) le nombre des représentants et j'aurais, par suite, moitié moins de passions politiques»

j.   «Je me réserverais la nomination des présidents et des vice-présidents»

k   «Au lieu de sessions permanentes, je réduirais à quelque mois la tenue de l'assemblée»

l   «comme chef du pouvoir exécutif, j'ai le droit de convoquer, de dissoudre le Corps législatif, et (...) en cas de dissolution, je me réserverais les plus longs délais pour convoquer une nouvelle représentation.»

m   «Il n'est pas bon que la personne du souverain soit constamment en jeu»

n   «des grandes magistratures qui environnent le trône»

o   «c'est à ce rôle que vous destinez le Sénat et le Conseil d'Etat»

p   «les articles (...) susceptibles de différentes intérprétations»

q   «je fais des décrets qui ont force de lois»

r   «...le droit de défaire ce que vous avez fait (...), de changer votre constitution (...), ou même de la faire disparaitre»

s   «l'heure où je me ferai proclamer roi n'est plus qu'une affaire d'opportunité. Je le serai avant ou après avoir promulgué ma constitution»

t   «le Conseil d'Etat? (...) Ce n'est qu'un Comité de Rédaction. Quand (...) fait un règlement, c'est le souverain qui le fait; quand il rend un jugement, c'est le souverain qui le rend»

u   «Vous faites la loi: 1° sous la forme de proposition au Corps législatif; vous la faites, 2°, sous forme de décrets; 3° sous forme de sénatus-consultes; 4° sous forme de règlements généraux; 5° sous forme d'arrètés au Conseil d'Etat; 6° sous forme de règlements ministériels; 7° enfin sous forme de coups d'Etat.»

v   «la liberté de la presse, du droit d'association, de l'indipéndence de la
     magistrature, du droit de suffrage, de l'élection (...) et de beaucoup d'autres
     choses encore qui devront disparaître ou être profondément modifiées»

w   «Il faut (...) commetre une seule fois toutes les rigueurs (...); car plus tard il ne
     pourra plus varier (...); si c'est en mal (...) vous n'ètes plus à temps (...); si c'est
     en bien, vos sujets ne vous sauront aucun gré d'un changement qu'ils jugeront
     être forcé»

x   «Le pays est encore sous la terreur de vostre coup d'Etat»

y   «vous ne demandez rien et (...) vous prenez tout.»

z   «Le pays fermera volontairement les yeux»

aa   «les libertés que je supprime, je prometterai solennellement de les rendre après
     l'apaisement des partis.»

ab   «on attendra toujours»

ac   «A quoi servirait la politique, si l'on ne pouvait gagner par des voies obliques le
     but qui ne peut s'atteindre par la ligne droite?»

ad   «Les bases de mon établissement sont posées»

X [1472]

Слово свобода, которое **можно толковать разнообразно,** мы определим так, когда придет наше время[1473]: «190**свобода есть право делать то, что позволяет закон (a)».** **Подобное толкование**[1474] в то же[1475] время **послужит нам**[1476], потому что **законы будут разрешать**[1477] только то, **что будет согласоваться** (b) с[1478] вышеозначенной[1479] программой[1480] и с[1481] той[1482], которую еще доложу вам[1483]. С прессой мы поступим следующим образом[1484]. **Она служит пылкому возгоранию**[1485] нужных нам **страстей, или**[1486] **эгоистическим**[1487] **партийностям; она бывает** пуста, **несправедлива, лжива, и большинство людей не понимает**[1488], **чему она** в действительности[1489] **служит** (c). **Мы ее** окончательно[1490] **оседлаем**[1491], **равно**[1492] **как и всю**[1493] печать (d), ибо **какой смысл нам**

[1472]   K omitt.; A1, N, B: **Еще протокол** [B add.: **(14)**]; A2: **XII.**

[1473]   A2, N omitt.: когда...

[1474]   A2, N add.: этого слова

[1475]   A2, N, B omitt.

[1476]   N add.: к тому, что вся свобода окажется в наших руках

[1477]   N: разрушать

[1478]   A2, N omitt.: то, что.... & add.: желательное нам по

[1479]   A1, N: вышеизложенной; B: вышеизложенною

[1480]   K: програмой; A2, N: программе

[1481]   K, A1 omitt.

[1482]   B: тою

[1483]   A2, N omitt.: и с той...

[1484]   N add.: -Какую роль играет теперь пресса?

[1485]   N: разгоранию; B: возгаранию

[1486]   N add.: же

[1487]   A2, N: эгоистичным

[1488]   A2: понимают; N add.: вовсе

[1489]   A2, N omitt.

[1490]   A2, N omitt.

[1491]   B add.: обуздаем- газеты

[1492]   B omitt.

[1493]   A2, N omitt.: равно... & add.: и накинем на нее [N: возьмем в] крепкие возжи, равно и на всю [N: то же сделаем и с остальной печатью]

избавиться[1494] **от нападок прессы, если мы останемся мишенью**[1495] **для брошуры и книги** (e). Но[1496] мы устроим[1497] так, что[1498] ныне дорого стоящий **предмет**[1499] **гласности** (f) по причине[1500] необходимости его цензуровать[1501], превратится в предмет, дающий статью дохода государству нашему[1502]. Для этого[1503] **мы** обложим **прессу**[1504] особым **марочным налогом и взносом** (g)[1505] при учреждении органов[1506] и[1507] типографий, каковые залоги будут штрафным источником, гарантирующим наше правление от нападок[1508] прессы[1509], за которые она будет штрафована[1510] под предлогом, что штрафуемый орган волнует умы без повода и основания[1511]. **Партийные газеты**, пожалуй, **не пожалели бы**[1512] **денег** (h), но[1513] мы их[1514] будем закрывать по

[1494] N: избавляться

[1495] K omitt.

[1496] A2, N omitt.

[1497] B: устроимся; A2, N: превратим

[1498] A2, N omitt.: так,...

[1499] N: продукт

[1500] N: дорогой, благодаря

[1501] N: цензуры

[1502] A2, N omitt.: превратится... & add.: в доходную статью для нашего государства

[1503] A2, N omitt.

[1504] A2, N: ее

[1505] A1, B add.: залога [B: залогов]; A2, N: взносами залогов.

[1506] N add.: печати

[1507] A2, N, B: или

[1508] A1: нападений; A2, N omitt.: каковые... & add.: которые гарантируют [N: должны будут гарантировать] своим существованием [N omitt.] наше правительство от всяких нападений со стороны

[1509] K: пресы

[1510] A2, N omitt.: за которые... & add.: которая будет штрафоваться за таковые [N: За возможное нападение мы будем штрафовать безпощадно]; B: оштрафована

[1511] A2, N omitt.: под предлогом... & add.: Такое положение принесет [N: Такие меры, как марки, залоги и штрафы, ими обезпеченные, принесут] огромный доход правительству [N add.: Правда,]

[1512] A2, N omitt.: пожалуй, не.... & add.: могли бы не пожалеть

второму нападению (i) на нас[1515]. **Никто не может**[1516] безнаказанно **касаться ореола**[1517] **нашей правительственной непогрешимости** (j) и под вышесказанным предлогом и[1518] по[1519] недоказанности нападок, **будем закрывать упорствующие издания** (k)[1520]. Но когда нам надо будет изменить какой-нибудь[1521] пункт наших установлений, то на них будут нападать наши[1522] органы, и, так как они дадут веские[1523] доказательства недостатков, то им это будет сходить,[1524] послужит еще к тому, что будут говорить, что все же свободоговорение мотивированное и справедливое не возбраняется нами[1525]. Ведь[1526] ни одно оповещение не будет исходить и[1527] проникать в массы[1528] без нашего контроля, потому что и теперь[1529] **все**[1530] новости получаются несколькими[1531] **агентствами, в**[1532] которых и[1533] централизуются[1534] со всех концов

[1513] A1: тогда; A2: так

[1514] A2: эти издания

[1515] K, A1, B omitt.: их будем.. & add.: объявим, что

[1516] A2, N: будет

[1517] K, B: органа

[1518] B: или

[1519] A1 omitt.

[1520] A2, N omitt.: и под предлогом ...и & add.: Предлог для прекращения издания мы заявим том-де, что [N omitt.: мы заявим...] закрываемый [N add.: де] орган волнует умы без повода и основания

[1521] A1, B: либо

[1522] A2, N omitt.: Но когда... & add.: [N add.: Прошу вас заметить, что] Среди нападающих на нас будут и нами учрежденные

[1523] B: весские

[1524] A1 add.: с рук, что; B add.: что

[1525] A2, N omitt.: и, так как... & add.: [N add.: но] они будут нападать исключительно на пункты, предназначенные нами к изменению

[1526] A2, N omitt.

[1527] A2, N omitt.: исходить...

[1528] A2, N: общество

[1529] N add.: уже нами достигается тем,

[1530] A2 omitt.: и теперь...

[1531] B: немногими

[1532] K: у

[1533] A2, N: они

мира[1535]: эти агенства, как нами созданные учреждения, огласят[1536] только то, что[1537] им предпишем (l)[1538]. **Каждый пожелавший быть издателем, типографщиком, или библиотекарем, должен[1539]** будет получить[1540] диплом, установленный для **получения права на эти занятия[1541], который[1542]** будет отбираться (m) у провинившихся лиц[1543]. Благодаря таким порядкам[1544], **орудие мысли превратится в** воспитательное **средство[1545]** в руках **нашего правления** (n). Тогда оно[1546] уже не допустит народные мысли[1547] заблуждаться[1548] в дебрях и мечтах[1549] о благодеянии[1550] прогресса[1551], ибо эти[1552] дороги ведут к

[1534] К, В: централизируются

[1535] А2, N: света

[1536] А2, N omitt.: как... & add.: будут [N add.: тогда уже всецело] нашими учреждениями и будут оглашать

[1537] А1, А2 add.: мы

[1538] N add.: Если теперь мы съумели овладеть умами гоевских обществ до той степени, что все они почти смотрят на мировые события сквозь цветные стекла тех очков, которые мы им надеваем на глаза, если теперь для нас ни в одном государстве не существует запоров, преграждающих нам доступ к так называемым гоевской глупостью государственным тайнам, то что же будет, тогда, когда мы будем признанными владыками мира в лице нашего всемирного царя?!...Вернемся к будущности печати.

[1539] А2, N: вынужден

[1540] А2, N: добыть на это [N add.: дело]

[1541] А2, N omitt.: для получения...

[1542] А2 omitt.; А2, N add.: в случае провинности этих лиц диплом [N omitt. этих лиц диплом & add.: немедленно же]

[1543] А2, N omitt.: отбираться... & add.: отобран

[1544] А2: такими мерами; N: При таких мерах

[1545] А2, N: сделается [N: станет] воспитательным средством

[1546] А2, N omitt.: правления.. & add.: правительства, которое

[1547] А2, N: народную массу

[1548] В: заноситься

[1549] А1, А2, В: дебри и мечты

[1550] N: благодеяниях

[1551] К: прогреса

[1552] А2 omitt.: ибо эти... & add.: которые суть; N add.: Кто из нас не знает, что эти призрачные благодеяния- прямые

анархии в отношениях[1553] людей между собою и по отношению[1554] к власти, потому что прогресс[1555] выдвинул мысли[1556] об[1557] эмансипации, не установив границы ее. Все[1558] либералы имеют тенденцию сделаться[1559] все требовательнее, то есть превратиться в анархистов[1560] мысли, коль еще[1561] не дела. Они все более гонятся[1562] за призраками свободы и впадают только[1563] в своесловие,[1564] в анархию[1565] протеста. Перейдем к[1566] прессе. **Мы ее обложим, как и всю печать, марочными сборами** с листа, и залогами.[1567] **Книги, имеющие**[1568] **менее 300 листов**[1569]**, мы**[1570] **запишем в разряд брошюр** (о) и обложим их двойным сбором,[1571] для того[1572], чтобы[1573] **сократить** все **пристежки к журналам** (р)[1574], а **с другой стороны, чтобы вынудить**[1575] **писателей сочинять**

[1553] A2, N omitt.: ведут... & add.: к [N add.: нелепым] мечтаниям, от которых родились анархические отношения

[1554] N omitt.: по...

[1555] K: прогрес

[1556] A1: вел мысль; A2: навел на мысль; N: или лучше идея прогресса навела на мысль; B: ввел мысль

[1557] N: о всякого рода

[1558] N add.: так называемые

[1559] B: становиться

[1560] A2, N omitt.: имеют... & add.: суть анархисты, то

[1561] A2, N: если

[1562] A2, N: Каждый из них гоняется

[1563] A2, N: впадая исключительно

[1564] A2, N add.: то есть

[1565] A1, A2, B add.: из за; N add.: ради

[1566] B add.: повременной

[1567] A2, N add.: а

[1568] A2 add.: не

[1569] B: 600 страниц; A2, N: -в двойном размере

[1570] A2, N add.: их

[1571] A2 omitt.: и обложим...

[1572] N omitt.: и обложим...

[1573] N add.: с одной стороны

[1574] A2 add.: которые суть худший яд; N omitt.: все пристежи... & add.: число журналов, которые собой представляют худший печатный яд

[1575] A2: это вынудит; N omitt.: стороны... & add.: эта мера вынудит

такие **длинные** и скучные **произведения**[1576], **которые**[1577], при их[1578] дороговизне, **мало будут читать** (q). Так мы заменим нашими дешевыми журналами всю книжную торговлю[1579]. **Налог угомонит пустое литературное влечение** (r) и[1580] поставит[1581] литераторов в зависимость от нас. **Если**[1582] **найдутся желающие писать против** нами намеченного направления[1583], то[1584] **не найдется желающих**[1585] **печатать** (s) их произведения. **Прежде чем принять для печати какое либо произведение**[1586], издатель или типографщик справится (t), может ли он[1587] воспроизводить[1588]. **Таким образом, нам заранее будут известны**[1589] **готовящиеся против нас**[1590] **козни** (u)[1591], забежав[1592] вперед с толкованиями[1593] на затронутую[1594] тему[1595], разобьем впечатление о ней ранее ее появления[1596]. Литература и **журналистика**

[1576] A2, N omitt.: сочинять... & add.: к таким длинным произведениям

[1577] A2, N: что их особенно

[1578] A2 omitt.

[1579] A2, N omitt.: Так мы... & add.: А то, [N: То же] что мы сами будем издавать на пользу умственного направления в намеченную нами сторону будет дешево и будет читаться нарасхват

[1580] A2, N: а наказуемость

[1581] A1: постановит

[1582] N add.: и

[1583] A2, N omitt.: нами... & add.: нас

[1584] A2 omitt.

[1585] A2: найдутся желающие; N: охотников

[1586] K, A1, B omitt.: Прежде чем... & add.: Получив заказ

[1587] B: его

[1588] A2, N omitt.: справится... & add.: придет [N: должен будет придти] к [N: ко] властям просить разрешения на это

[1589] A2 omitt.: нам... & add.: мы будем ведать заранее

[1590] A2 omitt. против нас & add.: нам

[1591] A2, N add.: и [N add.: мы] разобьем их,

[1592] K, A1, B omitt.: Таким образом... & add.: а если мы будем видеть, что нельзя отказать в этом, то [B add.: мы] забежим

[1593] A2, N: объяснениями

[1594] A2, N: трактуемую

[1595] A1, B add.: и

[1596] A2, N omitt.: разобьем...

суть[1597] **важнейшие** воспитательные **силы**[1598]; **вот почему наше правление**[1599] **будет**[1600] **собственником** большинства **журналов** (v), а другие им[1601] будут закуплены субсидиями. Этим мы приобретем[1602] громадное влияние[1603]: **если будут** издаваться[1604] **30**[1605] **журналов, то 25 будут издаваться нами**[1606] **и так далее в том же роде** (w)[1607]. Но, так как[1608] этого публика не должна[1609] подозревать (x), то[1610] наши[1611] журналы будут самых противоположных друг другу[1612] мнений: **это вызовет**[1613] **доверие** (y) и привлечет к ним наших[1614] противников, которых мы занесем в списки таковых, благодаря этой хитрости[1615]. **На первом плане поставятся**[1616] органы официального[1617] характера: они будут всегда стоять[1618] **на страже государственных**[1619] интересов, а[1620]

[1597] N omitt.: суть & add.: две

[1598] K, B: орудия

[1599] A2, N: правительство

[1600] A2, N: сделается

[1601] B: остальные же

[1602] A2, N omitt.: а другие... & add.: Этим нейтрализуется [N: будет нейтрализовано] вредное влияние частной прессы и приобретется

[1603] A2, N add.: на умы

[1604] A1, B: издаваемы

[1605] A2, N omitt.: будут... & add.: мы разрешим десять

[1606] A2, N omitt.: 25 будут... & add.: сами учредим тридцать

[1607] K, A1, B omitt.: и т. д...; A2 omitt.: в том же...

[1608] A2, N omitt.

[1609] A2, N omitt.: публика не... & add.: не должны в публике [N add.: отнюдь]

[1610] A2: вот почему

[1611] N: почему и все издаваемые нами

[1612] N: по внешности направлений и

[1613] A2, N: что возбудит к ним; B: возбудит

[1614] N add.: ничего не подозревающих

[1615] A2, N omitt.: которых... & add.: которые [N add.: таким образом,] попадутся нам [N: в нашу западню] и будут отмечены [N: обезврежены]

[1616] K, B: у нас будут стоять; A1: у нас будут

[1617] B: оффициального

[1618] A1 omitt.: органы... будут & add.: журналы всегда стояшие

[1619] A2, N: наших

[1620] N: и

потому[1621] не[1622] иметь влияния[1623]. На втором- станут[1624] официозы[1625], роль которых будет[1626] в объединении[1627] равнодушных и тепленьких[1628]. В третьих выступят[1629] антиподы мнений[1630], которые будут говорить по крайней мере одним органом[1631] в голосе каждой партии (z)[1632]; эти партии[1633] примут их[1634] за своих и придут к ним открывать[1635] свои карты. Третий разряд нашей прессы будет[1636] аристократом, республиканцем, революционером, анархистом (aa), консерватором и т. д.[1637]: как индийский божок Вишну, мы[1638] будем[1639] иметь сто рук, из коих[1640] каждая будет щупать пульс у какого-нибудь[1641] из

[1621] A1 add.: они и

[1622] A1, B add.: будут

[1623] A2, N omitt.: не иметь... ; A2 add.: самому не сильно будут влиять; N add.: их влияние будет сравнительно ничтожно

[1624] K, A1, A2, B: Во вторых, будут

[1625] A2: оффициозного характера

[1626] A2 add.: привлечении и; N add.: заключаться

[1627] N: привлечении

[1628] B: тепловатых

[1629] A1, A2, B: станут те

[1630] A1, B: мнения; A2 omitt.

[1631] K omitt.: по крайней мере....

[1632] A2 omitt.: в голосе... & add.: о каждом мнении; N omitt.: В третьих... & add.: На третьем- мы поставим как бы нашу оппозицию, которая хотя бы в одном из своих органов будет представлять собою как бы наш антипод

[1633] A2: которые и

[1634] N: Наши действительные противники в душе примут эту кажущуюся оппозицию

[1635] N: откроют нам

[1636] A2, N omitt.: Третий... & add.: Эти [N: Все] наши газеты будут [N add.: всевозможных направлений-]

[1637] A2, N omitt.: аристократом... & add.: аристократами, республиканцами, революционерами, даже анархистами- [N: аристократического, республиканского, революционного, даже анархического-] пока [N add.: конечно] будет жить конституция [N add.: Они,]

[1638] A2 omitt.

[1639] N: будут

[1640] N: которых

общественных мнений (ab); когда пульс ускорится в борьбе от противоречия[1642], то рука поведет его[1643] по направлению к[1644] нашей цели, потому что[1645] заволновавшийся[1646] субъект теряет рассудительность и хладнокровие[1647], легко поддается управлению[1648], в надежде с его помощью скорее победить врага[1649]. **Те партизаны**[1650], **которые будут предполагать**[1651], **что повторяют мнение газеты своего лагеря, будут повторять**[1652] то, что **наши** агенты написали для того[1653], чтобы их[1654] сильнее взволновать[1655]. **Воображая, что они следуют за флагом**[1656] **своей партии, они пойдут за тем флагом, который мы повесим** (ac)[1657] для них. Чтобы направлять в этом смысле наши[1658] газетные милиции, мы должны будем[1659] особенно тщательно организовать это дело. **Под названием** центрального **отделения печати, мы учредим** литературные **собрания, в которых** наши агенты **будут** незаметно **выдавать**[1660] пароль и **сигнал** (ad)[1661] литераторам[1662].

[1641] A2: либо; N: любого

[1642] A2, N omitt.: в борьбе...; В: противоречий

[1643] A2, N omitt.: то... & add.: то [N: тогда] эти руки поведет [N: поведут мнение]

[1644] A1 omitt.

[1645] A2, N: ибо

[1646] N: разволновавшийся

[1647] A2, N omitt.

[1648] A2, N: внушению.

[1649] A2, N omitt.: в надежде...

[1650] N: Тартарены

[1651] A2, N: думать

[1652] A2, N add.: наше мнение, или

[1653] В: умышленно

[1654] K omitt.

[1655] A1: волновать; A2, n omitt.: что наши... & add.: которое нам желательно

[1656] N: органом

[1657] A1, A2, N, В: вывесим

[1658] K omitt.

[1659] N omitt.

[1660] N, В: давать

[1661] A2, N: сигналы

[1662] A2 omitt.

Обсуждая и осуждая[1663] **наши начинания**[1664] **всегда лишь**[1665] **поверхностно, никогда**[1666] **не затрагивая**[1667] **сущности**[1668] **таковых**[1669], **наши органы будут вести пустую перестрелку** (ae) с официальными[1670] органами[1671]: это послужит к тому[1672], чтобы дать нам пощупать точку[1673], на которой стоит общественное мнение по поводу того или другого вопроса, а во вторых, даст[1674] нам[1675] высказаться более подробно по этому вопросу[1676], чем[1677] возможно[1678] сделать в официальном[1679] распоряжении[1680], в котором управлению[1681] не подобает выяснять[1682] свои распоряжения. Кроме всего этого,[1683] их[1684] нападки **покажут, что как будто свободоговорение**[1685] **не запрещено** (af). Другие наши[1686] органы будут на все нападки доказывать, что

[1663] A2, N: противореча

[1664] A2, N: нашим начинаниям

[1665] A2, N omitt.

[1666] A2, N omitt.

[1667] N, B: затрогивая

[1668] A2: но затрогивая сущность

[1669] N: существа их

[1670] A1, A2, B: оффициальными

[1671] A2, N: газетами

[1672] A2, N omitt.: это... & add.: для того [N add.: только],

[1673] B: почву

[1674] B: сверх того будет давать

[1675] A2, N omitt.: пощупать... & add.: повод

[1676] A2, N omitt.: по этому...

[1677] A1 add.: то

[1678] A2, N: мы могли бы это

[1679] A1, B: оффициальном

[1680] A2, N: оффициальных заявлениях

[1681] A1: направлению; B: правлению

[1682] A1: пояснить; B: пояснять

[1683] A2, N omitt.: в котором... & add.: [N add.: Конечно,] когда для нас будет выгодно высказываться [N: это]

[1684] N: эти

[1685] B add.: и

[1686] A2, N omitt.: покажут... & add.: [N add.: на нас] сыграют еще [N add.: и] ту роль, из которой [N: что] подданные увидят, что свободоговорение,

нападающие[1687] пустословят **и не приводят основателных аргументов против**[1688] **наших распоряжений** (ag).[1689] По мере надобности, **мы будем**, через прессу,[1690] **возбуждать и успокоивать**[1691] **умы в политических вопросах, убеждать или сбивать**[1692], печатая **то правду, то ложь, данные или их опровержения** (ah)[1693], если[1694] будут плохо[1695] приняты[1696]. Мы будем побеждать наших противников наверняка, ибо[1697] у них не будет, вследствие вышеприведенных причин[1698], органа[1699], в котором им привелось[1700] бы высказаться до конца; **мы же будем**[1701] **всегда опровергать**[1702], и[1703] до конца, справедливо или несправедливо, **последним словом** (ai) влияя на недальновидных гоев[1704]. Брошенные[1705]

[1687] повидимому, не стеснено [N: будут уверены в полной свободе свободоговорения] а нашим агентам это даст повод говорить [N: утверждать] что выступающие против нас
A2, N omitt.: будут на все...; A2 add.: лишь

[1688] A2, N omitt.: и не приводят... & add.: так как не находят [N: могут найти] настоящих поводов к существенному обвинению [N: опровержению]

[1689] A2, N add.: Такие незаметные [N add.: для общественного внимания, но верные] мероприятия всего успешнее поведут общественное мнение [N: внимание] и доверие в сторону нашего правительства. Благодаря им

[1690] A2, N omitt: через...

[1691] K, A1, B: успокаивать

[1692] N add.: с толку

[1693] A2: опровержение

[1694] A2 add.: они

[1695] N omitt. если будут... & add.: смотря по тому, хорошо или дурно они

[1696] A2, N add.: щупая [N: всегда осторожно ощупывая] почву, прежде чем ступить на нее.

[1697] A2, N: так как

[1698] A2, N: вышесказанных мероприятий против прессы

[1699] A2, N: органов [N add.: печати в распоряжении]

[1700] A2, N: в которых они могли

[1701] B add.: в состоянии

[1702] A1, B: опровергнуть

[1703] A1, A2, B: их

[1704] A2 omitt.: и до конца... & add.: до основания; N omitt.: мы же будем... & add.: Нам не нужно будет даже опровергать их до основания.

[1705] N add.: нами

пробные камни (aj) в третьем разряде нашей прессы[1706] мы будем энергично опровергать в официозных[1707], в случае надобности. Уже[1708] **ныне в журналистике**[1709] **существует**[1710] **масонская**[1711] **солидарность** и пароль[1712]. **Все** органы[1713] **связаны между собою профессиональной**[1714] **тайной и**[1715], **подобно древним авгурам, ни один** из членов[1716] журналистики[1717] **не выдаст тайны своих ведений** (ak), если нами[1718] не постановлено их оповещать[1719]. **Ни один журналист не решится предать** этой тайны, **ибо**[1720] ни один журналист[1721] не допускается в число литературных знаменитостей[1722], без того, чтобы[1723] его прошлое не **имело бы**[1724] **какой нибудь постыдной раны**... (al) Эти раны были бы тотчас же[1725] раскрыты. **Пока эти раны составляют тайну немногих, ореол журналиста привлекает мнение большинства страны- за ним шествуют с восторгом** (am)[1726]. Нужда, самомнение,[1727] гордость и проч.[1728] служат порукой, что, в погоне за успехом, журналист

[1706] К: пресы

[1707] А1, А2, N, В: оффициозах

[1708] N add.: и

[1709] А1, А2, N, В: формах [N add.: хотя бы французской] журналистики

[1710] К: существуют

[1711] К omitt.; А1: массонская

[1712] А2: с паролем; N: в пароле

[1713] N add.: печати

[1714] К: професиональной; В: профессиональною

[1715] А2, N omitt.

[1716] А2, N, В: член

[1717] А2, N: ее

[1718] А2, N omitt.

[1719] N: оповестить

[1720] К, А1, В omitt.: Ни один журналист... & add.: Это потому, что

[1721] А2, N: из них

[1722] А2, N omitt.: число... & add.: литературу

[1723] N add.: все

[1724] А2 omitt.

[1725] А2 omitt.

[1726] К, А1, В: ...было[бы] порукой его покорности сигналу и паролю

[1727] А1 add.: и

[1728] В: другие поруки

подчинится общему обычаю солидарности, суть ключи к литературнной дороге, на которую многие великие, но непокорные паролю умы не попали. Ныне[1729] **наши расчеты простираются на влияние в провинции** (an)[1730], где[1731] нам необходимо пролить[1732] те[1733] стремления, которые нам нужно будет скоро[1734] **обрушить**[1735] **на столицы в которых мнение может опоздать** (ao)[1736], ибо там оно созидается[1737] разом-действием...[1738] Пока мы еще не в полном праве, надо, чтобы[1739], **столицы оказывались окутанными**[1740] **провинциальным мнением** (ap) народов[1741], то есть большинством[1742]. Когда наступит период нашего полного права[1743], мы не допустим[1744] **разоблачения**[1745] **в прессе**[1746]

[1729] N omitt.: Нужда, самомнение...

[1730] A2, N omitt.: на влияние... & add.: особенно на провинцию

[1731] A2, N: в которой [N: ней]

[1732] A1, B: породить; A2: пробудить ту веру; N: возбудить

[1733] N add.: упования и

[1734] A2, N: которые [N: с которыми мы] всегда можем [N: могли бы]

[1735] A2: обратить; N: обрущиться

[1736] A2 omitt.: в которых & add.: которых мнение может и запоздать

[1737] A2: создается

[1738] A2: add.: Нам нужно, чтобы иногда; N omitt.: на столицы & add.: столицу, выдавая их столицам за самостоятельные упования и стремления провинции. Ясно, что источник их будет все тот же- наш. Нам нужно, чтобы иногда

[1739] A2, N omitt.: надо, чтобы; N add.: полной власти

[1740] A1: окутаны

[1741] A2, N: народа

[1742] K omitt.: в которых мнение...; A2: его большинства; N: большинства, подстроенного нашими агентами. A1, A2, N, B add: [A2, N add.: Нам] Нужно, чтобы в известные психологические моменты [A2, N: в психо-логический момент; B: в известные психологические моменты], столицам уже [N: бы] не пришлось обсуждать то [B: того], что является совершившимся фактом с момента [A2: факта, совершившегося тем; N: факта уже по одному], когда [B: как] провинциальное большинство его приняло [A2, N: что он принят мнением провинциального большинства]

[1743] A2, N omitt.: наступит... & add.: мы будем в период нового режима, переходного к нашему воцарению

[1744] A2, N: [N add.: нам] нельзя будет допускать

общественной безчестности (aq),[1747] чтобы думали, что новый режим так всех удовлетворил, что даже преступность изсякла. Преступления будут[1748] оставаться лишь[1749] в ведении[1750] случайных свидетелей их[1751]...

QUOTATIONS FROM JOLY'S *DIALOGUE*

a. «Le mot de liberté est un mot auquel on attache des sens fort divers (...) "La liberté est le droit de faire ce que les lois permettent."»

b «Je m'accomode très bien de cette définition (...) mes lois ne permettront que ce qu'il faudra»

c «La presse (...) n'est jamais au service que de passions violentes, égoïstes, exclusives; elle (...) est injuste (...); vous ne ferez jamais comprendre à la grande masse d'un pays à quoi elle peut servir.»

d «...aux moyens (...) de la museler (...). Ce n'est pas seulement le journalisme que j'entends refréner (...) l'imprimerie elle-même.»

e. «ce ne serait pas la peine d'échapper aux ataques du journalisme s'il fallait rester en butte à celles du livre.»

f «les entreprises de publicité»

g «je soumettrai les feuilles (...) à ce que vous appelez (...) le timbre et le cautionnement.»

h «les partis politiques ne regardent pas à l'argent»

i «je vous avertirai (...) deux fois»

j «à une condition, (...) que vous ne viendrez pas (...) déconsidérer mon pouvoir»

k «Quand vous m'attaquerez (...), je vous supprimerai»

l «Comment les nouvelles arrivent-elles? Par un petit nombre d'agences qui centralisent les renseignements qui leur sont transmis des quatre parties du monde. Eh bien, on doit pouvoir soudoyer ces agences, et (...) elles ne donneront de nouvelles que sous le contrôle du gouvernement.»

[1745] A1: разоблачение

[1746] K: пресе; A2, N: прессой

[1747] A2, N add.: надо

[1748] A2, N omitt.: Преступления... & add.: Такие [N omitt.] случаи [N: проявления преступности] должны

[1749] A2, N omitt.

[1750] A2, N add.: их жертв и

[1751] A2, N add.: не более.

m   «j'obligerai ceux qui voudront exercer la profession d'imprimeur, d'éditeur ou de libraire à se munir d'un brevet (...) que le gouvernement pourra toujours leur retirer»

n   «Les instruments de la pensée deviendront les instruments du pouvoir!»

o   «j'étendrai aux livres, le timbre qui frappe les journeaux (...). Un livre (...) qui n'aura pas (...) trois cents pages (...) ne sera qu'une brochure.»

p   «je raréfie par l'impôt cette nuée (...) des annexes du journalisme»

q   «de l'autre, je force (...) des compositions longues et dispendieuses qui (...) se liront à peine»

r   «Le fisc découragera la vanité littéraire»

s   «s'il est des écrivains assez osés pour écrire des ouvrages contre le gouvernement, ils ne puissent trouver personne pour les éditer»

t   «Avant de donner le jour à des ouvrages nouveaux, les imprimeurs, les éditeurs (...) viendront s'informer»

u   «de cette manière le gouvernement sera toujours informé utilement des publications qui se préparent contre lui»

v   «Puisque c'est une si grande force que le journalisme, (...), mon gouvernement (...) se ferait journaliste»

w   «S'il y en a dix pour l'opposition, j'en aurai vingt pour le gouvernement; s'il y en a vingt...»

x   «il ne faut pas que la masse du public puisse soupçonner cette tactique»

y   «auront le plus d'ascendant sur l'opinion»

z   «Au premier rang je mettrai (...) journeaux dont la nuance sera (...) officielle, et qui (...) défendront mes actes à outrance. Ce ne sont pas ceux-là (...) qui auront le plus d'ascendant (...). Au second rang je placerai (...) journeaux dont le caractère ne sera (...) qu'officieuse et dont la mission sera de rallier (...) hommes tièdes et indifférents (...). C'est dans les catégories (...) qui vont suivre (...) dans chaque parti.»

aa   «j'aurai un organe aristocratique (...), un organe républicain (...), un organe révolutionnaire (...), un organe anarchiste»

ab   «Comme le dieu Wishnou, ma presse aura cent bras, et ces bras donneront la main à toutes les nuances d'opinion sur la surface entière du pays»

ac   «Ceux qui croiront parler leur langue parleront la mienne, ceux qui croiront agiter leur parti agiteront le mien, ceux qui croiront marcher sous leur drapeau marcheront sous le mien.»

ad   «j'instituerai (...) sous le titre de division (...) de la presse un centre (...) d'où partira le signal»

ae   «jamais les bases (...) de mon gouvernement ne seront attaqués (...); ils ne feront qu'une polémique d'escarmouche» af   «vous voyez bien qu'on est libre, qu'on peut parler»

ag   «...qu'il est injustement attaqué»

ah   «J'excite ou j'endors les esprits, je le rassure ou je les déconcerte (...) le pour et le contre, le vrai et le faux.»

ai   «je puis infliger, au besoin, les désaveux les plus énergiques»

aj   «...ballons d'essai»

ak   «le journalisme est une sorte de franc-maçonnerie: (...) sont tous (...) rattachés les uns les autres par (...) la discrétion professionnelle; pareils aux anciens augures, ils ne divulguent pas (...) le secret de leurs oracles.»

al   «Ils ne gagneraient rien à se trahir, car ils ont (...) des plaies (...) honteuses»

am   «dans un certain rayon de personnes, ces choses ne seront pas un mystère; mais (...) la grande majorité de la nation marchera avec la confiance la plus entière sur la trace des guides»

an   «C'est à la province qu'est réservée la plus grande partie de son influence»

ao   «la capitale (...) sera en retard»

ap   «le mouvement extérieur qui l'envelopperait»

aq   «j'enverrai défendre aux journeaux d'en [quelque méfait de fonctionnaire public] parler»

XI [1752]

Насущая нужда заставит[1753] гоев молчать и быть нашими покорными слугами. Когда мы им позволим что нибудь[1754] обсуждать, то[1755] для того лишь[1756], чтобы под шумок таких обсуждений нам провести[1757] желательные[1758] меры незаметно и поднести[1759] их, **как совершившийся факт** (a)[1760]. Затем наши агенты отвлекают[1761] мысли на новые вопросы (мы, ведь, приучили людей искать все нового[1762])... и вот эти вопросы привлекут опять внимание[1763] вершителей[1764] судеб, какими являются наивные политиканы[1765], которые никак[1766] не могут еще[1767] понять, что[1768] не смыслят ничего в том, что берутся обсуждать, потому что[1769]

[1752]   K omitt.; A1, N, B: **Еще протокол** [B add.: **(15)**]; A2: **XIII**

[1753]   N: Нужда в насущном хлебе

[1754]   B: либо

[1755]   B add.: это

[1756]   A1, B omitt.

[1757]   A2, N omitt.: Когда... & add.: Взятые из числа их к нам в [N omitt.: к нам в] агенты в [N add.: нашу] прессу будут обсуждать по нашему приказу то, что нам неудобно издавать прямо [N: непосредственно] в оффициальных документах, а [N add.: тем временем,] под шумом поднявшегося обсуждения мы [N add.: возьмем да и] проведем

[1758]   N add.: нам

[1759]   A2, N: поднесем [N add.: публике]

[1760]   A1, A2, N, B add.: никому в голову не придет [A2, N add.: никто не посмеет] требовать отмены уже [N: раз] установленного [A2, N: решенного], да еще представляемого [N add.: тем более, что оно будет; A2, N: представлено] как улучшение

[1761]   A2, N: А тут пресса отвлечет

[1762]   B: новое

[1763]   A2, N omitt.: и вот... & add.: на обсуждение [N: этих новых вопросов] бросятся [N: набросятся те из безмозглых]

[1764]   A2: вершители

[1765]   A2, N omitt.: какими...

[1766]   A2 omitt.; N: до сих пор

[1767]   N omitt.

[1768]   A1, A2, N, B add.: они

[1769]   A2: так как; N omitt.: потому...

вопросы политики[1770] доступны только тем, кто руководит[1771] ею в течение[1772] веков по определенному плану, тем, которые ее создали, ввели в употребление, как экипаж, на котором[1773] везут людей в неведомые места.[1774] Добиваемся мы их[1775] мнения[1776] только[1777] **не для действий** наших, **а для слов** (b)[1778]... При этом не забываем провозглашать[1779], что **служим лишь социальному**[1780] **благу** (c). Чтобы ныне[1781] отвлечь[1782] внимание от настоящей[1783] политики, мы поставили[1784] вопросы промышленности и торговли на почву якобы политики[1785]. **Массы соглашаются бездействовать** (d), отдыхать от якобы политической деятельности (к которой мы же их приучили, чтобы бороться при их посредстве[1786] с гоевскими правительствами),

1770 A2, N add.: никому не

1771 A2, N omitt.: только... & add.: кроме руководящих

1772 A2, N: уже много

1773 A1, B add.: опи

1774 A2, N omitt.: по определенному... & add.: создателей ее

1775 A2, N omitt.: Добиваемся... & add.: Из [N add.: всего] этого вы увидите, что, добиваясь; B omitt.

1776 A2, N, B add.: толпы, [A2, N add.: мы]

1777 A2, N add.: облегчаем ход нашего механизма, и вы можете заметить, что; B omitt.

1778 A2, N omitt.: не для... & add.: действиям, а словам, выпущенным нами по тому или другому вопросу, мы как бы ищем апробации.

1779 A2, N omitt.: При этом... & add.: Мы постоянно провозглашаем

1780 A2, N omitt.: служим... & add.: руководимся во всех своих [N: наших] мероприятиях надеждой, соединенной послужить [N add.: с уверенностью общему]

1781 A2, N omitt.

1782 A2: отвлекать

1783 A2, N omitt.: внимание... & add.: слишком беспокойных людей от обсуждения вопросов

1784 A2, N: [N add.: теперь] проводим новые якобы вопросы ее

1785 A2 omitt.: промышленности...; N omitt.: и торговли... & add.: промышленные; на этом поприще пусть [N add.: себе] беснуются.

1786 A2: через них

лишь под условием новых занятий (e)[1787], а чтобы они вообще не предавались слишком умственным занятиям и не впали в деловитость[1788], **мы настроили для них всяких увеселительных заведений**, в которых они спешат перебывать и все испытать[1789]... Скоро **через прессу**[1790] мы будем[1791] предлагать[1792] состязания в искусстве, в[1793] спорте,[1794] **изобретениях** (f), и[1795] окончательно отвлечем[1796] умы от[1797] вопросов, которыми мы желаем сами заниматься[1798]. Отвыкая все более и более[1799] от самостоятельного мышления по общественным вопросам[1800], люди заговорят в унисон с нами[1801], потому что мы одни будем[1802] предлагать новые идеи[1803], конечно, через таких лиц, с которыми повидимому мы не солидарны[1804]. Когда наше правление будет признано и интернациональное правительство учреждено, то[1805]

[1787] К, А1, В omitt.: Массы соглашаются...н & add: гои позаймутся новой задачей; N add.: в которых мы им указываем как бы то же политическое направление

[1788] А2, N omitt.: а чтобы... & add.: чтобы они сами до чего бы [N: нибудь] не додумались

[1789] А2, N omitt.: настроили... & add.: их еще отвлекаем увеселениями, играми, забавами, страстями или интересами [N: народными домами]

[1790] К: пресу

[1791] А2, N: станем

[1792] А2, N add.: конкурсные

[1793] N omitt.

[1794] А1, В add.: в

[1795] А2, N omitt.: изобретениях... & add.: в произсводстве всякого рода [N: всех видов] эти интересы

[1796] А2, N: отвлекут

[1797] А1, В add.: обсуждения

[1798] В: заняться; А2, N omitt.: которыми... & add.: на которых нам пришлось бы с ними бороться. И [N omitt.]

[1799] А2, В omitt.: и более

[1800] А2, N omitt.: по ...

[1801] А1: ними

[1802] А2, N: станем

[1803] А2, N: направления мысли. Но [N omitt.]

[1804] А2, N omitt.: мы... & add.: нас не почтут солидарными

[1805] А2, N omitt.: и интернациолальное...

роль[1806] **утопистов будет**[1807] **сыграна** (g)[1808]; но пока они еще и[1809] нам полезны, ибо направляют[1810] умы на фантастические теории, якобы прогрессивные, отвлекая их от сущности[1811]: **мы ведь**[1812] **вскружили**[1813] **головы идеей прогресса** (h)[1814]... И не нашлось ни одной головы[1815] среди гоев, которая уразумела бы[1816], что истина одна, что она не может прогрессировать[1817], если она истина, что в прогрессе[1818] есть[1819] отвлечение от истины, во всех случаях, в которых он не касается[1820] материальных изобретений[1821]: что[1822] прогресс,[1823] служит к затемнению[1824] истины[1825], чтобы ее никто не знал, кроме нас, избранников Божих, хранителей истины о тайне человеческих отношений и блага их, открытой[1826] нами до поры победы в мирном завоевании мира[1827]. Когда мы воцаримся,[1828] наши ораторы будут

[1806] N add.: либеральных

[1807] N add.: окончательно

[1808] A2: окончена

[1809] B omitt.

[1810] A2, N omitt.: но пока... & add.: до тех пор они нам сослужат хорошую службу, поэтому мы еще будем направлять

[1811] A2, N omitt.: фантастические... & add.: всякие измышления фантасти-ческих теорий, новых [N: и] якобы прогрессивных:

[1812] A2, N add.: с полным успехом

[1813] A1, B add.: все; N add.: безмозглие гоевские

[1814] K: прогреса; A2, N omitt.: идеей... & add.: прогрессом

[1815] A2, N omitt.: не нашлось... & add.: и нет ума

[1816] A2, N: который бы увидел

[1817] K: прогресировать

[1818] K: прогресе

[1819] A2, N omitt.: что истина... & add.: что под этим словом кроется

[1820] A1, A2, N, B omitt.: он не...; A1 add.: которые не касаются; A2, N, B add.: где дело не касается [N, B: идет не о]

[1821] N, B: изобретениях

[1822] A2, N: ибо истина одна, в ней нет места прогрессу, но [N omitt.]

[1823] K: прогрес; N add.: как ложная идея

[1824] K: затемению

[1825] A2: ее

[1826] A1: сокрытое; B: скрытой

[1827] A2, N omitt.: истины о тайне... & add.: ее

толковать истину и **великие проблемы человеческого строя** (i)[1829], указывая на заблуждения гоевских правлений, которые[1830] привели нас[1831] ко[1832] благу нашего царства[1833]. Кто заподозрит[1834], что все эти ошибки были созданы и[1835] подстроены нашей воспитательной[1836] программой, согласно[1837] политическому плану, измышленному нашими мудрецами с Соломоном во главе, для мирного завоевания мира нашей короне дома царя Давида[1838].

[1839]Нам нежелательно, чтобы существовала какая-либо религия[1840], кроме нашей о едином **Боге**, с Которым связана **наша судьба**, Его избранного племени[1841], и[1842] **объединена**[1843] **с судьбою**[1844] **мира** (j)[1845]. Поэтому мы должны стремиться до тех пор стереть с лица земли[1846] всякую другую[1847] веру[1848]. Если от наших трудов в этом направлении[1849]

[1828] A2, N add.: то

[1829] A2, N omitt.: истину... & add.: о великих проблемах, которые переволновали человечество

[1830] A1: которыми мы; B add.: мы

[1831] A1, B omitt.

[1832] K: к

[1833] A1: наше царство; A2, N omitt.: указывая... & add.: для того, чтобы его в конце концов привести к нашему благому правлению

[1834] N add.: тогда

[1835] A2, N omitt.: ошибки... & add.: проблемы были

[1836] B: нашею воспитательною

[1837] A2, N omitt.: нашей... & add.: нами по

[1838] A2, N omitt.: измышленному... & add.: о котором [N: которого] никто не заподозрел [N: раскусил] в течение [N: течении] многих веков?!...

[1839] A2, N add.: **XIV** [N: **Еще протокол**] Когда мы воцаримся

[1840] A2, N omitt.: чтобы... & add.: будет существование другой религии

[1841] A1, A2, N, B omitt.: избранного...; A1 add.: избранием нашего племени; A2, N add.: его избранием

[1842] N add.: Которым та же наша судьба

[1843] B add.: через нас

[1844] N: судьбами

[1845] B add.: ибо только по нашей Вере мы -избранное Богом племя...

[1846] A2, N omitt.: стремиться... & add.: стараться [N omitt.] разрушить

[1847] B: ... иную

[1848] A2: всякое верование; N: всякие верования

родятся[1850] атеисты, то как переходная степень к нашей вере[1851] это не может нам мешать[1852], а скорее[1853] послужит для примера следующим поколениям, которым мы будем проповедывать религию[1854] Моисея[1855]. Мы укажем[1856] мистическую правоту[1857] ее, которая оказалась столь сильной, что в течение веков привела все народы к нашему царству[1858].

QUOTATIONS FROM JOLY'S *DIALOGUE*

a «comme un évenement officiel»

b «ce sont les paroles bien plus que les actes...»

c «l'on s'occupe sans cesse de l'amélioration du sort des classes ouvrières»

d «Je m'attacherais (...) à ces questions [*l'industrie*], (...) pour (...) la politique»

e «les masses consentent à être inactives (...) à une condition (...) d'une activité incessante»

f «par des nouveautés, par des surprises, par des coups de théâtre (...) dans la presse (...) toutes sortes de projets, de plans»

g «je ne lasserais rien à inventer à (...) vos utopistes»

h «je personnifie le progrès (...) le peuple m'adore»

i «des grands problèmes qui agitent l'humanité»

j «l'invocation de la Divinité, en associant (…) ma propre étoile à celle du pays»

[1849] A2, N omitt.: наших... & add.: этого

[1850] A2 add.: совершенные; N add.: современные

[1851] A2 omitt.: к нашей вере; N omitt.: степень... & add.: ступень

[1852] A2, N: помешает нашим видам

[1853] A2, N omitt.

[1854] A2 omitt.: следующим; N omitt.: для примера...; A2, N add.: [N: примером] тем поколениям [N: для тех поколений] которые будут слушать проповеди [N add.: наши] о религии

[1855] A2, N add.: которая привела [N: приведшей] своей стойкой и обдуманной системой к покорению всех народов нам: в этом

[1856] N: подчеркнем и

[1857] N: правду

[1858] A2, N omitt.: которая... & add.: в которой, скажем мы, основывается [N add.: вся] ее воспитательная сила...

XII [1859]

Если[1860] мы воцаримся[1861], мы будем при каждом удобном[1862] случае[1863] **сравнивать наше** благое **правление**[1864] **с прошлыми** безалаберными **администрациями** (a)[1865]... **Благодеяния**[1866] **покоя,** хотя и вынужденнаго веками-[1867] волнения, **послужат**[1868] к новому[1869] **рельефу** сказанного блага.[1870] **Ошибки гоевских царств**[1871] **будут нами**[1872] **описываться в самых ярких красках и**[1873] **мы посеем такое презрение и**[1874] **отвращение** (b) к ним, что народы предпочтут покой и мир[1875] в крепостном состоянии правам пресловутой свободы, столь измучившим[1876] их в течение веков[1877], истощив[1878] самые источники[1879] существования, попираемые[1880] проходимцами, неведающими[1881], что творят. Безполезные дефекты[1882] перемены правлений[1883] на которые[1884] мы

[1859] K omitt.; A1, B: **Еще протокол** [B add.: **(16)**].

[1860] B: Когда

[1861] A2, N omitt. Если... & add.: Тогда

[1862] A2, N omitt.

[1863] A2, N add.: публиковать статьи, в которых будем

[1864] K, A1: направление

[1865] A2, N omitt.: безалаберными...

[1866] A2: Благодеяние

[1867] A2 omitt.: и... & add.: несколько вынужденного после веков

[1868] A2: послужит

[1869] A2: особенному

[1870] K, A1, B omitt.: Благодеяния...

[1871] A2, N: администраций

[1872] A1 omitt.

[1873] A2, N omitt.

[1874] A2, N omitt.: презрение...

[1875] A2, N omitt.: и мир

[1876] A1, B: измучившей

[1877] A2, N omitt.: в течение веков

[1878] N: и истощившим

[1879] N add.: человеческого

[1880] A2, N: которые попирались [N: эксплоатировались] толпою

[1881] A2, N: проходимцев, не знающих [N: неведавших]

[1882] A1: Фактически; B: дефакто; A2, N omitt.

их[1885] подбивали, когда подкапывали их строй[1886], до того им[1887] надоедят[1888], что они предпочтут принять[1889] все то, что им навяжем[1890], лишь бы не рисковать переиспытать[1891] пережитые невзгоды и волнения, тем более, что[1892] мы будем, публичною[1893] критикой,[1894] особенно подчеркивать ошибки управления[1895] гоевских правлений, столько веков промучивших человечество недостатком[1896] сознания истинных благ[1897], в погоне[1898] за фантастическими социальными улучшениями[1899], не замечая, что, улучшая быт некоторых, их[1900] меры[1901] ухудшали всеобщие отношения и порядок строя[1902], на котором[1903] основывается человеческая жизнь. Наши принципы и меры будут иметь за себя[1904] то[1905], что они будут истолкованы и

[1883] К: направлений

[1884] A2, N: к которым

[1885] N: гоев

[1886] A2: государства; N: государственные здания

[1887] A2, N: народам

[1888] A1, B add.: до тех пор; A2, N add.: к тому времени

[1889] A2, N: терпеть от нас

[1890] A2, N omitt.: то, что...

[1891] A2, N: переиспытывать

[1892] A2, N omitt.: тем более, что; A2 add.: A

[1893] A1: публичной

[1894] A2, N omitt.: публичною... ; N add.: же

[1895] A2, N: исторические

[1896] A2, N: отсутствием

[1897] A2, N, B omitt.: сознания... & add.: сообразительности на истинные [N: во всем, что касается истинного; A2, N add.: его] блага

[1898] A2: гоняясь

[1899] A2, N: проектами социальных благ

[1900] B: эти

[1901] A2, N omitt.: улучшая... & add.: эти проекты все более

[1902] A2, N omitt.: всеобщие... & add.: а не улучшали положения [N: положение] всеобщих отношений

[1903] A2, N: которых

[1904] A2, B add.: в свою пользу

[1905] N omitt.: Наши принципы... & add.: Вся сила наших принципов и мероприятий будет заключена в том

выставлены[1906], как[1907] контраст[1908] разложившимся[1909] старым порядкам общественного строя. Наши философы будут **обсуждать** и критиковать[1910] все недостатки гоевских **верований** (с)[1911], чем они нам ответить не смогут[1912] по отношению[1913] к[1914] нашей вере[1915], потому что[1916] никто ее тайн[1917] не знает[1918], кроме наших талмудистов и раввинов[1919], а они[1920] никогда не выдадут[1921] ее[1922], потому что на ней[1923] основана сила управления паствой[1924] нашей[1925]. Мы **создали**[1926] **безумную, грязную, отвратительную литературу** особенно[1927] **в странах**, называемых **передовыми**,[1928] после вступления нашего[1929] во власть, **мы**[1930] **ее не запретим** (d), а[1931] будем ее искоренять строгой[1932]

[1906] N omitt.: будут... & add.: нами выставятся и истолкуются

[1907] N add.: яркий

[1908] B add.: с

[1909] N omitt.

[1910] A2 omitt.

[1911] B add.: в

[1912] B: могут

[1913] A2, N omitt.: чем они... & add.: но никто никогда не станет обсуждать

[1914] B omitt.

[1915] K, B: веры

[1916] A2, N omitt.: к нашей вере & add.: нашу веру с ее настоящей [N: истинной] точки зрения, так как

[1917] A2, N: основательно

[1918] A2, N: узнает

[1919] K: равинов

[1920] A2, N omitt.: талмудистов... & add.: которые

[1921] A2, N: посмеют выдать

[1922] B: их; A2, N: ее тайны

[1923] B: них

[1924] B: паствою

[1925] A2, N omitt.: потому что...

[1926] A2: создадим

[1927] A2, N omitt.

[1928] A2, N, B add.: еще некоторое время

[1929] A2 omitt.

[1930] A1 omitt.

[1931] B: но

критикой[1933], чтобы она, как остаток гоевских рук[1934], рельефнее обрысовывала[1935] **контраст того, что раздаваться** будет **с нашей выси** (e)[1936], с тем, что исходило из грязного болота гоевских царств[1937]. **Наши умные люди,** воспитанные для руководства гоями, **будут составлять речи, проекты, записки, статьи, которыми мы будем влиять на умы** (f), направляя их к намеченным нами понятиям и знаниям.[1938]

[1939]Когда мы наконец воцаримся окончательно посредством[1940] государственных переворотов, всюду подготовленных к одному и тому же дню, после окончательного признания невыгодности[1941] всех существующих[1942] в то время гоевских правлений[1943] (что может быть не скоро, может быть **к концу века** (g) и далее[1944])... **мы искореним** всякое семя крамол и **заговоров** против правления[1945]. **Во первых[1946], мы** немилосердно **казним всех, кто встретит[1947] с оружием в руках[1948] наше**

[1932] В: строгою

[1933] A2, N omitt.: ее не запретим...критикой & add.: станем поощрять ее существование

[1934] A2, N omitt.: как остаток...; В: руин

[1935] A2, N: обрисовала

[1936] В: высоты; A2, N omitt.: того, что... & add.: речей, программ, которые раздадутся с нашей вышки [N: высот наших]

[1937] A2, N omitt.: с тем, что...

[1938] K, A1, B omitt.: Наши умные люди...

[1939] A1, N, В: **Еще протокол** [B add.: **(17)**]; A2: **XV**

[1940] N: при помощи

[1941] A2, N, В: негодности

[1942] K: ществующих

[1943] A1 omitt: после окончательного признания...; A2, N omitt.: в то время... & add.: правительств

[1944] A2, N omitt.: что может быть... & add.: что будет через [N omitt.: что... & add.: еще] не мало времени, а может быть, до того времени пройдет [N add.: и] целый век

[1945] A1, В: правлений; A2, N omitt.: искореним... & add.: постараемся, чтобы не было уже заговоров против нас

[1946] N omitt.: Во первых; A2, N add.: для етого

[1947] A2: тех, которые встретят; В: не встанет

[1948] B add.: за

воцарение (h). **Факт учреждения**[1949] какого либо **тайного общества будет наказуем**[1950] **смертной**[1951] казнью (i), **а существующие**[1952] (j), нам известные и послужившие[1953], **мы** раскассируем[1954], и **вышлем**[1955](k) в далекие[1956] континенты [1957]**тех**[1958] масонов[1959], **которые слишком много знают**, или совсем сократим их число,[1960] а **те**[1961], **которых** мы почему либо **помилуем**[1962], **будут оставаться**[1963] под постоянным страхом[1964] посылки[1965], **потому что**[1966] **будет издан закон, по которому все бывшие**[1967] **участники**[1968] в тайных обществах[1969], хотя бы не существующих уже[1970], **изгоняются из**[1971] центра **нашего управления** (l)-

[1949] N: Всякое новое учреждение

[1950] A2 add.: тоже; N: тоже наказано

[1951] B: смертною

[1952] A2 add.: же; N: те из них, которые ныне существуют

[1953] A1 add.: нам; N: известны и нам служат и служили

[1954] K: раскасируем

[1955] B omitt.: и... & add.: ; мы сошлем

[1956] A2, N add.: от Европы

[1957] A1 add.: Мы сократим число

[1958] N: Так мы посутпим с теми гоями из

[1959] K, A1: массонов; A2 add.: -гоев

[1960] A2, N omitt.: или совсем...

[1961] N: те же; B: тех

[1962] K, A1, B: которым позволим остаться в Европе

[1963] K: находиться

[1964] A2, N: в постоянном страхе

[1965] A2, B: высылки; N: перед высылкой

[1966] N: Нами

[1967] K, A1, B omitt.: все бывшие... & add.: уличенные

[1968] K: в участии; A1: за принадлежности; B: в принадлежности

[1969] B: к тайным обществам; A2, N: тайных обществ

[1970] B: существующим более; A2, N omitt.: хотя бы...

[1971] N: подлежат изгнанию как

из[1972] Европы. **Решения**[1973] нашего правительства **будут**[1974] безаппеляционным и **окончательным судом**[1975].

[1976]**В гоевских странах**[1977], **в которых мы посеяли** такие глубокие **корни разлада** и протестантизма[1978], **можно**[1979] **водворить порядок только беспощадными мерами,** доказывающими неукоснительную власть; **нечего смотреть на** падающие **жертвы, приносимые**[1980] для будущего **блага** (m), а и[1981] достиженье такового[1982], хотя бы[1983] путем жертвоприношения, есть[1984] обязанность всякого[1985] правления, которое сознает, что не только в привилегиях[1986], но и[1987] в обязанностях есть[1988] его миссия[1989] и[1990] что от последних зависит[1991] его существование,[1992] благополучие и незыблемость[1993] правления в ореоле[1994] могущества,

---

[1972]   A1 omitt.

[1973]   A1: решение

[1974]   A1: будет

[1975]   N: окончательны и безаппелляционны.

[1976]   B omitt. usque ad: ...и храбростью. (2014)

[1977]   A2: государствах; N: обществах

[1978]   A1: протеста

[1979]   A2, N: возможно

[1980]   K, A1: они приносятся

[1981]   A1 omitt.

[1982]   A2, N: В достижении блага

[1983]   A1 add.: и

[1984]   N: заключена

[1985]   A1, A2 omitt.

[1986]   A1, N: привиллегиях

[1987]   A1 omitt.

[1988]   A1: состоит

[1989]   K: мисия

[1990]   A1 omitt.

[1991]   A2, N omitt.: есть... & add.: состоит

[1992]   A1 add.: и

[1993]   A1 omitt.: и незыблемость & add.: что суть незыблемости; A2, N omitt.: благополучие... & add.: что [N omitt.] главное суть дела. [N: главное дело] для незыблемости

[1994]   N omitt.: в... & add.: укрепления ореола

который[1995] достигается[1996] только **величественной непоколеби-мостью**[1997] **власти** (n), которая через силу свою приобретает мистический[1998] престиж и делается неприкосновенной[1999]: вспомните[2000], как **залитая кровью Италия не коснулась волоса с**[2001] **головы Силлы**[2002], **который пролил**[2003] **эту кровь** (o), потому что[2004] Силла[2005] был герой[2006] в глазах[2007] истерзанного им[2008] народа[2009]. Народ не в силах коснуться[2010] того, кто[2011] гипнотизирует его[2012] своею силой[2013] и храбростью[2014]. До нашего воцарения **мы**, напротив, размножим и **создадим** фран[2015]-масонские **ложи** во всех странах мира:

[1995] N: а ореол этот

[1996] A1 omitt.: который... & add.: достигаемого

[1997] A2: в величественной непоколебимости

[1998] A1 omitt.

[1999] A2, N omitt.: через... & add.: при етом как бы неприкосновенна [N: носила бы на себе признаки неприкосновенности] от мистических причин [N add.:- от Божьего избрания. Таково было до последнего времени русское Самодержавие- единственный в мире серьезный враг наш, если не считать Папства]

[2000] A1, A2, N add.: пример того

[2001] K omitt.: волоса с; A1 omitt.: с

[2002] K: Силы; A1: Суллы

[2003] A1 omitt.: который... & add.: пролившего

[2004] N omitt.

[2005] K: Сила; A1: Сулла

[2006] A1, A2, N omitt.: был герой & add.: обоготворился своею мощью

[2007] N add.: хотя и

[2008] N omitt.

[2009] A1, A2, N add.: а храбрость его возврата [A2: храбрый его возврат; N: мужественное еще возвращение] в Италию поставила [A2: ставил; N: ставило] его вне прикосновенности

[2010] A2, N omitt.: в силах... & add.: касается

[2011] A1, A2: который

[2012] A1: людей

[2013] A1 add.: духа; N: силою

[2014] A2, N add.: духа. Пока же

[2015] A2, N: франк

втянем в них всех могущих быть выдающимися деятелями[2016], потому что в этих ложах **будет** наше[2017] **главное**[2018] **справочное место** и средство влиять на деятелей[2019]... **все эти ложи будут централизированы**[2020] **под одно,**[2021] неведомое **управление** (р), которое состоит из наших мудрецов. Каждая ложа будет[2022] иметь своего[2023] представителя, прикрывающего собой сказанных мудрецов[2024] от которых[2025] они[2026] будут[2027] получать[2028] пароль и программы[2029]. **Там**[2030] **мы завяжем** узел **всех революционных** и либеральных **элементов, которые** будут **извлечены**[2031] **из всех слоев общества. Самые тайные политические замыслы будут нам известны** и попадут под наше руководство в самый день их возникновения. В число[2032] членов[2033] лож[2034] будут зачислены и втянуты[2035] почти все агенти руководители[2036] национальной, а главное,[2037] международной

[2016]   A1: деятелей; A2, N: и существующих выдающихся деятелей

[2017]   N omitt.

[2018]   A1 omitt.

[2019]   K: деятелелей; A2, N omitt.: влиять... & add.: влияющее

[2020]   A2, N: мы централизируем

[2021]   N add.: одним нам известное, всем же остальным

[2022]   A2, N: Ложи будут

[2023]   B: явного

[2024]   B omitt.: прикрывающего... & add.: служащего ширмою сказанным мудрецам; A2, N omitt.: сказанных мудрецов & add.: сказанное главное [N omitt.] управление масонства

[2025]   A1, A2, N: которого

[2026]   A2, N omitt.; B: он

[2027]   N, B: будет

[2028]   N: исходить

[2029]   K: програмы; N: программа; B: программу

[2030]   A2, N: В этих ложах

[2031]   A2, N omitt.: которые... & add.: состав их будет состоять

[2032]   A1, A2, N, B: числе; A2 add.: их

[2033]   N add.: этих

[2034]   A2 omitt.

[2035]   A2, N omitt.: зачислены...

[2036]   A2, N omitt.

[2037]   A2, N omitt. & add.: и

полиции,[2038] служба которой[2039] для нас незаменима, так как она[2040] может, под предлогом крамолы[2041], распорядиться с непокорными[2042] и прикрыть[2043] наши действия[2044], создавать предлоги к неудовольствиям, и т. д.[2045]

QUOTATIONS FROM JOLY'S *DIALOGUE*

a   «Je voudrais que l'on comparât à chaque instant les actes de mon règne à ceux des gouvernements passés»

b   «...faire ressortir mes bienfaits (...) mettre en relief les fautes de ceux qui m'ont précédé (...) une sorte d'anthipatie, d'aversion»

c   «la doctrine du libre examen»

d   «Dans les pays les plus avancés (...) donner naissance à une littérature folle, furieuse, effrénée, presque immonde (...) il suffira (...) de ne pas la gêner»

e   «un contraste (...) avec la dignité du language qui tomberait des marches du trône»

f   «publicistes (...) la rédaction de (...) communications (...) dont l'impression serait (...) très forte sur les esprits»

g   «Avant un siècle»

h   «ne craignez-vous rien des complots?»

i   «déporter (...) ceux qui ont accueilli, les armes à la main, l'avénement de mon pouvoir»

j   «Le fait d'organiser une société secrète (...) sera puni rigoureusement....mais les sociétés existantes?»

k   «J'expulserai (...) ceux qui seront notoriement connus»

l   «Ceux que je n'atteindrai pas resteront sous le coup d'une menace perpetuelle, car je rendrai une loi qui permettra au gouvernement de déporter (...) quiconque aura été affilié»

m   «La décision d'un gouvernement (...) est (...) un jugement»

[2038] A2, N add.: так как ее

[2039] A2, N omitt.

[2040] A2, N omitt.: так как... & add.: в том [N: отношении], что она [N: полиция]

[2041] A2, N omitt.: под предлогом... & add.: не только [N add.: по своему]

[2042] A2, N add.: но

[2043] A2: прикрывать

[2044] A1, A2, N, B: деяния

[2045] A1, B: п.

n   «Dans les pays incessamment troublés par les discordes (...) il faut ramener la paix par des actes de vigueur impacables; il y a un compte de victimes à faire pour assurer la tranquillité, on le fait».

o   «l'aspect de celui qui commande devient (...) imposant»

p   «Après avoir couvert de sang l'Italie, Sylla pur reparaître (...) personne ne toucha un cheveu de sa tête.»

q   «un moyen d'information (...) J'entrevois la possibilité de donner, à (...) ces sociétés, une (...) existence légale ou plutôt de les centraliser (...) je nommerai le chef suprème.»

r   «Par là je tiendrai dans ma main les divers éléments révolutionnaires (...) Les gens (...) appartiennet (...) à toutes les classes, à tous les rangs; je serais mis au courant des intrigues les plus obscures de la politique».

s   «sera (...) une annexe de ma police»

XIII [2046]

В тайные общества[2047] **поступают** всего охотнее аферисты, карьеристы[2048] и[2049] **легкомысленные** (а)[2050], с которыми нам не трудно будет вести дело и завести[2051] по нашему усмотрению[2052] механизм масонской[2053] машины. **Если этот мир замутится,**[2054] это будет **значить**[2055], **что нам нужно было** (b) его замутить, чтобы расстроить слишком большую солидарность или помешать самостоятельному действию[2056]... **Если же среди него возникнет какой либо**[2057] **заговор, то во главе**[2058] **станет** никто другой[2059], как **один из** вернейших слуг **наших** (с): таким образом мы воспользуемся[2060] масонским двигателем[2061] и поведем человечество, зная[2062] конечную цель всякого политического и социального[2063] действия; гои же не ведают ничего далее[2064] непосредственного результата всякого распоряжения[2065]; они

[2046] A1, A2, N, B omitt.

[2047] A1, A2, N, B add.: обыкновенно

[2048] N: каррьеристы

[2049] A2 add.: большей частью; N add.: вообще люди, по большей части

[2050] A1, A2, B: легкомысленники

[2051] N: ими заводить

[2052] A2, N omitt.: по нашему...

[2053] A1: массонской; A2, N: проектированной [N add.: нами]

[2054] A2, N add.: то

[2055] A2, N: означать

[2056] A2, N omitt.: или помешать...

[2057] A2, N omitt.: какой либо

[2058] A1, A2, N, B add.: его

[2059] A1, B: иной

[2060] A1: поведем; A2, N omitt.: таким образом... & add.: Естественно, что мы, а не кто [N: никто] другой, поведем; B: руководим

[2061] A1, B: масонскими [A1: массонскими] действиями; A2: масонским действием; N: масонские действия

[2062] A1, A2, N, B omitt.: и поведем... & add.: ибо мы знаем, куда ведем [A1, B add.: человечество], знаем

[2063] A2, N omitt.: политического...

[2064] A2, N: даже

[2065] A2, N omitt.: всякого...

задаются[2066] минутным рассчетом или удовлетворением[2067] самолюбия, исполнением[2068] задуманного непосредственно, и[2069] не замечают[2070], того[2071], что задумывают не иначе, как по нашему внушению, нашей инициативе, которая их наводит[2072] на мысль... Гои идут в ложи из любопытства или в надежде[2073] пробраться к общественному пирогу, а некоторые лишь[2074] для того, чтобы иметь возможность высказать перед публикой, хотя бы в небольшом сборище[2075], свои[2076] мечтания: эти последние ищут[2077] рукоплесканий, на которые мы все[2078] щедры, потому что для нас полезно приучать их к[2079] эмоции успеха[2080]...
[2081]Конечно, мы создаем его[2082], чтобы потом[2083] пользоваться рождающимся от него[2084] самообольщением, с которым люди незаметно[2085] воспринимают наши внушения, преподносимые им с каждением и похвалами их уму и сообразительности. Эти люди не

[2066] N add.: обыкновенно

[2067] A2, N omitt. или... & add.: удовлетворения

[2068] A2, N: в исполнении

[2069] A2, N omitt.: непосредственно...

[2070] N: замечая

[2071] B omitt.

[2072] A2, N omitt.: того, что... & add.: даже того, что задумывают-то не по собственной [N: самый замысел не принадлежал их] инициативе, а после того, как мы их наведем [N: а нашему наведению]

[2073] N add.: при их помощи

[2074] N omitt.

[2075] A2, N omitt.: хотя бы...

[2076] A2, N add.: несбыточные и беспочвенные

[2077] A2, omitt.: последние ищут & add. ждут; N omitt.: эти... & add.: они жаждут эмоции успека и

[2078] A1, A2, N, B: весьма

[2079] A2 omitt. потому что & add. и

[2080] N omitt.: потому что...

[2081] B omitt. usque ad: потребность к каждению (2092)

[2082] A1 omitt.; A2, N omitt.: Конечно,... & add.: Мы им, конечно [N omitt. & add.: затем и] даем этот успех

[2083] A2, N omitt.

[2084] A2, N: отсюда

[2085] A2: незаметнее

остерегаются внушений, в[2086] уверенности, что наши рукоплесания на столько доказали их талант и непогрешимость воззрения[2087], что у них столько ума собственного, что нет места в их голове для чужого мышления[2088]. Вы не можете себе представить, как умнейших из гоев можно легко[2089] привести[2090] к бессознательной наивности, развив[2091] их самообольщение и потребность к каждению.[2092] **Эти тигры по виду имеют бараньи души, а в головах их ходит сквозной ветер** (d)... Мы посадили их теперь[2093] на конька **мечты о поглощении**[2094] **человеческой индивидуальности в символическую единицу**[2095] **коллективизма** (e).[2096]

[2086] A2, N omitt.: преподносимые... & add.: не остерегаясь их, в [N add.: полной]

[2087] K, A2, N, B: возрения

[2088] A2, N omitt.: наши рукоплескания... & add.: их непогрешимость выпускает только [N omitt.] свои мысли, а воспринять [N: чужих уже] не может...

[2089] A2, N omitt.

[2090] A1: провести

[2091] A2, N omitt.: развив... & add.: при самообольщении [N: условии самообольщения, & add.: вместе с тем,] и; A2, N, B add.: как легко их обезкуражить [B add.: самообольщенных простачков] малейшей неудачей, [N, B add.: хотя бы] прекращением аплодисментов И [B add.: и каждения их авторитету; как легко] привести [B add.: их] к рабскому [N: рабьему; B add.: уже почти сознательному] повиновению ради возобновления [B add.: силы] успеха... Насколько наши пренебрегают успехом, лишь бы провести свои планы, настолько гои готовы пожертвовать всякими планами, лишь бы получить успех... [B omitt.: Насколько наши...] Это [N: Эта их психология] значительно облегчает нам задачу их направления [B: руководства ими].

[2092] A1 add.: успеха.

[2093] A2, N omitt.

[2094] B: превращении

[2095] N: символической единицей

[2096] K, A1 omitt.: Эти тигры...; A2, N, B add.: Они еще не разобрались и [B: Можно наверняка рассчитывать, что они] не разберутся, что в этой мысли- N: этот конек есть явное; B add.: им нами навеянной, зиждится] нарушение главнейшего закона природы, создавшей [B add.: которая создала] единицу, непохожую на другие [B: всякого вида] с самого [B omitt.] сотворения мира, именно, в целях индивидуальности... Если мы

Из этого вы видите,[2097] насколько[2098] наши древние мудрецы были прозорливы, когда создавали планы порабощения гоев и преподали[2099] нам правило, не останавливаться перед средствами и не считать числа приносимых жертв, при достижении серьезной и целесообразной задачи[2100]. Мы[2101] не считали падающих на нашем пути гоев, за то мы сохранили наших в целости и[2102] дали им на земле такое место[2103], о котором они и[2104] мечтать[2105] не могли в то время, когда наши мудрецы составляли программу[2106] их действий[2107] на десятки веков[2108]... Наибольшие[2109] жертвы из числа наших, которые нам пришлось так и совершать[2110], оберегли[2111] нашу народность от гибели. Смерть есть

могли их привести [B: довести гоев] к такому [N add.: безумному] ослеплению [B: до такого ослепления], это [N add.: то не] доказывает [N add.: ли это с поразительной ясностью], до какой степени ум гоев не развит человечески по сравнению с нашим умом [B: значит степень их ума в сравнении с нашим умом недоразвита человечески], что [N add.: ?! это то, главным образом,] и гарантирует наш успех [B: а стоит на степени животного, что доказывает наше избрание и дает нам гарантию успеха]

[2097] A2, N omitt.: Из этого...

[2098] A2, N add.: же

[2099] A1 omitt.: планы порабощения...

[2100] A1: цели; A2, N omitt.: создавали планы... & add.: говорили, что достигая [N: для достижения] серьезной цели не следует останавливаться перед средствами и считать число приносимых [N: ради этой цели] жертв; B omitt.: целесообразной задачи & add.: полезной нам цели

[2101] A1, A2, B add.: и

[2102] A2, N omitt.: падающих... & add.: жертв из числа семени скота- гоев, очень много [N: хотя и] пожертвовали [N add.: многими] из своих, но зато [N add.: и теперь уже]

[2103] N: такое положение

[2104] B omitt.

[2105] B add.: бы

[2106] K: програму

[2107] B: действия

[2108] A2, N omitt.: в то время...

[2109] A1, A2, B: Небольшие; N: Сравнительно немногочисленные

[2110] B: принести; A2, N omitt.: которые нам...

[2111] B: сберегли

неизбежный конец для всякого, лучше же[2112] приблизить этот конец для тех, которые мешают[2113] нашему делу, чем для[2114] наших братий-[2115] созидателей[2116] этого[2117] дела...

Но вернемся к масонам[2118]. Мы их ныне уже казним за непослушание, да еще[2119] так, что только[2120] братия[2121] может заподозрить экзекуцию[2122], да пожалуй и[2123] сами они[2124], для публики же[2125] они умирают вполне[2126] естественной[2127] смертью[2128]... Умирают эти лица[2129], когда нужно. Братья[2130] не смеют[2131] протестовать. Таким образом[2132] **мы вырвали из среды масонства**[2133] корень **протеста против наших распоряжений** (f). Проповедуя гоям либерализм, в то же время мы держим свой народ[2134] в неукоснительном послушании: ибо где послушание, там порядок,[2135] там мир и благоденствие[2136].

2112   A2, N omitt.

2113   A2, N: [N: к тем], кто мешает

2114   A1 add.: тех

2115   A2 omitt.

2116   N : к нашим, к нам, создателям

2117   B: нашего

2118   A1: массонам

2119   A2, N omitt.: Но вернемся... & add.: Мы казним масонов

2120   A1 add.: лишь

2121   A2, N omitt.: только... & add.: никто, кроме братии [N: братий] об этом не

2122   A2, N omitt.

2123   A2, N omitt.: да... & add.: даже

2124   N: жертвы казни

2125   A2, N omitt.: для... & add.: все

2126   A1 omitt.

2127   B: естественною

2128   A2, N omitt.: вполне... & add.: как бы от нормального заболевания

2129   A1: люди; A2, N omitt.: Умирают...

2130   B: Братия; A2, N: Зная это, [N add.: даже] Братия в свою очередь

2131   A1, A2, N, B: смеет

2132   A2, N: Такими мерами

2133   A1: массонства; A2, N add.: самый

2134   A2, N add.: И [N add.: наших] агентов

2135   A1, B add.: а где порядок,

2136   A2, N omitt.: ибо где...

QUOTATIONS FROM JOLY'S *DIALOGUE*

a   «Ce monde (...) des sociétés secrètes est rempli de cerveaux vides»

b   «S'il s'y agite quelque chose, c'est ma main qui remue»

c   «s'il s'y prépare un complot, le chef c'est moi»

d   «Ces tigres ont des âmes de mouton, des têtes pleines de vent»

e   «Leur rêve est l'absorption des individus, dans une unité symbolique.»

f   «Les sociétés secrètes existeront dans les conditions que je viens de dire ou elles n'existeront pas»

XIV [2137]

Под нашим влиянием сократилось до минимума исполнение гоевских законов. Ныне[2138] престиж закона[2139] подорван **либеральными толкованиями** (a), введенными нами в общество гоев[2140]. В важнейших политических и принципиальных[2141] вопросах, **суды** решают так,[2142] как мы[2143] предписываем, видят дела в том свете, в который[2144] мы их облекаем для гоевской **администрации**[2145] через подставных лиц[2146], газетным мнением или **другими путями** (b)[2147]. Даже сенаторы и высшая административная власть[2148] слепо повинуются[2149] нашим советам и мнениям[2150]; и[2151] еще раз доказываю вам[2152] тем самым[2153], что[2154] животный ум гоев не способен к анализу и наблюдению, а тем более к предвидению того,[2155] к чему может клониться вопрос своей[2156]

[2137] K, A2, N omitt.; A1: **Еще протокол** [B add.: **(18)**]

[2138] A2, N omitt.

[2139] A1: законов

[2140] A2, N: эту сферу

[2141] N add.: делах и

[2142] A2 omitt.

[2143] A1, A2, N, B add.: им

[2144] A2: как; N: каким

[2145] N add.: конечно

[2146] A2, N add.: с которыми общего как бы не имеем-

[2147] A1 add.: в составлении которых мы как бы не имеем части; B add.: в начертании которых мы как бы не имеем части

[2148] A1, A2, N, B: администрация; A1, B add.: гоев

[2149] A1: повинуется

[2150] A1, B: мнению; A2, N omitt.: повинуются... & add.: принимают наши советы

[2151] A1, B omitt.

[2152] K omitt.

[2153] A1 omitt.: вам тем самым

[2154] A2, N omitt. и еще... & add.: Чисто

[2155] A2 omitt.

[2156] A1, B: своею

постановкой. Ум гоев инстинктивно животный[2157], он зрит[2158], но[2159] не предвидит[2160], изобретает[2161] же исключительно материальные[2162] изобретения[2163]. Ясно из этого, что сама природа нам предназначила руководить ими[2164] и править миром.

QUOTATIONS FROM JOLY'S *DIALOGUE*

a   «restreindre (...), dans le sens de la liberté, les dispositions de lois»

b   «l'action des tribuneaux (...) se trouve en contact (...) avec l'administration, par la voie...»

[2157]   N omitt.: вопрос... & add.: известная постановка вопроса... A2, N add.: В этой разнице способности мышления между ими [N: гоями] и нашими можно ясно узреть печать избрания [N: избранничества] и человечности, в различии [N: отличие] от инстинктивного, животного ума гоев.

[2158]   A2, N: Они зрят

[2159]   A2: не

[2160]   A2, N: предвидят, и не

[2161]   A2, N: изобретают

[2162]   A: материальное

[2163]   A1 omitt.; A2, N omitt.: же исключительно... & add.: мысль [N omitt.] (a [N omitt.] разве [N add.: только] материальные вещи)

[2164]   A2, N omitt.

XV [2165]

Когда наступит время нашего открытого правления, время проявлять его благотворность, **мы переделаем все законодательства** (a), ныне существующие[2166]. **Наши законы будут кратки** (b), ясны и[2167] незыблемы: без всяких толкований, так как[2168] их всякий будет[2169] твердо знать, потому что[2170] главная черта, которая в них будет проведена, это послушание начальству в градационном[2171] отношении[2172]. Тогда[2173] злоупотребления иссякнут, вследствие ответственности[2174] всех до единого перед высшей властью представителя власти. Злоупотребления[2175] властью[2176] ниже этой последней инстанции будут так беспощадно наказываться, что у всякого отпадет охота экспериментировать[2177] свои силы... Мы будем[2178] неукоснительно следить за каждым действием администрации, от которой зависит ход государственной машины, ибо[2179] распущенность в ней порождает распущенность всюду[2180]. Укрывательство, солидарное попустительство среди служащих[2181], все это зло исчезнет после первых

[2165] K, A2, N omitt.; A1, B: **Еще протокол** [B add: **(20)** (sic!; *rectius:* 19)].

[2166] A2, N omitt.: ныне...

[2167] A1, A2, N, B omitt.

[2168] A2, N: что

[2169] N add.: в состоянии

[2170] A2, N omitt.: потому...

[2171] A1, A2: грандиозном

[2172] N omitt.: в градационном... & add.: доведенное до грандиозной степени

[2173] N add.: всякие

[2174] A1: соответственности

[2175] N add.: же

[2176] N add.: лежащей

[2177] K: эксперементировать

[2178] B add.: так

[2179] B omitt.

[2180] A1, A2, N, B add: почему [A2, N omitt.; B: что] ни один случай незаконности или злоупотребления властю [A2, N, B omitt.] не останется без примерного наказания

[2181] A2, B, N add.: между служащими; N add.: в администрации

же примерных наказаний[2182]. Ореол нашей[2183] власти требует целесообразных хотя бы[2184] жестоких наказаний за[2185] нарушение ее[2186] престижа ради личной выгоды[2187] кого бы то ни было[2188]. Потерпевший за такое нарушение несоразмерно вине своей[2189] будет как бы солдатом, падающим на административном поле в[2190] пользу неукоснительности[2191] власти, т. е. порядка[2192], ради сохранения престижа[2193], принципа и закона, которые не могут допускать[2194] отступления от[2195] общественной дороги на личную тех, кто руководит[2196] общественной[2197] колесницею...[2198] Нашим судьям будет внушено[2199], что желая похвастать собственным[2200] милосердием и казаться либеральными[2201], они являются сами нарушителями закона[2202] о правосудии, который создан для примерного назидания людей[2203] за проступки, а не для

[2182] A2, N omitt.: примерных... & add.: примеров [N add.: сурового] наказания

[2183] A2: Наш

[2184] A2, N: т. е.

[2185] A2, N add.: малейшее

[2186] A2, N add.: высшего

[2187] A1: личных выгод

[2188] A2, N omitt.: кого бы...

[2189] A2, N omitt.: за такое... & add.: хотя бы несоразмерно [N: и не в мере] своей вины

[2190] A2, N: на

[2191] A1, B: неукоснительной; A2, N omitt.

[2192] A1, B add.: от этого [B: нее] зависящего

[2193] A2, N omitt.: т. е. порядка...

[2194] A2, N omitt.: могут... & add.: допускают

[2195] A2, N, B: с

[2196] A2, N, B: от самих же [B omitt.] руководящих [N: правящих]

[2197] A1, B: общественною

[2198] A1, A2: колесницей; A1, A2, N, B add.: Например,

[2199] A1, B: хорошо понятно; A2, N omitt: нашим... & add.: наши судьи будут знать

[2200] A2, N: глупым

[2201] A1, B: или быть либералами; A2, N omitt.: и казаться....

[2202] A2, N omitt.: являются... & add.: нарушают закон

[2203] A1, A2, N, B add.: наказаниями

выставки мягкости[2204] душевных[2205] нравов[2206] судьи. Такие порывы хороши[2207] в частной жизни, а не на общественной почве, являющейся воспитательной основой[2208] жизни... **Наш судебный персонал будет служить не далее[2209] 55[2210]-ти летнего возраста** (с); во первых потому, что **старцы упорнее держатся предвзятых мыслей[2211] и труднее подчиняются** руководству и[2212] **новым распоряжениям** (d), а во вторых[2213] **это нам доставит[2214] возможность[2215] перемещения персонала, который мы лучше согнем[2216] этим под нашей[2217] волей** (e)[2218]: те, которые пожелают[2219] удержаться[2220] на своих местах[2221], должны будут[2222] слепо повиноваться, чтобы этого заслужить. [2223]Наши[2224] судьи будут избираемы[2225] из[2226] среды[2227] крепких волею;

[2204] A2, N omitt.

[2205] N: духовных

[2206] A1, B: порывов; A2, N: качеств

[2207] A2, N: Эти качества уместно показывать

[2208] A1, A2, N, B omitt.: являющейся... & add.: каковая [A2: которая] есть воспитательная основа [N: представляет собою воспитательную основу] человеческой

[2209] N: долее

[2210] A2: 35

[2211] A2, N: мнений

[2212] A2, N omitt.: и труднее... & add.: менее способны повиноваться

[2213] N add.: потому, что

[2214] A2 add.: такую

[2215] N add.: такой мерой достигнуть гибкости

[2216] A2, N omitt.: мы лучше... & add.: легче согнется

[2217] A1, B: нашею

[2218] A2 omitt.: этим под нашей волей & add.: такой мерой; N: нашим давлением

[2219] N: кто пожелает

[2220] A1, B: задерживаться; A2, N: задержаться

[2221] N: своем месте

[2222] N: должен будет

[2223] A2, N add.: Вообще же

[2224] A2 omitt.

[2225] A1: избираются; A2, N, B: выбираемы [N add.: нами]

[2226] A1, B omitt.

[2227] A2, B: среди

они[2228] **будут** твердо **знать**[2229], **что их роль карать и применять законы** (f), а никак не в том, чтобы[2230] мечтать о проявлении своего[2231] либерализма за счет государственного воспитательного плана, как[2232] ныне воображают[2233] гои, не понимающие, что всякое милосердие есть[2234] попустителство, вселяющее в[2235] преступника надежду[2236] на оправдание[2237]. Мера[2238] перемещений[2239] еще[2240] **будет подрывать коллективную**[2241] **солидарность** (g)[2242] сослуживцев и подчинит их еще больше правительству[2243], от которого будет зависеть их судьба. Молодому поколению[2244] судей будет нами[2245] привито уважение к[2246] ненарушимости установленного порядка[2247] отношений наших подданных между собою и необходимости карать всякие нарушения этого порядка- немилосердно[2248]. Ныне, гоевские судьи творят

[2228] A2, N omitt.: крепких... & add.: только тех, которые

[2229] A2 omitt.: твердо знать & add.: ведать

[2230] A2, N omitt.: никак... & add.: а не

[2231] A2, N omitt.

[2232] A2, N add.: это

[2233] A1: делают

[2234] A1 add.: всякое

[2235] A1, B: сеющее расчет

[2236] A1, B omitt.

[2237] B: безнаказенность; A2, N omitt.: не понимающие....

[2238] B: Система

[2239] A2, N: перемешения

[2240] B add.: более

[2241] K: колективную

[2242] N omitt.: подрывать...солидарность & add.: служить и к подрыву коллективной солидарности

[2243] A1, A2, N, B omitt.: подчинит... & add.: привяжет всех к интересам правительства

[2244] A1, A2, N, B: Молодое поколение

[2245] A2, N omitt.

[2246] A1, B omitt.: привито... & add.: воспитано со взглядом [B: во взглядах]

[2247] A2, N omitt.: привито... & add.: воспитано во взглядах о недопущении таких злоупотреблений, которые бы нарушили [N: могли бы нарушить] установленный порядок

[2248] A2, N omitt.: и необходимости...

поблажки всяким преступлениям, оправдывая[2249] виновных из либерализма и милосердия...[2250] Они не имеют[2251] никакого[2252] представления о[2253] назначении и ответственности своей должности[2254]. Назначая их на такие воспитательные должности[2255], их[2256] правители[2257] не заботятся внушить[2258] им чувство[2259] долга и сознания[2260] дела, которое от них требуется. Как животные выпускают[2261] своих детей на добычу, так и гои дают[2262] подданым доходное место[2263], не думая о необходимости растолковать[2264] им[2265], для чего[2266] это место создано,[2267] какова его роль в социальной[2268] машине...[2269] От того то правления гоев[2270] разрушаются[2271] собственными силами тех[2272] в руках которых находятся[2273] нити от[2274] существования гоевских

[2249]   A1 omitt.; B: оправданию

[2250]   A1, B add.: ибо

[2251]   A2, N omitt.: оправдывая... & add.: не имея

[2252]   A1, B: точного; A2 omitt.; N: правилного

[2253]   A2, N add.: своем

[2254]   A1, B add.: потому что; A2 omitt.: и ответственности... & add.: потому что

[2255]   A2 omitt.: такие... & add: должность

[2256]   A2 omitt.

[2257]   N omitt.: и ответственности... & add.: потому что теперешние правители, при определении судей на должность

[2258]   A1, A2, B: внушать

[2259]   A1, A2, N: чувства

[2260]   A2, B: сознание

[2261]   A1, A2, N, B: животное выпускает

[2262]   A2, N, B add.: своим

[2263]   N: доходные места

[2264]   A2, N omitt.: о необходимости

[2265]   A1 omitt.

[2266]   A1, A2, N, B: на что

[2267]   B add.: и

[2268]   A1: государственной

[2269]   A2, N omitt.: какова...

[2270]   A2, N: их; N add.: и

[2271]   A1: разрушается

[2272]   A1, B: теми

[2273]   A2 omitt.: тех в руках... & add.: -держателями

правительств, т. е.[2275] через деяния[2276] собственной[2277] администрации... Почерпнем же в примере результатов этих действий еще один урок для нашего[2278] правления. Мы искореним, когда придет время нашего правления[2279], либерализм со[2280] всех[2281] важных постов[2282], от которых зависит приучение[2283] наших подданных[2284] общественному строю, дающему порядок непоколебимый[2285]: на эти посты попадут только те, которые будут воспитаны нами для административного руководства[2286]. На замечания[2287] Д. А.[2288], что отставка[2289] старых служащих дорого стоит государству[2290], скажу, во первых, что им дадут взамен[2291] частную службу, или занятие[2292]; во вторых замечу, что в наших руках[2293] все мировые деньги, что я докажу при обсуждении финансовых вопросов: а[2294] в третьих, в то время будут интернациональные деньги, т. е. воистину обменный знак, облегчающий обмен, а не затрудняющий его, как нынешняя система, созданная нами

[2274] A1, B omitt.; A2 add.: его

[2275] A2 omitt.: т. е.; N omitt.: тех...

[2276] A1: деяние; N: действия

[2277] A2 omitt.: деяниа... & add.: действия своей же; N: своей; B add.: же

[2278] A2, N: своего

[2279] A2, N omitt.: когда придет...

[2280] A1, B: изо; A2, N: из

[2281] A1, A2, N, B add.: стратегических

[2282] N add.: нашего управления

[2283] A1, A2, N, B: воспитание

[2284] N omitt.: наших... & add.: подчиненных нашему

[2285] A2, N omitt.: дающему...

[2286] A2, N: правления [N: управления]

[2287] A2, B: замечание; N add.: возможное

[2288] A2: д′ A; N omitt.

[2289] A2: отставки

[2290] A1, B omitt.; A2: дорого стоят; N: будет дорого стоить казне

[2291] A2, N, B add.: теряемой; A2, N omitt.: дадут... & add.: найдут предварительно

[2292] A1 add.: a; A2, N omitt.: или... & add.: a

[2293] N add.: будут сосредоточены

[2294] B omitt.

для окончательного разорения[2295] гоев нуждой...[2296] и[2297] нам нечего будет[2298] бояться дороговизны... **Наш абсолютизм будет** во всем последователен, а потому **непоколебим**[2299] **в каждом своем постановлении. Наша**[2300] **воля будет уважаема**[2301], исполняема, потому что[2302] она, в сознании своей силы[2303], **будет игнорировать всякий ропот** (h), всякое недовольство, искореняя всякое[2304] проявление таковых[2305] примерным[2306] наказанием[2307]. Мы упраздним **кассационное**[2308] **право** (i), которое перейдет в исключительное распоряжение[2309] правящего, ибо мы[2310] должны искоренить мысль, что допустимо[2311] неправильное решение[2312] назначенных[2313] нами судей.

[2314]Если же[2315] подобное произойдет, то мы[2316] кассируем[2317] это[2318] решение[2319], но с таким примерным наказанием судьи за непонимание

[2295] A1: раззорения; B: раззорения и закабаления

[2296] B: нуждою

[2297] A1, B omitt.

[2298] A2, N omitt.: т. е. воистину... & add.: следовательно, не нашему правительству

[2299] A2, N omitt.

[2300] A2, N add.: великая

[2301] A2 add.: и; N add.: и беспрекословно

[2302] N omitt.

[2303] A2, N omitt.: в сознании...

[2304] A1 omitt.

[2305] A2, N: их

[2306] A1, B: действием-; A2, N: в действии

[2307] A1, A2, N, B add.: примерного свойства

[2308] K: касационное

[2309] A2, N add.: наше- в ведение

[2310] A2, N add.: не

[2311] A2, N omitt.: искоренить... & add.: допустить [N add.: возникновение] мысли у народа что было [N: чтобы могло состояться]

[2312] N add.: у

[2313] A2: поставленных

[2314] B omitt.: Если же usque ad: своих подданных- детей. (2355)

[2315] N add.: что либо

[2316] A1 omitt.; A2, N add.: сами

[2317] K: касируем

своего долга и назначения, что эти случаи[2320] не будут часто повторяться[2321]... Повторяю, что[2322], мы будем особенно следить за каждым шагом[2323] нашей[2324] администрации, от[2325] которой зависит порядок социального строя; за ней[2326] только и надо следить правителю[2327], чтобы народ был им[2328] доволен, и пребывал в послушании[2329]. Всякий[2330] в праве ожидать[2331] от хорошего правления и[2332] хороших ставленников[2333]. **Наше правление будет**[2334] **патриархальной, отеческой**[2335] **опекой**[2336] (i). Народы[2337] будут рады,

[2318]
A2, N omitt.

[2319]
A1 add.: через правящего

[2320]
A2 add.: и

[2321]
A2, N omitt.: будут... & add.: повторятся

[2322]
A2, N add.: ведь

[2323]
A2, N omitt.: следить... & add.: знать каждый шаг

[2324]
A1 omitt.

[2325]
A2, N: за

[2326]
A2, N omitt.: зависит...

[2327]
A2, N omitt.

[2328]
A2, N: нами

[2329]
A1 omitt.: пребывал... & add.: хорошо служил ему своим послушанием.

[2330]
A2, N omitt.: и пребывал... & add.: ибо он

[2331]
A2, N: требовать

[2332]
A1, A2 omitt.

[2333]
A2, N: хорошего ставленника

[2334]
A2, N add.: иметь вид

[2335]
K, A1: отечественной

[2336]
A2, N: опеки; A1, A2, N add.: со стороны [A2, N add.: нашего] правителя;- народ наш и все остальные [A2, N omitt.: и все...] подданные увидят в лице его отца, озаботищегося о каждой нужде, о каждом действии, о каждом отношении своих подданных, между собой и к нему [A2, N omitt.: своих подданных...; A2 add.: друг к другу и к нему; N add.: как подданных друг к другу, так и их к правителю]: тогда они настолько проникнутся мыслью, что им невозможно обходиться без Его [A2, N: этого] попечения и руководства [N: руководительства], если они желают жить в покое [A2, N: спокойствии] и мире, что они признают и санкционируют [A2, N: omitt.] Его [N: нашего правителя] самодержавие с благоговением [N add.: близким к обоготворению], особенно когда убедятся, что его [A2, N:

что[2338] все урегулированно[2339] в их жизни, что в таком регулировании[2340] выражается такая же заботливость о благе народа, какую проявляют[2341] разумные[2342] родители, желая воспитать[2343] своих детей в чувстве долга и принципе[2344] послушания: ведь, народы по отношению к[2345] нашей политике[2346] вечно несовершеннолетние дети[2347], как равно[2348] их правления... Как видите, **я основываю**[2349] **деспотизм лишь**[2350] **на праве** (j) и долге[2351]... на праве понуждать к исполнению[2352] долга, что[2353] есть прямая обязанность правительства, которое действительно печется о благе и мире[2354] своих подданных- детей[2355].

Такое правление[2356] **имеет право сильного** (k) над несведущими. Оно[2357] обязано[2358] пользоваться этим правом[2359] для[2360] направления

наши] ставленники лишь исполнители его власти, слепо повинующиеся ему, а не узурпаторы этой власти, как это является ныне у гоев; [A2, N omitt.: лишь исполнители... & add.: не заменяют его властью своею, а лишь слепо исполняют его предписания].

[2337] A1, A2, N: Они

[2338] A2, N add.: мы

[2339] K: урегулировано; A2, N: урегулировали

[2340] A1: такой урегулириовке

[2341] A2, N omitt.: что в таком... & add.: как это делают

[2342] A2, N: умные

[2343] A2, N: которые хотят воспитывать

[2344] A1, A2: принципа; N omitt.

[2345] A2 omitt.; N add.: тайнам

[2346] A2, N: политики

[2347] N add.: точно также,

[2348] N: и

[2349] A2, N add.: наш

[2350] A2 omitt.

[2351] A1: долга

[2352] A1: вынуждать исполнение; A2, N: Право вынуждать исполнение

[2353] A2, N omitt.

[2354] A2, N omitt.: действительно... & add.: есть отец [N add.: для]

[2355] A2, N omitt.

[2356] A1: Правительство; A2, N: Оно

[2357] K omitt.: имеет....

[2358] A2, N omitt.: над... & add.: для того, чтобы

человечества к природою[2361] намеченному[2362] строю- послушанию[2363]. Все в мире повинуется[2364], коль[2365] не людям[2366], так обстоятельствам[2367], во всяком случае[2368] всему что[2369] сильнее его[2370]... Так будем же[2371] мы этим сильнейшим[2372], будем[2373], не задумываясь, жертвовать отдельными лицами[2374], нарушителями наших планов и порядков, потому что[2375] в этом[2376] воспитательная задача, чтобы искоренить зло и противодействие[2377] примерными наказаниями[2378]. Когда царь от дома Давида,[2379] царь израильский, наденет[2380] корону[2381], поднесенную ему Европой[2382], он сделается патриархом мира. [2383]Жертвы, принесенные ради возведения его на престол[2384], не

2359 A1, A2, B: им

2360 A2, N: во благо

2361 A1: природой

2362 A2: определенному; N: природно-определенному

2363 A2: послушания

2364 A2: слушатся; N: находится в послушании

2365 A2, N, B: если

2366 A2: людей; N: у людей

2367 A1, B add.: или природе; A2, N add.: то [N add.: у] обстоятельств или [N add.: у] своей натуры

2368 A2: во всех случаях

2369 B omitt.: во всяком... & add.: чему нибудь

2370 A1, B: себя; A2: сильнейшего; N: у сильнейшего

2371 A1, B omitt.; A2: только

2372 A1, B add.: безраздельно; A2, N add.: ради блага

2373 A2, N: Мы обязаны

2374 A2, N: личностями

2375 A2, N omitt.: наших... & add.: [N add.: установленного] порядка, ибо

2376 A1, B: том; N omitt.: потому... & add.: в примерном наказании зла лежит великая

2377 A2 omitt.: и противодействие

2378 N omitt.: чтобы искоренить...

2379 A1: Давидова; A2, N omitt.: царь от...

2380 N add.: на свою священную голову

2381 A1 add.: мира

2382 A2, B: Европою

2383 A2, N add.: Необходимые

достигнут количества тех[2385] жертв, которые принесены были[2386] в течение веков манией величия и[2387] соревнованием гоевских правителей[2388].

QUOTATIONS FROM JOLY'S *DIALOGUE*

a   «Vous allez (...) détruire l'organisation judiciaire?»

b   «Quant aux lois nouvelles (...) auront été rendues sous forme de simples décrets»

c   «Je rendrai un décret qui mettra les magistrates à la retraite, quand ils seront arrivés à un certain âge.»

d   «Il fait disparaître cet esprit de résistance (…) si dangereux dans des compagnies judiciaires qui ont conservé le souvenir (…) Il introduit dans leur seine une masse d'éléments nouveaux (…) toutes favorables à l'esprit qui anime mon règne.»

e   «...places de magistrats qui deviennent vacantes (...) entraînent un déplacement dans tout le personnel de la justice (...) on se rapproche plus étroitement du gouvernement»

f   «Ils savent que le gouvernement aime l'ordre (...) et il ne s'agit que de les servir (...) en faisant bonne justice»

g   «…l'esprit collectif disparaît»

h   «…l'irrévocabilité de mes décisions, malgré les murmures 9…) qui agit ainsi toujours sûr d'imposer le respect de sa volonté»

i   «...je vais vous parler de la cour de cassation»

j   «votre gouvernement devient de plus en plus paternel. Ce sont là des moeurs (…) presque patriarcales»

k   «je prends mon point d'appui (…) dans le droit»

l   «Dans le droit du plus fort»

[2384] A2, N omitt.: принесенные... & add.: им принесенные [N: присвоенные], вследствие их целесообразности, никогда

[2385] A2: жертв; N omitt.: количества... & add.: числа жертв

[2386] A2, N: принесенных

[2387] N omitt.

[2388] A2: администраций; N: правительств. A2, N add.: Он [N: Наш царь], будет непрестанно в обращении [N: находиться в непрестанном общении] с народом, говоря ему с трибуны речи, которые разнесутся [N: молва будет разносить] на весь мир в тот же час.

XVI [2389]

С **целью уничтожения** во дни нашего правления[2390] **всякой коллективной**[2391] **силы**[2392], кроме нашей[2393], **мы обезвредим** первую ступень коллективизма[2394]- **университеты** (a), для начала. Мы перевоспитаем состав[2395] их[2396] новым направлением[2397]. **Начальство и преподаватели**[2398] для таковых[2399] будут подготовляемы[2400] тайными программами[2401] действий, от которых они безнаказанно не отступят ни на иоту. Они **будут** назначаться с особенною осторожностью и будут **поставлены в полную зависимость от правительства** (b). **Мы исключим из предметов**[2402] преподавания государственное право, как и все, что **касается политических вопросов** (c)[2403]: эти предметы будут преподаваться в особых школах[2404], немногим десяткам лиц[2405], кончившим университет, с выдающимися способностями[2406], которые и попадут в число[2407] посвященных. **Университеты**[2408] **не должны**

[2389] K omitt.; A1, N, B: **Еще протокол** [B add.: **(20)**]

[2390] A2, N omitt.: во дни...

[2391] K: колективной

[2392] A1, A2, N, B: всяких коллективных сил

[2393] A2, N: наших

[2394] K: коллективизма

[2395] A2, N omitt.: для начала... & add.: перевоспитав

[2396] A2: его

[2397] N: в новом направлении.; A2, N add.: Их

[2398] N: начальства и профессоры

[2399] A2, N omitt.: для...

[2400] A1, B add.: полными, но; A2, N add.: для своего дела полными [N: подробными]

[2401] K: програмами

[2402] N omitt.

[2403] A1, A2, N: политического вопроса

[2404] A2, N omitt.: в особых...

[2405] B: лицам

[2406] A2, N omitt.: кончившим... & add.: избранных по выдающимся способностям

[2407] A2, N omitt.: которые... & add.: из числа

[2408] A1, A2, B add.: же

выпускать[2409] **молокососов, стряпающих планы конституций**[2410]**, как** комедии и[2411] **трагедии** (d), занимающихся[2412] вопросами политики, в которых и отцы[2413] их ничего не смыслят[2414]. **Плохо направленное ознакомление** большого количества[2415] лиц с вопросами якобы[2416] политики **создает утопистов и плоких подданных** (e), как вы[2417] можете усмотреть это[2418] из примера всеобщего воспитания[2419] гоев этим вопросам[2420]. В их воспитание нам необходимо[2421] было ввести все те брожения[2422], от которых нарушился[2423] их строй.[2424] Когда[2425] мы будем у власти,[2426] мы исключим[2427] всякие смущающие предметы из воспитания[2428] и **постараемся сделать**[2429] **из молодежи послушных детей начальства, любящих правящего** (f), как опору и надежду на мир и покой. Классицизм[2430], как и всякое **учение**[2431] о[2432] **древней истории,** в

[2409]   N add.: из своих стен

[2410]   A2: конституции

[2411]   A omitt.; A2, N: или

[2412]   A1, N, B: занимаясь; A2: заниматься

[2413]   A2, N, B add.: то

[2414]   N: смыслили

[2415]   N: числа

[2416]   A2, N omitt.

[2417]   N add.: сами

[2418]   A1, A2, N omitt.

[2419]   B: обучения

[2420]   A1 omitt.: этим вопросам; A2, N: в этом направлении

[2421]   N: надо

[2422]   A2, N: начала

[2423]   A1, B: испортился; A2, N: которые [N add.: так блистательно] надломили

[2424]   A1, B add.: Знание якобы политики толпою сильнее всего замутили [B: замутило] этот строй

[2425]   A2, N add.: же

[2426]   A2, N add.: то

[2427]   A2, N, B: удалим

[2428]   B: образования

[2429]   A2, N: сделаем

[2430]   K: Класицизм

[2431]   B: преподавание; N: изучение

[2432]   A2, N, B omitt.

которой больше[2433] дурных, чем хороших примеров, **мы заменим изучением**[2434] программы[2435] будущего и **настоящего** (g)[2436]. Мы вычеркнем из памяти людей все факты прежних веков, воспоминание о которых нам нежелательно[2437], и оставим[2438] из них только те, которые обрисовывают все ошибки гоевских правлений. Учение о практической системе отношений[2439], обязательном строе, о необходимости избегать[2440] дурных примеров эгоизма[2441], которые сильнее всего[2442] сеют зло[2443], и другие подобные вопросы воспитательного характера будут стоять в первых номерах[2444] программы[2445], составленной по отдельному плану для каждого класса[2446] и не обобщающей[2447] преподавания... [2448]Каждый общественный класс[2449] должен[2450] быть воспитан[2451] в строгих разграничениях[2452], соответствующих[2453] его[2454]

[2433] A2, N: более

[2434] A1, A2: учением; B: обучением

[2435] K: программы; A1, B: программе

[2436] A2, N omitt.

[2437] A2, N omitt.: воспоминание... & add.: которые нам не желательны

[2438] A1, A2, N, B: оставив

[2439] A2, N omitt.: системе... & add.: жизни, [N add.: об]

[2440] A2, N omitt.: о необходимости... & add.: об отношениях людей друг к другу, об избежании [N: избежания]

[2441] A2, N: эгоистических

[2442] A2, N omitt.: сильнее...

[2443] A2, N: заразу зла

[2444] N, B: нумерах; A1, A2, N, B add.: [A1, B add.: нашей] преподавательной [N: преподавательской]

[2445] K: программы

[2446] K: класа; A1, A2, N, B: звания

[2447] A1, A2, N, B omitt. & add.: ни под каким видом не обобщая

[2448] A1, A2, N, B add.: Этот вопрос заключает [N: Такая постановка вопроса имеет] особую важность, потому что [N omitt.]

[2449] K: клас

[2450] A1, A2, N, B: каждое общественное звание должно

[2451] A1, A2, N, B: воспитано

[2452] A1, B add.: знания

[2453] A1, B: соответствующего; A2, N: согласно

[2454] A1, A2, N, B omitt.

назначению и труду. Случайные гении всегда умели[2455] проскользнуть в высшее звание[2456]; а[2457] ради этой редкой случайности нельзя наталкивать[2458] в чужие ряды бездарности, отвлекая их несоответственным воспитанием от[2459] присущих им[2460] по рождению занятий[2461], так сказать применяя[2462] колесо общественной машины к функциям или к частям механизма[2463] к которым оно не подходит[2464]. Вы уже[2465] знаете[2466], чем кончилась[2467] для гоев попытка нарушить Богом определенную судьбу и место каждого человека, и[2468] уравнять в правах неуравнимое[2469]. Чтобы ореол правящего[2470] крепко запечатлелся[2471] в сердцах и умах[2472] подданных, надо, чтобы[2473] во время его правления[2474] преподавалось[2475] народу ведение[2476] о его деятельности[2477], значении[2478], благоначинаниях на пользу человечества

[2455] A2, N add.: и сумеют [N: съумеют]

[2456] A2, N: другие звания

[2457] N: но

[2458] A2, N omitt.: нельзя... & add.: пропускать

[2459] A2, N omitt: отвлекая... & add.: отнимая их [N: места] у [N: от]

[2460] N: этим рядам

[2461] A2, N: и заниятию [N add.: -совершенное безумие...]

[2462] A1, B: отвлекая

[2463] A1, B omitt.: к функциям... & add.: от его функций в другие места

[2464] A1, B: приходится, а в приложении к ним дезорганизует ход общественной машины; A2, N omitt.: так сказать...

[2465] A1, B omitt.; A2, N: сами

[2466] A1, B: узнаете

[2467] A2, N: все это кончилось

[2468] A1, B omitt.

[2469] A1, B add.: безнаказанно- распределение прав; A2, N omitt.: попытка... & add.: допустивших это [N add.: эту вопиющую бессмыслицу...]

[2470] A2, N omitt.: ореол... & add.: правящий

[2471] A2, N: засел

[2472] A2, N add.: своих

[2473] A2, N omitt.

[2474] K: направления

[2475] A2, N omitt.: правления... & add.: деятелности преподавать всему

[2476] A1: сведения; A2, N omitt. & add.: [N add.: в школах И] на площадях

[2477] A2, N omitt.

или народа[2479]. **Мы уничтожим всякое свободное преподавание**. Все источники образования будут сосредоточены в руках правительства. Но **будет** якобы **свободное чтение лекций**, дозволенное[2480] в учебных заведениях[2481], **в праздничные дни** (h), когда ученики с родителями будут допущены **как бы для клубного сборища** (i), для обмена мыслей с преподавателями по вопросам[2482] философии[2483].

[2478] A2, N add.: и делах [N: деяниях], о всех его

[2479] A2, N omitt.: на пользу...

[2480] A2, N omitt.: Все источники... & add.: Учащиеся будут иметь право [N add.: вместе] с родными собираться, как в клуб-,

[2481] A2: учебные заведения

[2482] A1 add.: о

[2483] K omitt.: Мы уничтожим....; A2, N omitt.: в праздничные дни... & add.: во время этих собраний, по праздникам, учителя [N: преподаватели] будут читать [N add.: якобы] свободные лекции; A1, A2, N, B add.: о человеческих отношениях [A2, N: вопросах человеческих отношений], о необходимости соблюдения определенного места в общественном строе [A2, N omitt.: о необходимости...], о законах примера и репрессалий [N: о репрессалиях], рождающихся при бессознательности людей, не ведающих правила [B: правил; A2, N: от бессознательных] отношений, и наконец для ознакомления с новыми теориями [A2, N: о философии новых теорий], еще не проявленных [N: явленных] миру, но [A2, N omitt.] которые [N: Эти теории] нам необходимо возвести [A2, N: мы возведем] в догмат веры, потому что в этом [A2: как в; N omitt.] переходная степень [A2: переходную степень] к нашей вере. Я вам доложу [A2, N: прочту] основания этих теорий по окончании изложения программы наших [A2, N: нашей программы] действий в [A2, N add.: настоящем и в] будущем. Словом, зная по опыту N: из многовекового опыта], что людьми надо руководить [A2, N: люди живут и руководятся] идеями и теориями [A2, N omitt.] что таковые [A2: последние; N: идеи эти] всасываются [N add.: людьми; A2 add.: только] через образование [A2, N: воспитание], преподаваемое [A2, N: даваемое] во всех возрастах [N: при помощи воспитания, даваемого всем возрастам] с одинаковым успехом, лишь при употреблении [A2, N omitt.: лишь...]

Пользуясь[2484] различными приемами[2485] внушения[2486], **мы поглотим и конфискуем[2487] в нашу пользу последние проблески независимости мысли** (l) людей[2488], которую мы веками утилизируем[2489] в нужном нам[2490] направлении[2491], которая[2492] стала[2493] окончательно[2494] обуздываться наглядной[2495] системой, долженствующей[2496] превратить гоев в немыслящих, послушных животных, неспособных «без наглядности» сообразить что-нибуд;[2497] …Во Франции Буржуа, один из лучших наших агентов, уже провозгласил новую программу[2498] наглядного воспитания. Теперь, когда мы в силе, нам не нужны мыслители-гои, а нужны работники, какими всегда будут материалисты, алчные поклонники[2499] земных благ[2500].

[2484] A2, N omitt.: Пользуясь... & add.: но лишь [N: конечно, только] различными приемами

[2485] A1, B omitt.: Пользуясь... & add.: различных приемов

[2486] A2, N omitt.

[2487] K: сумеем поглотить и направить; A1, B: съумеем поглотить и конфисковать

[2488] A2, N omitt.

[2489] A1, B: направляем

[2490] A1: нужное нам; B: полезном для нас

[2491] A1: направление, вследствие чего люди; A2, N omitt.: утилизируем... & add.: уже давно направляем на нужные нам предметы [N add.: и идеи].

[2492] A2 add.: уже

[2493] A1 omitt.: которая... & add.: стали; A2: начала

[2494] A2 omitt.

[2495] B: наглядною

[2496] B: долженствующею; A2: имеющей; N omitt.: которая... & add.: Система обуздания мысли уже в действии в так называемой системе наглядного обучения, имеющей

[2497] A1, A2, N, B omitt.: неспособных... & add.: ожидающих наглядности, чтобы сообразить обстоятельство [A2, N: ее]

[2498] K: програму

[2499] A1, B: потребители

[2500] A2, N omitt.: Теперь...

QUOTATIONS FROM JOLY'S *DIALOGUE*

a   «...la destruction des forces collectives. (...) vous n'avez encore porté la main (...) sur l'Université»

b   «... les membres des corps enseignants (...) sont nommés par le gouvernement (...) ils en dépendent»

c   «...je regarde comme très importante de proscrire, dans l'enseignement du droit, les études de politique constitutionelle»

d   «...au sortir des écoles, les jeunes gens (...) se mêlent de faire des constitutions comme on fait des tragédies»

e   «Avec ces notions mal digérés, (...) on prépare des faux hommes d'Etat, des utopistes»

f   «Il faut que (...) soient élevés dans le respect des institutions établies, dans l'amour du prince»

g   «...négliger l'histoire contemporaine. Il est au moins aussi essentiel de connaître son temps que celui de Périclès»

h   «...réagir contre l'enseignement libre (...) on peut (...) utiliser les loisirs»

i   «voulez-vous donc que j'autorise des clubs?»

j   «vous absorbez, vous confisquez à votre profit même les dernières lueurs d'une pensée indépendante»

XVII [2501]

Адвокатура создает людей холодных, жестоких, упорных, **беспринципных, становящихся** во всех случаях на[2502] **чисто легальную** (a) почву.[2503] Они все относят[2504] к выгоде защиты, а **не к социальному благу** (b)[2505] результатов ее...[2506] Поэтому[2507] они[2508] не отказываются ни от какой защиты, ищут[2509] оправдания преступника[2510] во что[2511] то ни стало; в погоне за оправданием, они вносят каз[у]истику в юриспруденцию[2512], чем и деморализуют[2513] суд, уничтожая значение его и назначение[2514]... **Мы поставим эту профессию** в узкие рамки, заключим[2515] ее[2516] **в сферу**[2517] **исполнительного чиновничества** (c). Они не будут иметь[2518] права общения с тяжущимися, или обвиненными[2519], как и судьи[2520], получая дела[2521] от суда[2522], и[2523] разбирая их по

[2501] K omitt.; A1, N, B: **Еще протокол** [B add.: **(21)**]; A2: XVII

[2502] add.: безличную

[2503] K omitt.: становящихся...

[2504] A2, N: приучились относить

[2505] A1, B add.: от

[2506] K omitt.: а не к социальному...

[2507] A2, N omitt.

[2508] N add.: обыкновенно

[2509] N: домогаются

[2510] A2, N omitt.

[2511] A1, A2, N, B add.: бы

[2512] A1, B omitt.: оправданием... ; A2, N omitt.: в погоне...; A2, N, B add.: таковым они придираются [A2, N: придираясь] к мелким гвоздкам [A2, N, B: загвоздкам] риспруденции

[2513] A2, N omitt.: чем & add.: этим они; K, A1: деморализует

[2514] A2, N omitt.: уничтожая... & add.: Поэтому; B omitt.: Мы поставим usque ad: творят ныне гои (2544)

[2515] A2, N: которые заключат

[2516] A2: их

[2517] A2: сферы

[2518] A2 omit: не... & add.: будут лишены; N omitt.: Они не... & add.: Адвокаты будут лишены наравне с судьями

[2519] A2, N omitt.: или обвиненными

[2520] A1, A2, N: omitt.: как и... & add.: наравне с судьями

документам и докладным запискам, защищая[2524] клиентов после публичного[2525] допроса их[2526] по выяснившимся фактам[2527]. Гонорар они будут получать, не по качеству[2528] защиты, а по размеру дела, они[2529] будут[2530] докладчики дел в пользу правосудия на перевесе[2531] прокурору[2532], который докладывает[2533] в пользу обвинения[2534]. Такими мерами[2535], установится честная, беспристрастная защита, которая поведется[2536] не казуистически[2537], из интереса, а по убеждению. Эти же меры послужат к устранению подкупов[2538] товарищей, их соглашения[2539] дать выигрыш дела[2540] тому[2541], кто более[2542] платит из двух тяжущихся, не взирая на правоту той или иной[2543] стороны, как это творят ныне гои[2544]... **Духовенство**[2545] гоев **мы**[2546] **позаботимся**[2547]

[2521] N add.: только

[2522] A2: последних

[2523] N omitt.

[2524] N add.: своих

[2525] A2, N omitt.

[2526] N add.: на суде

[2527] A1 add.: искусно подобранным.

[2528] A2, N omitt.: по... & add.: взирая на качество

[2529] A2, N omitt.: а по... & add.: Это

[2530] N add.: простые

[2531] A1, A2: в перевес

[2532] A2: прокурора

[2533] A2, N: будет докладчик [N: докладчиком]

[2534] A2, N add.: это сократит судебный доклад

[2535] A1 add.: уже; A2, N: Таким образом

[2536] A2, N omitt.: которая... & add.: веденная

[2537] A2, N omitt.

[2538] A2, N omitt.: Эти же меры & add.: Это [N add.: между прочим] устранит существующие [N: практикующиеся] ныне подкупы

[2539] A1, A2, N: соглашение

[2540] N: делу

[2541] N: только того

[2542] A1: больше; A2: только; N omitt.

[2543] A1 omitt.: той или иной

[2544] A2, N omitt.: из двух тяжущихся...

[2545] A1, A2, N, B: Священничество

дискредитировать[2548] и этим **подорвать**[2549] **его влияние** (d)[2550], которое препятствует[2551] нам. С каждым днем влияние священников[2552] на народы падает- всюду провозглашается[2553] свобода совести: следовательно[2554] какие нибудь[2555] годы нас отделяют от момента полного крушения христианской веры[2556], самой опасной для нас противницы по теориям о духовном мире и будущей жизни...[2557] А с другими справиться будет легко[2558], но об этом говорить преждевременно. Мы поставим[2559] клерикализм[2560] в такие узкие рамки, чтобы[2561] его[2562] влияние совсем исчезло[2563]. Когда время придет[2564] уничтожить папский двор, то **палец** от незримой руки **укажет** (e) народам в сторону этого двора, а[2565] когда[2566] последние[2567] бросятся на

[2546] N add.: уже

[2547] А1, А2, В: позаботились; N: озаботились

[2548] В: дискредитовать

[2549] А1, В: раззорить; А2, N: разорить

[2550] А1, А2, N, В: их миссию [А1: миссии]

[2551] А1, А2, N, В: которые [А2, N, В: которая] ныне [А1, А2, В: omitt.] могли [А2, N, В: могла] бы препятствовать А2, N: очень мешать]

[2552] А2, N: его

[2553] А2, N: провозглашена [N add.: теперь]

[2554] А1, В: только

[2555] А2, N omitt. какие... & add.: только

[2556] А2, N: религии

[2557] А2, N omitt.: самой опасной...

[2558] А2, N omitt.: справиться... & add.: [N add.: же религиями] справимся еще легче

[2559] А2, В: поставили

[2560] N add.: и клерикалов

[2561] А1, А2, В: что

[2562] А2, N: их

[2563] А1, А2, N, В omitt.: совсем... & add.: пойдет [А2, N, В: пошло] обратно к [А2, N, В omitt.] своему первоначальному [N: прежнему; А2 omitt.]

[2564] А2, N add.: окончательно

[2565] N omitt.

[2566] А2 add.: эти

[2567] N, В: [N add.: же] народы

него[2568], **мы выступим как бы защитниками**[2569] его (f), чтобы помешать слишком[2570] сильному "кровопусканию"[2571]. Это нам откроет его двери[2572], **мы пробьемся**[2573] туда[2574] и уже **оттуда не удалимся** (g)[2575], пока не подточим его основания[2576]. **Царь Иудейский будет тем, чем некогда был папа** (h). Он будет вселенским[2577] патриархом[2578] интернациональной церкви, нами учрежденной[2579]. Но пока мы перевоспитаем людей для этой веры[2580], через переходные верования[2581], мы открыто и насильственно[2582] не затронем существующие церкви, а будем уничтожать их[2583] **критикой, возбуждающей раскол**[2584] (i). Вообще,[2585] наша пресса[2586] должна[2587] изобличать государственные дела религии, неспособности[2588] гоев, не[2589] солидарность[2590] с нами[2591], в

2568   A2, N: туда

2569   K: защитникиками

2570   B omitt.

2571   A2, N omitt.: помещать... & add.: не допустить до сильных кровопусканий

2572   A2, N omitt.: Это... ; A2 add.: этим; N add.: Этой диверсией

2573   A1, A2, N, B: проберемся

2574   N: в самые его недра

2575   A2, N: выйдем

2576   A2 omitt.: подточим & add.: источим; Λ1, Λ2, N, B omitt.: его... & add.: всю силу этого места.

2577   A2, N omitt.: тем, чем... & add.: настоящим папой [N: папою] вселенной,

2578   A2 add.: нашей

2579   A2, N omitt.: нами...

2580   A1, A2, N, B omitt.: людей... & add.: юношей [N: юношество] в эту веру [A2: в новые переходные вераы, а затем и в нашу; N: в новых переходных верах, а затем и в нашей]

2581   A1: переходное верование; A2, N omitt.: через...

2582   A2, N omitt.: и насильственно

2583   A2, N omitt.: уничтожать их & add.: с ними бороться

2584   A2: расколы

2585   N add.: же современная

2586   K: преса

2587   A2, N: будет

2588   B: неспособность

2589   A1: на

2590   B: солидарных

самых бесцеремонных[2592] выражениях, чтобы[2593] их унизить ныне[2594], как они унижали наше племя в течение веков[2595]... Наше царство будет **апологией**[2596] **божка Вишну**, в котором находится олицетворение его. В наших **ста руках будут**[2597] **все пружины** (j)[2598] социальной машины.[2599] **Мы будем все знать** и ведать[2600] без помощи **официальной**[2601] **полиции**, которая ныне, в выработанной нами системе,[2602] мешает правительствам ведать истину[2603]. При нашей программе[2604] воспитания[2605], **треть подданных наших будет**[2606] **наблюдать за остальными** (k)[2607] и докладывать[2608] о них.[2609] **Наши агенты** будут из числа[2610] **высшего**[2611] и

[2591]   A2, N omitt.: не солидарность... ; N add.: и все это

[2592]   N: беспринципных

[2593]   N add.: всячески

[2594]   A2 omitt.

[2595]   A2 omitt.: в течение...; N omitt.: ныне... & add.: так, как это умеет делать только наше гениальное племя

[2596]   A1: аппологией; A2: апологиею

[2597]   A2, N: будет

[2598]   A2, N: по пружине

[2599]   B omitt.: Наше.... машины.

[2600]   A2, N omitt.: знать... & add.: видеть

[2601]   A1, A2, B: оффициальной

[2602]   A1, A2, N, B omitt.: ныне... & add.: в той форме ее прав, которые [N: которую] мы выработали для гоев, только [A2, N omitt.]

[2603]   A2, N omitt.: ведать истину & add.: видеть

[2604]   K: програме

[2605]   A2, N omitt.

[2606]   A1, B: будут добровольно

[2607]   A1, A2, N, B add.: из чувства долга, [N: из] принципа государственной службы каждого, как ныне треть наших братьев наблюдает за остальными [A2, N omitt.: как ныне]

[2608]   A1, B: докладывает

[2609]   A2, N omitt.: и докладывать... & add.: Тогда не будет постыдно; A1, A2, N, B add.: Быть шпионом и доносчиком на всякое отступление считается у нас похвальным [A1, B omitt.: на всякое отступление... & add.: будет не постыдно, а похвально], что будет и тогда, но уже для всех [A1, N omitt.: что будет... & add.: Но неоснованные доносы и указания [N omitt.] будут

низшего общества, из среды веселящегося административного, **издательского, типографского мира**, в числе их будут[2612] **книгопродавцы** (l), приказчики[2613], рабочие, кучера, лакеи и т. д. Эта бесправная, неуполномоченная на всякое[2614] самоуправство, а, следовательно и бесправство[2615] полиция будет[2616] свидетельствовать и докладывать, но проверки[2617] ее докладов как равно[2618] и аресты будут производиться[2619] группой[2620] контролеров по делам полиции; аресты же[2621] будут производиться корпусом жандармов и городской полиции[2622]. Такой надзор[2623] искоренит злоупотребление[2624] властью,

---

наказуемы, чтобы не развилось [N: развелось] злоупотребление этим правом.

[2610] A2, N add.: как

[2611] N add.: так

[2612] A2, N omitt.: издательского... & add.: класса, издатели, типографы

[2613] A1: прикащики

[2614] N: какое либо

[2615] N omitt. и... & add.: безвластная

[2616] N add.: только

[2617] A2, N: а проверка

[2618] A2 omitt.: ее докладов...; N omitt.: докладов... & add.: показаний

[2619] A1 add.: ответственной; A2, N: зависеть

[2620] K: групой

[2621] A2 omitt.; N add.: самые

[2622] A1: полицией & add.: роль которой будет заключаться кроме того в наблюдении за порядками; A2, N omitt.: группой контролеров & add.: от ответственной группы контролеров по делам полиции, самые же [A2 omitt.] аресты будут производить жандармский корпус и городская полция; B omitt.: Наши агенты...; A1, A2, N, B add.: Недонесший о виденном или [A2, N: и] слышанном по вопросам политических действий или проектов [A2, N omitt. политических... & add.: политики тоже] будет привлечен [N: привлекаться; B: привлекаем] к ответственности за укрывательство, если будет доказано, что он имел названные сведения [A2, N: в этом виновен; N add.: Подобно тому]. Как ныне наши братья [N add.: под собственною ответственностью] обязаны доносить кагалам [A2, N: кагалу] на [A2, N add.: своих] отступников от исполнения наших законов [A2, N omitt.: от исполнения & add.: или замеченных в чем-либо противном; N add.: кагалу], так же, под собственною ответственностью,

силой, подкупом, который[2625] мы ввели нашими соблазнами[2626] в привычку[2627] гоев[2628], которым[2629] разожгли своенравие и алчность агентов[2630] водворения порядка, возбудили в них все разрушительные наклонности, первая из которых-[2631] взяточничество[2632], и породили[2633] те беспорядки в верхних слоях, которые произвели[2634] недовольства[2635] меньших[2636] классов[2637].

будут доносить все наши подданные, соблюдая [A2, N: так в нашем всемирном царстве будет обязательно для всех наших подданных соблюдать] долг государственной службы [N add.: в этом направлении]

[2623] A1, A2: Такое постановление; N: Такая организация

[2624] A2, N: злоупотребления

[2625] A1, A2: которые; N: все то, что

[2626] A1: советами и; A2, N: советами, теориями человеческих [N: сверхчеловеческих] прав; A1 add.: -сильному пользоваться своей силой

[2627] N: привычки

[2628] A1, A2, N add.: но как [N add.: же] бы нам [A2, N add.: иначе; N add.: было] добиться возникновения [A2, N: увеличения] причин к введению беспорядков в администрацию и учреждения [A2, N omitt. к введению... & add.: к беспорядкам среди их администрации] как не такими [A2, N: этими] путями

[2629] B omitt.: Такой надзор... & add.: Подложив гоям приманки либерализма и подкупа, мы

[2630] A2, N omitt. которым... & add.: через агентов [N: В числе же этих путей один из важнейших- это агенты]

[2631] A2, N omitt.: возбудили... & add.: разжигая их своенравие и все разрушительные наклонности, в числе коих первая [N: поставленные в возможность в своей разрушительной деятельности проявлять и развивать свои дурные наклонности- своенравие, своевластие и в первую голову]

[2632] B: взятничество

[2633] K: продлили

[2634] B: вызвали

[2635] B: недовольство

[2636] A1: низших

[2637] A1, B add.: и общую потасовку...; A2, N omitt.: и породили...

334 *Appendix: The Russian Text of the* Protocols

QUOTATIONS FROM JOLY'S *DIALOGUE*

a   «Cette profession (...) développe des caractères froids et opiniâtres dans leurs principes, des esprits dont la tendance est de rechercher (...) la légalité pure».

b   «L'avocat n'a pas (...) le sens élevé des nécessités sociales»

c   «je rendrai un décret qui (...) soumettra (...) les avocats à recevoir du souverain l'investiture de leur profession.»

d   «Le clergé (...) Prenez garde au prêtre: (...) son influence est partout»

e   «...d'indiquer du doigt...»

f   «d'être le défenseur de l'Eglise»

g   «...l'y ramèneraient et l'y maintiendraient toujours»

h   «Pourquoi le souverain ne sarait-il pas pontife»

i   «Je pourrais provoquer (...) un schisme»

j   «...l'apologue du dieu Wishnou; vous avez cent bras (...) et chacun (...) touche un ressort.»

k   «...pourrez vous aussi tout voir? —Oui, car je ferai de la police (...) la moitié des hommes verra l'autre»

l   «Ma police (...) Hommes de plaisirs et de bonne compagnie (...) imprimeurs et libraires»

XVIII [2638]

Если во время нашего царства нам понадобится[2639] усилить[2640] меры охраны нашей власти[2641], **мы устроим симуляцию беспорядков** (а)[2642], или мнимую демонстрацию недовольных групп[2643]. Эта демонстрация[2644], руководимая хорошими ораторами[2645], увлечет баранье человеческое стадо[2646]. И[2647] мы получим[2648] **повод**[2649] к **обыскам** (b)[2650], и с помощью[2651] гоевской полиции[2652] отделяемся от наших противников, отозвавшихся[2653] на призыв наших агентов-провокаторов[2654]. Большинство заговорщиков действуют[2655] **из любви к искусству** (с)[2656], ради краснобайства[2657]. Поэтому[2658] мы не будем их

[2638] K omitt.; A1, N: **Еще протокол** [B add.: **(22)**]

[2639] A1, B: придется; A2, N omitt.: Если... & add.: Когда нам надо [N: нужно] будет

[2640] A2, N add.: строгие

[2641] A2, N omitt.: нашей... ; N add.: (страшнейший яд для престижа власти)

[2642] K, A1, B omitt.: симуляцию...; A1, B add.: выражение якобы неудовольствия

[2643] K: груп; A2, N omitt.: мнимую... & add.: проявление неудовольствий

[2644] A1, B: эти неудовольствия

[2645] A1, B omitt.: руководимая... & add.: будут выражать хорошие ораторы; A2, N omitt.: Эта демонстрация... & add.: выражаемых через [N: при содействий] хороших ораторов

[2646] A1, A2, N, B omitt.: увлечет...; A1, B add.: за которыми пойдут бараны человеческого стада; A2, N add.: К ним [N: этим ораторам] примкнут сочувствующие

[2647] A2 add.: так

[2648] N omitt.: И мы... & add.: Это даст нам

[2649] A1, A2, B: нить

[2650] K: репресям

[2651] A1, B: якобы надзору со стороны наших слуг из; A2, N: надзору со стороны наших слуг из числа

[2652] A1, B add.: руками которой мы

[2653] A1, B add.: будто бы

[2654] A2, N omitt.: отделяемся... & add.: Так как

[2655] A2: действует; B add.: лишь

[2656] K, A1, B: [A1 add.: в] таинственности

[2657] A1, A2, N, B: [A1, B add.: и] для [N: ради] говорения

трогать[2659] до появления порыва к деятельности против нас[2660], а лишь **введем в их среду наблюдательные элементы** (d)... Но[2661] надо не забывать[2662], что престиж власти усиливается, если она обнаруживает[2663] заговоры против себя.[2664]

[2665]**Наш правитель будет охраняться**[2666] только **самой неприметной стражей,** если[2667] необходимо будет его охранять, **потому что не надо допускать**[2668] и[2669] **мысли что**[2670] **против него будет действовать**[2671]

[2658] A2, N: то,

[2659] A2, N: тревожить

[2660] A2, N omitt.: порыва... & add.: с их стороны действия [N: действий]

[2661] A1, A2, N, B omitt.

[2662] A2, N: помнить

[2663] A1, A2, N, B omitt.: усиливается... & add.: умаляется, если она проявляет [N: обнаруживает] на показ публики [A2, N: часто]

[2664] A1, A2, N, B add.: В этом есть признание [B: допущение мысли о возможности] своей [A2: своего бессилия... или, хуже того; N omitt.: есть признание... & add.: заключена презумпция бессилия, или, что еще хуже,] неправоты, дающей повод [B add.: к] неудовольствиям, и- бессилию [A2 omitt.: дающей повод...; B: слабости]. Вам известно, что мы излагали [A2, N: разбили; B: унизили] престиж царствующих гоев, частыми покушениями [A2: тем, что, покушаясь часто] на них со стороны наших [A2, N: их жизнь через своих] агентов, слепых баранов [A2, N add.: нашего стада], которых было [N omitt.] легко несколькими либеральными фразами двинуть на всякие преступления с политическим престижом, что [N: двинуть на преступления, лишь бы они имели политическую окраску] мы вынудили и подговорили гоев [B: гойских; A2, N omitt.: и подговорили гоев]-правителей признать свое бессилие открытыми мерами охраны [N omitt.: открытыми мерами... & add.: в объявлении открытых мер охраны и этим погубим престиж власти]

[2665] B omitt.: Наш правитель usque ad: ... страны. (2691)

[2666] K: охраниться

[2667] A1 add.: уже

[2668] A2, N omitt:: если необходимо...& add.: мы не допустим

[2669] A1 omitt.

[2670] A2: чтобы

[2671] A1, A2, N omitt.: будет...& add.: существует [A2: существовала; N: могла существовать] такая

крамола (e), да еще такая[2672], с которой он сладить не может[2673] и вынужден от нее прятаться. Если[2674] мы, подобно гоям[2675], допустили[2676] подобную[2677] мысль, то[2678] подписали бы этим[2679] приговор коль[2680] не ему[2681], то его династии в недалеком будущем[2682]. Наш правитель будет[2683] пользоваться своею[2684] властью[2685] только для блага[2686] народов[2687], а отнюдь не для своих или династических выгод. При такой окраске его деятельности он, конечно, будет пользоваться уважением, доверием народов, которые будут его ограждать, с сознанием, что от него зависит[2688] благополучие каждого гражданина[2689], ибо от него[2690] будет зависеть порядок общественного строя, мир и благоденствие страны[2691].

[2672] A2, N omitt.: да еще...

[2673] A2, N omitt.: сладить... & add.: не в силах бороться

[2674] A2, N add.: бы

[2675] A2, N omitt.: подобно... & add.: как это делали [N add.: и делают] гои

[2676] A1 add.: бы

[2677] A2, N: эту

[2678] A2, N add.: тем самым мы

[2679] A2, N omitt.

[2680] A1, A2, N: если

[2681] N add.: самому

[2682] A1 add.: ибо каждый, с долей храбрости, мог бы расчитывать настигнуть прятающегося.; N add.: По строго соблюдаемой внешности

[2683] A1 add.: повидимому; A2 add.: кроме того

[2684] A1: своей

[2685] A2 add.: повидимому

[2686] A2, N: пользы

[2687] N: народа

[2688] A2, N omitt.: При такой... & add.: Поэтому, [N add.: при соблюдении этого декорума] власть будет уважаться и ограждаться [N add.: самими подданными], ее будут боготворить сознавая [N: в сознании], что с ней связано

[2689] A2, N add.: государства

[2690] A2, N: нее

[2691] A2, N omitt.: мир и... & add.: Если [N omitt.] охранять царя открыто, то [N omitt.] значит признать слабость организации его сил [N: силы]

[2692]**Наш правитель будет**[2693] **всегда в народе**[2694] **окружен**[2695] **толпой как бы любопытных, мужчин и женщин**[2696] **которые займут**[2697] **первые ряды около**[2698] **него, по виду**[2699] **случайно, а сдерживать будут**[2700] **ряды остальных** (f)[2701] **якобы**[2702] **из уважения к порядку**[2703]. Для своего существования ореол власти требует, чтобы каждый человек[2704] мог сказать: «**Кабы**[2705] **знал**[2706] **об этом**[2707] **сам**[2708] **царь**» или «**царь об этом узнает** (g) **сам**[2709]»...

[2692]   K omitt.: Наш правитель usque ad: узнает сам (2709)

[2693]   A2 add.: только

[2694]   A1, B omitt.: всегда... & add.: в случаях не полной безопасности; A2 omitt.: в народе

[2695]   A1, B add.: нами, якобы

[2696]   A1, A2, B omitt.: толпой как бы... & add.: любопытными, мужчинами и женщинами

[2697]   A1, B omitt.: которые... & add.: якобы случайно попадающими в

[2698]   A1, B: близ

[2699]   A2 omitt.: около... & add.: как бы

[2700]   A1, B omitt.: по виду... & add.: сдержавающие

[2701]   B omitt.

[2702]   A2 omitt.

[2703]   A1, A2, N, B add.: показывая [A2: который (N: Это) посеет] пример сдержанности, требуя того же и от [N omitt.: требуя... & add.: и в] других. Если же среди публики [A2: народа; N: в народе; B omitt.: среди...] окажется проситель [A2, N add.: старащийся подать свое (N omitt.) прощение, пробиваясь через ряды,] то [A2, N add.: первые ряды; B add.: они] обязаны ему помочь передать просьбу [A2, N omitt.: обязаны... & add.: должны принять это прошение; B: прошение], но якобы, чтобы не нарушить ряды, они должны взять это прошение из рук просителя [A2, N omitt.: но якобы...] и на глазах его [A2, N: просителя] передать таковое по назначению. Это необходимо для того, чтобы подданные знали, что [A2, N omitt.: таковое... & add.: его правителю, чтобы все знали, что подаваемое доходит до назначения (N: по назначению), что, следовательно] существует контроль царствующего [A2, N: самого правителя]

[2704]   A2, N: народ

[2705]   A1: Если бы; A2: Как бы; N: Когда бы

[2706]   A1: узнал

[2707]   A2: это

Мы будем беспошадны к политическим преступникам[2710], ибо **если допустить побудительные причины**[2711] **к простым преступлениям**[2712], **то нет извинения для преступлений против власти** (h)[2713]. Мы снимем[2714]

[2708]   N omitt.

[2709]   A1, A2, N omitt. & add.: С оффициальной охраной [N: учреждением официальной охраны] исчезает мистический престиж власти, ибо [A1 omitt.] каждый при [N add.: наличности известной] смелости чувствует [N: считатет] себя хозяином ее судьбы [A2 omitt.; N: над ней], крамольники чувствуют [N: крамольник сознает] свою силу и [A2 omitt.; A2, N add.: при случае] караулят [N: караулит] момент покуситься на недоверяющую себе власть [A2: нее; N: для покушения на власть...]; A1, A2, N, B add.: Понятно [A2, N omitt.] для гоев мы проповедывали иное, что [A2, N, B: но за то; N add.: же и; B: теперь] нам видно [A2, N: можем видеть пример] до чего [B add: мы] их довели [A2: привели] меры открытой охраны [B: своими советами].

[2710]   A2, N omitt.: Мы будем... & add.: У нас преступники будут арестованы как только проявятся виновными [N omitt.: как только... & add.: при первом более или менее обоснованном подозрении]: нельзя из боязни могущей быть [N: произойти] ошибки представлять [N: предоставлять] возможность побега при подозрении [N: подозреваемым] в политическом проступке [N: или преступлении], в котором [N: к которым] мы будем по истине беспошадны [N: беспошадными]

[2711]   A1 omitt.: допустить... & add.: и можно отнести причины побуждившие их; A2, N omitt.: ибо; N add.: еще можно, с известной натяжкой

[2712]   N: рассмотрение побудительных причин в простых преступлениях

[2713]   A1, A2, N, B omitt.: преступлений... & add.: заниятия [N: лиц занимающихся] вопросами, в которых никто, кроме правительства, ничего понять не может. [A1, B add.: Я говорю о нашем Правительстве, ибо гоевские правления ничего не смыслят в двигательных причинах...; A2, N add.: Да и правительства-то не все понимают ее (N: истинную политику); A2 add.: **XIX**; N add.: **Еще протокол**] Но, [A2, N omitt.] если мы не будем допускать [A2, N: допустим] самостоятельного занятия вопросами политики [A2, N: политикой], то напротив, будем поощрять [N add.: всякие] проекты [A2, N: петиции] и доклады по вопросам общественного быта и улучшения [B: улучшений] его [A2, N add.: с предложениями на усмотрение правительства всяких проектов для улучшения народного быта], потому что это нам [A2 add.: всегда] будет открыват; [A2, N:

престиж доблести с политического преступления. Для этого[2715] **мы посадим**[2716] **политического преступника**[2717] **рядом с ворами, с убийцами** (i)[2718] и всякими другими[2719] отвратительными и грязными преступниками[2720], на скамьи[2721] подсудимых. Тогда **общественное мнение сольет в своем представлении**[2722] **политическое**[2723]

откроет] недостатки строя или [A2, N add.: же] фантазии наших подданных. На все поданное [A2, N: которые] для нашего усмотрения [A2, N omitt.: для...], мы будем отвечать, коль не [A2 omitt.; N.: или] исполнением, то [A2, N: или] толковым опровержением, имеющим доказать [A2: которые бы доказали; N: которое доказало] докладчику его [A2, N: разсуждающего неправильно] близорукость... При нашем режиме всякое [A2, N omitt.] крамольничество будет лишь лаем [A2, N: есть не что (N: ничто) иное, как лай] моськи на слона, [B add.: раз] наше правление будет [B omitt.; A2, N: для правительства] хорошо организовано [A2, N: организованного] не с полицейской, а с общественной стороны [A2: части],- полицейские меры ожесточают и вызывают усиление крамолы, а общественные репрессии искореняют их [A2, N omitt.: полицейские меры...]. Моська лает на слона, пока не сознает [A2, N: не сознавая] его силы и назначения, поэтому [A2, N: значения, то] ее [N omitt.] только стоит [A2: на первых порах] примерно оповестить о том и о другом [N: на добром примере показать значение того и другого], чтобы она [A2, N add.: тогда она перестанет (N: как моськи перестанут) лаять (N add.: a), станет (N: станут) завиляла] [A2, N: вилять] хвостом и спряталась бы в кусты [A2, N omitt.: и спряталась...] как только [A2: когда] завидит [N: завидят] слона...

[2714] A2, N: Чтобы снять

[2715] A2, N omitt.: Для...

[2716] K, B: посадили

[2717] A1, B: политических преступников; A2, N omitt.: политиуческого...; A2 add.: таковой; N add.: его

[2718] A2, N omitt.: рядом... & add.: на ряду с воровством, убийством

[2719] A1, B omitt.

[2720] A2, N omitt.: всякими... & add.: всяким отвратительным и грязным преступлением

[2721] A2, N: скамью

[2722] A1, A2, B: воображении

[2723] A2: это

преступление[2724] с обыкновенным преступлением[2725] и заклеймит[2726] его одинаковым презрением (j). Мы старались[2727], чтобы[2728] гои не узрели такой способ[2729] борьбы с крамолою[2730]. Поэтому[2731] через прессу[2732] и в речах,[2733] мы старались рекламировать идею о необходимости отдельных, примерных наказаний крамольников, а одновременно[2734] рекламировали мученичество якобы за общее благо принятое[2735] на себя[2736]... Это увеличивало[2737] число[2738] баранов в нашем инвентаре[2739].

QUOTATIONS FROM JOLY'S *DIALOGUE*

a   «...il y aura des complots simulés»

b   «...elles permettent (...) des perquisitions»

c   «...d'amour de l'art»

d   «...ma police soit parsemée dans tous les rangs de la société»

[2724] N omitt.: политическое... & add.: этот разряд преступлений

[2725] A1, A2, N, B omitt.: обыкновенным...; A1, A2, B add.: позорным покушением простого преступления; N add.: позором всякого другого

[2726] A1, A2, B: оклеймит

[2727] A2, N add.: и [N add.: надеюсь] достигли того

[2728] A2, N: что

[2729] A2: не поняли способа такой; N: постигли такого способа

[2730] A1, A2, N, B: крамолой

[2731] N: Для этого

[2732] K: пресу

[2733] N add.: косвенно,- в умно составленных учебниках истории,

[2734] A2, N omitt.: старались...

[2735] K: принятыми; N omitt.: за общее... & add.: за идею общего блага крамольниками

[2736] A1, B add.: последними; A2 add.: крамольниками

[2737] A2: увеличило; N: Эта реклама увеличила

[2738] A2, N: контингент

[2739] A1 omitt.: число... & add.: количество цисла; A2, N, B omitt.: баранов...; A1, A2, N, B add.: либералов-мучеников за якобы правду [A2, N omitt.: -мучеников...] и ставило [A2: поставило; N: поставила] тысячи гоев баранов в ряды баранов нашего [N add.: живого] инвентаря [B omitt.: нашего... & add.: наших послушных] рабов [A2 add.: -баранов; N omitt.: рабов]

e   «...du souverain (...) il faut qu'elle soit environnée (...) d'innombrables agents (...) cette milice secrète soit (...) dissimulé pour que le souverain n'ait pas l'air d'avoir peur»

f   «...un prince qui sort dans les rues pouvait avoir l'air d'un simple particulier, qui se promène, sans garde, dans la foule, alors qu'il est environné de deux ou trois mille protecteurs»

g   «...Si le roi le savait (...) Le roi le saura»

h   «celui qui entreprend quelque chose contre le gouvernement est (...) plus coupable que celui qui commet un crime (...) ordinaire»

i   «le journaliste insolent sera confondu (...) avec le simpe larron (...) le conspirateur s'assiéra (...) côté à côté (...) avec le meurtrier»

j   «l'opinion publique (...) finira par confondre les deux genres dans le même mépris»

XIX [2740]

Сегодня[2741] коснемся[2742] **финансовой программы**[2743], которую я отложил к концу[2744] моего[2745] доклада, **как труднейший** (a) и[2746] важнейший[2747] завершительный[2748] пункт наших планов.

[2749]Посдтупая[2750] к этим вопросам[2751], я вам[2752] **напомню, что говорил вам о том, что итог наших действий разрешится вопросом цифр** (b)...

Когда мы воцаримся, наше самодержавное правительство **будет избегать, ради принципа самосохранения, чувствительно обременять массы налогами** (c), ни минуты[2753] не забывая[2754] роль[2755] отца и покровителя, -иудейского патриарха[2756]. Но так как **государственная организация стоит дорого** (d), то все таки[2757] придется[2758] добывать[2759] средства. Поэтому надо[2760] тщательно выработать вопрос равновесия в этом отношении[2761].

[2740] K omitt.; A2: **XX**; A1, N, B: **Еще протокол** [B add.: **(23)**].

[2741] N add.: мы

[2742] A1, A2, B: будем касаться

[2743] K: програмы

[2744] A1, A2, N, B: на конец

[2745] A2, N: своего

[2746] A1, A2, N, B omitt.

[2747] N omitt.

[2748] A1, A2, N, B add.: и решительный

[2749] K omitt.: Поступая к этим вопросам usque ad: цифр

[2750] A2, N: Приступая

[2751] A2: ним

[2752] A2, N omitt.

[2753] A2, N omitt.

[2754] A1, A2, B add.: свою

[2755] N: своей роли

[2756] A2, N omitt.

[2757] A1, A2, N, B: же

[2758] A1, B: надо; A2: нужно

[2759] A2, N omitt. придется... & add.: нужно [N: необходимо] получить нужные на это [N: для этого]

[2760] A2, N: надобно [A2 omitt.] особенно

[2761] A1, A2, N, B: предмете

[2762]Наше Правление, в котором **Царствующий**[2763] **будет иметь легальную фикцию принадлежности Ему всего, что находится в Его государстве** (что легко будет провести на деле[2764]), **всякое изъятие сумм будет только** (e) регулировать[2765] их обращение[2766] в государстве.

[2767]Налоги[2768] лучше всего собирать в виде проценты с собственности[2769]. Богатые должны сознавать, что их прямая[2770] обязанность предоставить часть своих излишков на общее государственное[2771] пользование, которое им служит гарантией безопасного[2772] владения[2773] остальным имуществом[2774] и права[2775] наживы,[2776] -честной, в те времена[2777], ибо контроль над имуществом необходимый для взимания податей[2778], устранит грабежи на законном основании[2779]. Эта социальная[2780] реформа должна идти сверх[2781], чтобы

[2762] K omitt.: Наше Правление usque ad: в государстве.

[2763] A2, N: царь

[2764] A2, N omitt: будет... & add.: перевести на дело; A2 add.: то

[2765] A2: регулирование; N omitt.: всякое... & add.: может прибегнуть к законному изъятию всяких сумм для регулирования

[2766] A2, N: обращения

[2767] A1, A2, N: Из этого следует, что; B omitt.: Налоги usque ad: строя (2806).

[2768] A2, N: покрытие налогов

[2769] N omitt.: собирать... & add.: производить; A1, A2, N omitt.: в виде проценты... & add.: с возрастающего [N: прогрессивного] % [A2, N: налога] на собственность, таким образом подати можно будет собрать без раззорения и стеснения [A2, N: будут уплачиваться без стеснения или разорения в соразмерном % владения]

[2770] A2, N omitt.

[2771] A1, A2, N: общегосударственное

[2772] A2 omitt.: служит...; N omitt.: которое... & add.: так как государство им; A2, N add.: гарантирует безопасность

[2773] A1: на безопасное владение

[2774] A1 add.: своим

[2775] A1, A2, N: право честной

[2776] N add.: говорю-

[2777] A2, N omitt.: в те времена

[2778] A1: податных; A2, N omitt.: необходимый...

[2779] A2 add.: и

[2780] A1: специальная

ее не вызвали[2782] снизу...[2783] Она необходима как залог мира и благоденствия[2784] народов[2785]. Налог на[2786] бедняка есть семя революций[2787] и служит к ущербу государства[2788]. Налог на капиталы[2789] уменьшит рост богатств[2790] в частных руках, в которые[2791] ныне мы их стянули для противовеса правительственной силе гоев, их[2792] государственным финансам. Но[2793] во время нашего царства такое положение вещей будет более чем нежелатеьно[2794]. Налог, увеличивающийся в процентном отношении к капиталу, принес[2795] гораздо[2796] больший доход, чем нынешный поголовный или цензовый, который полезен для нас, ибо он дает повод нам к возбуждению неудовольствия[2797] против правительств и волнению[2798] толпы.[2799]

[2781] A1, A2: сверху

[2782] A1: вынудили

[2783] A2, N omitt.: чтобы... & add.: ибо ей наступает время-

[2784] A1: благоденствие

[2785] A2, N omitt.: и благоденствия...

[2786] A2, N: с

[2787] A2, N: революции

[2788] A1, A2, N add.: теряющего крупное за погоней на мелкоту... [N: в погоне за мелочью (A2: мелкотой...). Независимо от этого (A2: Кроме того),]

[2789] A2, N: с капиталистов

[2790] N: богатства

[2791] A1, A2, N: которых

[2792] A2, N omitt.

[2793] A1 omitt.

[2794] A2, N omitt.: Но во время...

[2795] A1: принесет

[2796] A2, N: даст много

[2797] A1: неудовольствий

[2798] A: волнения

[2799] A2, N omitt.: ибо... & add.: теперь [A2 omitt.] только для возбуждения неудовольствий и волнений среди гоев. A1, A2, N add.: Сила, на которую мы будем [A2, N: наш царь будет] опираться, состоит в равновесии и гарантии мира, ради которых капиталисты должны будут поступиться [A2, N: надо (N: необходимо), чтобы капиталисты поступились] долей своего дохода для правильности хода [A2, N: своих доходов, ради безопасности действия] государственной машины.

Государственные нужды должны оплачивать те, которым эти платежи[2800] не в тягость и[2801] с которых есть что[2802] взять... Такая мера уничтожит еще антагонизм классов,[2803] ненависть бедняка к богачу, в котором[2804] бедняк будет усматривать необходимую[2805] поддержку финансам государства, т. е. нужную функцию машины социального строя[2806]. Чтобы интеллигентные[2807] плательщики не слишком горевали о новых платежах, на них возложенных[2808], им **будут**[2809] **давать подробные отчеты в них** (f)[2810], за исключением тайных[2811] сумм, которые будут употребены[2812] на нужды трона и[2813] учреждений. Царствующие не будут[2814] иметь своих[2815] имуществ, раз все, что в государстве, составляет их[2816] достояние, а то одно противоречило бы[2817] другому: факт обладанья специальными собственными средствами отрицал бы[2818] право владения[2819] всем[2820].

2800   A2, N: это

2801   A1 omitt.

2802   A1 add.: и легко

2803   К: класов; A2, N omitt.: еще...

2804   A1: этой мере

2805   A2, N omitt.: бедняк... & add.: он увидит нужную финансовую

2806   A1: быта; A2, N omitt.: финансам... & add.: для государства, -увидит в нем устроителя мира и благоденствия, раз [N: так как] он [N add.: будет видеть, что им] уплачивает [N: уплачиваются] нужные для [N add.: них] достижения их [N omitt.] средства.

2807   К: интелегентные

2808   A2, N omitt.: на них...

2809   N add.: в назначении этих платежей

2810   A2, N omitt.: в них

2811   N: конечно, таких

2812   A1, A2, B: целиком [B: огулом; A2 omitt.] раздроблены [N: распределены]

2813   N add.: административных

2814   A2, N: Царствующий не будет

2815   B omitt.

2816   A2, N: есть [N: представляет собою] его

2817   A1: противоречит

2818   A1, A2, N, B omitt.: omitt.: обладанья... & add.: собственных сумм [N: средтсв] уничтожил бы де-факто

2819   A2, N add.: на [A2 add.: всеобщее] владение

²⁸²¹Налоги будут взиматься следующим образом:²⁸²² купля, получение денег или наследства²⁸²³, будут²⁸²⁴ оплачиваться марочным сбором, прогрессивным²⁸²⁵, по расчету сумм.²⁸²⁶ Фондовая касса государства²⁸²⁷

2820 A2, N omitt.; A1, A2, N add.: Но [N omitt.] кроме царя и признанного наследника Его, все царские родные [A2, N omitt.: кроме... & add.: родственники его (N: царствующего), кроме (N add.: его) наследников, которые тоже на попечении (N: также содержатся на средства) государства,] должны становиться в рядыı [N add.: государсвтенных] служащих для защиты трона [A2, N omitt.: для...] и [A2, N: или] трудиться [N add.: для того], чтобы получить права [A2, N: право] собственности: привилегия [A1, N: привиллегия] царской крови не должна служить поводом [A2, N omitt.] для хищения государственной казны.

2821 В omitt: Налоги будут usque ad: по расчету сумм (2826).

2822 A2, N omitt.: Налоги будут...

2823 A1: наследство

2824 A2: будет

2825 К: прогресивным

2826 A2, N omitt.: по расчету...; A1, A2, N add.: Незаявленная [A2, N add.: этим сбором], непременно именная передача собственности, денежной и [A2, N: или] другой, оставит на прежнем владельце [A2: составит за прежним владельцем; N: возложит на прежнего владельца] платеж % налога, за время считающегося [A2 omitt.] нахождения у него [N.: от передачи] этих сумм [N add.: до обнаружения уклонения от заявления о передаче]. Передаточные росписки [A2: расписки] должны будут [A2, N omitt.] еженедельно представляться местному казначейству или указанному месту [A2, N: в местное казначейство], с обозначением имени, фамилии, отчества, [A2, N add.: и] постоянного местажительства [N: местожительства] бывшего и нового владельца имущества. Такая [A2, N.: Эта] именная передача собственности будет [A2, N omitt.: собственности... & add.: должна] начинаться с определенной суммы, превывающей обыкновенные расходы купли и продажи [N.: по купле и продаже] необходимого, которые будут оплачиваться [A2 add.: лишь] марочным сбором, определенным [A2, N add.: определенного %] с единицы. Считайте [A2: Сосчитайте; N: Рассчитайте-ка], во сколько раз такие налоги превысят нынешние сборы с бедноты и мелкоты, жертв поголовной системы [A2, N omitt.: превысят... & add.: покроют доходы гоевских государств]

должна[2828] содержать определенный комплект запасных сумм, а **все**[2829], **что будет собрано сверх того**[2830], **должно обязательно**[2831] **возвращаться** (g) в обращение; на эти суммы будут устраиваться общественные работы. Работы создаваемые государством[2832] крепко привяжут[2833] рабочий класс[2834] к государственным интересам.[2835] Деньги существуют для обращения и всякий застой их губительно отзывается на ходе государственного механизма, для которого они служат «смазывающим средством» застой «смазки» может остановить правильный ход этого механизма. Замена части обменных[2836] знаков[2837] процентными бумагами произвела[2838] такой застой,[2839] последствия которого[2840] стали уже весьма[2841] заметны. Мы учредим[2842] отчетный двор, в котором[2843] правитель во всякое время найдет полный отчет государственных

2827   B add.: государства

2828   A2, N add.: будет

2829   A2, N add.: то

2830   N: этого комплекта

2831   N: будет

2832   A1, A2, N, B omitt.: Работы... & add.: Исхождение [N: Инициатива; A2, N add.: таких] работ [N add.: исходящая] из государственного источника [N: государственных источников]

2833   A1, A2, N, B: привяжет

2834   K: клас

2835   A1, A2, N, B add.: и к царствующим- олицетворяющим эти интересы [A2, N omitt.: олицетворяющим...]. Из этих же сумм часть должна будет пойти [A2, N: omitt.: должна... & add. выделена; B: пойдти] на премии изобретательности и производства, потому что [N: Отнюдь] не следует сверх определенных сумм [N add.: и] (широко рассчитанных) задерживать хотя бы единицу в государственных кассах, ибо

2836   B: денежных

2837   A1, A2, N: обменного знака; B add.: находящихся в обращении

2838   B add.: уже

2839   A2 add.: и

2840   A1, B: этого застоя; A2, N: этого обстоятельства

2841   A2, N omitt.: стали... & add.: теперь уже достаточно

2842   N: тоже нами будет установлен

2843   N: и в нем

приходов и расходов[2844], за исключением текущего, еще не составленного месячного отчета или[2845] предыдущего, еще не доставленного. Единственное лицо, которому не выгодно[2846] грабить государственные кассы[2847], это их собственник, правитель[2848], вот почему только[2849] его контроль может устранить[2850] утраты или растраты.[2851] Экономические кризисы были созданы[2852] нами[2853] для гоев, именно путем извлечения[2854] денег из обращения. Громадные капиталы собирались[2855], извлекая деньги из государств, которые[2856]

[2844] B omitt.: и расходов

[2845] A2, N: и

[2846] A2, N: не будет интереса

[2847] K: касы

[2848] A1: собственнику, правителю

[2849] A2, N omitt.

[2850] A2, N omitt.: может... & add.: устранит возможность

[2851] A1, A2, N, B add.: Представительство и этикет [A2, N: в приемах ради этикета], отнимающее драгоценное время у правительства [A2, N, B: правителя] и отвлекающие его внимание от более серьезного дела [A2, N omitt.: и отвлекающие...], будут нами упразднены [A2, N: будет упразднено (N add.: для того,) чтобы], Наш [A2, N omitt.] правитель ни минуты не оторветя [B: оторвет] от контроля и своей обязанности ясно соображать [A2, N omitt.: ни минуты... & add.: имел время на контроль и соображение (N: соображения)], чего сделать нельзя при постоянной заботе о соблюдении этикета и представительства, превращающих царствующух в манекенов [A2, N omitt.: чего сделать...]. Наш правитель не будет раздроблять свою мощь на поручения [A2, N: Тогда его мощь не будет уже раздроблена на поручение] временщикам [N: временщиков; A2, N add.: окружающих для блеска и пышности престол и], не заинтересованным [N, B: заинтересованных] в общегосударственных [A2: вообще в государственных] интересах, а скорее [A2: больше] в своих собственных [N: только в своих, а не в общегосударственных интересах]...

[2852] A1, B: подстроены; A2, N: произведены

[2853] A1, B omitt.

[2854] A1, A2, N, B omitt.: именно... & add.: ничем иным, как извлечением

[2855] A2, N: застаивались

[2856] N add.: к ним же и

были вынуждены[2857], благодаря этому, занимать у самых себя[2858]. Эти займы[2859] удручили[2860] финансы государств платежами процентов и закрепостили их[2861]. Нынешний выпуск денег[2862] не соответствует поголовной потребности, а потому не может удовлетворить всем рабочим нуждам. Выпуск денег в наше время будет[2863] согласоваться с приростом человечества[2864], причем со дня рождения ребенок будет считаться потребителем денег наравне со взрослыми, но за то умершие дадут повод к сокращению их[2865] на сумму, точно высчитанную[2866] только[2867] человеческой потребностью на[2868] них, соответственно с дороговизной[2869] времени, по которой будут высчитаны индивидуальные потребности[2870] для всего человечества, во всем мире[2871]. Вы знаете, что золотая валюта была гибелью для принявших ее государств именно потому, что[2872] она сокращала[2873] количество денег в обращении, тем

[2857]   A1, A2, B omitt.: которые... & add.: которых мы [A2: и] вынудили

[2858]   A1, A2, B omitt.: самых...; B add.: нас; A2, N omitt.: благодаря...; N add.: обратиться за займами

[2859]   A2: тайны

[2860]   N: отяготили

[2861]   A1, A2, N, B add.: тем самым нашим [A2, N: названным] капиталом [N: капиталам]. Концентрация промышленности из рук кустарей в руки [N: руках] капиталистов, высосала все народные соки и [A2, N, B: а] затем и государственные.

[2862]   A2 add.: вообще

[2863]   A2, N omitt.: в наше... & add.: должен

[2864]   A2, N: населения

[2865]   A1, B: таковых

[2866]   B: высчитанной

[2867]   B omitt.

[2868]   B: потребности в

[2869]   B: оценкою

[2870]   B add.: выпуска. Такой пересмотр выпуска денег есть существенный вопрос

[2871]   A2, N omitt.: ребенок... & add.: необходимо считать и детей, как их потребителей. Пересмотр выпуска есть существенный вопрос для всего мира.

[2872]   A2, N omitt.: именно... & add.: ибо

[2873]   B: сократила

более, что золотое обращение[2874] дало[2875] нам возможность выбрать золото и[2876] еще больше[2877] сократить это обращение[2878] денег[2879]... У нас будет иной порядок, мы введем валюту[2880] (стоимость[2881] рабочей силы), будь она деревянная или бумажная, это безразлично, ибо обменный знак не должен быть ценностью, он должен только отвечать[2882] стоимости нормальных, а не фантастических потребностей людей[2883].

[2884]Расчетами по прибавлению выпускных денег на рождающиеся головы и убавление их в зависимости от числа умерших[2885] будет

[2874]   A1 add.: введенное тоже

[2875]   B omitt.: тем более... & add.: а выпуск золота в обращение дал

[2876]   B add.: этим

[2877]   A omitt.; B: более

[2878]   B omitt.: это обращение... & add.: количество обращающихся

[2879]   A2, N omitt.: сокращала количество... & add.: тем более не могла удовлетворить потреблению денег обращением [N omitt.] что мы изъяли, сколько было можно [N: возможно], золото из обращения.

[2880]   A2, N omitt.: будет иной... & add.: должна быть введена валюта

[2881]   A2, N: стоимости

[2882]   A1: быть потребителем; B: быть показателем

[2883]   A2, N omitt.: это безразлично... & add.: то-есть [N: Мы произведем] выпуск денег по нормальным потребностям каждого подданного, прибавляя его количество с каждым родившимся человеком, убавляя его с каждым умершим; A1, B add.: Представляя из себя ценность, деньги вынуждают людей изнемогать от лишних, не необходимых трудов [B: в непроизводительных трудах], для приобретения этой ценности от небольшой группы капиталистов, собравшей ее в свои руки для того, чтобы ею угнетать и закрепощать себе остальных людей; A1 add.: мы же будем править открыто, а потому нам необходимо будет, чтобы частные лица могли управлять другими, хотя бы деньгами: но этот вопрос я вам подробно опишу в конце доклада об общих наших проектах и планах.

[2884]   B omitt.: Расчетами usque ad: в каждом городе и деревне (2887)

[2885]   A2, N omitt.: по прибавлению...

заведывать каждый[2886] округ по докладам статистиков в каждом городе и деревне[2887].

[2888]Реформы[2889] гоевских финансовых оснований[2890] мы облечем в такие формы, что они никого не встревожат. Мы укажем на необходимость[2891] реформ, вследствие того беспорядочного сумбура, до которого их довели якобы гои[2892]... Мы укажем на то, что их финансовые распорядки[2893] дошли до того, что у них нет точного бюджета... **Сначала они назначают простой бюджет**[2894], который растет из года в год по следующей причине. Этот **бюджет**, видите ли, **дотягивается**[2895] **только до половины года; затем**[2896] требуют **поправочный**[2897] **бюджет**, который растрачивают через три месяца,

---

[2886] A2, N add.: департамент [N add.: французское административное деление], каждый

[2887] A2, N omitt.: по докладам... ; A1, A2, N add.: Чтобы не было задержек в выдачах сумм [A2, N: в выдаче денег] на государственные нужды, как они, так и время их выдачи будут определяться Правителем, потому что Он лучше всех будет ведать состояния касс [A2, N omitt. как они... & add.: суммы и срок выдачи их будут определяться указом правителя: этим устранится протекторат министерства финансов одним учреждениям (N: над одними учреждениями) в ущерб другим]. Бюджеты получек [N: доходов] и расходы для Него [A2, N omitt.] будут вестись рядом, чтобы они не затемнялись вдали друг от друга

[2888] K omitt.: Реформы usque ad: для себя (2950)

[2889] В: Когда-же мы станем управлять явно, то..... реформу; A2, N add.: проэктированные нами

[2890] N omitt.: финансовых... & add.: учреждений и принципов

[2891] A1 add.: таких

[2892] A1 add.: же; A2, N omitt.: их довели... & add.: дошли финансовые безпорядки у гоев

[2893] A1: беспорядки

[2894] A2, N omitt.: Мы укажем... & add.: из коих [N omitt.] первый непорядок [N add.: укажем мы,] состоит в том, что у них начинают с назначения простого бюджета

[2895] A2, N omitt.: видите ли... & add.: дотягивают

[2896] A2: тогда

[2897] A1, В omitt.: затем... ; A1, В add.: тогда назначается; В add.: добавочный

после чего просят[2898] **дополнительный**[2899] **бюджет, и все это оканчивается ликвидационным бюджетом** (h)... А так как бюджет[2900] следующего года назначается согласно сумме[2901] общего подсчета, то ежегодное увеличение[2902] нормы простирает[2903] до[2904] 50% в год, вследствие чего[2905] **через десять лет утраивается**[2906] **годовой бюджет** (i)... Такими то[2907] приемами, допущенными[2908] беспечностью гоевских государств, опустели их кассы, затем наступивший период займов добрал остатки и привел их[2909] к банкротству. Вы[2910] понимаете, что такое хозяйство, внушенное[2911] нами гоям, не может продолжаться[2912] нами... Всякий заем ведь[2913] доказывает государственную немощь и непонимание государственных прав, а между тем займы, как Дамоклов меч, висят над головою[2914] правителей, которые[2915], вместо того, чтобы брать у своих поданных на особые нужды временным налогом, идут[2916] с протянутой рукою просить милостыни[2917] у наших банкиров... Внешние

[2898]   A1, B: дают

[2899]   A2: пополнительный

[2900]   A1: бюджета

[2901]   A: сумм

[2902]   A1, A2, N omitt.: ежегодное... & add.: ежегодно [A2, N: ежегодный] отход от [A2 omitt.]

[2903]   A1: норм простирается

[2904]   A2, N: простирается на

[2905]   A1, A2, N omitt.: вследствие... & add.: отчего

[2906]   A1, A2: устраивается

[2907]   A1 omitt.

[2908]   N omitt.: Такими... & add.: Благодаря таким приемам, допущенным

[2909]   A2 add.: всех; N: все государства гоев

[2910]   A2, N add.: отлично

[2911]   A2: выделенное

[2912]   N: быть ведено

[2913]   A2, N omitt.

[2914]   B: со стороны тех

[2915]   A1: Правителя, который

[2916]   A1: идет; A2, N add.: временным налогом; B: не умеют удовлетворить потребности в деньгах иначе, как только обращаясь

[2917]   A2, N : милостыню

займы суть пиявки, которых отнять[2918] от государственного корпуса[2919] нельзя, пока их не отбросят сами государства, а[2920] последние[2921] не отрывают, а все присаживают[2922] их к себе увеличивая дань, платимую сказанным[2923] банкирам... Поэтому[2924] должны неизбежно свалиться от собственного[2925] кровопускания...

Разберем[2926], **что такое**[2927] заем (j), да еще внешний...

Это есть[2928] **выпуск правительственных векселей, заключающих**[2929] **обязательство уплачивать обусловленный рост на капитал**[2930]**... Если заем пятипроцентный**[2931]**, то через двадцать лет государство** понапрасно[2932] **выплачивает процентную сумму, равно всей сумме займа**[2933]**, в сорок лет оно выплачивает двойную сумму, а**[2934] **в шестьдесят лет**[2935]**- тройную,**[2936] **долг же остается все таким непокрытым долгом** (k), как и был[2937]... Из этого расчета очевидно[2938], что при поголовной форме налога, государство черпает последние

[2918]   B: которые не отпадут

[2919]   N: тела; A2, N add.: никак

[2920]   B: но; A2, N add.: пока они сами не отпадут, или государство [N add.: само] их не сбросит; но эти

[2921]   N: гоевские государства

[2922]   N add.: а все продолжают их присаживать

[2923]   B: нашим

[2924]   A2, N: так что они

[2925]   N: погибнуть, истекая от добровольного

[2926]   A2,N: В сущности

[2927]   N: что же иное представляет собою

[2928]   A2 omitt.; N: Заем- это

[2929]   A1, A2, N: содержащих процентное

[2930]   A1: обязательства; A1, A2, N omitt.: уплачивать... & add.: соразмерно сумме заемного капитала

[2931]   A1, A2, N: оплачивается 5%

[2932]   N: напрасно

[2933]   A1, A2, N omitt.: равно... & add.: равную взятому займу

[2934]   N omitt.

[2935]   A1, A2, N omitt.

[2936]   A1 add.: и т. д.; A2, N add.: а

[2937]   A2, N omitt.: как...

[2938]   A1: видно

гроши из карманов[2939] бедняков, плательщиков податей, чтобы расплачиваться с иностранными богачами, у которых оно взяло деньги[2940] взаймы, вместо того, чтобы собрать на те же[2941] нужды те же гроши, но[2942] без приплаты процентов этой неоплатной[2943] дани[2944]... Пока займы были внутренние[2945], гои только перемешали деньги из карманов бедняков[2946] в карманы богатых[2947] подданных[2948], но когда мы подкупили кого следовало, чтобы они подстроили перенос займов[2949] на внешнюю почву, то все государственные богатства потекли в наши кассы, и все гои стали платить нам дань подданства, незаметно для себя[2950]... Застой денег в наше время[2951] не будет допущен, а потому не будет государственных бумаг[2952], чтобы проценты не поедали государственную[2953] мощь в пользу пиявок дармоедов[2954]. Выпуск[2955]

[2939] N omitt.: из карманов

[2940] A1 add.: в

[2941] A2, N omitt.: те же & add.: свои

[2942] A1, A2, N omitt.

[2943] A1: неиссякаемой

[2944] A2, N omitt.: приплаты... & add.: процентных приплат

[2945] A1: внутренними

[2946] A2, N: кармана бедняка

[2947] A1 add.: своих же

[2948] A2, N omitt.: богатых... & add.: богачей

[2949] A2, N omitt.: они подстроили... & add.: перевести займы

[2950] A2, N omitt.: незаметно...; A1, A2, N, B add.: Если легкомыслие царствующих гоев, по отношению [N, B: в отношении] государственных дел, и продажность их [N, B omitt.] министров или непонимание их [N, B omitt.] в финансовых вопросах, было причиной задолжания вцех стран [A2, N, B omitt. было... & add.: других правящих лиц задолжили свои страны (B: закабалили все народы нам)] нашим кассам неоплатными долгами, и поставило [B: поставили] все финансовые вопросы в зависимость от нашего руководства- якобы научного... -то надо знать, сколько N: же] это нам стоило труда, времени [A2, B omitt.] и денег...

[2951] A2, N: нами

[2952] A2, N add.: процентных, кроме одной процентной [N: однопроцентной] серии

[2953] A2 add.: народную

[2954] N: отдавали государственной мощи на высласывание пиявкам

процентных[2956] бумаг будет предоставлен только[2957] промышленным компаниям, которым будет не трудно оплачивать[2958] проценты с прибыли[2959]. Государство же прибылей не имеет, ибо[2960] занимает деньги на траты[2961], а не на операции... Промышленные бумаги будут покупаться и правительством, которое таким образом[2962] превратится в заимодавца и будет получать проценты на свои деньги вместо того, чтобы их платить. Таким образом оно может сократить подати на сумму получаемых выгод от покупки процентных бумаг промышленных компаний[2963]. Такая мера еще более послужит[2964] к прекращению застоя денег, тунеядства и лени[2965], которые нам были полезны в гоевском строе, но не могут быть желательны нашему правлению[2966].

Как ясна[2967] продажность, подлость, или[2968] недомыслие чисто животных мозгов гоевских голов[2969], которые не подумали, что когда нибудь их осудит[2970] мир, за то[2971] что[2972] они брали взаймы[2973] у нас, под

[2955] A2, N: Право выпуска

[2956] A1 omitt.

[2957] A2, N: исключительно предоставлено

[2958] A1, B: платящим

[2959] A2, N, B: к прибылей

[2960] A2, N: которые [N: которых] государство не вырабатывает на занятые деньги, подобно этим компаниям, ибо оно

[2961] B: расходы

[2962] A2, N omitt.

[2963] A2, N omitt.: и будет... & add.: из расчета из нынешнего плательщика дани по займам

[2964] B: служит

[2965] A2, N omitt. еще более... & add.: прекратит застой, тунеядство и лень

[2966] A2, N: omitt.: в гоевском... & add.: у [N add.: самостоятельных] гоев, но нежелательны в нашем правлении

[2967] A2, N: ясно

[2968] A1: и; A2, N omitt.: продажность...

[2969] A2, N omitt.: гоевских... & add.: гоев

[2970] A1, B: будет судить

[2971] A1 omitt.: за то; A2, N omitt.: которые не... ; N add.: выразившееся в том

[2972] A2, N add.: когда они

[2973] A1: займы

платежи процентов и учетов, и как будто игнорировали,[2974] что[2975] те же деньги, да еще с приплатой процентов, им придется черпать из своих же[2976] карманов для расплаты с нами[2977]; что, следовательно[2978], проще было[2979] взять[2980] деньги прямо у своих, чем записываться данниками по отношению к нам на[2981] суммы процентных платежей в год[2982]. Но[2983] это же доказывает гениальность нашего человеческого[2984] ума, благодаря которому[2985] мы сумели[2986] так представить и осветить[2987] дело займов в глазах гоев[2988], что они сочли[2989] их выгодными[2990] для себя...

[2991]**Наши финансовые положения**[2992], когда время придет их толковать[2993], **под освещением вековых опытов**, проделанных[2994] нами с[2995] гоевскими государствами, **будут отличаться ясностью и определенностью**,[2996] покажут[2997] пользу наших нововведений... **Они**

[2974] A2, N, B omitt.: и учетов... & add.: они не подумали [N, B: думали]

[2975] A2, N add.: все равно

[2976] A2, N add.: государственных

[2977] N: ними

[2978] N omitt.

[2979] A2 omitt.

[2980] A2 add.: нужные

[2981] B add.: ежегодно возрастающие

[2982] B omitt.: в год; A2, N omitt.: чем записываться....

[2983] N omitt.

[2984] A1 omitt.; A2, N: избранного

[2985] A2, N omitt.: благодаря... & add.: [N add.: в том,] что

[2986] A2, N add. им

[2987] A2, N omitt.: и осветить

[2988] A2, N omitt.: в глазах гоев

[2989] A1: считали; A2: увидели; N: усмотрели

[2990] A2, N: выгоду в таковых [N: в них даже]

[2991] K omitt.: Наши финансовые usque ad: герои и богатыри (3009)

[2992] A2, N omitt.: финансовые... & add.: разсчеты, представляемые [N: которые мы представим]

[2993] A2, N omitt.: их толковать

[2994] A1: проделанные

[2995] A2, N: над

[2996] A2 add.: и; N add.: и воочию

[2997] N add.: всем

положат конец тем злоупотреблениям, которыми[2998] мы овладели гоями[2999], но которые не могут быть допущены в нашем царстве. Мы так обставим расчетную[3000] систему, что **ни правитель, ни мельчайший чиновник не будут**[3001] **в состоянии отвести**[3002] **малейшую сумму**[3003] **от ее назначения, или**[3004] **направить ее по другому направлению** (l), как то[3005], которое будет значиться в[3006] определенном плане действий... Без определенного[3007] плана управлять нельзя: шествуя по неопределенной дороге и с неопределенным запасом, погибают в дороге[3008] герои и богатыри[3009]...

Гоевские правители, которых мы когда то посоветовали отвлечь от государственных интересов и[3010] занятий-[3011] приемами, этикетами, увеселениями, были лишь ширмами нашего правления, потому что доклады и[3012] отчеты окружающих[3013] их временщиков составлялись[3014] по внушению[3015] наших агентов[3016], и каждый раз[3017] удовлетворяли недальновидные умы обещаниями, что де[3018] **в будущем предвидятся**

[2998] N: благодаря которым

[2999] N: владели; B: погубили гоев

[3000] N: разсчетную

[3001] N: будет

[3002] A2, N: вывести

[3003] A2, N: малейшей суммы незаметно

[3004] A2: если

[3005] N: кроме того

[3006] A2, N add.: раз

[3007] A2, N add.: же

[3008] A2, N: пути

[3009] N: богатыры

[3010] A2, N omitt.: интересов и

[3011] A2, N add.: представительными

[3012] A2, N omitt.: потому что...

[3013] A2, N: замещающих на поприще дел

[3014] A2, N add.: для них

[3015] A1, B: под внушениями

[3016] K omitt.: и каждый раз usque ad: трудолюбие их народов; A2, N omitt.: по внушению... & add.: нашими агентами

[3017] B add.: успешно

[3018] A2, N omitt.

сбережения (m) и улучшения... С чего сбережения?- с новых[3019] налогов?- могли спросить и не спросили гои[3020], читающие[3021] отчеты и проекты... Вы видите[3022] до чего их довела такая безпечность; до какого финансового расстройства они дошли, не смотря на удивительное трудолюбие их народов...

QUOTATIONS FROM JOLY'S *DIALOGUE*

a   «Il reste (...) le plus difficile de tous les problèmes (...) celui de vos finances»

b   «...je me souviens de vous avoir dit che tout, en définitive, se résoudrait par une question de chiffres»

c   «était astreint, par le principe de son gouvernement, à n'imposer que de faibles tributs à ses sujets»

d   «votre gouvernement coûtera cher»

e   «il y a une fiction légale (...) le souverain est censé posséder tous les biens de ses sujets»

f   «rendre visibles à tous les yeux les éléments de recettes et de dépenses»

g   «les crédits non employés doivent être annulés»

h   «le budget (...) au commancement de l'année (...) Quand on est arrivé à la moitié de l'année (...) on présente (...) un budget rectificatif. Arrive ensuite le budget supplémentaire (...); vient enfin la liquidation»

i   «au bout de dix ans, on peut (...) tripler le budget»

j   «Comment se font les emprunts?»

k   «...des émissions de titres contenant obligation de la part du gouvernement, de servir des rentes proportionnées au capital qui lui est versé. Si l'emprunt est de 5 p.c. (...), au bout de vingt ans a payé une somme égale au capital emprunté; au bout de quarante ans une somme double; au bout de soixante ans une somme triple et, néanmoins, il reste toujours débiteur de la totalité du même capital.»

l   «Notre système de comptabilité, fruit d'une longue expérience, se distingue par la clarté et la certitude de ses procédés. Il met obstacle aux abus et ne donne à personne, depuis le dernier des fonctionnaires jusqu'au chef de l'Etat (...) le moyen de détourner la somme la plus minime de sa destination, ou d'en faire un emploi irrégulier»

[3019]   B omitt.

[3020]   A2, N omitt.

[3021]   A2, N add.: наши

[3022]   A2, N: знаете

m   «L'amortissement va bientôt fonctionner»

XX [3023]

В дополнение[3024] к доложенному[3025] на прошлом собрании, сделаю[3026] еще кое какие пояснения[3027] о внутренних займах. О внешних[3028] говорить не стану[3029], потому что[3030] для нашего[3031] государства не может быть[3032] внешнего займа[3033], как у[3034] гоевских государств, которые[3035] питали[3036] наши кассы[3037] национальными деньгами[3038]... Мы пользовались нерадивостью правителей и продажностью администраторов, чтобы, ссужая гоев[3039] вовсе ненужными им деньгами[3040], получать с них за это[3041] двойные и[3042] тройные[3043] суммы[3044]. Итак[3045], вот подробное изложение хода гоевских[3046]

[3023] К omitt.; А1, N, B: **Еще** [N: **Следующий] протокол** [B add.: **(24)**]; А2: **XXI**.

[3024] А2, N omitt.

[3025] А2, N add.: вам

[3026] А1, А2, N, В: прибавлю

[3027] А2, N omitt.: кое какие... & add.: подробное объяснение

[3028] А2, N add.: же я

[3029] А1: станем; А2, N omitt.: не стану & add.: более не буду

[3030] А2, N add.: они нас питали национальными деньгами гоев,

[3031] А2, N add.: же

[3032] А1, А2, N, В omitt.: может быт & add.: будет

[3033] А1, В omitt.: займа; А2, N omitt. внешнего займа & add.: иностранцев, т. е. чего-либо внешнего

[3034] А1, В omitt.: как у... & add.: [В add.: а] исходя из

[3035] А1: эти деньги; В: они

[3036] А1: питают

[3037] К: касы

[3038] А1: средствами гоев; В add.: гоев; А2, N omitt.: как у гоевских...

[3039] А1: гоям; А2: им; N: гоевским правительствам

[3040] А1, А2: ненужные [А2: государству; N: государств] деньги

[3041] А2, N omitt.: с них...

[3042] А1, А2, N, В omitt.

[3043] А1, В add.: и более; А2, N add.: и бо́льшие

[3044] В add.: на то, что мы ссудили...; А2, N, В add.: но кто [В add.: же] бы мог делать то же [В: проделать что либо подобное] по отношению нас [N, В: к нам]?!

[3045] В omitt.

государственных[3047] займов. Объявляя о совершении такового[3048], правительство открывает[3049] подписку на процентные бумаги, то есть[3050] на свои векселя, а[3051] **чтобы они были доступны почти всем**[3052], **им назначают цену от 100 до 1.000** (a). При этом делается еще[3053] скидка с номинальной цены[3054] для первых подписчиков. **На другой день уже**[3055] **искусственно поднимается цена на них, якобы потому, что де**[3056] все **бросились на покупку** (b)[3057]... **Через несколько дней** говорят, что[3058] **будто бы кассы**[3059] **казначейства переполнены,**[3060] **денег некуда девать** (зачем же было их столько[3061] **брать?**... [c]); подписка якобы **превышает во много раз выпуск займа...** (d) **В последнем заявлении** кроется[3062] **весь эффект**[3063]: **вот де какое доверие к векселям правительства** (e), делающего заем[3064]... Но когда эта вся[3065] комедия сыграна, то[3066] **восстает**[3067] **факт образовавшегося**[3068] **тяжелого пассива** (f)[3069]... Для

[3046] A1 omitt.

[3047] A2, N omitt.: Итак... & add.: Поэтому буду излагать подробности только одних внутренних

[3048] N, B omitt.: совершении такового; N add.: заключении; A2, N add.: такого займа; B add.: займе

[3049] A2, N: государства открывают

[3050] A2 omitt.: то есть

[3051] N: Для того

[3052] A2, N: для всех; A2 add.: они

[3053] N omitt.

[3054] A2: номинала; N omitt.: с номинальной цены

[3055] A2, N omitt.

[3056] K: не; A2, N omitt.

[3057] A1, B add.: их; A2, N omitt.: бросились... & add.: бросаются раскупать их

[3058] A2, N omitt.: говорят, что

[3059] K: касы

[3060] N add.: и

[3061] A2, N omitt.: было столько

[3062] A2, N omitt.: последнем... & add.: этом-то [N omitt.: то]

[3063] K: ефект

[3064] A2, N omitt.: делающего заем

[3065] A2, N omitt.: эта вся

[3066] A1 omitt.

[3067] N: возникает

уплаты процентов приходится[3070] прибегать к новому займу, не погашающему[3071], а лишь увеличивающему[3072] капитальный долг; а[3073] когда кредит истощен, приходится **новыми налогами** (g) покрывать не заем, а только[3074] проценты по нем... Налоги же[3075] эти суть[3076] **пассив, употребляемый на покрытие пассива** (h)[3077]... Далее **наступает время конверсий** (i). Но эти последние[3078] уменьшают платеж процентов[3079], а не покрывают долгов... Кроме того, они не могут быть сделаны без согласия заимодавцев, потому что[3080] при объявлении о[3081] конверсии **предлагается возврат денег тем, которые не согласны**[3082] **конвертировать проценты** (j)[3083] со[3084] своих бумаг[3085]. Но[3086] **если бы все** выразили[3087] несогласие и **потребовали** бы[3088] **свои деньги** назад, **то правительство было бы поймано**[3089] **на** собственную **удочку** (k), протянутую для ловки других...[3090] и оказалось бы несостоятельным[3091]

3068	N add.: и притом весьма
3069	K: пасива
3070	A1: придется
3071	A1, A2, N, B: новым займам непогашающим
3072	A1, A2, N, B: увеличивающим
3073	N: же
3074	A2 add.: все
3075	A2, N omitt.
3076	N omitt.
3077	K: пасив (...) пасива
3078	N omitt.: эти... & add.: они
3079	B omitt.: платеж... & add.: проценты
3080	A2, N omitt.: потому что
3081	A1 omitt.
3082	A2, N: кто не согласен
3083	B: процентов
3084	A1: с
3085	A2, N omitt.: проценты... & add.: свои бумаги
3086	N omitt.
3087	N add.: свое
3088	A2, N, B omitt.
3089	A2, N: правительства были бы пойманы
3090	A2, N omitt.: протянутую...
3091	A2, N: оказались [N: сказались] бы несостоятельными

уплатить все вытребованные[3092] деньги. [3093]По счастью, несведущие в финансовых делах гоевские[3094] **подданные всегда предпочитали** потери на курсе и **уменьшение процентов риску**[3095] **новых помещений** (l) своих[3096] денег, чем и дали[3097] возможность[3098] правительствам не раз **погасить**[3099] **пассив в несколько миллионов** (m). Ныне[3100], при внешних займах[3101], таких штук повторить нельзя: гои знают[3102], что если они объявят конверсию, то[3103] мы потребуем[3104] свои[3105] деньги целиком, а происшедшее от сего[3106] банкротство всего лучше докажет народам, что нет[3107] связи между интересами их правителей и их интересами[3108]: обращаю ваше сугубое внимание на это обстоятельство[3109]. Ныне все внутренние **займы консолидированы так называемыми летучими долгами, т. е.**[3110] **такими, которых срок**[3111] **уплаты более или менее близкий** (n)[3112]: они[3113] состоят из денег, положенных в сберегательные

[3092] A2, N omitt.: все & add.: предложенные; B: затребованные

[3093] A2 add.: Но

[3094] A2: их; N: гоевских правительств

[3095] B: исканию

[3096] A2, N omitt.; B add: для

[3097] B: давали

[3098] N: этим

[3099] A2, N: сбросить [N add.: с себя]; B: сбрасывать

[3100] A2, N: Теперь

[3101] A2, N: долгах

[3102] A2, N omitt.: повторить... & add.: сделать [N: выкинуть] гои уже не могут, зная

[3103] A2, N omitt.: если они...

[3104] A2, B: затребуем

[3105] A2, N: все

[3106] A2, N omitt.: целиком, а... & add.: назад. Таким образом, признанное

[3107] A2, N omitt.: народам... & add.: стране [N: странам] отсутствие

[3108] A2, N omitt.: их правителей... & add.: народов и их правлений

[3109] N add.: и на следующее

[3110] A2 omitt.

[3111] N: сроки

[3112] A2, B: близок; N: близки

[3113] N: Долги эти

кассы и т. н.[3114] запасные[3115]. Находясь долгое время в распоряжении правительства, эти фонды улетучиваются[3116] для уплаты процентов на заграничные долги[3117], а вместо них на равную сумму положена[3118] в кассы[3119] эта рента[3120]. Последняя покрывает[3121] все прорухи[3122] в государственных кассах гоев. Когда мы взойдем на престол мира, то все подобные кунштюки[3123], как[3124] несоответствующие нашим интересам, будут уничтожены бесследно, как равно[3125] фондовые биржи: ибо[3126] мы не допустим колебать престиж нашей власти колебанием[3127] цен на наши ценности, которые будут нами объявлены[3128] законно[3129], в цене полной их стоимости, не допуская никакого[3130] ни[3131] понижения ни[3132] повышения: потому что[3133] повышение дает повод к понижению их[3134]...

3114 A2, N omitt.: т. н.

3115 A2: сберегательных и запасных кассах

3116 A1: исчезают

3117 N: по заграничным займам

3118 A1: кладется; A2, N, B: положены

3119 K: касы

3120 A1, B: эти ренты & add.: Эта; A2, N: вклады ренты

3121 A2, N omitt.: последняя... & add.: [N add.: Вот] эти [N add.: то] последние [N add.: и] покрывают

3122 A2: прорехи

3123 A2: меры; N: финансовые извороты; B: кундштюки

3124 A2 omitt.

3125 N add.: будут уничтожены и все

3126 A2, N: так как

3127 A1: колебаниями

3128 A2, N omitt.: будут... & add.: мы объявим

3129 A2, N, B: законом

3130 A2, N omitt.: не допуская... & add.: без возможности [N add.: их]

3131 B omitt.

3132 A2, N: или

3133 A2, N omitt.

3134 A1 omitt.: повод к...; B omitt.: их & add.: Мы начали изменения цен на; A1, B add.: гоевские ценности с повышения, от которого скоро перешли к понижению их...; A2, N omitt.: их & add.: с чего мы и начали с ценностями [N: в отношении к ценностям] гоев

Биржи будут заменены нами[3135] **грандиозными кредитными казенными учреждениями** (о), назначение которых будет заключаться[3136] в таксировании промышленных ценностей, согласно правительственным соображениям.

Эти учреждения **будут в состоянии выбросить на рынок на 500 миллионов**[3137] **промышленных бумаг в один день, или скупить на столько же** (р): таким образом все промышленные предприятия станут в зависимости от нашего правления[3138]. Вы можете себе представить, какую мощь мы этим проявим[3139].

QUOTATIONS FROM JOLY'S *DIALOGUE*

a   «et pour que chacun puisse acheter des rentes, on (...) vend depuis 10 francs de rente (...) jusqu'à cent mille francs»

b   «Le landemain (...) la valeur de ces titres est en hausse (...), comme on dit: (...) l'on se rue de tous côtés pour en acheter»

c   «En quelques jours les coffres du Trésor regorgent; on reçoit tant d'argent qu'on ne sait où le mettre; cependant on s'arrange pour le prendre»

d   «...la souscription dépasse le capital des rentes émises»

e   «C'est le coup de théatre ménagé (...) le public est frappé de cette confience du pays dans le gouvernement»

f   «...mais ne vous préoccuperez pas de payer enfin?»

g   «...il y a d'abord l'impôt»

h   «...le passif employé à payer le passif»

i   «...il y a ce que l'on appelle la conversion»

j   «Consentez à cette réduction ou recevez le remboursement du capital que vous m'avez prêté»

k   «Si tout le monde demandait son argent (...) le Trésor serait pris au lacet»

l   «les rentiers (...) aiment mieux un revenu moindre et un placement sûr.»

m   «l'on se débarrasse (...) d'un passif de plusieurs centaines de millons»

[3135]   A2, N omitt.: будут... & add.: мы заменим

[3136]   N: состоять

[3137]   К: милионов

[3138]   A2 omitt.: зависимости... & add.: зависимость от нас; N omitt.: нашего... & add.: нас

[3139]   A2, N: составим себе через это...; В: приобретем

n   «...consolide (...) les dettes (...) que l'on appelle très pictoresquement la dette flottante, parce qu'elle se compose de créances (...) qui sont à une échéance plus ou moins rapprochée»

o   «...de gigantesques établissements de crédit»

p   «Capables de jeter pour 400 ou 500 millions de titres sur la place, ou de raréfier le marché dans les mêmes proportions»

XXI [3140]

Во всем, что до сих пор мною доложено вам, я старался тщательно обрисовать вам[3141] тайну всего[3142] происходящего пред нами[3143] с той[3144] высоты, на которой мы стоим[3145]. Мне остается добавить немного. Вам известно, что[3146] **в наших руках величайшая современная**[3147] **сила- золото: в два дня мы можем достать его в каком угодно количестве** (а) из наших хранилищ. **И мы** этим путем **докажем**[3148] что наше правление предназначено миру[3149] Богом[3150]. Неужели таким богатством мы не докажем, **что** преходящее[3151] зло, которое[3152] мы вынуждены были делать[3153] **послужило к истинному благу** (b)[3154]? Все будет приведено[3155] в порядок[3156]: и при некотором насилии[3157] мы в первый же момент[3158]

[3140] K omitt.; A1, N, B: **Еще протокол** (B add.: **(25)**) A2: **XXII**.

[3141] A2, N omitt.

[3142] N omitt.; B: ныне

[3143] A1, A2, N, B omitt. & add.: бывшего раньше [A2, N omitt.; B: ранее] и текущего

[3144] A1, B: нашей; A2 omitt.

[3145] A1, A2, B omitt.: на которой... ; N omitt.: пред нами... ; A1, A2, N, B add.: образующего [A2: в; N: стремящегося в; B: образуя] будущий [N omitt.] поток [N add.: великих, грядущих уже в близком будущем событий]; тайну законов [N add.: наших] отношений и финансовых операций. На эту тему

[3146] A2, N omitt.: Вам известно...

[3147] B omitt.

[3148] A1, A2, B, N omitt.: И мы... & add.: Как же [N: Неужели еще] нам не доказать [N: доказывать]

[3149] A2, N omitt.; A1, B add.: самим

[3150] A2, N: от Бога

[3151] A1: проходящее; N: все то; A2 omitt.

[3152] N add.: столько веков

[3153] A2, N: творить [N add.: в конце концов]

[3154] K omitt.: Неужели таким... ; A1, B: хорошему результату; A2: добру результата

[3155] A1, B: придет; A2: на приведение всего; N: -приведению всего

[3156] A2, N: к порядку...

[3157] A1, A2, N, B: хотя и [A2 omitt.: хотя...] через некоторое насилие

[3158] A2, N omitt.: в первый... & add.: а [N: но] он все же будет установлен. Мы

съумеем доказать, что **мы благодетели, вернувшие расстерзанной земле** настоящее благо[3159] и **свободу** (c) личности, которая[3160], при соблюдении[3161] нами[3162] установленных[3163] законов, будет ограждена от частного насилия и злоупотребления, и будет[3164] пользоваться покоем и[3165] миром[3166]. Мы докажем[3167], что **свобода не состоит в распущенности** (d) и в праве[3168] на разнузданность, как равно **достоинство и сила**[3169] человека **не состоят**[3170] в **праве**[3171] провозглашать[3172] принципы, суть которых ему самому не понятна[3173], что **свобода**[3174] **не состоит** в праве волновать себя и других, безобразничая и ораторствуя[3175] беспрепятственно[3176] **в безпорядочных сборищах** (e)[3177]; что[3178] **свобода состоит** в неприкосновенности личности, соблюдающей все законы[3179] общежития честно и точно[3180].

[3159] N: истинное добро

[3160] A2, N: которой

[3161] N: условии, конечно, заблюдения

[3162] B omitt.

[3163] A1 add.: правил и

[3164] A1: люди будут; A2, N omitt.: будет ограждена...& add.: мы дадим

[3165] A1, B: в труде; A2, N omitt.

[3166] A1: мире; A2, N, B add.: достоинством отношений

[3167] A2, N: выясним при этом

[3168] A2: права

[3169] A2: силе

[3170] A1, N, B: состоит

[3171] A1, A2, N, B add.: каждому

[3172] N add.: разрушительные

[3173] A2, N omitt.: суть которых... не понятна & add.: в роде свободы совести, равенства и т. д. [N: им подобным]

[3174] A2: она; N add.: личности, отнюдь

[3175] N omitt.: и... & add.: ораторством

[3176] N omitt.

[3177] N: скопищах; A2, N add.: а

[3178] N add.: истинная

[3179] A2: соблюдении всех законов

[3180] K omitt.: что свобода...; A1, A2, N, B add.: а [A2, N omitt.] что [N add.: человеческое] достоинство- [A2 add.: заключается; N add.: заключено] в сознании своих прав и своего бесправия, в уважении чужой личности ради

Наша власть будет славною (f)[3181] и[3182] могущественною[3183], потому что она[3184] будет править и руководить, а не плестись за ораторами и коноводами[3185], выкрикивающими утопии[3186], называя их[3187] принципами[3188]. Наша власть будет вершителем порядка, в котором лежит тайна счастья[3189] людей... Ее[3190] ореол внушит мистическое благоговение народам[3191], которые и преклонятся перед[3192] нею[3193], **ибо**[3194] **истинная сила никогда не теряет своего**[3195] **права** (g)[3196].

Чтобы народы привыкли к послушанию, **их надо воспитывать в**[3197] **скромности** (h), с которой рука[3198] об руку идет кротость. Поэтому мы

того, чтоб [B: чтобы] заслужить уважение себе [A2, N omitt.: в уважении...], а не в [N add.: одном только] фантазировании на тему собственного [A2, N: своего] я.

[3181] A1: славной

[3182] A1, A2, N, B: потому что она будет

[3183] A2, N: могущественна

[3184] A1, B omitt.: потому что; A2, N omitt.: потому что она

[3185] A2, N: лидерами

[3186] A2: принципы; N: безумные слова

[3187] N: которые они называют великими; B: называемые

[3188] A2 omitt.: называя их; A2, N add.: [N add.: и] которые [N add.: ничто иное, говоря] по совести надо назвать [N omitt.] утопией [N: как утопия]

[3189] A2, N omitt.: лежит... & add.: и заключается [N add :.все] счастье

[3190] N: этой власти

[3191] A2 omitt.: мистическое... & add.: преклонение мистического благоговения народов; N omitt.: благоговение... & add.: поклонение ей и благоговение перед ней народов

[3192] K: пред

[3193] A2, N omitt.: которые...

[3194] N omitt.

[3195] A1: свои

[3196] K omitt.: ибо истинная...; A2: своих прав; N omitt.: никогда не теряет...; A1, A2, N, B add.: [N add.: не поступается никаким правом, даже Божественным:] никто не смеет приступит к ней и надеяться [A2, N: чтобы; B: не имея надежды] отнять [B add.: и] пяди от [N: хотя бы пядь] ее мощи. ; A1, N, B add.: **Еще протокол** (B add.: **(26)**); A2 add.: **XXIII**.

[3197] A2, N: приучать [N: приучить] к

[3198] B omitt.

законом сократим[3199] производство предметов роскоши[3200]. Этой[3201] мерой[3202] мы сейчас не[3203] улучшим нравы, деморализованные[3204] соревнованием на почве роскоши. **Мы восстановим кустарное производство** (i), которое обессилит[3205] фабрикантов, ныне зазнавшихся от жирных капиталов,[3206] которые[3207] часто двигают[3208] массовыми[3209] мыслями против нас[3210]. Главная выгода от этого еще в том, что[3211] народ кустарь не знает безработицы, что[3212] его связывает с[3213] крепостью власти, роль[3214] которой- ограждать каждого подданного[3215] от обиды[3216] со стороны других. Ведь[3217] **безработица- это**[3218] **самая опасная вещь для правительства** (j). Для нас роль безработицы[3219] будет сыграна, как только власть перейдет открыто[3220] в наши руки. Пьянство

3199   A2, N omitt.: с которой... & add.: а потому сократим [N: сократить] промышленное

3200   A1, B add.: которые усугубляют нервность, [B add.: и] заносчивость

3201   B: Этою

3202   A2, N: Этим

3203   B: же; A2, N omitt.: сейчас не

3204   B: испорченные

3205   A2, N: подорвет частные капиталы

3206   A2 omitt.: ныне...

3207   N omitt.: ныне... & add.: Это необходимо еще и потому, что крупные фабриканты

3208   N add.: хотя и не всегда сознательно

3209   K: масовыми; A1, N: масс

3210   A2, N: правительства

3211   A2, N omitt.: Главная...

3212   N: а это

3213   A1, A2, N B add.: потребностью [A2: существованием] порадка, и [N, B: а] следовательно [A2, N add.: и] с

3214   B: назначение

3215   A1 omitt.

3216   A1: обид

3217   A1 omitt.; A2, N omitt.: роль которой...

3218   A1, A2, N omitt.

3219   A2, N: ee

3220   N omitt.

тоже будет воспрещено[3221] законом и наказуемо строжайше[3222], как преступление против человечности людей, превращающихся в животных под влиянием алкоголя. Повторяю еще раз, подданные готовы[3223] слепо повиноваться[3224] только сильно[3225] организованной и[3226] независимой от них мощи[3227] в которой они чувствуют не только[3228] цепь, но и[3229] защиту, и[3230] поддержку против[3231] социальных бичей...[3232] Владыка, который сменит ныне существующие правления, действующие[3233] среди деморализованных обществ, отрекающихся даже от Божеской[3234] власти, из среды которых выступает[3235] со всех сторон огонь анархии, прежде всего должен будет[3236] приступить к заливанию этого всепожирающего пламени: поэтому он обязан будет[3237] убить такие общества,[3238] чтобы вновь воскресить их в лице правил и[3239] организованного и обученного[3240] войска, сознательно борющегося с[3241]

[3221] A2, N: запрещено

[3222] A2, N omitt.

[3223] A2, N omitt.

[3224] A2, N: повинуются

[3225] A2, N, B: сильной

[3226] A2, N omitt.: организованной.. & add.: вполне

[3227] A2, N: руке; B: власти

[3228] A2, N, B omitt.: не только

[3229] N omitt.: цепь... & add.: мечь на

[3230] A1, A2, B omitt.

[3231] A2, N add.: ударов

[3232] A1, A2, N, B add.: На что им [N add.: нужна] ангельская душа в лице их правителя [N omitt.: лице... & add.: царе; A2 omitt.: ангельская... & add.: зреть на ангельскую душу своего царя]; они знают, что его роль представительство [B: назначение- проявление; A2, N omitt.: они знают... & add.: Им надо видеть в нем олицетворение] силы и мощи...

[3233] N: влачащие свое существование

[3234] A1: Божьей

[3235] A2: наступает

[3236] A2, N omitt.

[3237] A2, N omitt.

[3238] N add.: хотя бы залив их собственною кровью

[3239] A1, A2, N, B: правильно

[3240] A2, N omitt.: и...

заразной болезнью[3242], могущей[3243] гангренировать[3244] общественный организм[3245]. Этот избранник Божий, назначенный[3246] свыше, **сломит**[3247] **безумные силы, движимые**[3248] **инстинктом**, а не разумом, **животностью** (k)[3249], а не человечностью[3250]. Тогда[3251] мы скажем[3252] народам: благодарите Бога и **преклонитесь перед**[3253] **носящим на лице своем печать предопределения** (l)[3254], к которому сам Бог вел его звезду в течении веков[3255]...

[3241]   A1, B add.: собственной [B: собственною]

[3242]   A2, N omitt.: с заразной... & add.: со всякой заразой

[3243]   N, B: могущею

[3244]   A2, N: изъязвить

[3245]   A1, A2, B: корпус; N: государственное тело

[3246]   A2, N: назначен

[3247]   A1, A2, N: чтобы сломить

[3248]   A1: движения; A2: двигающиеся

[3249]   A1: жестокостью

[3250]   A1, A2, N, B add.: Эти [B: каковые] силы [A2, N, B add.: теперь торжествуют в проявлениях грабительства и всякого насилия (A2, B omitt.: теперь... & add.: проявляются в грабительстве шествующем (B add.: и разбойничестве, шествующие), под личиною принципов совести [N: свободы] и прав (B: права). Они (B: Эти силы)] разрушили все социальные порядки [A2, N add.: чтобы на них (N omitt.) воздвигнуть трон царя иудейского] И [A2 omitt.; N, B: но] их роль сыграна, ибо [B: как только] благодаря такому разрушению можно было [B: будет] воздвигнуть трон Царю Иудейскому [B: Царя Иудейского]; но [B omitt..] с момента достижения этой цели нам надо будет сметать с пути нашей власти все для нас [B: нее] вредное, чтобы на ее пути не встретилось [A2, N omitt.: ибо... & add.: будет в момент воцарения его; тогда их надо будет смести с его пути, на котором не должно лежать] ни сучка ни задоринки...

[3251]   N add.: то

[3252]   A2, N: нам можно будет сказать

[3253]   A1: пред

[3254]   A2, N add.: людей

[3255]   K omitt.: Этот избранник Божий... ; A1 add.: уготовляя ее...; A2, N omitt.: в течении... & add.: чтобы никто иной, как он, освободил вас [N: кроме него, не мог освободить нас] от [N add.: всех] вышеуказанных сил [N add.: и зол]

QUOTATIONS FROM JOLY'S *DIALOGUE*

a   «Vous avez entre les mains la plus grande puissance des temps modernes, l'argent. Vous pouvez en procurer à peu près autant que vous voulez»

b   «...montrer enfin que le bien peut sortir du mal»

c   «mes bienfaits (...) j'ai rendu à un pays déchiré (...) la liberté»

d   «La liberté ne consiste pas dans la licence»

e   «la dignité et la force ne consistent dans l'insurrection et le désordre»

f   «Mon empire (...) sera glorieux»

g   «car la force n'abdique jamais ses droits»

h   «d'introduire (...) la décence»

i   «Je donnerai à l'esprit d'entreprise un essor prodigieux»

j   «Mon gouvernement lui procurerait du travail»

k   «Je contiens des forces insensées qui n'ont d'autre mobile, au fond, que la brutalité des instincts»

l   «inclinez-vous devant celui qui porte à son front le signe fatal de la prédestination»

XXII [3256]

Сегодня[3257] перейду **к способу укрепления династических корней царя Давида, до последних слоев земли** (a)[3258]. Это укрепление будет состоять[3259] в системе, которая послужила к сохранению[3260] за нашими мудрецами ведения[3261] всех мировых дел[3262]. Несколько членов[3263] от семени Давида[3264] будут подготовлены[3265] на царство и управление народами, уготовляя[3266] для последних[3267] царей и наследников[3268] не по прямому[3269] наследственному праву, а по выдающимся способностям, посвящая их в сокровенные тайны[3270] политики, то есть[3271] планов[3272] управления, но[3273] с тем, чтобы никто, кроме них[3274], не ведал этих тайн[3275]. Правление не может быть поручено непосвященным в

3256   К omitt.; А1, N, В: **Еще протокол** [В add.: **(27)**]; А2: **XXIV.**

3257   А2, N: Теперь

3258   К omitt.: до последних...

3259   А2 omitt.; N: заключаться

3260   А2, N omitt.: в системе... & add.: прежде всего в том, в чем [N add.: до сего дня] заключалась сила сохранения

3261   А1: ведение

3262   А1, А2, N, В add.: направление [А2, N: направления] и воспитание [А2, N, В: воспитания] мысли человечества до сего дня [N omitt.] следовательно направление всей политики мура [А2, N omitt.: следовательно...]...

3263   А1: человек

3264   N: Давидова

3265   А1: подготовляемы; А2, N: готовить

3266   А1: приготовляя

3267   А2, N omitt.: на царство...

3268   А1 add.: их (наследование будет; А2 add.: выбираемых; N add.: выбирая; В add.: их, но

3269   А1, А2, N omitt.

3270   В: тайники

3271   А2 omitt.: то есть

3272   N: в планы

3273   N: однако

3274   N omitt.

3275   А1: этой тайны; А2, N add.: [N add.: Цель такого образа действий та,] чтобы все знали, что

сказанные тайны и в искусство[3276], осуществлять планы[3277] так, чтобы никто не узрел[3278] замысла...[3279]
[3280]Этим немногим[3281] лицам будет преподано практическое применение названных планов, через[3282] сравнение многовековых опытов и наблюдений[3283] над политико-экономическими выводами[3284], вынесенными из этих опытов[3285]. Прямые наследники часто будут устраняемы[3286] от восшествия на трон[3287], если в учебное время они[3288] выкажут[3289] легкомыслие, эгоизм[3290], мягкость и другие качества делающие их[3291] неспособными к управлению, которое в их[3292] руках губит их власть[3293].

[3276] A2, N omitt.: сказанные... & add.: тайники его искусства; B: эти тайны

[3277] A1, B: их проводить в действие

[3278] A1: мог узреть

[3279] A2, N omitt. осуществлять... & add.: Только

[3280] B omitt.: Этим немногим usque ad: губит их власть (3293)

[3281] A2, N omitt.

[3282] K, A1: чрез

[3283] A2, N: все наблюдения

[3284] A1, A2, N , B: ходами и социальными науками

[3285] A2, N omitt.: вынесенными...; A1, A2, N, B add.: то есть [A2 omitt.; N: -весь, словом,] дух [A1: двух] законов, [A2, N add.: непоколебимо] установленных [B add.: установленный] самой [N, B: самою] природой [A2, N, B: природою] с целью [A2, N: для] урегулирования человеческих отношений [B: человеческими отношениями]

[3286] A1, A2: отстранены

[3287] A1, N: престол

[3288] A2 omitt.

[3289] A1: выказывают; A2: выскажут

[3290] A2, N omitt.

[3291] A1: царствующих; A2, N: [N add.: свойства- губители власти] которые делают

[3292] A1 omitt.

[3293] A2, N omitt. которое... & add.: вредных [N: а сами по себе вредны] для царского назначения губителей власти [N omitt.: губителей...]; A1, A2, N add.: Только безусловно способные к твердому [A2 add.: и; N add.: хота бы и до жестокости] неукоснительному управлени [N: правлению], получат бразды правления [N omitt. & add: его от наших мудрецов]... Но [N omitt.]

Планы[3294] действий текущего момента, а тем более будущего, **будут тайною**[3295] даже для тех[3296], которых будут называть[3297] **ближними**[3298] советниками (b) нашего царя[3299].

Все будут видеть[3300] в лице царствующего[3301], владеющего собою[3302] с непоколебимой волей[3303], **как бы судьбу с ее неведомыми путями** (c). **Никто не будет знать**[3304], какова цель распоряжения[3305] царя (d)[3306], а потому **никто**[3307] не посмеет стать поперек (e) неведомого предначертания[3308]...

в случае заболевания упадком воли, трусостью [A2, N omitt.] или иным видом неспособности, Цари должны будут [A2, N add.: по закону] передавать бразды правления в новые, способные руки ибо мы никогда не допустим, чтобы наши Цари служили ширмами для управления временщиков, роль которых должна быть в точном исполнении предписаний сведующего, а не самоуправства, личным и коллективным [A2, N omitt.: ибо мы... и коллективным & add.: Царские].

3294   К: План

3295   A1: тайной; A2, N: неведомы

3296   A2, N omitt.: для... & add.: тем

3297   N: назовут

3298   A1: ближайшими

3299   A2, N omitt.: нашего...; A1, A2, N, B add.: лишь [A2, N add.: Только царь да просвещавшие [A2: посетившие; N: посвятившие; B: посвящавшие] его учителя [A2, N: трое] будут ведать уготованное для грядущего [A2, N omitt.: ведат... & add.: знать грядущее]

3300   A2, N: узрят

3301   A2, N: царя

3302   A1: собой; N add.: и человечеством

3303   A2, B: волею

3304   A2, N: ведать

3305   B: распоряжений

3306   A2, N omitt.: какова... & add.: чего царь желает достигнуть своим распоряжением [N.: своими распоряжениями]

3307   A2 omitt.; N add.: и

3308   A2, N omitt. & add.: пути; A1, A2, N, B add.: Повторяю, что конечно необходимо [A2, N: Понятно, что надо (N: нужно)] чтобы умственный резервуар Правителя [A2, N: царей] соответствовал величиине плана [A2, N: вмещаемому (N add.: в нем) плану] управления: [A2, N add.: вот] почему

a   «les (...) moyens à l'aide desquels je pousserai jusqu'aux dernières couches du sol les racines de ma dynastie»

b   «Je ne communiquerais mes projets (...) ses ministres eux-mêmes ne savaient rien»

c   «la puissance souveraine est une image de la puissance (...) de la Providence (...) dont les voies sont inconnues»

d   «je veux que mes desseins soient impénétrables»

e   «les ennemis mêmes (...) tremblassent de le renverser»

он не будет входить [А2, N: восходить; N: всходить] на престол иначе, как по испытании его [А2Ь после испытания; А2, N: своего] ума нашими [А2, N: названными] мудрецами. Чтобы народ знал и любил своего Царя надо [N: необходимо], чтобы он лично [А2, N omitt.] беседовал на площадях с так называемою чернью [А2, N: с своим народом]; ничто, как это, не скрепляет [А2, N add.: Это произведет (N: производит) нужное скрепление; В: ибо только это может скрепить] две силы [А2, N: двух сил] мира [А2, N omitt.] ныне [А2 omitt.] отделенные [А2, N: отделенных] нами друг от друга террором, потому, что нам надо было стать посреди них для того, чтобы влиять на ход той и другой силы [В add.: отдельно; А2, N omitt.: потому, что...; А2, N add.: когда надо было (N: Этот террор был нам необходим до времени для того), чтобы в отдельности каждая из них подпала (N: обе эти силы подпали) под наше влияние]...; А1, А2, N add.: Кончив свой доклад тем, что [А2, N omitt.: Кончив...] Царь Иудейский так воспитан, чтобы ни коим образом не был сладострастным [А2, N omitt.: так воспитан... & add.: не должен находиться под властью своих страстей, особенно же- сладострастия:] чтобы не [А2, N: ни] одной стороной [А2, N: своего характера он должен] не давать животным инстинктам власть [N: власти] над своим умом: сладострастие же [А2, N: хуже всего] расстраивает умственные способности и ясность взглядов, отвлекая мысли на мелочи жизненного пути [N: на худшую и наиболее животную сторону человеческой деятельности].Опора человечества, какою должен быть наш Царь, будет себя [А2 omitt.; N: в лице Всемирного Владыки от святого семени Давида; А2, N: должна] приносить в жертву своему народу, со всеми личными влечениями, отказываясь от них ,чтобы быть безупречным [А2, N omitt.: со всеми... & add.: все личные влечения. Она должна быть примерно безупречна (N omitt.: Она... & add.: Владыка наш должен быть примерно безупречен)].

От [3309] переводчика [3310]

Изложенные протоколы написаны[3311] сионскими представителями (не смешивайте с представителями сионистского движения)[3312], и[3313] выхвачены[3314] из целой книги протоколов[3315], все содержание[3316] которой[3317] переписать не удалось по случаю[3318] краткости времени, данного на прочтение их переводчику этих протоколов. К ним было приложено еще небольшое прибавление и план завоевания мира евреями мирным путем[3319]. Этот[3320] рисунок и протокол[3321] добыты[3322] из тайных хранилищ сионской главной канцеляри, ныне находящейся на французской территории[3323]. На приложенном рисунке[3324] значится[3325] весь политический план Сиона по отношению к имеющим быть

[3309] В: **Примечание**

[3310] A1, A2, N omitt.

[3311] A1, B: подписаны; A2, N omitt.: Изложенные... ; A2 add.: Подписали; N add.: Подписано

[3312] A2, N omitt.: не смешивайте...движения & add.: 33 [N add.: степени]

[3313] В: Они; A2, N: Эти отчеты [N: протоколы]

[3314] N: были тайно извлечены (или похищены)

[3315] A2 add.: переданных мне

[3316] В: всего содержания

[3317] A1 omitt.: все содержание которой & add.: которые полностью

[3318] A1, B omitt.

[3319] A2 omitt.: все содержание... & add.: **Препроводительное письмо.** Имею честь представить при сем рисунок шествия евреев на завоевание мира и пояснение сего.

[3320] A2: наш

[3321] A1: протоколы; B omitt.: Этот... & add.: Эти протоколы и чертеж

[3322] A2 omitt.: и протокол... & add.: добыт; N omitt.: все содержание... & add.: Все это добыто моим корреспондентом

[3323] K: территории; A2 add.: и о чем, конечно, глава русского тайного агентства за границей, еврей Эфрон, и его агенты, евреи же, еще не сообщили нашему министерству.

[3324] B omitt.: приложенном... & add.: упомянутом чертеже

[3325] В: значился

пройденным этапам[3326] этого шествия[3327] и способам перехода от одного к другому.[3328]

Сказанный[3329] политический план[3330] осуществляется с[3331] 929 года[3332] до Р. Х., он[3333] был[3334] измышлен Соломоном и[3335] мудрецами иудейскими в теории: по мере же[3336] исторических событий,[3337] разрабатываем[3338] и дополняем[3339] посвященными в этот план[3340] последователями. Эти мудрецы решили мирно завоевать мир для Сиона, с мудростью[3341] символического змия[3342], главу которого должно было

[3326] A1: этапами

[3327] A1: пути

[3328] A2, N omitt.: по отношению... & add.: Франция потребовала у Турции, как главный пункт своих предписаний [N omitt.: как главный...] льгот [N: льготы] для школ и религиозных учреждений всех вероисповеданий, которые в Малой Азии будут поддерживаемы французской дипломатией. Пункт этот, понятно [N: Конечно, это требование льготы], не касается католических учреждений, изгоняемых из Франции несколькими последними составами ее правительства, а доказывает лишь, что дрейфусаровская дипломатия выступает за интересы Сиона и открывает путь для колонизации французскими евреями Малой Азии; ведь [N omitt.] Сион всегда завоевывал себе места и влияния [N: влияние] через свой рабочий скот с человеческими лицами, как называет Талмуд все не-еврейское человечество.

[3329] N omitt. & add.: По данным тайного еврейского Сионизма

[3330] N add.: мирного завоевания вселенной

[3331] A2 omitt.:   Сказанный... & add.: и осуществление его; N omitt.: осуществляется... & add.: еще за

[3332] N: лет

[3333] A2: каковой план; N omitt.

[3334] A1, B omitt.

[3335] A2, N add.: другими

[3336] B omitt.; N: развития

[3337] A1, N add.: был

[3338] B: разрабатывается

[3339] N: пополняем; B: дополняется

[3340] N: в это дело

[3341] A1, A2, N, B: хитростью

[3342] A2: змея

составлять посвященное в планы мудрецов правительство евреев (всегда замаскированное[3343] даже для[3344] своего народа), а туловище-народ иудейский. Переползая[3345] в государственные[3346] недра, змий[3347] этот подтачивал и[3348] пожирал[3349] все не еврейские государственные силы, по мере их роста на разных континентах, но особенно[3350] в Европе,[3351] что[3352] он должен делать и в будущем, при точном следовании по[3353] предначертаниям плана до тех пор, пока цикл пройденного им[3354] пути не сомкнется возвратом головы[3355] змия[3356] на Сион, то есть,[3357] пока этот[3358] змий не заключит[3359] в сферу[3360] своего круга всю Европу[3361], а через нее и весь[3362] мир, пользуясь всеми силами, завоеванными[3363] экономическим путем, чтобы завлечь в сферу[3364] своего цикла[3365] остальные страны[3366]. Так как[3367] возврат[3368] главы

[3343]   N: замаскированные

[3344]   A2, N: от

[3345]   A2: проницая; N: Проникая; B: Проползая

[3346]   N omitt.

[3347]   A2: змей

[3348]   A1, B: или

[3349]   A2, N add.: (свергая их)

[3350]   A1: в особенности

[3351]   A2 omitt.: на разных...

[3352]   N omitt.: на разных... & add.: Это же

[3353]   A2 omitt.

[3354]   A1: ими

[3355]   A1, A2, N, B: главы

[3356]   A2, N: его

[3357]   A2, N omitt.: то... & add.: и

[3358]   A2, N: таким образом

[3359]   A2, N add.: не сосредоточит

[3360]   A1, A2, N: сфере

[3361]   N: всей Европы

[3362]   K: весть; A2, N: остальной

[3363]   N: завоеванием и

[3364]   N omitt.: завлечь... & add.: подчинить своему влиянию, влиянию

[3365]   A2: влияния; N add.: и

[3366]   A1, A2, B: континенты; N: контингенты

[3367]   A1, N omitt.: Так как

змия[3369] мог[3370] совершиться лишь[3371] по[3372] развалинам[3373] государственной мощи всех европейских стран,[3374] через падение этой мощи[3375] от экономического расстройства и разорения[3376], всюду вносимого[3377] Сионом[3378] с помощью[3379] нравственного упадка и растления[3380], с помощью[3381] распутных[3382] евреек,[3383] испанок[3384]... то эти[3385] женщины в руках Сиона служат приманкой для тех, которые, благодаря им, всегда нуждаются в деньгах, а потому охотно[3386] торгуют совестью, чтобы добыть денег во что бы то ни стало...[3387]

3368 A1: Движение

3369 A2: змея; A2, N add.: в Сион

3370 A1: могло

3371 N: только

3372 A2, N, B add.: сглаженным

3373 N: равнинам

3374 A2, N add.: то есть

3375 A2 add.: и

3376 A1, B: раззорения

3377 N omitt.: падение... & add.: экономическое расстройство и разорение, всюду вносимое

3378 A2 add.: через упадок и нравственное растление

3379 A1: путем

3380 A2, N, B omitt.: с помощью... & add.: через [N add.: духовный] упадок и нравственное [B omitt.] растление [N add.: главным образом]

3381 A1: при помощи

3382 A1, A2, N, B: omitt.

3383 A1, B add.: выдающих себя за француженок, итальянок; A2, N omitt. евреек & add.: еврейских женщин, под маскою француженок, итальянок,

3384 A1 add.: и пр. [B: и т.д.], являющих самыми лучшими носительницами [A2 N omitt. и пр... & add. лучших вносительниц] распутства нравов [N: в нравы руководителей народов] с места на место [A2 N omitt.]; A2 add.: Ныне в числе агентш Сиона считаются: Отеро, Сахарет, Сарра Бернар и др.

3385 A1, A2 omitt.: то; N omitt.: то эти

3386 A2, N omitt.

3387 A1, A2, N, B add.: Деньги же [A2, N add.: эти], собственно говоря, только ссужаются таким торговцам совестью, и [A2, N add.: им, ибо; B omitt.] быстро возвращаются [B: возвращаясь] в руки, ссужавшие [B: ссудившие]

Конечно[3388], для успеха предприятия надо было, чтобы ни государство[3389], ни отдельные личности не заподозрили[3390], какую роль они играли[3391] в руках Сиона: и потому[3392] иудейские[3393] правители учредили из себя[3394] якобы религиозную касту, ревнивую блюстительницу[3395] моисеевых законов и талмудических[3396] предписаний. И вот[3397] все поверили, что маска[3398] моисеевых законов есть истинный руль управления[3399] евреев,[3400] никто не стал присматриваться к деятельности этого самоуправления: никто не замечал[3401], как велись национальные дела[3402] народа без территории[3403], тем более, что глаза всех отводились[3404] на золото, из за которого все спорили, пока евреи потихонько[3405] забирали его в свои кассы[3406]...

их, потому что с помощью тех же женщин, растрачиваются скоро после их получения. Денег ищут опять... [B omitt.] и вот [A2, N omitt.: ссужавшие их... & add.: подкупающего Сиона, через тех же женщин, а (N add.: между тем); B add.: транжиры опять ищут денег, и] рабы Сиона [A2, N: Сиону] приобретены...

3388   N: Естественно, что

3389   A1, A2, N, B: государства

3390   K: заподозрели; A2, N: подозревали

3391   A2: она играла

3392   A1, A2, N, B omitt. и... & add. поэтому

3393   A2, N: сионские

3394   N: своей среды

3395   A2, N add.: чистоты

3396   N: талмудистских

3397   N omitt.

3398   B: личина

3399   A1, A2, N, B omitt.: истинный... & add.: истинная личина [B: сущность] самоуправления [N: истинное самоуправление]

3400   A1, B add.: Поэтому

3401   A1: заглянул; B: обратил внимания на то,

3402   A1 add.: этого

3403   A1, B: бестерриториального; A2, N omitt.: никто не замечал...

3404   A2, N omitt.: всех... & add.: были отведены

3405   A1, B: незаметно

3406   K: касы

Поэтому[3407] то[3408] и была предоставлена[3409] полная свобода действия[3410] в[3411] экономическо-политических[3412] интригах Сиона[3413].

Первый этап змия[3414] в Европе был в 429 г. до Р. Х.[3415] в Греции, где во времена Перикла[3416] он начал подтачивать величие и мощь этой страны.

Второй этап был в Риме во времена Августа (с 63 г. до Р. Х. до 14 г. после Р. Х[3417]), где он пробыл 16 веков и где положил начало кредито[3418]-политической мощи евреев.[3419]

Третий этап был[3420] в Мадриде[3421], во времена Карла V (с 1558 по Р. Х.)[3422].

Четвертый этап был[3423] в Париже в 1700[3424], во времена Людовика XIV[3425].

Пятый[3426] в Лондоне с 1814 г., после падения Наполеона.

Шестой[3427]- в Берлине, с 1871 г., после[3428] франко-прусской[3429] войны.

[3407] A1, B: а потому

[3408] A1, B: им; A2, N omitt.: из за которого... & add.: доставляемое кастой, которой

[3409] B add.: Сиону

[3410] A1, A2, N, B: действий

[3411] A2, N add.: ее

[3412] B: экономически-политичсских; A2, N: политическо [N: политико]-экономических

[3413] A2 omitt.: интригах... & add.: интересах; N, B omitt.: Сиона; N add.: По графическому изображению шествия символического змия,

[3414] A2: змея; N: его

[3415] B omitt.: в 429 г. & add.: (469 до 429 г. до Р. Х)

[3416] K add.: I

[3417] K, A1, A2, N: с 69 г. до Р. Х.

[3418] A1: кредитов

[3419] A2, N omitt.: где он...

[3420] A2, N omitt.: этап был

[3421] A1: Мадрите

[3422] A2, N: в 1552 г. после [N: по] Р. Х.; B: с 1500 до 1556 г. по Р. Х.

[3423] A2, N omitt.: этап был; B omitt.: был

[3424] B: (1638-1715 по Р. Х.)

[3425] A1 add.: -го

[3426] B add.: этап

[3427] B add.: этап

[3430]Седьмой[3431] - в С.[3432]-Петербурге, над которым[3433] нарисована ныне[3434] глава змия[3435], а год водворения ее там[3436] значится[3437] с[3438] 1880 г.[3439]. Все выше[3440] названные[3441] государства, пройденные змием,[3442] действительно подточены в своем основании[3443] либерализмом и экономическим расстройством, внесенными евреями[3444]. Далее глава змия движется[3445] или[3446] двинулась по указанному стрелками пути[3447] на Москву, Киев, Одессу[3448]. Константинополь значится[3449] восьмым и последним этапом[3450] до Иерусалима. Следовательно[3451], осталось

3428   A2: с

3429   A2: германской

3430   A2 add.: а

3431   B add.: этап

3432   A1, A2, N omitt.

3433   A1: на котором

3434   N: теперь

3435   A2: змея

3436   A2 omitt.: водворения...

3437   A1: значит

3438   A1, B omitt.

3439   N omitt.: а год... & add.: под датой 1881 год

3440   B omitt.

3441   A1, A2, N omitt.: выше названные

3442   A2: змеем; N add.: не исключая Германии с видимой ее мощью

3443   N add.: конституционным

3444   A2, N omitt.: внесенными евреями & add.: В экономическом отношении пощажены Англия и Германия, но только до времени, пока не совершится бесповоротного завоевания России, на которую устремлены все усилия.

3445   B: двинется

3446   A2, N omitt.: движется или & add. еще не

3447   A2, N omitt.: по указанному... & add.: но на рисунке стрелками показан его [N omitt.] путь

3448   A1, A2, B add.: Кстати достойно внимания, что Одесса [A2 add.: уже] обстраивается, ожидая гостей...; N add.: Нам теперь хорошо известно, в какие гнезда воинствующего еврейства обратились эти города.

3449   B: значился; N: причислен к

3450   N: восьмому и последнему этапу

3451   N omitt.

змию[3452] немного пройти[3453] до сомкнутия[3454] цикла через соединение главы его[3455] с хвостом. Чтобы указанное «проползание» совершилось беспрепятственно, были проведены следующие меры[3456]. Прежде всего была создана[3457] обособленность евреев[3458], чтобы[3459] никто не проник в их[3460] среду и не открыл тайны[3461] из[3462] патриотической работы, вредной для приютивших их стран[3463]. И вот им[3464] пророчески объявили[3465], что они избраны[3466] самим[3467] Богом из среды людей, чтобы владеть землею[3468], нераздельным[3469] царством. Кроме того[3470] внушали[3471], что только евреи сыны Божии[3472] и они одни достойны названия «человека»[3473], остальные же люди созданы[3474] как рабочий

[3452] A2: змею

[3453] A2, N: уже проползти; B: пройдти

[3454] N add.: рокового

[3455] A2 omitt.; N omitt.: соединение... & add.: сомкнутие головы

[3456] A1, A2, N, B add.: для воспитания и образования евреев [A2, N omitt.],- рабочих этого трудного дела, чтобы работа их [B omitt.] вышла наиболее благотворной [B omitt.: наиболее... & add.: чистою; A2, N omitt. чтобы... & add.: с целью получить чистую работу].

[3457] A1, A2, N, B: подстроена

[3458] A2 omitt.; N: еврейского племени

[3459] A1, A2, N, B: дабы

[3460] N: его

[3461] A1: тайну; A2: тайн

[3462] A1, B: их

[3463] A2, N omitt.: из патриотической... & add.: их [N: его] деяний

[3464] N omitt.: И вот... & add.: Ему

[3465] N: было возвещен

[3466] N: оно избрано

[3467] K: самым

[3468] A1, A2: землей; B add.: как

[3469] A2, N: безраздельным сионским

[3470] A1, A2, B add.: им

[3471] A1: внушили; N omitt.: Кроме... & add.: Ему внушено было

[3472] B: Вечного Существа

[3473] A1, B: Человеков

[3474] A2, N add.: Богом только

скот и рабы для[3475] евреев, а[3476] человеческие лица им даны[3477] для того, чтобы евреям не были слишком противны их[3478] услуги, заключайшиеся в созидании[3479] престола Сиона[3480] над всем миром[3481]. Раз[3482] им[3483] было внушено, что они высшие существа, или[3484] сверхчеловеки,[3485] то[3486] поэтому они[3487] не могут сочетаться браком[3488] со скотским племенем- с другими народами, которые по сравнению с евреями суть скоты. Такие[3489] принципы, внушаемые воспитанием[3490] в тайных и явных школах и в семьях иудейских, были причиной самовозвеличения евреев над остальным человечеством[3491], самообоготворения[3492] их, якобы[3493] сыновья Божиих[3494]. Обособленности евреев[3495] еще[3496] служила кагальная

[3475] A2, N omitt.

[3476] N: же

[3477] A2, N add.: только

[3478] A2, N omitt.: не были... & add.: было не противно принимать от них

[3479] A2, N, B omitt.: заключаюшиеся; A2 add.: а роль их заключается в завоевании; N add.: для воспитания и образования; B add.: необходимые для созидания

[3480] A1, A2, N, B: Сиону

[3481] A1, A2, N, B add.: (смотри Sanh [A1: §§], 91, 21, 1051)

[3482] A1: Так как; B: Еще

[3483] A2, N omitt.: Раз... & add.: Евреям

[3484] A1, B: как бы; A2 omitt.

[3485] N omitt.: или...

[3486] A2, N, B: что

[3487] A1 add.: и

[3488] A1, B omitt.; N omitt.: сочетаться... & add.: сливаться

[3489] A2, N omitt.: скотским племенем... & add.: скотскими племенами- другими народами [N: других народов]. Эти [N omitt.]

[3490] N omitt.: внушаемые... & add.: этих мер, при посредстве воспитания

[3491] A2, N omitt.: были... & add.: внушали [N: внушили] евреям самовозвеличение над остальными людьми

[3492] A1: самоубоготворения; A2: самобоготворение; N: самообоготворение

[3493] A2, N omitt.: их, якобы; A1, A2, N, B add.: по праву

[3494] A1, A2, N, B add.: (см. Jihal [A1 omitt.; A2, B: Sihal] 67, 1, Sanh [A1 omitt.] 58, 2)

[3495] A2, N: сионского народа

[3496] A2: кроме того; N omitt.

система, вынуждавшая каждого еврея оказывать поддержку[3497] соотечественникам[3498], независимо от[3499] поддержки, которую они все получают от местного управления[3500] Сиона, носящего разные[3501] названия- кагала, консистории, комитета по еврейским делам, канцелярии по сборам податей и проч. и проч.[3502], прикрывающих[3503] сионскую администрацию от взоров других правительств, всегда усердно охранявших и[3504] охраняющих почему-то сионское самоуправление, сделавшееся благодаря этому вполне автономным[3505], якобы религиозным[3506]. Считая всех неевреев[3507] своим рабочим скотом (см.[3508] Арам-Хайм, п. А, стр.1; Эбен-Гайзер, п. 44, ст. 8, 24; Иебанот, 98, 25; Катубот, 3, в , 34; Санхедрин, 74 и 30, Кидушин, 68, в)[3509], созданным[3510] для возвеличения Сиона,[3511] евреи[3512] и обращаются с

[3497] A2, N omitt.: оказывать... & add.: поддерживать

[3498] B: единоплеменникам; A2, N: соотечественника

[3499] A1, A2, N, B add.: той

[3500] A1, A2, N: самоуправления; B: отделения

[3501] N: различные

[3502] A omitt.: и проч.

[3503] A1, B: прикрывающие; A2, N: прикрывавшими и прикрывающими

[3504] A2, N omitt.: охранявших и

[3505] A2, N omitt.: сделавшееся...

[3506] A2, N: религиозное; A1, B add.: несмотря на предостережения многих; A1, A2, N, B add.: Вышеприведенные [N add.: многовековые] внушения [A2 add.: которым подвергались евреи] повели [N: повлияли; B: определили] материальную жизнь евреев [A2: и их материальную жизнь; N: и на принципы еврейской материальной жизни]

[3507] B add.: лишь

[3508] A2 omitt.: всех... ; N omitt.: Считая всех... & add.: Читая

[3509] A1, A2, N, B: Орах-Хаим [A2, N: Хопаим], § 14, стр. 1; Эбен-Гаэзер [N: Гаэзар], § 44, стр. 8, 24 [A2 omitt.; N: 1I1]; и [A2, N, B omitt.] Иебамот [A2: XXXIV Иебаскот; N: XXXVi Ебамот], 98, 25 [A2, N omitt.]; [A2, N add.: XXV] Катубот [A2: Кетубош; N: Кетубат], 3, в, 34 [A2, N: 3 б]; [A2, N add.: XXXIV] Санхедрин, 74 в. 30 [A2, N: omitt.]; [A2, N add.: XXX] Кидушин [A2: Кадумин; N: Кадушин], 68 в [A2, N: a]

[3510] A1: созданы; A2: созданными; N: созданные

[3511] N add.: мы видим, что

[3512] N add.: с нами обращались

ними^{3513} как с таковыми^{3514}; собственность и^{3515} даже жизнь народов они считают своим достоянием и распоряжаются ими^{3516} по своему усмотрению, когда^{3517} это можно сделать безнаказанно. Администрация^{3518} их это санкционирует отпушением^{3519} всех злодейств, содеянных евреями против неевреев. Такое отпущение производится^{3520} в день Иом-Кипура^{3521} (еврейского нового года), давая вместе с тем разрешения^{3522} на таковые же деяния для наступающего года^{3523}... Помимо всего сказанного, желая усилить^{3524} непримиримость и ненависть своего народа к другим народам^{3525}, сионская администрация удачно пользовалась движением антисемитизма^{3526}, полезного Сиону в том отношении, что будя ненависть^{3527} в сердцах евреев, он^{3528} вызывал к ним жалость^{3529} в сердцах многих христиан^{3530} как^{3531} к несправедливо

3513   A2 omitt.: и... & add.: с ними обращались; N omitt.: с ними & add.: действительно

3514   N: со скотами

3515   B omitt.

3516   A2, N: расправляются с ними

3517   N add.: конечно,

3518   A2, N add.: же

3519   A1: отпушение

3520   A2, N omitt.: Такое отпущение...

3521   A2: Иомо-Кошгура; N: Сем- Кемпура

3522   A1, N, B: разрешение

3523   A2, N omitt.: для... & add.: [N add.: и] в наступающем году

3524   A2, N: возбудить

3525   A1, A2, N, B omitt.: к другим... & add.: против остальных людей

3526   К: антисемизма; A1, A2, N, B omitt.: удачно... & add.: по временам [A2 omitt.] выдавала христианам [A2, N: гоям] некоторые правила Талмуда, чем возбуждала антисемитизм

3527   A1, A2, N, B omitt.: полезного... & add.: который [N: Этот антисемитизм] служил Сиону тем, что кроме ненависти

3528   A2, B omitt.

3529   A1, A2, N, B omitt.: вызывал... & add.: создавал жалость [N: чувство жалости]

3530   A1, A2, N, B omitt.: многих.. & add.: нужных отдельных лиц

3531   A2, N, B: якобы

гонимому племени[3532]. Застращивая еврейскую массу[3533] (глава Сиона[3534] никогда не страдала[3535] от антисемитизма[3536] в своей автономии и[3537] цельности[3538]), руководители Сиона еще больше подчиняли ее себе[3539]. Антисемитизм[3540] удерживал массу[3541] в[3542] повиновении[3543] пастырей[3544] стада[3545], которые[3546] умели во время защитить[3547] свой народ[3548]. Но главная заслуга антисемитизма[3549] заключается[3550] в том, что он разбрасывал еврейский народ во все концы мира, что дало возможность создать всемирный союз сионистов,[3551] ныне сбросившего[3552] маску,

[3532] A1, A2, N, B add.: а [A2, N: И] это последнее чувство многих затянуло в число служащих Сиону. Гоняя [B: Гоня] и

[3533] K: масу; A1, A2, N: еврейский плебс; B: чернь

[3534] A2, N add.: еще

[3535] A1, B: пострадала; A2, N: пострадал

[3536] K: антисемизма; A2, N: этого; A1, A2, N, B add.: ни в своих законах, ни

[3537] A1 add.: в; A2, N omitt. автономии и & add.: административной

[3538] A1, A2, N, B: целости учреждения [A2, N omitt.]

[3539] A1, A2, N, B omitt.: руководители Сиона...

[3540] K: Антисемизм

[3541] K: масу; A1, A2, N: [A2, N add.: этот] плебс; B: чернь

[3542] N add.: бсспрекословном

[3543] A2, B add.: у; A1, N add.: у своих

[3544] A2, B add.: сего

[3545] A1 omitt.

[3546] A2 omitt.: которые; N omitt.: стада, которые; A2, N add.: потому что они всегда успешно

[3547] A1 omitt.: умели защитить & add.: защитили

[3548] A1, A2, N, B add.: да и не мудрено, так как они ведь [N: пастыри эти] сами набрасывали на него [A2, N omitt.; B add.: как] собак антисемитов [A2, N: гонщиков [N: гончих] (гоев-хриастиан)], которые отлично загоняли им их [A2, N omitt.] стадо, делая [A2, N: и делали] его послушным, слепым исполнителем предписаний Сиона [A2, N: пастырей; N add.: направленных к созданию всемирного союза Сиона]

[3549] K: антисемизма

[3550] B: заключалась

[3551] A2, N omitt.: Но главная заслуга...

[3552] B: сбросивший; A2: Всемирный Союз Сиона сбрасывает свою; N: уже начавшего сбрасывать с себя

потому что[3553] он[3554] достиг положения сверхправительства[3555], имея возможность[3556] незаметно руководить[3557] по своему усмотрению,[3558] нитями, исходящими из всех канцелярий[3559] мира. Ныне крепкий трон Сиону[3560] воздвигнут,- остается возвести лишь[3561] царя иудейского. Этому царству не будет границ, потому что оно сумело расположиться интернационально.[3562] Главным завоевательным средством[3563] в руках евреев[3564] было золото[3565], а для сего надо[3566] было не только добыть его[3567], но и увеличить его ценность. Вздорожанию[3568] золота послужила[3569] золотая валюта, а наживе его[3570] послужили[3571] международные[3572] распри, как это доказала[3573] история Ротшильдов, напечатанная[3574] в Париже[3575]. Этими-то распрями[3576] создалась

[3553] N omitt.

[3554] N add.: по его мнению, уже

[3555] B add.: к которому стремился

[3556] A1, A2, N, B omitt.: Имея возможность; A1, B add.: двигая; A2, N add.: двигающего

[3557] A1, A2, N, B omitt.: руководить... & add.: для всех не-евреев

[3558] A1, A2, B add.: всеми

[3559] A2, N omitt.: нитями... & add.: канцеляриями всего

[3560] A1: Сиона

[3561] A1: его; B add.: на него

[3562] A2, N omitt.: Ныне крепкий трон... & add.: Конечно

[3563] A1, A2, N, B: Главное завоевательное средство

[3564] A2, N: Сиона

[3565] A1, A2, N, B: [N add.: всегда] полагалось в золоте

[3566] A1: надобно

[3567] B: таковое

[3568] A1, A2, B: Удорожанию

[3569] A1: послужило

[3570] A2 omitt.; B add.: евреями

[3571] A1 omitt.; N omitt.: наживе... & add.: переходу его в Сионские кассы-

[3572] A2, N add.: и внутренние

[3573] A2, N: доказывает

[3574] B: опубликованная

[3575] A2, N add.: газетой [N: в газете] *«Libre Parole»*.

[3576] A1 add.: и

монопольная сила капиталов[3577], под флагом[3578] либерализма и[3579] социально-экономических[3580] вопросов[3581]. В избирательной борьбе евреи стали[3582] действовать[3583] подкупом[3584] большинства голосов[3585]. Массы[3586], вечно[3587] нуждающиеся, или жадные[3588] интеллигенты[3589], недальновидные либералы и тому подобный слепой народ[3590]- тоже хорошо послужили[3591] Сиону. Поэтому для последнего[3592] самым

[3577] A1, A2, N, B: капитала

[3578] A2, N: флагами

[3579] B omitt.; A1, A2, N add.: научно разработанных

[3580] B: социального и экономического

[3581] N omitt.: социально-экономических вопросов & add.: экономических и социальных теорий; A1, A2, N, B add.: Присвоение титула "научности", разным теориям, [A2 add.: и] оказывало и оказывает [N: продолжает еще оказывать] все более [A2, N omitt.; B: все чаще] Сиону немаловажные услуги... Например: экономическая теория [B: экономические теории] о баллотировочных системах, дала [B: дали; A2, N omitt.: Например... & add. Балотировочные (N: Баллотировочные) системы давали] возможность провести [A2, N: проводить; N add.: в жизнь] все, что [N: чего только не] для возвеличения Сиона было желательно [A2, N: желало сионское начальство].

[3582] A1, B omitt.: В избирательной... &add.: Начальство евреев начало [B: стало]

[3583] A2, N omitt.: В избирательной... ; A2 add.: действующее; N add.: действуя всегда

[3584] A1, A2, N, B add.: или подговором [A2, N add.: нужных лиц (N: людей) и]

[3585] A1, A2, N, B add.: [A2, N add.: толпы,] как [A2, N: лишь] только ему удалось подстроить так, что этому большинству было дано [A2, N omitt: подстроить... & add.: дать; N add.: общественное или политическое] значение решающего постановления [B omitt.: так... & add.: что постановления этого большинства получили значение решающее] по вопросам народного бытия [A2, N: этому большинству]

[3586] A1, B: Толпы

[3587] A2, N omitt.: Массы, вечно

[3588] B: алчные; A2, N omitt.: или жадные

[3589] K: интелегенты

[3590] A2, N omitt.: слепой... ; A2, N, B: люд

[3591] A1: служили и служат

желательным, удобным государственным строем[3593] является[3594] республиканское управление[3595], оно[3596] дает[3597] полный простор деятельности армии Сиона - анархистам, называемым социалистами, мысли и дела. Таково[3598] дело рук бестерриториального[3599] народа, составляющего каплю в океане человечества, но располагающего силой кагала и капитала и властью невидимого правительства[3600].
Отсюда ясно, за кем должны[3601] остаться победа и руководство миром[3602].

[3592]   A2, N omitt.: Поэтому; N add.: Для Сиона же

[3593]   A1, A2, N, B: самый желательный и удобный государственный строй [A2, N: вид государственного управления]

[3594]   A1, B: есть; A2, N omitt.

[3595]   A2, N: республиканский режим; A1, B add.: потому что

[3596]   A1: он

[3597]   A2, N omitt.: оно & add.: дающий

[3598]   A1: Все вышеизложенное; B: Все вышеизложенное есть

[3599]   K: бестериториального

[3600]   A1, B omitt.: но располагающего силой... & add.: потому, что он обладает [B: но обладающего] идеальнейшим правительством, каждый член которого ознакомлен с планом действий, выработанных [B: выработанным] веками, от которого он отступать не может. "Гоевская"-же политика является политикой случайных обстоятельств, подстроенных евреями, а клонится она не к усовершенствованию дела [B: дел] государства, а к ведению борьбы из за алчности и [B: a] часто к личной выгоде администраторов.

[3601]   A1, B: должна

[3602]   A1, B add.: Перевод с французского. 1901 г. Декабря 9-го; A2, N omitt.: называемым социалистами... & add.: Отсюда его усердная пропаганда либерализма, проводимая преданною [N: преданной] Сиону прессой, которая тщательно игнорирует [N add.: уже достаточно] выяснившийся факт, что в республике нет свободы личности, потому что там существует свобода давления толпы большинства над меньшинством, хотя бы и не правым. Слепо следующая [N: Большинство же всегда следует] за агентами капитала Сиона, рекламированными расклейкой [N: расклейками] афиш и газетными статьями, на которые Сион [N add.: по завету Монте Фиоре] не скупится в пользу своих агентов. Пресса игнорирует и то [N add.: конечно, не без инспирации с известной стороны], что единственно [N add.: только] самодержавие правителя [N: царя] страны беспристрастно, ибо для него каждый подданный одинаково сын его земли; он [N: и что одно самодержавие] дает свободу личности, ограждая ее от давления бессмысленной толпы. Только самодержавному правителю не выгодно предоставлять стихийному насилию толпы [N add.: свободу] гнуть [N add.: своим] большинством [N add.: такие] столпы, которые могут выйти из всех слоев его государства, как бывало выходили у нас, в России, и в нужное время поддерживали Русь (Минин, Князь Пожарский и многие другие) [N omitt.: как бывало...]. Кто хочет добыть или сохранить свободу личности, тот не должен требовать свободы для толпы, которая стирает лучших людей тем, что, как стадо баранов, гонится [N add.: в республике] не за [N add.: своими] истинными пастырями, а за агентами Сиона, как это ясно показал [N: показывает теперь] республиканский строй [N add.: несчастной] Франции. Ныне не заметно для себя или добровольно, но все государства мира повинуются распоряжениям [N add.: воровского] сверхправительства, т. е. Сиона, который подстраивает их соглашения (концерты), ибо [N add.: у него] все государственные векселя на неоплаченные [N: неоплатные], все увеличивающиеся суммы в его руках... Сион таксирует ценности, имущества [N add.: в том числе и земельные], аттестует и рекламирует деятелей, неудобных и нежелательных для себя подводит [N: отдает] под опалу начальствующего [N: опеку начальства] или общественного мнения посредством тайных доносов и подвохов [N: прибегая для того или к тайным доносам и подвохам] или через свою прессу,- [N: или] лучше сказать, через всемирно расположившуюся [N: всемирную] агентуру его прессы, в которую не вошли только единичные издания. Ныне Сион своей рекламой составляет [N: изобретает так называемые] "идеи времени", "теории науки", дает или не дает ход людям, их произведениям, изобретениям, ибо и биржа и торговля, и дипломатия- [N add.: все] в его руках. Всем этим он руководит для перевоспитания людей на материалистическую практику, которой убиваются [N: материалистической подкладке, которою убивается] душа, принцип [N: принципы], творчество, превращая всех адептов материализма [N: которой все адепты превращаются] в механических деятелей, искателей одних материальных благ, то есть [N omitt.] ради наживы делающихся слепыми и не рассуждающими рабами, служащими капиталу [N: раболепными прислужниками капиталов] Сиона. Таким образом, этот капитал, государственными долгами поглотивший [N: эти капиталы Сиона, системой государственных долгов поглотившие] остальные [N add.: народные капиталы], это бесчувственное и человеконенавистное [N: человеконенавистическое] сверхправительство налагает [N: налагают] на всех не-евреев тяжкие цепи небывалого крепостного состояния. Настает конец свободе [N: свободы] народной, а, следовательно, и личной, каковой [N: которой] не может быть там, где денежный рычаг дает царствовать толпе и ее насилию над бесправным, хотя [N add.: и] более достойным и разумным меньшинством, которому не дается возможность воспрепятствовать процветанию панамских и дрейфусаровских клик, потому что эти клики поддерживаются рекламой капитала, как лучшие его агенты по бессовестности к собратьям- гоям-христианам... Поэтому Сион оповещает их имена расклейкой афиш перед каждыми выборами и газетными статьями, в которых обещают, что эти благодетели народа сделают все, что угодно избирателям, как только попадут в палату депутатов. На практике же давно и вполне выяснилось, что напр., во Франции за всю республиканскую эру (построенную Сионом, как это доказывает история Ротшилдов)   [N omitt.: которому не дается...] еще ни один избранник толпы [N: что Франция всей своей республиканской эрой обязана Сиону, и в ней еще ни один до сих пор ее избранников] не исполнил того, что обещал, если требования его избирателей не согласовались с предначертаниями правительства Сиона [N: сионского]. И все это дело рук народа бестерриториального, но тем не менее с идеальнейшим правительством [N omitt.: И все это... & add.: Что же сталось с несчастной Францией!... «Имеющий уши слышати, да слышит!»].

Bibliography

ABBREVIATIONS

AA.VV.= various authors

ACS = Archivio Centrale dello Stato (Rome)

Amfiteatrov mss. = Fond A., Manuscripts Dept., Lilly Library, Indiana University (Bloomington, Ind., USA)

AS MAE = Archivio Storico del Ministero degli Affari Esteri (Rome)

ASV = Archivio Segreto Vaticano, Città del Vaticano (Rome)

Berner Prozess = Bern Trial Records. WL (Tel Aviv)

BNF = Bibliothèque Nationale de France (Paris)

ČOIDR = Čtenija Obščestva Istorii Drevnostej Rossijskix

DBF = *Dictionnaire de Biographie française*

DBI = *Dizionario Biografico degli Italiani*

DNB = *Dictionary of National Biography*

GRB = *Gosudarstvennaja Rossijskaja Biblioteka* (M.)

KLE = *Kratkaja Literaturnaja Enciklopedija*, M. 1962-1978

Nikolaevsky mss. = Fondo N., Hoover Institution, Stanford, California (USA)

PSB = *Polski Słownik Biograficzny*, Warsaw 1935-

PSM = *Protokoly Sionskix Mudrecov*

PSS = *Polnoe Sobranie Sočinenij*

RISS = Revue Internationale des Sociétés Secrètes

RNB = *Russkaja Nacional'naja Biblioteka* (St. Petersburg.)

RP = *Russkie pisateli* 1800-1917, M. 1989

RXD = Russkoe Xristianskoe Dviženie

SS = *Sobranie Sočinenij*

SSRLJa = *Slovar' Sovremennogo Russkogo Literaturnogo Jazyka*, M. 1950– 1965

TODRL = *Trudy Otdela Drevne-Russkoj Literatury*

WL = Wiener Library

PRIMARY SOURCES

Amfiteatrov, A.
1906   *Proisxoždenie antisemitizma. I čast'. Evrejstvo i socializm. II čast' Evrejstvo kak dux revoljucii.* Berlin.
"Axeron"
1920   Očerki iz rossijskogo Dekamerona. *Varšavskoe slovo.* 17 July.
Brafman Ja.
1869   *Kniga Kagala.* Vil'na. French trans. *Livre du Kahal.* Odessa 1873; Polish trans. *Żydzi i Kahaly.* Lwow 1874; German trans. *Das Buch vom Kahal.* Leipzig 1928.
Brant, E.
1926–1929 *Ritual'noe ubijstvo u evreev.* 3 vols. Beograd.
Butmi de Kacman, G.
1896   Zolotaja valjuta. *Novorossijskij Telegraf.*
1897a   *K voprosu o denežnoj reforme (Soobraženija sel'skogo xozjaina).* St. Petersburg. German trans. *Zur Währungsfrage. Betrachtungen eines südrussischen Landwirthes.* Berlin.
1897b   *Zolotoj monometallizm.* St. Petersburg.
1898a   *The monetary question in Russia.* Washington.
1898b   *Kapitaly i dolgi.* Preface by S. Šarapov. St. Petersburg. German trans. *Kapital und Schulben.* Preface by W. von Karhopf. Berlin 1899 (?).
1904a   *Zolotaja valjuta. Sbornik statej i rečej.* St. Petersburg.
1904b   *Itogi finansovogo xozjajstva s 1892 po 1903.* St. Petersburg.
1905a   Istoričeskaja spravka ob Iudejax. *Zarja,* 9 July 1905 (*Russkoe delo,* 23 July).
1905b   Po povodu stat'i M. I. Dragomirova ob Evrejax. *Moskovskie vedomosti,* 27 August.
1906a   *Vragi roda čelovečeskogo (Obličitel'nye reči 1).* St. Petersburg.
1906b   *Šuler (Obličitel'nye reči 2).* St. Petersburg.
1906c   (with N.L.) *Konstitucija i političeskaja svoboda (Obličitel'nye reči 3).* St. Petersburg.
1906d   *Rossija na rasput'i: kabala ili svoboda? (Obličitel'nye reči 4).* St. Petersburg.
1906e   (with N.L.) *Fran-Masonstvo i Gosudarstvennaja izmena (Obličitel'nye reči 5).* 2 vols. St. Petersburg. Czech. trans. *Svoboda zednářství a velezrada.* Prague 1907.
1906f   *Frankmasony: Iudei v masonstve i revoljucii.* St. Petersburg.

1906 g   *Zemlja Božija.* St. Petersburg.
1906h   *Den'gi, Zemlja i Volja.* (n.p.).
1906i   *Gosudarstvennaja duma ili Zemskij sobor?* (n.p.).
1914   *Rimskaja kurija o ritual'nyx ubijstvax* and *"Bez predrassudkov,"* in Butmi, N. 1914b.

Butmi, N.
1914a   *Kabala, eresi i tajnye obščestva* (edited by G.B.), St. Petersburg; Czech trans. by J. Hora. *Kabbala, sekty a tajné spolky.* Prague 1925.
1914b   *Dogmat krovi* (with two appendices by G. B.). St. Petersburg.

Chamberlain, H. S.
1913   *Die Grundlagen des XIX Jahrhunderts.* Munich 1899; French trans. *La genèse du XIX siècle.* Paris 1913; English transl. *The Foundations of the Nineteenth Century.* 1966.

Demčenko, Ja.
1906   *Evrejskoe ravnopravie ili russkoe poraboščenie?* Kiev.

Herzl, Th.
1990   *Journal 1895–1904.* Paris.
1992   *Der Judenstaat* (1896); Russian trans. *Evrejskoe gosudarstvo.* St. Petersburg. 1896; Ital. trans. *Lo stato ebraico.* Genoa 1992.

Joly, M.
1864   *Dialogue aux enfers entre Machiavel et Montesquieu.* Brussels.

Kruševan, P.
1882   *Razorennoe gnezdo.* St. Petersburg.
1896   *Delo Artabanova.* Moscow.
1897   *Prizraki.* Moscow.
1903   *Bessarabija.* St. Petersburg.
1911   [Prijatel'] *Provincial'nye očerki.* Kishinev.

Leont'ev, K.
1875   *Vizantizm i slavjanstvo.* Moscow.

Ljutostanskij, I.
1902–1905 *Talmud i evrei.* 3rd ed. 4 vols. St. Petersburg.

Men'šikov, M.
1899   *Kritičeskie očerki.* St. Petersburg.
1900   *Narodnye zastupniki i drugie nravstvenno-bytovye očerki.* St. Petersburg.
1901   *Načala žizni.* St. Petersburg.
1902a   *Dumy o sčast'e.* St. Petersburg. (Rpt. Stavropol' 1995).
1902b   Pis'ma k bližnym. XVI. Zagovory protiv čelovečestva. *Novoe vremja,* 7 (20) April.

| 1906 | *Krasnoe znamja.* St. Petersburg. |

1908   *Drevnie dokumenty po evrejskomu voprosu.* Xar'kov.
1993   M. O. Men'šikov. Materialy k biografii. *Russkij arxiv.* Vol. 4. Moscow.

Nečvolodov, A.
1894   *Očerki javlenij vojny v predstavlenii polkovodca Napoleona.* Warsaw.
1906   *Ot razorenija k dostatku.* St. Petersburg.
1907   *Russkie den'gi.* St. Petersburg.
1910   *Skazanija o Russkoj zemle.* St. Petersburg. (2nd ed., Moscow 1991).
1924   *L'Empereur Nicolas II et les Juifs.* Paris; Ital. trans., abridged, *Giuda senza maschera.* Florence 1926 (2nd ed. 1931).

Nilus, S.
1899   *Koren' zla.* Moscow.
1902   *Golos very iz mira toržestvujuščego neverija.* Moscow.
1903   *Dux božij, javno počivšij na otce Serafime Sarovskom.* Moscow.
1903   *Velikoe v malom.* Moscow.
1904a   *Služka Božiej Materi i Serafimov (N. A. Motovilov).* Moscow.
1904b   *Otec Egor Čekrjakovskij.* Moscow.
1905   *Velikoe v malom i Antixrist(...).* Carskoe Selo.
1907   *Sila Božija i nemošč' čelovečeskaja.* Sergiev Posad
1908a   *Marko Fraceskij.* Sergiev Posad.
1908b   *Žatva žizni.* Sergiev Posad.
1909a   *Odin iz tex nemnogix, kogo ves' mir nedostoin.* Sergiev Posad.
1909b   *Zvezdy pustyni.* Sergiev Posad.
1909c   *Dlja čego i komu nužny pravoslavnye monastyri.* Sergiev Posad.
1909d   *Nebesnye pestuny.* Sergiev Posad.
1911a   *Svjatynja pod spudom.* Sergiev Posad.
1911b   *Bliz grjaduščij Antixrist.* Moscow.
1911c   *Velikoe v malom. Bliz grjaduščij Antixrist.* Sergiev Posad (2nd ed. 1912).
1916   *Na beregu Bož'ej reki.* Sergiev Posad.
1917   *Bliz est', pri dverex.* Moscow.
1995   *Nejzvestnyj Nilus.* Edited by R. Bagdasarov and S. Fomin. 2 vols. Moscow.

Osman Bey
1868   *La Turquie sous le règne d'Abdul-Aziz (1862–1867).* Paris.
1870a   *Wild life among the Koords.* London.
1870b   *Slavery in Turkey.* London.

1871   *Progrès de l'hellènisme.* Braila.

1873a   *La conquète du monde par les juifs.* Bâle; German trans. *Die Eroberung der Welt durch die Juden.* Bâle 1873; Russian trans. *Pokorenie mira evrejami.* Odessa 1874, and *Zavoevanie mira evrejami.* Warsaw 1880; Polish trans. *Zawojowanie świata przez Żidów.* Lwów 1876; English trans. *The Conquest of the World by the Jews.* St. Louis 1878; Ital. trans. *Gli ebrei alla conquista del mondo.* Venice 1880 (2nd ed. 1883, 3rd ed. Bologna 1939).

1873b   *Ženščiny v Turcii.* St. Petersburg; French trans. *Les Femmes en Turquie.* Paris 1877; English trans. *Modern Women of Turkey.* Cosmopolitan 1891; German trans. *Die Frauen in der Türkei.* Leipzig 1904.

1874   *Turki i ix ženščiny.* Bulgarian trans. *Turcite i texnite ženy.* 1888; 2nd ed., 1992.

1877a   *Les Anglais en Orient 1830–1876.* Paris; Italian trans. *Gli inglesi in Oriente.* Trieste 1882, Venice 1882.

1877b   *Tureckij provodnik dlja russkogo soldata.* Tiflis.

1879   *Luttes sur le Rhin et sur le Danube entre Latins, Germains et Slaves.* Paris.

1881   *Les Imans et les derviches.* Paris.

1883   Rivelazioni sull'assassinio dello Czar Alessandro II. *Gazzetta d'Italia.* Chaps. 1–18, 4 September 1883–8 December 1883; Chap. 19, 18. January 1884); German trans. *Enthüllungen über die Ermordung Alexanders II.* Bern 1886; French trans. *Révélations sur l'assassinat d'Alexandre II.* Geneva 1886.

1889a   *Madre e Patria vendicate.* Turin 1889; German trans. *Wie ich Mutter und Vaterland rachte.* Berlin 1889.

1889b   *Les Russes en 1877–78.* Berlin.

1890a   *Il genio dell'Islamismo.* Turin.

1890b   *La guerre à l'horizon.* Lyon.

1890   *The Armenian Question and the Rule of Abdul Hamid.* (n.p.) Cited in Woods, H. F. *Blackmailing the Sultan. Refutation of the Calumnies in Osman Bey's Anonymous Pamphlet.* 1890.

1891   *Il ministro Giers in Italia. Caccia all'Ebreo in Russia.* Milan.

1894a   *Les Caserios invisibles (Dans Carnot, on a voulu frapper la France).* Dijon.

1894b   *Chasse à l'homme en pays civilisés.* Nice.

1894c   *Partage de l'Afrique selon la fable d'Ésope.* Nice.

1895   *Tod Alexanders II und Alexanders III.* Bern.

1896   *La crise orientale 1895–96.* Philippopoli.

L'excommunié Comte Léon Tolstoï. Nice, April 14.

Šmakov, A.

1897   *"Evrejskie reči."* Moscow.

1912   *Meždunarodnoe tajnoe pravitel'stvo.* Moscow. 2nd. ed., 1999.

Tajna evrejstva

1895   *Tajna evrejstva* (1895). In Delevskij 1923.

Wolski [Vol'skij], K.

1887   *Evrei v Rossii. Ix byt, celi i sredstva.* St. Petersburg. French trans. *De la Russie juive.* Paris.

Ževaxov, N.

1907–1909 *Materialy dlja žizneopisanija Sv. Ioasafa, Episkopa Belogorodskogo i Obojanskogo.* 3 vols. Kiev. 2nd ed. *Žitie Sv. Ioasafa.* Novi Sad 1929.

1909a   *Nikolaj Nikolaevič Nepljuev.* St. Petersburg.

1909b   *Knjažna Marija Michajlovna Dondukova-Korsakova.* St. Petersburg.

1910a   *Stroiteli ducha žizni v oblasti živopisi i architektury. I. Izakevič i A. Ščusev.* St. Petersburg.

1910b   *Reči.* Moscow.

1911a   *Verujuščaja intelligencija o tolkovanii Evangelija.* St. Petersburg.

1911b   *Bari. Putevye zametki.* St. Petersburg.

1912   *Na rodine Prepodobnogo Sergija Radonežskogo.* Moscow.

1913   *Akty i dokumenty Lubenskogo Mgarskogo Spaso-Preobraženskogo Monastyrja.* Kiev.

1914   *Probuždenie Sv. Rusi.* St. Petersburg.

1923–1928 *Vospominanija.* Vol. 1. Munich 1923; Vol. 2. Novi Sad 1928.

1926a   *Evrejskij vopros.* New York.

1926b   *Pamjati grafa A. Čerep-Spiridoviča.* New York.

1926c   *Izabell-Florens Chapchud.* New York.

1928   *Svetloj pamjati štatmejstera Vysosčajšego Dvora F. V. Vinberga.* Paris.

1929   *Pričiny gibeli Rossii.* Novi Sad.

1930   *La verità su Rasputin* [fragment of Ževaxov 1923]. Bari.

1934a   *Rab Božij Nikolaj Nikolaevič Ivanenko.* Novi Sad.

1934b   *Svetloj pamjati knjazja A. Širinskogo-Šichmatova.* Novi Sad.

1934c   *Korni russkoj revoljucii.* Kišinev.

1936   *Sergej Aleksandrovič Nilus: kratkij očerk žizni i dejatel'nosti.* Novi Sad.

1939   *Il retroscena dei 'Protocolli di Sion."* Rome.

1942	*Memorie della Rivoluzione russa 1917.* Trans. by Ževaxov, 1923. Milano.
1944	*Colloquio del grande santo russo Serafino di Sarov con N. A. Motovilow.* Preface by Prince N. D. Gevakhow. Rome.
1992	*Evrejskij terror v Rossii.* [fragment of Ževaxov 1923]. In *Sergiev Possad.*
1993a	*Vospominanija* [rpt. by Ževaxov 1923–1928]. Moscow.
1993b	*Pričiny gibeli Rossii* [rpt. by Ževaxov 1934]. Voronež.

SECONDARY SOURCES

Amal'rik, A.

1984	*Rasputin* (1982). Ital. trans. Torino.

Arendt, H.

1966	*The Origins of Totalitarianism.* New York.

Avrex, A.

1990	*Masony i revoljucija.* Moscow.
1991	*P. A. Stolypin i sud'by reform v Rossii.* Moscow.

Barrucand, P.

1992	Dossier (1. *Lettre à P. A. Taguieff*; 2. *Propagande secrète anti-juive au XIX siècle dans l'Église Catholique*). Typescript. Paris.

Begunov, Ju.

1996	*Tajnye sily v istorii Rossii.* St. Petersburg.

Benigni, U. [FER]

1921	I documenti della conquista ebraica del mondo. Parte prima. I protocolli dei saggi Anziani di Sion. *Fede e Ragione,* Supplement to 13–21, 23–26 (27 March–26 June).

Bostunič, G.

1921	*Pravda o Sionskix Protokolax.* Mitrovica.
1922	*Masonstvo i russkaja revoljucija.* Beograd.
1928	*Masonstvo v svoej suščnosti i projavlenijax.* New ed. of Bostunič 1922. Beograd.

Briman, Š.

1998	Počtovoe bjuro Sionizma, ili fakty v podderžku versii rimskogo professora. *Okna* (suppl. to *Vesti,* Jerusalem), 18 June.

Bulgarin, F.

1990	*Sobranie sočinenij.* Moscow.

Capaldo, M.
1990a   Sulla datazione di un'iscrizione pseudo-salomonica ad opera di Costantino. In AA. VV. *Filologia e letteratura nei paesi slavi. Studi in onore di Sante Graciotti*. Rome.
1990b   Rispetto del testo tràdito o avventura congetturale?. *Europa Orientalis* 9.
Čerep-Spiridovič, A.
1926   *The Secret World Government or "The Hidden Hand."* New York.
Charles, P.
1939   *Les Protocoles des Sages de Sion.* Paris-Tournai 1938; Ital. trans. *I Protocolli dei Savi di Sion.* Brescia 1939; Eng. trans. "The Learned Elders of Zion." In *The Bridge. A Yearbook of Judaeo-Christian Studies* (New York). 1 (1955); Polish. trans. "Prawda o Protokolach Mędrców Syjonu," *Znak*, 4–5 (1990).
Cohn, N.
1969   *Warrant for Genocide. The Myth of the Jewish World Conspiracy and the Protocols of the Elders of Zion.* London 1967; French trans. *Histoire d'un mythe. La "Conspiration" juive et les Protocoles des Sages de Sion.* Paris 1967; Italian trans. *Licenza per un genocidio. I «Protocolli degli Anziani di Sion»: storia di un falso.* Torino 1969; German trans. *Die Protokolle der Weisen von Zion. Der Mythos von der jüdischen Weltverschwörung.* Berlin 1969 (2nd ed. Edited by M. Hagemeister. Zürich 1998); Russian trans. *Blagoslovenie na genocid: mif o vsemirnom zagovore evreev i "Protokolax Sionskix mudrecov."* Moscow 1990.
Confino, A.
1938   *Les Protocoles des Sages de Sion.* Alger.
Creutz, W.
1934   *Le Péril Juif.* Paris [n.d., but: 1934].
De Felice, R.
1961   *Storia degli ebrei italiani sotto il fascismo.* Turin.
1966   *Mussolini il fascista.* Vol. 1. Turin.
1990   *Mussolini l'alleato.* (Vol. I, *L'Italia in guerra*). Turin.
Delevskij, Ju.
1923   *Protokoly Sionskix mudrecov. Istorija odnogo podloga.* Berlin.

De Michelis, C. G.
1996   "Il principe N. D. Ževaxov" *Studi Storici*, 3.
1997a   "Un professionista dell'antisemitismo ottocentesco: Osman Bey." *La Rassegna mensile di Israel* 2.
1997b   "Les Protocoles des sages de Sion. Philologie et histoire." *Cahiers du monde russe* 38 (3).
1997c   "Russia e Italia." In *Storia della civiltà*. Vol. 2.
1999   "Una storia che si ripete." *La Repubblica,*" 21 November.
De Vaux, R.
1964   *Le istituzioni dell'Antico Testamento*. Italian trans. Casale.
Dudakov, S.
1989   "Vladimir Solov'ev i Sergej Nilus.*"* in AA.VV. *Russian Literature and History.* Jerusalem.
1992   "E. A. Šabel'skaja." In AA.VV. *In Honour of Professor Victor Levin. Russian Literature and History*. Jerusalem.
1993   *Istorija odnogo mifa. Očerki russkoj literatury XIX–XX veka.* Moscow.
Ebrei in Italia
1997   AA.VV. *Gli ebrei in Italia. Storia d'Italia.* 11. Edited by C. Vivanti. Turin.
Eco, U.
1994   "Protocolli fittizi." In *Six Walks in the Fictional Woods*. Italian trans. *Sei passeggiate nei boschi narrativi.* Milan.
Evola, J.
1940   Revised ed. of Ževaxov 1939. *Bibliografia fascista* 15, no. 5.
Ford, H.
1939   *The International Jew* (1921), Italian trans. *L'ebreo internazionale.* 2nd ed. Milan 1938.
Fry, L.
1921   "Sur l'authenticité des Protocols. Achad ha-Ham et le Sionisme." *La vieille France* 218 (31 March–6 April.   Italian trans. "Su l'autenticità dei 'Protocolli dei Savi Anziani di Sion'." *La Vita Italiana,* 15 July.
1931   *Waters flowing eastward.* Paris. French transl. *Le retour des flots vers l'Orient. Le Juif, notre maître.* Paris.
Ganelin, R.
1992   "Černosotennye organizacii, političeskaja policija i gosudarstvennaja vlast' v carskoj Rossii." In *Nacional'naja pravaja.*
Gentile, F.
1972   "Machiavelli e Montesquieu." In *Studi machiavelliani.*

Hagemeister, M.
1991   "Wer war Sergej Nilus?" *Ostkirchliche Studien* 40, no. 1; French trans. "Qui était Serguei Nilus?" *Politica hermetica* 9 (1995).
1995a   "Die 'Protokolle der Weisen von Zion' Einige Bemerkungen zur Herkunfft und zur aktuellen Rezeption." In *Russland und Europa. Historische un kulturelle Aspekte eines Jahrhundert—problems.* Leipzig: Rosa Luxemburg-Verein.
1996   "Sergej Nilus und die "Protokolle der Weisen von Zion." *Jahrbuch für Antisemitismusforschung* (Berlin) 5.
1997   "Die 'Protokolle der Weisen von Zion' und der Basler Zionistenkongress von 1897." In aa.vv. *Der Erste Zionisten-kongress von 1897—Ursachen, Bedeutung, Aktualität.* Basel-Freiburg.

Helebrandt, R.
1991   *Sionské protokoly.* Slovak trans. *Kniežatá zloby (Protokoly siónskich mudrecov).* Bratislava.

Janov (Yanov), A.
1981   *Détente after Brezhnev* (1977); *The Russian New Right* (1978), Italian trans. *La nuova destra russa.* Florence.

Jouin, E.
1920–1922   *Le péril judéo-maçonnique.* Vol. 1: *Les "Protocols" des Sages de Sion.* Vols. 2–3: *La Judéo-Maçonnerie et l'Eglise Catholique.* Vol. 4: *Les Protocols de 1901 de G. Butmi.* Paris.

Klier, J. D.
1995   *Imperial Russia's Jewish Question, 1855–1881.* Cambridge.

Laqueur, W.
1991   *Russia and Germany Hitler's Mentors* (1965), Russian trans. *Rossija i Germanija nastavniki Gitlera.* Washington 1991.

Literatura o evrejax
1995   *Literatura o evrejax na russkom jazyke, 1890-1947.* Edited by V. Kel'ner and D. El'jasevič. St. Petersburg.

Luč sveta
1920   *Luč světa. Literaturno-političeskoe izdanie. God pervyj. Kn. III.* May. Berlin.

Makarov, N.
1884   *Polnyj Russko-francuzskij Slovar'.*
1887   *Dictionnaire Français-Russe.*

Małyński, E.
1928   *La grande conspiration mondiale.* Paris.

Masanov, I.
1956–1960   *Slovar' psevdonimov.* 4 vols. Moscow.

Menzogna (La)
1994   *La menzogna della razza. Documenti e immagini del razzismo e dell'antisemitismo fascista.* Edited by F. Jesi Center. Bologna.

Miccoli, G.
1997   "Santa Sede, questione ebraica e antisemitismo." In *Ebrei in Italia.*

Miljukov, P.
1931   *Očerki po russkoj kul'ture.* Vol. 2, 2. Paris.

Mutti, C.
1976   *Ebraicità ed Ebraismo.* Padua.

Nacional'naja pravaja
1992   AA.VV. *Nacional'naja pravaja prežde i teper'. Istoriko-sociologičeskie očerki.* Vols. 1–3. St. Petersburg.

Pichetto, M. T.
1983   *Alle radici dell'odio. Preziosi e Benigni antisemiti.* Milan.

[Polovinkin S.]
1995   *Sergej Aleksandrovič Nilus (1862–1929). Žizneopisanie.* Moscow.

Preziosi, G.
1921   [S. Nilus]. *L'Internazionale Ebraica. Protocolli dei "Savi Anziani" di Sion.* Rome.

1938   *L'internazionale ebraica. I "protocolli" dei "savi anziani" di Sion.* Rome 1937 [republ. 1938 and 1939].

1942   "Le fantasie del principe Gevakhow." *La Vita Italiana* 6.

Programmy
1995   *Programmy političeskix partij Rossii. Konec XIX-načalo XX vv.* Moscow.

Radziwiłłowa, K.
1921   "Le Protocoles des Sages de Sion." *La Revue Mondiale* 6 (15 March).

Raskin, D.
1992   "Ideologija pravogo radikalizma v konce XIX-načale XX vv." In *Nacional'naja pravaja.*

Reznik, S.
1988   "Usluga za uslugu (P. A. Kruševan)." In idem. *Krovavaja karusel'.* Washington.

Rollin, H.
1991   *L'Apocalypse de notre temps* (1939). 2nd ed. Paris.

Romano, S.
1992   *I falsi protocolli.* Milan.
Šafarevič, I.
1991   *Rusofobija* (1989). In *Est' li u Rossii Buduščee?* (Moscow 1991); Italian trans. *La setta mondialista contro la Russia.* Parma.
Sarfatti, M.
1997   "Gli ebrei negli anni del fascismo." In *Ebrei in Italia.*
Slavjane i ix sosedi
1994   AA.VV. *Slavjane i ix sosedi. Vyp. 5. Evrejskoe naselenie v Central'noj, Vostočnoj i Jugo-Vostočnoj Evrope.* Moscow.
Starcev, V.
1996   *Russkoe političeskoe masonstvo načala XX veka.* St. Petersburg.
Stepanov, S.
1992   *Černaja sotnja v Rossii /1905-1914 gg./.* Moscow.
Storia della civiltà
1977   AA.VV. *Storia della civiltà letteraria russa.* Edited by M. Colucci and R. Picchio. Turin.
Strižëv, A.
1993   "Nikolaj Davidovič Ževaxov. Biografičeskij očerk" In Ževaxov 1993a.
Taguieff, P. A.
1992   *Les Protocoles des sages de Sion.* Vol. 1: *Introduction à l'étude des Protocoles.* Vol. 2: *Études et documents.* Paris.
Tazbir, Ja.
1992a   *Protokoły mędrców Syjonu. Autentyk czy falsyfikat.* Warsaw; Czech trans. Olomouc. 1996.
1992b   "Najnowsze publikacje na temat Protokołów mędrców Syjonu." *Dzieje Najnowsze* 24, no. 4.
Vitte, S.
1923   *Vospominanija.* 2 vols. Berlin.
Vol'skij, A.
1993   *Prophètes et visionnaires de Russie* (1985); Italian trans. *I veri protocolli.* Parma.
Webb, J.
1976   *The Occult Establishment.* La Salle, Ill.

Zolotonosov, M.
1995   "U istokov subkul'tury russkogo antisemitizma." in AA.VV.
         Evrei v Rossii. Istorija i kul'tura (Trudy po iudaike 3). St.
         Petersburg.

EDITIONS OF THE PSM

Russian
K   "Programa zavoevanija mira evrejami." in *Znamja* 1, no. 190 (28
         August [10 September]): 2; 2, no. 191 (29 August [11
         September]): 2; 3, no. 192 (30 August [12 September]): 2; 4, no.
         193 (31 August (13 September]): 1–2; 5, no. 194 (1 [14]
         September): 1–2; 6, no. 195 (2 [15] September): 1–2; 7, no. 196
         (3 [16] September): 2; 8, no. 197 (4 [17] September): 2; 9, no.
         200 (7 [20] September): 2.
L   *Iudejskie tajny.* In Ljutostanskij 1904. Vol. 2.
A1   1905. "Vyderžki iz drevnix i sovremennyx protokolov Sionskix
         mudrecov Vsemirnogo obščestva Fran-Masonov." In *Koren'*
         našix bedstvij. St. Petersburg.
A2   1905. *Drevnie i sovremennye protokoly sobranij "Sionskix*
         Mudrecov." Moscow.
N   1905. *Protokoly sobranij Sionskix mudrecov.* In Nilus 1905.
B   *Protokoly izvlečennye iz tajnyx xranilišč Sionskoj Glavnoj*
         Kanceljarii. In Butmi 1906a.
B3   Idem. In Butmi 1906a (*3-e izdanie, obrabotannoe*).
D   *Protokoly sionskix mudrecov.* In Demčenko 1906.
R1   *Tajny politiki (Vyderžki iz rečej...sionizma).* In Begunov 1996,
         102–14.
R2   1905. "Tajny politiki (Reč' odnogo iz rukovoditelej...Sionizma)."
         Mirnyj Trud 8.
R3   1906. "Reč' odnogo iz rukovoditelej...Sionizma." *Samoderžavie*
         1–5.
R4   1906. *Evrejskaja politika i ee rezul'taty.* Kremenčug.
I   1917. *Izvlečenie iz protokolov I-go Sionistskogo kongressa.*
         Moscow. In Begunov 1996, 66–71.

English
The Jewish Peril. Protocols of the Learned Elders of Zion. Trans. by G.
     Shanks. London 1920.
B. Brasol, ed. *The Protocols and World Revolution.* Boston 1920.

H. A. Houghton, ed. *Praemonitus praemunitus. The Protocols of the Wise Men of Zion.* New York 1920.

Protocols of the Meetings of the Learned Elders of Zion. Trans. by V. Marsden. London 1921.

Italian

S. Nilus. *L'Internazionale ebraica Protocolli dei "Savi Anziani" di Sion.* In Preziosi 1921.

I Protocolli dei saggi Anziani di Sion. In Benigni 1921.

Anon. 1938. *Chi sono questi ebrei! I Protocolli dei saggi di Sion. Sensazionale documentario.* Milan.

Anon. N.d. (but: 1943). *Il grande pericolo nel contenuto dei Protocolli dei "Savi Anziani" di Sion.* Centro fiorentino per lo studio del problema ebraico. Florence.

N.a. 1972. *I Protocolli dei Savi di Sion. Testo integrale pubblicato nel 1095* [*sic!*] *da Sergio A. Nylus, preserved and catalogued in the British Museum Library.* Lucera.

German

N.a. 1919. *Die Geheimnisse der Weisen von Zion.* Trans. by. G. zur Beek. Charlottenburg.

French

La conspiration juive: "protocols," procès verbaux des reunions secrètes des sages d'Israel. Trans. by U. Gohier. *La Vielle France.* Paris 1920.

Les "Protocols" des sages de Sion. Trans. by E. Jouin. Paris (RISS) 1920.

"Les Protocols" des Sages de Sion. Trans. by R. Lambelin. Paris 1921. New ed. Beirut 1967.

Les protocoles des sages de Sion. Trans. by H. Coston. In Creutz 1934.

Polish

Baczność! Przeczytaj i daj innym (Protokuly posiedzeń mędrców Sjonu, rok 1897-1920) Trans. by J. Evrard. Warsaw n.d. (but: 1919).

Protokoly Mędrców Syjonu Trans. by B. Rudzki. Poznań 1937 (2nd ed. 1938. In Tazbir 1992a).

Other languages

Förlåten faller... Det tillkommande världssjälvhärskardömet enligt «Sions vises hemliga protokoll». Helsingfors 1919.

Utban a Világuralom Felé. Cion Bölcseinek Jegyzökönyvei. Trans. by I. Szabö. Vienna 1920.

Protokoly ze shromáždení Sionskych Mudrců. Trans. by F. Komrska. Prague 1926. In Tazbir 1996.

Di "Protokoln" fun Zikney Tsion. Preface by K. D. Warsaw 1934.

Index of Names

Italicized page numbers indicate the endnotes of each chapter.